LAUREL
Stage by Stage

by

"A.J" Marriot

Marriot Publishing

LAUREL – Stage by Stage

ISBN 978-0-9521308-5-7

First published March 2017

Second Print – October 2019

ISBN 978-1-78972-555-1

Marriot Publishing

Ciudad Quesada, Alicante, Spain

Text Copyright © by "A.J" Marriot 2016

Printed by "**Printondemand-worldwide.com**" Peterborough. PE2 6XD via Lulu.com

United Kingdom

Written, compiled and designed by "A.J" Marriot. Layout by "A.J" Marriot

COVER DESIGN by "A.J" Marriot

Cover artwork by Paul Wood (TT Litho, Rochester, Kent. ME1 1NN. www.ttlitho.co.uk)

All rights reserved

"A.J" Marriot is hereby identified as author of this work in accordance with Section 77 of the Copyright, Designs and Patent Act 1988

o-o-0-o-o

This book is sold subject to the condition that it shall not, by way of trade or otherwise, be lent, resold, hired out or otherwise circulated without the publisher's prior consent in any form of binding cover other than that in which it is published and without a similar condition – this condition being imposed on the subsequent purchaser.

o-o-0-o-o

PREFACE
by author "A.J" Marriot

The widely-held belief is that Stan Jefferson played in panto; toured with the Fred Karno company; formed 'The 3 English Comiques'; followed by 'The Keystone Trio,' then 'The Stan Jefferson Trio' — before touring in vaudeville with Mae Dahlberg between 1917 and 1921. If this is the sum of your knowledge, then prepare to be staggered by learning about the various stage acts and comedians Stan Jefferson was involved with, which are missing from previous accounts.

-----0-----

I am immensely fortunate to have been given full access to one of Stan Laurel's scrapbooks, which covers the years pre- 1925. For this, I am indebted to Rob Stone for granting me such a huge privilege. I had thought that the one hundred pages, containing a vast number of newspaper cuttings/clippings covering Laurel's solo stage tours, would fill in the missing dates and accounts I was looking for — AND, in chronological order. How wrong was I? If there is one person who ought not to have been given the task of cutting and pasting all those clippings into a book, it is STAN LAUREL. I will try to explain, using the oft-used jig-saw puzzle analogy:

When assembling a jig-saw puzzle, the most-common method is to lay out all the pieces, then place them in the correct position, whereupon it reveals a completed picture. So where does Laurel's method fall down? Well he laid out all the pieces (clippings) but then, whichever piece he picked up first, he pasted into the book. i.e. with no attempt whatsoever to place them in context. The final "picture" is the equivalent of the result you would get if you just picked any piece of a jig-saw puzzle from the box, and stuck it on the bottom left-hand corner of the work-board, and then just proceeded to place pieces, at random, until the allotted space was filled. Nightmare!

What made this an even greater nightmare is that Stan did not retain the titles, nor the dates, of the newspapers from which he had cut the reviews and/or adverts. Mentions of the other acts Laurel shared the bill with would have gone some way to helping track down the origin of the theatres played, and the dates; but, in most instances, Stan cut out only the references which mention him, personally. So, much as I have tried to complete the picture, there are still many theatre engagements for which the pieces will remain forever a puzzle. (Pun intended). If Hercules had been given the choice of re-assembling the scrapbook entries in chronological order, or completing the original twelve tasks for which he is fabled, he would have stuck with the twelve.

So, as you read through this book, don't display discontent at the missing dates, but celebrate the ones that are now revealed. After all, no-one has yet discovered a Roman mosaic floor in which all the tesserae are intact, but these are still finds to be celebrated.

When doing research for my first four books, contemporary newspapers were a valuable source of dates, venues, and reviews of the stage shows Laurel and Hardy did in both Britain, Europe, and the USA; plus Chaplin's stage shows. The major problem, then, was that I had to go through actual "hard" copies of the newspapers in the hope of finding the required information. In total, I spent over one hundred and fifty days in the British Newspaper Library (then in North London) skimming through newspapers from morning until they kicked me out at closing time. I also did my own "British Tours" when visiting other libraries — namely ones in North Shields, Blackpool, Liverpool, Birmingham, and Northampton. Plus, I visited many towns and cities to interview people who were a part of the story, and also do reconnaissance on the locations of hotels, theatres, houses, and buildings Laurel and Hardy had visited. These included: Ulverston (3 times), Glasgow (twice), Rutherglen, Edinburgh (twice), North Shields (twice), Tynemouth (twice), Newcastle (twice), Blyth (twice), York, Leeds, Bradford, Todmorden, Bolton, Morecambe (twice), Blackpool (3 times), Southport, Liverpool, Rhyl, Hanley (twice), Stoke, Barkston, Bottesford, Butlins Skegness (twice), Peterborough (twice), Coventry, Birmingham (twice), Northampton, Cardiff, Bristol, London (numerous times), Willesden, Ealing, Brixton, Lewisham, Finsbury Park, Camberwell (3 times), Lambeth, Southend (3 times), Margate (twice), Romney Hythe & Dymchurch Railway (3 times), Brighton, and Southsea. What a busy day that was.

LAUREL — Stage by Stage

Typical page from Stan Laurel's Scrapbook.
See how many clippings you can reconstitute into the right date, sketch, theatre, or film.

Preface

And if you think *that* is a great deal of miles to cover in the name of research, consider that, in order to gather information for "LAUREL and HARDY – The U.S. Tours," I flew to the States, where I spent two days in the New York Library, and two days in Philadelphia; after which I flew on to Puerto Rico, where I spent a further two days doing reconnaissance, followed by lighting visits to libraries in Antigua and St. Lucia.

Those days of doing research in the field have ended. I now have neither the time nor the energy. Imagine my utter joy therefore when, in setting about to compile this book, I learned of a number of on-line sites where one could actually access historical newspapers. Not only can one read scanned images of the original copies, but there is also a "Search" facility, whereby one types in the subject of the research and, in seconds, thousands of "finds" magically appear. Boy oh boy! this was going to be the easiest and fastest book ever researched and written. That's what I thought at first, anyway — until I learned the limitations of searches, and the cruel way in which a simple word search can throw up thousands of results which are of no relevance. Then there are those subjects which don't show up at all because they have more than one spelling or combination, or are simply mis-spelt at source. Here are just a few foibles of on-line searches I encountered:

Three of my main online searches, namely: – "Stan and Mae Laurel" – "Stan and May" – "Stanley and Mae" — did bring up many good results; but here are just some of the newspaper misprints which these searches did not pick up: "Dan & May Laurel" – "Dan Laurell" – "Stan and May Yaurel" – "Stan LAURELS May" – "Sam Laurel" — and "Mary Laurel." There are other variations. My favourite was an OCR translation of "Stan and May" which came out as "Islam and Ma" (I kid you not). Other searches, such as "Jefferson Hurley and Wren," also caused utter frustration, as did the searches for the titles of the sketches Laurel performed, but these will be revealed in the text.

As for the actual tours, those across the USA vary enormously from those undertaken in the UK — and I'm not just referring to the vast differences in miles travelled. In Britain, variety theatre tours ran from Monday to Saturday, almost without exception; whereas in America and Canada there were numerous permutations of the working week: Monday to Saturday did sometimes happen; but the following were more common — Monday to Wednesday, or Sunday to Wednesday; Thursday to Saturday, or Thursday to Sunday; but then comes Sunday only; or the pairing of any two consecutive days, and then, of course, single days. This makes it almost impossible to compile totally accurate date-sheets — although the ones published at the back of this book do represent the most definitive listing ever attempted in the one hundred years since those tours were undertaken.

Someone once said: "It is the duty of a writer to tell people something they didn't already know."

    I trust I have done my duty.

"A J" Marriot

Any mistakes are purely the responsibility of the author, and no doubt some of you will find mistakes. There may be errors where I have ventured into the world of solo films, but then this is not my area of expertise. Others may wish that I had expanded coverage on the Laurel films, or given CVs about other acts who appear in the narrative, but my goal was to keep Laurel as the focus of the picture. Just how many leaves does an artist have to paint on a tree, before you accept it as a tree?

Bouquets to the author at ajmarriot@aol.com (but not too many brickbats, please! I'm sensitive.) Corrections will be better received, and additions and amendments gratefully so.

I hope you get as much fun out of reading it, as I got out of researching it.

ACKNOWLEDGEMENTS

My main acknowledgment is to Rob Stone, who so generously supplied me with hi-res' copies of the hundreds of newspaper cuttings/clippings from one of Stan Laurel personal scrapbooks. (See Preface for further details!) These provided invaluable information on who, where, and what to search for; plus greatly enhanced the page illustrations in the book itself.

CHAPLIN SECTION

As Laurel spent the years 1910 to 1913 with Chaplin, some of the text is repeated from my book *"CHAPLIN – Stage by Stage"* for which I herewith also repeat my thanks to contributors:

I was lucky enough to spend time and correspondence with Fred Karno Jnr's widow, Olive, during her later years. I never asked her for anything, but she would often make me surprise gifts of items that she knew were of interest to me. Among these were scripts for some of the Karno sketches, extracts of which I am happy to share with readers of this book. Her son Michael was also generous enough to pass on further material to me, for which I am also grateful.

My gratitude also goes to descendants of the Karno Company members who toured America, for so kindly sharing their family archive photos and information: Valerie Gough, Vanessa Hussey Daley, Shorn Rah, Keith Ripley, June Russell, Tina Talbot, Hilary Snow, Linda Barber, Ian Smith, Sue Evans, Paul Duncan; Jane Koszuta and Karen Nesbitt (The Zanettos); and Marian Daniels, a great-niece of Muriel Palmer, who allowed me copies of the postcards, picturing the Karno Company, which Muriel sent home during the 1910-1912 U.S. Tours.

Then there were the "professional" guardians of personal collections. To Kate Guyonvarch and Claire Byrski, from 'Associated Chaplin' in Paris, who provided me with many rare and intriguing items from the Chaplin Archives up to and including 1913, I am greatly indebted for their extreme generosity. And to John Cahoon, Keeper of the 'Stan Laurel Collection' in the Los Angeles Natural History Museum, who allowed me images of the collection, I also acknowledge my appreciation. And to Chaplin biographer David Robinson for his friendship, generosity, and support.

For many of the reviews from Chaplin and Laurel's UK tours I am especially beholding to Catherine Comerford, Managing Director of *The Stage* newspaper, and Trevor Davies Production Manager, who very kindly provided me with CD copies of relevant volumes.

Thanks also to the following "Sons of the Desert":– Bram Reijnhoudt, Editor of the Laurel & Hardy Dutch magazine *Blotto*; and Wolfgang Guenther, Editor of the German *Two Tars* magazine.

And to the Libraries in England who were helpful in the extreme:

Stoke on Trent Archives – Janine Dawson; Portsmouth Central Library – Alan King; Wandsworth Local History – David Ainsworth; North Shields Local Studies – Eric Hollerton and Diane Leggett; Medway Archives – Jean Lear; Walsall Local History – Diana M. Wilkes.

And a Special Mention to the staff of the British Newspaper Library, Colindale, who, with unfailing grace, supplied me with literally thousands of newspapers.

UNITED STATES:

For the dates on the U.S. Karno Tours, I am grateful to my newly-found Scottish friend, Bob Dickson, who continually dispatched to me material that I would have struggled to find had I gone to the States myself. Bob also persuaded friends of his to do additional searches on my behalf. These people were: Spokane – Peter E. Nufer; Seattle – Samantha Everett; and Exeter – Carol Beers. Needless to say, without Bob and his friends' dedication in spending *weeks* in their various research centres, the account and date-sheets for the Karno US Tours would have been sadly depleted.

Others volunteers who, for neither fee nor favour, spent hours searching for information that only I was to benefit from are: Hooman Mehran; Hank Sykes, Richard Stewart; Mark Russell, Bill Oates, Bill Cassara, Brett Bradford, Steven Trodd, Gregg Nestor, Laurel Strumpf, and Matthew M. Bohn. The sole motivation of all these people was to assist towards generating a complete account of the early years of our beloved hero, Stan Laurel. They can now be justifiably proud of getting us ever-closer to that commendable aim.

To the *Ellis Island Foundation* I extend my utmost gratitude for access to the New York Immigration Records, which were invaluable in tracking the movements of the various Karno troupes across the great pond.

The following U.S. Libraries were helpful in the extreme:

LAUREL — Stage by Stage

St. Paul Central Library – Mark Kile; Baltimore Enoch Pratt Free Library – Don Bonsteel; Baltimore County Public Library – Valentina Pickens; Milwaukee Public Library – Brian Williams-Van Klooster; Minneapolis Public Library – Nathalie Hart; Kansas City Public Library – Sara J. Nyman; Cincinnati County Library – Joan Luebering; Butte-Silver Bow Public Library – anon; Duluth Public Library – David Ouse; Beverley Hills, Academy of Motion Picture arts – Susan Oka.

-----0-----

EUROPE

Bram Reijnhoudt (*ibid*) who passed on material he had acquired over a thirty-year period; and Marc De Coninck — Grand Sheik of the "Me and My Pal Tent" (Belgium) — who took it upon himself to visit libraries and spend days tracking down contemporary newspaper reports.

-----0-----

To Simon Louvish and Louis Morter – by whose perceptions and suggestions, the text of the Chaplin book greatly benefitted. Danny Lawrence (author) for comparing notes on Stan Laurel's boyhood years.

To Ross Owen (Scotland) for his valued publicity and marketing; and to Rob Lewis (Grand Sheik of the 'Helpmates UK' Tent) for his contribution, assistance and support in so many ways.

-----0-----

BIBLIOGRAPHY

"LAUREL or HARDY - The Solo Films," Rob Stone with David Wyatt (Split Reel)

"Mr. Laurel & Mr. Hardy," John McCabe (Signet USA)

"BABE – The Life of Oliver Hardy," John McCabe (Robson)

"The Comedy World of STAN LAUREL," John McCabe (Doubleday)

"LAUREL and HARDY – The Magic Behind the Movies," Randy Skretvedt (Moonstone)

"The Making of STAN LAUREL," Danny Lawrence (McFarland)

-----0-----

NEWSPAPER ARCHIVES

Genealogy Bank.com – Newspapers.com – FindMyPast.com – The Stage Archive – Old Fulton – California Digital Newspaper Collection – MyHeritage.com – Google News Archive – University of Alberta.

Other on-line ARCHIVES: lettersfromstan.com (Bernie Hogya)

-----0-----

IMAGE SOURCES

Author's Collection – Google images – Getty/Corbis/Keystone Images – Cine-Variety (Mike Lang) – Brian Clarry – Paul E. Gierucki – Bernie Hogya — John Cooper – Carl M. Cole – David Tomlinson.

> [Every effort was made to trace the present copyright holders of the photographs and illustrations contained within these pages. Anyone who has claim to the copyright of any of those featured, please make representation to the publisher, who will be only too pleased to give appropriate acknowledgement in any subsequent edition(s).]

It isn't that long ago when the only way to receive photographs was by negatives or prints being sent by post. Nowadays, with email, and especially with tens of thousands of related images available to download from the Internet, keeping tabs on the source of photographs is nigh on impossible. My sincerest apologies, therefore, to anyone I may have omitted to acknowledge as source.

CONTENTS

TITLE			i
COPYRIGHT			ii
PREFACE			iii
ACKNOWLEDGMENTS			vi
CONTENTS			viii
Chapter 1	Father of a Comic Genius	(1884 - 1894)	1
Chapter 2	Empire of Theatres	(1895 - 1907 pt1)	4
Chapter 3	Solo – So Low	(1907 pt2 - 1908 pt1)	16
Chapter 4	Home from Home	(1908 pt2 - 1909 pt1)	27
Chapter 5	Two Loaves and Something Fishy	(1909 pt2 - 1910 pt1)	37
Chapter 6	Variety to Vaudeville	(1910 pt2)	52
Chapter 7	The Eleventh Hour	(1910 pt3 - 1911 pt1)	60
Chapter 8	The Awakening	(1911 pt2)	66
Chapter 9	Way Out West	(1911 pt3)	76
Chapter 10	Rotten Dam	(1911 pt4 - 1912 pt1)	87
Chapter 11	Never Go Back	(1912 pt2 - 1913 pt1)	97
Chapter 12	Brotherly Love	(1913 pt2)	108
Chapter 13	One Flew West	(1913 pt3)	114
Chapter 14	The Lull Before the Lull	(1913 pt4 - 1914 pt1)	124
Chapter 15	Where Did He Went?	(1914 pt2 - 1915 pt1)	130
Chapter 16	Too Good to Be True	(1915 pt2)	140
Chapter 17	A Bit of Hurly-Burly	(1915 pt3)	147
Chapter 18	A Puzzle Within a Puzzle	(1915 pt4)	150
Chapter 19	Mae or May Not	(1915 pt5 - 1916 pt1)	157
Chapter 20	Life to the Max	(1916 pt2 - 1917 pt1)	164
Chapter 21	Stanonimity	1917 pt2	175
Chapter 22	The Roach Approach	(1918)	187
Chapter 23	Back in the Old Routine	(1919)	198
Chapter 24	A Special Kind of Nothing	(1920)	210
Chapter 25	Breaking News	(1921)	218
Chapter 26	I Wanna Be in Pictures	(1922 - 1927)	227
Chapter 27	Remember Me?	1928 onwards	234

THE END

Tour Date-Sheets	240
The Author – further reading	263

CHAPTER 1

FATHER OF A COMIC GENIUS

In America in the 1850s the Jeffersons *were* the drama theatre, with Joseph Jefferson playing 'Lord Dundreary' over eight hundred times. In later life, English-born Arthur Jefferson claimed to be a close relative of the American Jeffersons but, in truth, had no family connection. In fact, Arthur Jefferson could not lay claim to being related to *anyone* by the name of Jefferson – as his family name was Gough. To avoid lengthy and complicated notes about ancestry we will, in this account, retain Arthur's chosen name of Jefferson.

Two places of birth are often quoted for him. Many still believe he was born in Darlington, but more recent genealogy searches have ruled this out. *Our* Arthur Jefferson is confirmed as having been born in LICHFIELD, on September 12, 1862.

First sightings of Arthur in the theatrical world are from 1881, when he was based in Manchester. But then in March 1884, after a tour in the pantomime *Babes in the Wood*, an announcement in a trade paper revealed him to be living in Ulverston, Lancashire.

> MR. ARTHUR JEFFERSON, Comedy Character, and Burlesque, as Sergeant Copley in *Grelly's Money*. "Mr. Arthur Jefferson proved himself a capable comedian, his Sergeant Copley being worthy of high commendation." — *Barnsley Independent*.
> PoW, Salford, Oct. 15th, 6 nights

ABOVE: Review dated October 15, 1883
RIGHT: March 21, 1884

> **MR. ARTHUR JEFFERSON**
> Concluded on Saturday last most successful engagement of 10 weeks with Messrs. Roberts, Archer, and Bartlett, as the Baron, *Babes in the Wood* Pantomime. "Mr. Arthur Jefferson, as the Baron, was excellent." – *Era*.
> "Mr. Arthur Jefferson (a promising young actor) gave a capital representation of the Baron Graspall." – *Bedford Observer*.
> Now resting. 32, Oxford-street, Ulverston.

[AJM: A later boundary change placed Ulverston in Cumberland, which subsequently underwent a second name change, to Cumbria].

Arthur's spell of "resting" didn't last long as, on March 19, 1884, he married local girl Madge Metcalfe, whom he had first seen singing in the church choir in nearby Millom. He continued as a touring actor after the marriage, with his preferred roles being made known in this advert:

> **MR. ARTHUR JEFFERSON**
> Comedy, Character, Eccentric Old Men, and Burlesque.
> All arrangements, complete for the present. Address, 32, Oxford-st, Ulverston. Agent, D.S. Batchelor.

The Stage — May 30, 1884

It is interesting to note that, even though he was only in his early twenties, Arthur was specialising in "Eccentric Old Men." It makes me wonder if, when he reached his sixties, his speciality was playing men in their twenties.

In August 1884 Arthur placed an advert in *The Stage* containing the line: "… *all arrangements compete till March 1885* …" — meaning that he was fully booked up till that date. With the security of this work, the Jeffersons were able to upgrade their living accommodation, with a move from 32, Oxford-street, to 5 Soutergate, Ulverston. It also signalled the time to start a family, with the first fruit of their marriage emerging on February 3, 1885, a son – George Gordon Jefferson.

Fast forward three years to February 1888, where we find the Jeffersons domiciled at yet another Ulverston address — Lightburn Park. Madge is listed as resting — i.e. no professional engagements — while Arthur is on tour with the play *Romany Rye*. *The Stage* gave him the following review:

> **MR. ARTHUR JEFFERSON**
> Engaged by Gilbert Elliott, Esq.
> Scragger, *Romany Rye*.
> "Mr. Arthur Jefferson and — are deserving of more than passing mention for their effective performances" – *The Stage* – Feb. 24th.
> ---------
> Miss MADGE METCALFE (Mrs. J.), resting. Lightburn Park, Ulverston.

> **MR. ARTHUR JEFFERSON**
> *Romany Rye* tour
> Miss MADGE METCALFE (Mrs. J.),
> Aristocratic Comedy and Character Old Women.
> At liberty.
> Address, Prince's Bristol; or Lightburn Park, Ulverston.

ABOVE: *The Stage* — April 27, 1888
LEFT: Published March 2, 1988

Arthur's run in *Romany Rye* was to continue till June 1888, but, before it ended, Madge was found to be advertising for theatrical bookings of her own, with her speciality too being old characters. (See above, right!)

Previous accounts of Arthur's theatrical career in Ulverston tell of his having some involvement with the running of the Hippodrome, a wood-and-canvas theatre nicknamed "Spencer's Gaff." Not only was I unable to confirm this, but could not even find contemporary newspaper entries as to its existence. The only theatres I found listed in Ulverston during the Jefferson's residency were: Totten's, Prince's, and the Bell.

In July 1888, Madge Metcalfe's desire to become an actress paid off, as she had been engaged, along with her husband, in a touring play.

> **MR. ARTHUR JEFFERSON**
> Concludes on Saturday next third engagement
> With Brinsley Sheridan, Esq.
> Specially re-engaged in conjunction with
> **MISS MADGE METCALFE**
> (Mrs. J.)
> By Auguste Creamer, Esq.
> Clacton-on-Sea, July 30th, six nights.
> Permanent address, Lightburn-park, Ulverston.

> **BRADFORD – Prince's**
> July 14, 1898
> Arthur Jefferson's Company in *London by Day and By Night*, seen here before under the title *The Bootblack*. Miss Madge Metcalfe, under the somewhat repulsive character of 'Olga Snake,' acts with power and intelligence.

Not long thereafter the Jeffersons left Ulverston, in the North West, and moved to Bishop Auckland, County Durham – in the North East. Together they spent a couple of seasons touring with drama companies, during which time Madge became a most-accomplished actress, as this later review shows.

Sometime between 1889 and 1891, A.J and Madge were staying in professional lodgings at 15 High Tenters Street, Bishop Auckland; but then a move to South View, coincided with them settling down and Arthur starting a long-lasting working relationship with the local Theatre Royal.

When Madge became pregnant again, she feared there might be complications with the birth. Infant deaths were frighteningly all too common at that time, and so she wisely decided to return to Ulverston to have the child under her mother's supervision as a stand-in mid-wife. The decision was well taken as the baby was born a weakly child, having survived a difficult delivery – during which the mother's health was also impaired. As the baby was not expected to live, a christening was quickly arranged in the home.

The birth certificate recorded the child's name as "Arthur Stanley Jefferson" – date of birth – June 16th 1890, in Ulverston, Lancashire. The place of birth was given, confusingly, as "Foundry Cottages" – which was the name of at least two other terraces in the area. The actual address is 3, Argyle Street.

Madge feared that because of her health and lifestyle she would be unable to give proper care to the baby; and so, having to return to her husband's side, left him to be raised by his grandparents. This then was the beginning in the life of a little red-haired baby, who would go on to become one of the world's most famous comedians — STAN LAUREL.

CHAPTER 2

EMPIRE OF THEATRES

When he was sixteen months old, Stanley was taken to be with his mother, who was now living at 66 Princes Street, Bishop Auckland. It wasn't long, though, before he was returned to his grandparents' home in Ulverston, as Madge's skill and assistance in refurbishing the interiors of Arthur's two current theatres was far more valuable to her husband than her services as a mother.

The Theatre Royal, Consett, with Arthur Jefferson as 'lessee and manager,' was re-opened at the beginning of the 1892 Autumn season, followed two months later by the unveiling of the year-long transformation of the Theatre Royal, Bishop Auckland – renamed The Eden.

One year later Jefferson bought the lease for the Theatre Royal in Blyth; where, as with the theatre at Bishop Auckland, its re-establishment as a prestige venue was regarded as a serious attempt to lift the depression which existed in the town.

The earliest known photo of Arthur Stanley Jefferson.
[Taken Monday August 7, 1893]

[AJM: If you are wondering how I know when this photo was taken, it is because the studio address is embossed on the footer. And the only time Stan would have been at this address was on the day the Jeffersons opened the Theatre Royal, Blyth. See adverts for the Fine Art Photo Co. and the Theatre Royal, Blyth, which follow!]

Both adverts dated Monday August 7, 1893

Whilst "A.J" (the most-familiar of Arthur Jefferson senior's forms of address) was keeping his theatrical image alive, Madge had temporarily to forsake hers when – on December 16, 1894 – she gave birth to a daughter, Beatrice Olga. Stanley was brought over for the christening at St. Peter's Church, Bishop Auckland where, in a double ceremony on January 3, 1895, he was "received" into the church.

Arthur Jefferson's next acquisition was the Theatre Royal in North Shields, Tyneside, for which he staged a grand re-opening in August 1895. Within just a few months A.J's talents as manager, producer, writer, and comedy actor were to become firmly established in the minds of all his patrons, as the *Shields Daily News* of December 31st will testify:

> Last night the house at Mr Jefferson's cosy theatre, was crowded in every part to witness a new production by the popular lessee, entitled *The Orphan Heiress*. Mr Jefferson himself undertakes one of the characters, that of 'Ginger', and is responsible for most of the fun. His eccentricities and comicalities were very entertaining, and appealed to the risible faculties of the audience. We also see Mrs. Jefferson (Madge Metcalfe - a Shields' favourite), prominent in the cast, and she proved herself an able exponent of the part allotted to her.

Around October 1897, the complete Jefferson family joined Arthur, in North Shields, and began a new life at Gordon House, 8 Dockwray Square. Here Stanley was to spend what he was later to describe as the happiest days of his life. Some of his time there he recollected in letters written during his retirement years. The first one is to a life-time resident of North Shields, Vic Silver:-

-----0-----

```
                                              Nov. 12th.'55.
My Dear Vic:-
   Got a hell of a kick out of your letter of the 6th. inst.
enjoyed every line, re living those wonderful care-free days
with your vivid description, sprinkled with laughter & Tyneside
humour.

I don't remember going to King St. school, I first started at a
kindergarten at some house in Dockwray Square, it was down in a
basement, then went to a private school in Tynemouth, it was
called Gordon's - he was quite a character, he collected Cats,
don't think he ever let them out of the house - you could smell
the joint from Jarrow, the fish quay was like a garden of roses
compared. The old screwball used to write poetry & we had to
sit and listen to it all day long, his favourite one was "Ode
```

To The Tyneside" - used to add new verses to it every day & ask our opinion. I once told him I didn't like it & had to stand in the corner for an hour. Having so many cats I often wondered if he wrote "Kitten On The Keys"!

After this episode I was sent to a boarding school in Tynemouth I believe it was called Tynemouth College, the reason my folks had me board there was due to my always being in mischief & trouble at home, like setting fire to the house, (accidently of course) & falling into a barrel of fish guts in my best Sunday suit on the fish quay near the "Wooden Dolly", Drinking Gin (thought it was water) got cockeyed & many more escapades too numerous to mention. Think this was the forerunner of my film character!

[AJM: The reason Stan doesn't remember attending King Street School is because he knew it as 'Tynemouth College,' which he *does* remember.]

-----0-----

ABOVE: The Fish Quay – showing the 'herring girls' at work.

LEFT: The Wooden Dolly
Stan mentions the Wooden Dolly in other letters. The original was a carved wooden figure of a Cullercoats fishwife, looking much like a ship's figurehead. Fishermen going to sea would carve off a small piece of the figure, and keep it as a good luck charm on board ship. Needless to say, the original didn't last too long, and has been replaced several times over the years. Today, the site is marked by a dolly, made of fibre-glass.

A second letter, to Mary Rutter, brought forth more reminiscences:

June 7th.'57.

Dear Mary:-

Your mention of the Electric train rides to Tynemouth for a 1D return, bring back many happy memories, I [re]member I used to go to school in Tynemouth & ride the old steam train every day, that was quite an event for me to go by myself with my school bag strapped on my back - wearing knickers & cap! Sometimes I had to walk. I spent my fare on mint Black Bullets!

Theatre Royal, Prudhoe Street, North Shields

Stan's time in North Shields was also when he first got regular exposure to the world of theatre, and all the plays therein. His earliest memory was …:

> I was seven when I made my first appearance on stage. I was cast for the part of a newsboy in "The Lights o' London." Never shall I forget that first night. I spent hours with a make-up box, trying to add a little to my age; and, by the time I had finished, there were so many lines on my face that I looked like Clapham Junction. My one and only line in the play was, "Extra Special!" and I rehearsed it a dozen different ways. But when I came to speak it on the stage, my slight lisp—which you now all know about so well—caused me to make a noise like a soda syphon and this, together with my frightened expression, made the audience laugh so much that it killed a scene that was supposed to be tensely dramatic.
>
> (*Tit-Bits* – October 31, 1936)

[AJM: There doesn't appear to be a production of the play *The Lights o' London* during the time window Stan cites. Maybe he was referring to the similarly named *The Streets of London*, which was presented at the North Shields Theatre Royal during week commencing April 26, 1897. In 1906, Arthur Jefferson produced two more similarly titled plays – *The Rich and Poor of London*, and *London by Day and by Night* – which may have contributed to the confusion (in later years) as to which 'London' play Stan was in.]

Theatre Royal, Blyth

[Yet another option is that Stan was in *London by Day and by Night* when it played, not in North Shields, but at the Theatre Royal, Blyth – w/c January 2, 1899. Stan would have been nine-and-a-half, which is not too far removed from being seven, as far as memory goes. Plus, his mother and father were in the cast.]

> **BLYTH - Theatre Royal**
> January 1, 1899
> The visit of Mr Jefferson and his accomplished wife, supported by a powerful company, with the succesful drama *London by Day and Night*, has been a record one, full houses at early doors being the rule. Mr and Mrs Jefferson take the lead roles of 'Ginger' and 'Olga Snake,' respectively.

LEFT:
The Jeffersons – c1900

A.J, Gordon

Madge, Stanley, Sarah Metcalfe

Olga Beatrice

RIGHT:
Based on the 1901 Census, below, I can state without fear of contradiction, that the lady is called Mary.

Just when Arthur Jnr. had found happiness, and Arthur Snr.'s empire was flourishing, the family was struck by the tragic loss of Madge's newly-born son, Sydney Everitt, who died at only five months old. How lucky for the world that Madge had been so prudent at Stan's birth. The following year her heartbreak was somewhat softened when she bore another son, Edward Everitt (Teddy).

1901 CENSUS for 8 DOCKWRAY SQUARE

Name and Surname of each person	RELATION to Head of Family	Marriage Status	Age	PROFESSION or OCCUPATION	WHERE BORN
Arthur Jefferson	Head	M	38	Theatre Lessee & Manager	Lichfield, Staffs
Madge Jefferson	Wife	M	40		Yorkshire, Hawes
Gordon Jefferson	Son	S	16		Lancashire, Ulverston
Stanley Jefferson	Son	S	10		Lancashire, Ulverston
Sarah Metcalfe	M in law	M	69		Yorkshire, Hawes
Mary Ellis	Nurse	Widow	51	Monthly Sick Nurse	Yorkshire, Cropton
Mary C. Taylor	Servant	Widow	31	Domestic General	Northumberland, S. Shields
Mary J. Dakin	Servant	S	29	Domestic General	Durham, Shildon

Stan's longing to be an actor was not satisfied by having the occasional walk-on part in one of his father's productions, so he wrote and directed his own plays, with the casts recruited from family and friends. What follows is a copy of the script of one such play — *The Rivals of Dockwray Square*:

"The Rivals of Dockwray Square" by Stan Jefferson

Cast:

Beatrice Olga Jefferson as "Miss Olga Ran Ran"

Stan Jefferson as "Stupie"

Gordon Jefferson as "Ratty"

Gordon, Stan, and Olga acting out the play in the backyard of 8 Dockwray Square.
No doubt the props were borrowed from the Theatre Royal.

Scene 1

"The Rivals of Dockwray Square" Starring Miss Olga Ran Ran

The Choice - Ratty or Stupie?

Scene 2

Being stupid myself, I picked Stupie

Scene 3

Ratty being stupid too, decides to settle her choice once and for all - may the best man win.

Scene 4

Ran Ran (off stage) No! No! Not That!!

Scene 5

Ran Ran hurriedly entered, tripped over the rug - scenery fell down - they all recovered & continued the blood curdling scene

"Stop - I'll marry you both!"

PS posters at Waddingtons!

Scene 6

The rivals agree that half a loaf is better than none, and never the twain shall meet!

Scene 7

All's well that ends well. Ran Ran bakes an apple pie to celebrate

-----

But Stan, being the born-comedian he was, didn't limit his roles to drama. In these three unidentified portraits, taken in different years, he seems to be dressed for comedy roles.

| Could this be the page-boy role Stan spoke of? | The North East boy-comedian 'Little Stanley' drew cartoons, but it is not possible to say if that is who Stan is impersonating. | In the role of a "simple" comedian, (but too early for his time as a solo comic). |

In May 1900, news headlines worldwide were proclaiming the "Relief of Mafeking." Mafeking – a small town in South Africa, under British protectorship during the Boer War – had been besieged by the Boers for over seven months before finally being freed. This caused widespread celebrations, especially throughout Britain, which rivalled those for any latter-day Coronation or Royal Wedding. Commencing Saturday morning, May 19th, work was suspended, and people of all ages filled the streets. Everywhere was alive with colour: flags flew from every window ledge; and red, white, and blue bunting criss-crossed the streets.

In North Shields, three bands and a choir paraded in Dockwray Square. Swelled by hundreds of local residents, the whole entourage moved in procession out of the square and through the main streets of the town. For his enterprise in leading the pony on which was seated "Lord Roberts," one young showman was to receive the first of thousands of articles written about him throughout his life.

It is difficult to confirm whether 8 Dockwray Square is sixth, seventh, or even eighth from the left, as the photo was taken when some of the houses (off left) had been demolished.

> A conspicuous feature was seen at the head of the procession. Master Roland Park attired in full regimentals representing Lord Roberts, and mounted on a pony, was the central figure; he was attended by Masters Jefferson, Walton and Davidson attired in the uniform of the Imperial Yeomanry, and they made a perfect little picture, which excited much comment.
>
> (*Shields Daily News*)

That evening, every house in the borough was illuminated and, in Dockwray Square, the residents assembled to watch a re-enactment of a battle, staged by a hundred soldiers of the Civil Imperial Volunteers. This was followed by a huge bonfire and firework display, and dancing until the early hours.

-----0-----

DOCKWRAY SQUARE
North Shields
LEFT: The Jeffersons lived at No. 8, in the terrace on the left (in shadow).

BELOW: Stan and the boy on the pony are on the grass square in the middle of Dockwray, marked by an "X" in the photo left. Behind them is the 'High Lighthouse,' at the top of the bank of the River Tyne. Below is the North Shields Fish Quay.

Although the newspaper article states: " ... *at the head of the procession ... Master Roland Park attired in full regimentals representing Lord Roberts, and mounted on a pony, ...*" the boy in the photo with Stan is either Master Walton or Davidson. Inset, bottom left, *is* Roland Park.

-----0-----

Just to say that, whoever kitted out the four young lads in their authenticate uniforms deserves every praise. They are not exactly costumes you walk into a dress-hire shop and get off-the-peg.

[AJM: There has been some confusion as to which soldier in the Boer War the young Stan Jefferson was portraying. A contemporary newspaper account says only that: "Masters Jefferson, Walton and Davidson were attired in the uniform of the Imperial Yeomanry."

When Oliver Hardy visited North Shields with Stan, in 1932, he told one assembly that Stan was portraying General Buller. Yet another source believes he was Baden Powell (Yes, he of the later Scout movement). In the letter which follows, though, Stan reveals a hitherto previously unknown character:]

LAUREL – Stage by Stage

April 8th.'54.

```
Dear Mr. Newham:-
Thanks for your interesting letter, you are perfectly correct,
regarding my taking part in the celebration at North Shields on
the event of "Relief of Mafeking" in 1900. My Dad (Arthur
Jefferson) on the same night produced a show battle of Boers &
Britons in Dockwray Square - Fireworks & bonfires etc. with
impersonations of Lord (Bob) Roberts - Kitchener - Buller -
Kruger etc. & myself as bugler Dunne - I still have a photograph
of myself taken that day.
```

[AJM: Our good friend Bernie Hogya informs us: "The celebrated 14-year-old hero, 'Bugler Dunne,' was wounded at the Battle of Colenso (the third and final battle of the Second Boer War) and lost his bugle in the attack."]

-----0-----

During 1899 A.J. had been fully occupied with building a new theatre – near the site of the "old" Theatre Royal in Blyth – for which he staged a grand opening in February 1900. By July of that year, Jefferson was showing projected moving "living-pictures." These were short subjects, about 200 foot in length, shown preceding the plays at his theatres. He had gone all the way to London to see, with his own eyes, the stupendous machine "the Royal Randvoll," which projected the films; and, suitably impressed, taken it back to the North – the first of its kind. "And did the North like it?" asked the *Picturegoer* in a 1932 interview.

> "Not a bit!" replied Arthur. "And did Stan get excited? Not a bit! I don't remember a single display of enthusiasm on his part. In that black box lay his future fortunes, and he wasn't even interested."

By 1901 A.J's empire was at its largest. To the lesseeship of the Borough of Tynemouth Circus and Novelty Hippodrome, and the Theatre Royals in Blyth, Wallsend, Hebburn, and North Shields, he added the Metropole Theatre, Glasgow. This was looked upon with great excitement by those members of the local populace who were aware of his theatrical achievements. For those unaware, he placed the following newspaper announcement in the two main Glasgow newspapers:

Arthur Jefferson

August 5, 1901
THEATRE METROPOLE, GLASGOW
Ladies and Gentlemen, - Having secured a long lease of this Theatre, permit me to assure you that I shall strive hard not only to prove worthy the patronage accorded to and so justly deserved by my predecessors, but to augment same to the extent to which - after a fair trial - you may consider my efforts are entitled.
My Respectful Compliments.
ARTHUR JEFFERSON

Mrs. Arthur Jefferson

A.J. left the Metropole in the hands of an acting-manager, and continued to run his businesses from North Shields, but did make frequent visits to the Glasgow theatre.

Late the following year, 1902, the Jeffersons moved from Dockwray Square to 'Ayton House,' a substantial property on the edge of North Shields, where they were to stay for two-and-a-half years.

As some compensation for Stan's disappointment in having to leave Dockwray Square, A.J. had his stage-hands build a theatre in the attic of their new home, Ayton House. This allowed Stan to carry out his ambition to run his own repertory company, and acted as a social gathering place for the family – including cousins Mary and Nellie Shaw. Nellie recalled: *"Stan used to play the drums – not very well – and this served as the orchestra."* The project designed to enable our subject to learn his craft from an early age was, however, short lived. During a titanic on-stage-struggle in one play, between Stan and one of his school pals, an oil lamp was accidentally kicked over, and a fire started. Luckily it was soon contained, but A.J. decided the theatre should be closed.

LEFT: The lady may be one of the servants, Mary Taylor, with Stan outside *Ayton House*.

In a later letter, Stan described his schoolwear as follows:

```
I used to wear the black ribbed stockings & the garters, &
knickerbockers & the school bag on my back with straps over the
shoulders & the school cap with initials on the front - my bag
contained a sandwich & an apple & of course a marble bag.! More
important than books.
```

Stan soon found an audience elsewhere. Whilst attending the King James I Grammar School, Bishop Auckland (January 1902 to July 1903), he learned to his delight the perks one can receive from the art of making people laugh. Most comedians will tell you that the way they escaped being bullied at school, was to keep their would-be attackers amused. This also pays dividends with teachers, as they are unlikely to punish a child who enlightens the dull routine of school existence with genuine amusement. Stan was soon recognised as having this quality, and his services as an entertainer were sought after by pupils and masters, alike. In this instance, though, his popularity went against him as A.J. felt that Stan wasn't learning enough, due to the teachers' leniency, and had him transferred to Gainford Academy.

In 1905 the Jeffersons moved to Glasgow, because (Arthur said) of Madge's ill-health. A.J. left his North East theatres in the hands of acting-managers, and concentrated on running solely the Metropole. The Jeffersons' first address in Scotland is thought to be 187 Stonelaw Road, Rutherglen. Stan's education again suffered, but yet another move – from Stonelaw High School, Rutherglen (aka: Rutherglen Academy) to Queen's Park Secondary – proved futile, as he was forever playing truant. One of his hideaways was an old shed in Rutherglen, where he would play-act with other members of the entertainment troupe run by his friend, Willy Walker.

But then in February 1907, Stan got to play-act on the stage of the Metropole Theatre, in front of an audience of theatregoers, when his father produced, directed, and starred in his self-penned sketch *The Amateur Fire Brigade*.

Stan would have been keen to show off his talents as a music-hall comedian, but the bill reveals that his role required him to dress as a female, to play the Mayor's daughter — Evelina Clementine. At the time, he may have been a little reluctant to let his friends and family see him in drag, but the world has to be thankful that he went through with it, as it was to be the first time of many that audiences were to see him as a female character, both on stage and then later in film — a guise in which he enacted some of his greatest comedy scenes.

"THE AMATEUR FIRE BRIGADE"
On Saturday, February 9, 1907, was produced at the *Metropole*, Glasgow, a sketch by Arthur Jefferson, entitled:-
The Amateur Fire Brigade; or
The Fire Fighters of Frizzlington
Theopilus Fairhead .... Mr. James Albert
Susanhah .... Miss Vinnie Edmunds
Evelina Clementine ...... Master Stanley Jefferson
Percy Arthur Marmaduke .... Mr. Willie Albert
Rev. Reginald Letterspray ..... Reginald Hamilton
Joe Porter .... Mr. Fred Bernard
Scene one -
Club Room in "The Warriors Arms", Frizzlington
Scene two - Exterior of Brewery

THE AMATEUR FIRE BRIGADE - Or The Firefighters of Frizzlington,
A Sketch, by Arthur Jefferson, in 2 scenes.
(Metropole Glasgow 11.2.07)

CHARACTERS:
Theophilus Fairhead, Mayor of Frizzlington
Susannah, his wife
Evelina Clementine, his daughter
Willie Arthur Marmaduke, his son
Joe Porter, Landlord of the Warriors Public House
The Reverend Reginald Letterspray
Members of Fire brigade. Ballet troupe - waiters, crowd, etc.

Social gathering in pub to inaugurate formation of fire brigade, speeches, firemen kiss the ballet girls.

MAYOR: Theophilus - you are a disgrace - oh the hussies - as for you lot you're no more fit to be firemen than my umbrella - Firemen! Bah! - beasts - brutes - cannibals - hanimals and hyenas. (Exits)

LANDLORD (enters): Gentlemen, good news, your services are required - there's a blaze at the Marine stores - quick quick - there's not a moment to lose - the crowd are getting the engine out.

(Men are horrified at the idea and want to rush home, till told the blaze is not at the store, it's at the Brewery.)

Fire engine enters driven by son - an antiquated affair, groggy old horse - crowd cheer. No men on the engine.

POLICEMAN: Just in time sir. Where's the men?

SON: Good gracious they must have fallen off, will someone please go and look for them.

VOICES: Hurrah! Here they are - better late than never etc.

Men run on, some of them bandaged up. Here follows business ad lib. Men more intent on saving barrels of beer than lives - cheers as each barrel saved. Old man at top window continually calling for help but no notice taken of him. Sheet is held and just as person is going to jump, men remove it to another place, person falls on stage.

SON: Bring me a ladder quick. (Men bring him a ladder)

MAN: It's not long enough, Captain

SON: Then cut it in two you idiots and splice it.

(Crowd cheer, men saw ladder in two, tie it up, Captain goes up it breaks - he falls, crowd cheer)

SON: Where is the hose - give it to me - play on that side (men point hose at other side but no result)

MAN: It won't work Captain

SON: Give it to me - it's stopped up. Give me a pin - great heavens we shall be too late - No No - it's useless it won't work.

Boy: Please Captain, it isn't connected to the mains.

SON: Of course it isn't - what the blazes are you idiots thinking of? Go and fix it up.

MAN: Please Captain, we've forgotten how to do it.

SON: Well look at the book, where is it?

MAN: Where's the book?

(All look for manual, Mayor brings it, policeman tries to fix hose, then curate - it squirts in curate's face; Mayor is hauled up on rope to save girl he sees at window, but when her shawl comes off sees she's ugly, he pushes her out of window and calls for help.

Son and firemen haul Mayor out on rope.

[Facsimile of the script] [ABRIDGED]

-----0-----

When Stan left school, A.J. put him in full-time employment at the Met'. There, often finding himself on stage in front of a deserted auditorium, Stan would imagine himself to be one of his idols: Dan Leno, George Robey, or Tom Foy. During one such dream sequence, right on that very stage, Stan decided he had had enough of all this pretence, and determined to launch himself as a comedian. Unbeknown to his father, he spent several weeks in trying to build up an act. This he did by watching comedians at Glasgow music halls, and then stealing their songs and patter. When he felt he was ready, he boldly approached the manager of the nearby Britannia Music hall – A. E. Pickard – and got himself a place on one of his Friday night try-outs — of which the *Victualling Trades Review* said:

> The Britannia, the oldest music hall in town, presents a bill of fare equalled by few. Their amateur night every Friday is held in great repute by budding Dan Lenos.

At these "try-out" nights audiences were programmed to be derisory, but if the act was good enough they gave due credit; if not, the act got the "bird" — which involved being whistled at and booed, and sometimes being dismissed under a barrage of small missiles. If this sounds like a game of Russian roulette then the comparison is well drawn, and coming out of it "alive" was the thrill factor.

On one such evening, Stan duly sneaked out of the Metropole, without leaving word of his absence, so as to avoid being questioned about the parcel under his arm, for in it were his stage-clothes, props, and a stick of red grease paint. The latter was for painting Stan's nose red, of which he said: "*You couldn't be funny in those days, unless you had a red nose.*"

[AJM: Nor today, if "Comic Relief" is anything to go by.]

Stan with greased hair, red nose, stick-out ears, and blacked-out teeth. Date and venue unknown. Could this be his comedy debut at the Britannia?

As if the contents of the parcel weren't causing him enough worry, the thought of appearing at the Britannia was even worse. All comedians get attacks of nerves before a show but, like electrical impulses, they discharge from the comedian once he is at ease with his audience.

Stan takes over:

> I was terribly nervous, but determined to go through with it. My first verse and chorus seemed to go fairly well, and I was getting one or two ribald laughs with my patter. Gaining confidence, I glanced at the manager, who was standing in the corner of the stalls, to see how he was taking it.

(*Tit-Bits* – October 31, 1936)

It was at this exact moment that Jefferson Jnr. got an almighty shock, for standing at the back of the room was Arthur Jefferson—his father.

CHAPTER 3

SOLO – SO LOW

Stan had obviously overplayed his hand, for it needed no Sherlock Holmes to locate him that night. A.J's suspicions would have been aroused as to his son's recent Friday nights' disappearances, and a casual word with Madge, or the proprietor of the Britannia, Albert Ernest Pickard, would easily have solved the mystery.

The "Britannia Theatre of Varieties," to give it its full title, was part of a large complex known as the Panopticon; which, as its name would suggest [from the Greek meaning: "able to see everything in a single view"] incorporated the widest spectrum of attractions — wax tableaux; a Gypsy Palmist; bioscope pictures; slot-machines; electric rifle-shooting machine; a zoological collection of live animals; Roof Garden; an American Museum; and a Freak Show which, at various periods, boasted such curiosities as "The Bear Lady," "The World's Fattest Boy," "The World's Smallest Man," and "The Armless, Lady Midget."

Opening hours were 6a.m till 10p.m., and admission was a mere tuppence (two pence). If the exhibits weren't enough to justify the entrance fee, consider that there was a music-hall show, with four performances daily and which changed weekly.

Stan managed to stay coherent during his act, and resisted the temptation to flee the stage. More importantly, whether from audience sympathy or his display of talent, he received a good round of applause, after which, in his own words:

> I removed my make-up and rushed back to the Met' to hide from my father's wrath, but he was already there. He called me into his office, where, for what seemed like several minutes, neither of us spoke. Finally he glanced up at me and said, 'Not bad, son, but where on earth did you get all those gags?' Fearfully, I told him the whole story and waited for the storm to burst. Slowly, he rose to his feet, 'Have a whisky-and-soda?' he asked quite casually. At first I could not believe my ears, but when it dawned upon me I seemed to grow six inches in as many seconds. My boyhood was behind me – dad was accepting me as a man!
>
> Putting his arm around me he led me into the theatre bar, and, with eyes glistening, introduced me to his friends as 'My son, Stan – the new comedian.' Was I proud? I still think it was the greatest moment of my life.

[AJM: Sorry to say, but my own research leads me to believe that the Talent Show was not held on the stage of the Britannia Theatre, at all. In the above photo you can see a building on the left, in a process of construction. When completed, it was accessible via a doorway off the staircase leading to the balcony of the theatre, and it was here that the "second school of thought believes" the Talent Show took place, in a curtained-off room. The Britannia had a full music hall show running daily, and so it is unlikely that those who had just put in a good week's work would suffer the efforts of a batch of awful amateur acts. Friday night was heavy drinking and zero tolerance night, when even professional acts weren't always well-received; so to put amateurs in front of them, would be like throwing the Christians to the lions. As I say, it is only second school of thought, and so does not automatically rule out the first theory. Hey ho!

Another doubt is the oft-quoted date of June 1906. Taking in what is to happen next, Stan's Talent Show appearance was more likely mid-summer 1907.]

| Mark Sheridan | Ella Shields | Dan Leno | Stan Jefferson | George Robey |

WILL THE REAL STAN JEFFERSON PLEASE STAND UP!

The costume Stan is wearing in the above photo may well be the one he wore on the night. (The one described by John McCabe – in fact, the whole account of the appearance at the Britannia by John McCabe – I take with a pinch of salt). Stan would have had no problem in selecting what kind of comedic costume to wear, as contemporary comedians dressed in a pretty much standard uniform — as seen in the above. Even the male impersonators, like Ella Shields and Vesta Tilley, had the same concept of how a comedian should dress.

That the young Jefferson emerged unscathed from his traumatic first appearance made it one of the most significant milestones in the development of Stan Laurel "the comedian." Experiencing public humiliation in front of his father would have caused irreparable damage to the boy's ego, and halted progression into the next stage of his metamorphosis. As it was, A.J. now knew that his son was against following in his footsteps as a theatre manager, and was set on touring the halls — a profession he had hoped Stan would avoid after being warned of all the pitfalls and heartaches involved.

Jefferson senior may also have been aggrieved that his son was leaving the drama theatre to go into Music Hall. [Known in America as "Vaudeville" — later to become known in Britain as "Variety."] Drama had a history going back several hundred years, and was socially acceptable at most levels. Music Hall, however, was a fairly recent happening, and could scarcely be called cultural. Its roots lay in the pubs of London in the early nineteenth century, and it was to be as late as 1912, only after the first *Royal Performance* (Palace Theatre, London – July 1st), before it was considered to be truly "legitimate." Up till then, it had been frowned upon by the church and establishment alike. Also, most early music-hall venues were little more than taverns, so audiences drank throughout the evening, and were thus unable to appreciate the finer points of quality entertainment.

Accepting that Stan was determined to pursue a career in this medium his father decided to get him off to a good start, and used his status to obtain for Stan an introduction into the "Levy & Cardwell Pantomime Company."

Putting someone on a team does not guarantee them keeping their place, so Stan would still have to prove his worth if he were to stay. His immediate engagement was in the pantomime *The Sleeping Beauty*, for which rehearsals began in August 1907, after which it ran from August 12, 1907 to April 25, 1908. That's a staggering thirty-seven-week run. These days, few pantomimes barely survive longer than a couple of weeks either side of Christmas.

NEW CENTURY THEATRE
MOTHERWELL
MONDAY, October 14th. for 6 nights and
Matinee Saturday, October 19th. at 2 o'clock.
Mr. and Mrs. H. B. Levy and J. E. Cardwell's famous Juvenile
Pantomime Company in the original fairy spectacle.
"THE SLEEPING BEAUTY"
Full Chorus of 60.   Augmented Orchestra.
Grand Musical, Flower and Nations Ballets.
Specialities by Wee Georgie Wood, marvellous boy comedian and mimic; La Belle Annette, Ida Reenard, Myra Eyton.

Mr. and Mrs. H. B. LEVY'S COMPANIES.

Memorandum of Agreement made this 1st day of July 1907 between MR. AND MRS. HAROLD B. LEVY, Theatrical Managers of the one part, and Mr Arthur Jefferson of Glasgow being guardian of Stanley Jefferson of the other part.

WHEREAS the said MR. AND MRS. HAROLD B. LEVY agree to engage, and the said Stanley Jefferson agrees to accept an engagement at a salary of £1 5s per week from aug to Xmas and from Xmas to Easter weekly, to include all performances and matinees and to play the parts allotted them including specialities.

The said engagement to begin on or about August 19th 1907 and to be for the Tour from August 19th to Easter 1908 Inclusive Rehearsals to be given for two weeks commencing August 12th the said Stanley Jefferson further agreeing to provide all dresses wigs tights and shoes as the Management desires.

MR. AND MRS. LEVY agree to pay all train and boat fares (3rd class only) after commencement of tour until termination of engagement.

This Agreement being made subject to the following rules, regulations and conditions:

LIST OF RULES.

The handwritten part of the above Memorandum of Agreement reads:

> 1st day of July 1907. Mr. Arthur Jefferson of Glasgow being guardian of Stanley Jefferson. ... accept an engagement at a salary of 20s per week from Aug to Xmas and £1 5s. from Xmas to Easter ... The said engagement to begin on or about August 19th 1907. and to be for the Tour from August 19th to Easter 1908 inclusive. Rehearsals to be given for two weeks commencing August 12th.

THEATRE ROYAL

A pantomime which is practically performed by young persons calls from the critic the utmost leniency, were that needed to be exercised, but in the case of Messrs. Levy and Cardwell's juveniles there is so much that is really artistic that the spectator is charmed into forgetfulness that the performers who enchant his ear and beguile him of his dullness, are not full-grown and fully equipped histrionically and mentally. This is Messrs. Levy's second year with this pantomime. Last year *The Sleeping Beauty*, or *The Prince With the Golden Key*, came to us as a novelty in the domain of pantomime, and its success was assured. The company of young persons - some of them of very tender years, who yet babble and articulate in childish treble - have been well trained, and so effectively instructed that there is practically no suggestion of the automaton or the mechanical. The action is free and unconstrained, and the panto as a whole is a merry one, overflowing with the exuberance and charm of youth and beauty. The music has of course a certain music-hall lilt and tang, but there are one or two songs introduced worthy to be included in music of a higher character, and an added beauty is given to the melodies of the chorus of fresh young voices, sweet and tuneful. There is a spirit of boisterous good humour permeating the whole performance, and no-one can complain that the scenic setting is unattractive, and though both scenery and dresses did duty last season the tarnish and soil are not yet very visibly apparent. It specially appeals to children, and is not uninteresting to the elders. The chief performers are practically the same as before and they repeat their elaborated studies in pose, poetry of motion, and their grotesque studies in humour, to the evident amusement of young and old alike

As before, the performance of Wee Georgie Wood, the child comedian, the smallest performer of such prominence, ability, and self-possession we know, is the favourite with the audience. From the opening scene, where he appears in the nursery with his mechanical toys and his nurse, and he recalls to him the story of *The Sleeping Beauty*, to the final lowering of the curtain on the revels of 'Hyacinth Palace', he is the cynosure of all eyes, and the wonder of all who see him for the first time. Needless to say that the performances of the young persons associated with him are very clever in many ways, notably the acting and singing of Miss Kitty Trewitt as "The Prince"; Miss Isa Gibson as "The Sleeping Beauty"; Miss Flo Edwards as "Queen Claribel", with her fairy attendants Misses Irene Vivienne, Pearl Dewar, Cissie Reenan, Addie Gibson, Beattie Townsend. No less notable are the characters sustained by Misses Marie Lumberg, Trixie Wyatt, Daisy Wood, Hilda Large, Annie Brett, May Rutherford, Gertie Brumby. The comic men and fun-makers generally are up-to-date; namely Messrs. Graham and Barron, the Bros. Armstrong, Master Jack Harrison, Messrs. Adamson and Jefferson, and Rose Paley. Special mention must be made of Little Jeannie Brodie, the clever Scotch lassie, whose graceful dancing was much admired. She has won an abundance of medals, which she displayed in all their golden brilliance on her costume.

(*Ashton-under-Lyne Reporter* — January 25, 1908)

THE SLEEPING BEAUTY

1907

August 12	Lancashire	BACUP, New Court
August 19	Lancashire	CHORLEY, Grand
August 26		no trace
September 02	Lancashire	LANCASTER, Athenaeum
September 09	Scotland	LEITH, New Gaiety
September 16	Scotland	LEITH, New Gaiety
September 23	Durham	SOUTH SHIELDS, Royal
September 30	Durham	SUNDERLAND, King's
October 07	Scotland	GREENOCK, Alexandra
October 14	Scotland	MOTHERWELL, New Century
October 21	Yorkshire	CASTLEFORD, Royal
October 28	Wiltshire	SWINDON, Queen's
November 04	Cheshire	CREWE, Lyceum
November 11	Staffordshire	LONGTON, Queen's
November 18	Lancashire	DARWEN, Royal
November 25	Lancashire	TYLDESLEY, Royal
December 02	Lancashire	RAWTENSTALL, Grand
December 09	Yorkshire	MEXBOROUGH, Prince of Wales
December 16	Lancashire	WIDNES, Alexandra
December 23	Cheshire	STOCKPORT, Royal
December 30	Cheshire	STOCKPORT, Royal

1908

January 06	Manchester	SALFORD, Regent
January 13	Manchester	SALFORD, Regent
January 20	Lancashire	ASHTON-under-LYNE, Royal
January 27	Lancashire	ASHTON-under-LYNE, Royal
February 03	Lancashire	OLDHAM, Colleseum
February 10	Staffordshire	STAFFORD, Lyceum
February 17	Staffordshire	DUDLEY, Royal Opera House
February 24	Wallasey	SEACOMBE, Irving
March 02	Durham	JARROW, New Royal
March 09	Durham	SEAHAM HARBOUR, New Royal
March 16	Northumberland	BLYTH, New Royal
March 23	Cumberland	CARLISLE, His Majesty's
March 30	Durham	NORTH SHIELDS, Royal
April 06	Durham	CONSETT, New Royal
April 13	Durham	WEST STANLEY, Royal
April 20	Durham	HARTLEPOOL WEST, Grand and Opera House

-----0-----

In this production, the scene opens upon a nursery. A small boy is sat up in bed, surrounded by several mechanical toys. A nurse is by his bedside reading to him the story of *The Sleeping Beauty*. The boy falls asleep and, in his dream, his toys come to life. One of these was a golliwog, behind the black face of which was one Stanley Jefferson. In this guise, Stan faced the desperate task of trying to gain experience and show off his talents, whilst being allowed to do little more than follow the leading player around — a twelve year-old Wee Georgie Wood, in the role of 'Bertie Dalrymple.'

```
              THE SLEEPING BEAUTY
          Or "The Prince with the Golden Key"
          A pantomime in one act by H.B. Levy
     BERTIE of the King's Lifeguards
     QUEEN
     KING
     WICKED WITCH MALIGNIA
     GOOD FAIRY
     JULIUS CAESAR    ) Gollywog 1
     EBENEZER SNOW    ) Gollywog 2
```

SCENE 1:- A MODERN NURSERY
OPENING CHORUS OF AUTOMATONS:

    Objects of wonder we are to you,
    At which we are not surprised.
    By the one we are to amuse,
    We are now greatly prized.
    With wires we will appear to be,
    As near reality as can be.
    But we cannot move at will you see,
    Until we are wound up with a key.
    Now you see we are only toys,
    Made to please both girls and boys.

As the Fairy blesses the baby who is to be the Sleeping Beauty:-

BERTIE: What a pretty little baby!

EBENEZER: Ya! Ya! Ya! What are those in the sardine tins?

FAIRY: Now sisters come forward - on her your wishes bestow, have we not decreed, "to perfect woman you'll grow"?

WITCH ENTERS:-

KING: Who is this woman who has entered the royal abode?

GOLLYWOGS: She is a woman suffragist!

GOOD FAIRY: It's the Witch Malignia - "a woman of wickedness".

<u>LATER</u>

ENTER GOLLYWOGS WITH BERTIE, TO QUEEN.

EBENEZER: Please Mrs. Pankhouse - I mean Mrs. Queen, will you protect us?

QUEEN: How?

JULIUS: By calling out the Salford Militia...

LATER)

(THE GOLLYWOGS HELP THEIR MASTER TO ESCAPE THE WITCH.)

[Facsimile of the working script, highlighting Stan Jefferson's role of the gollywog 'Ebenezer Snow.']

(Abridged and edited.)

"The Sleeping Beauty."

WEE GEORGE WOOD, BOY COMEDIAN AND MIMIC.
THE SMALLEST ARTISTE ON THE STAGE.

CARLISLE - HIS MAJESTY'S THEATRE.
Lessees, Mr. Thos. Courtice and Mrs. R. Stewart.

Mr. and Mrs. H. Levy and J. E. Cardwell's juvenile company is the attraction this week in *The Sleeping Beauty*, a bustling, lively pantomime, well supplied with popular songs and pretty dances. A capital audience was attracted on the opening night. Wee Georgie Wood, a remarkably clever little comedian, made a tremendous hit. His cleverly rendered songs were heard all over the house, while his "business" and style would do credit to a long experienced artiste. Little Jeannie Brodie is a clever and dainty dancer, and she was warmly encored; Miss Kitty Trewitt made a dashing Prince, and Beauty was delightfully played by Miss Isa Gibson; The Brothers Armstrong are excellent comedians and dancers, and Messrs. Jack Adamson and Stanley Jefferson cause considerable laughter as two polliwogs; Messrs. Graham and Barron are smart knockabout artistes, and Miss Floe Edwards made a charming Fairy Queen; Jack Harrison and the Misses Rose Paley, Marie Lumberg, and Trixie Wyatt contributed capital performances.

The scenery was very pretty and effective, and the dresses bright and attractive.

SUNDERLAND – King's

There were a number of specialities introduced, including comedy and mimicry by Wee Georgie Wood, who after all made the hit of the night. First he was a charming little boy in petticoats; then a youngster in a velvet suit; next a jockey; after that, an old man; next a young gentleman in evening dress; and last of all a miniature Camille Clifford.

(September 30, 1907)

NORTH SHIELDS - THEATRE ROYAL
Lessee and Manager: Mr. Stanley Rogers;
Acting Manager, Mr. Horace Lee

Pantomime is again the attraction here this week, and Mr. and Mrs. H. B. Levy and Mr. J. E. Cardwell's company, with *The Sleeping Beauty*, has drawn large and delighted audiences. As 'Bertie Dalrymple', Wee Georgie Wood, a very smart little comedian, has made a tremendous hit; the Brothers Armstrong as the 'Queen' and 'Asbestos' are capital comedians and dancers; Messrs. Graham and Barron as 'Colonel Dreadnought' and 'Major Flashlight' have added greatly to the fun; and Messrs. Jack Adamson and Stanley Jefferson as 'Julius Caesar' and 'Ebenezer' are very clever.

Miss Kitty Trewitt as 'Prince Florizel' is much admired; Miss Isa Gibson makes a charming 'Beauty'; Miss Flo Edwards proves a delightful 'Fairy Queen'; Miss Rose Paley is good as 'the Nurse'; and Miss Daisy Thompson Wood an attractive 'King's Herald'.

Specialities are introduced successfully by Wee Georgie Wood, Little Jeannie Brodie (an excellent dancer), and Mlle. Adele; whilst the chorus and augmented orchestra, under the direction of Mr. Arthur Silver, perform their work well. The scenery and dresses are very pretty.

CONSETT - NEW THEATRE
Lessee: Mr Hugh Robertson;
Resident Manager Mr. Lloyd Clarence.

Messrs. Levy and Cardwell's company, with the pantomime *The Sleeping Beauty*, opened to a packed house on Monday. Miss Isa Gibson in the title-role was a complete success; whilst Miss Kitty Trewitt as "Prince Florizel" was very pleasing; Miss Marie Lumberg, as "Sir Alphonso", Miss Trixie Wyatt, and Miss Daisy Thompson Wood as the "Heralds" were well received. Master Jack Harrison as "King Dreadnought" and the Brothers Armstrong as the "Queen" and "Asbestos" were an excellent trio. Wee Georgie Wood as "Bertie Dalrymple" kept the audience in roars of laughter, his comic business being exceptionally funny. Master Jack Adamson as "Julius Caesar" and Master Stanley Jefferson as "Ebeneezer" were very good, and the dancing of Mlle. Adele quite a speciality. The Ballets were well arranged, and the scenery and dresses elaborate.

Despite the limitations of his role — plus the stiff opposition from the star turn, Wee Georgie Wood; and the well-polished routines of senior professional comedy double-acts the Armstrong Brothers, and Graham & Barron — the natural comedic talents of the young Jefferson still shone through, right from the very first show:

> Wee Georgie Wood is a miniature comic, his clever mimicking evokes much laughter. Messrs. Pat Sloan and Stanley Jefferson are amusing as the 'Golliwogs.'

After his original partner Paddy Sloan had been replaced, Stan was still able to extract the laughs, as these two reviews show:

> Master Jack Adamson as "Julius Caesar" and Master Stanley Jefferson as "Ebenezer" were very good.

---0---

> Messrs. Jack Adamson and Stanley Jefferson caused considerable laughter as two polliwogs 'Julius Caesar' and 'Ebenezer.'

[AJM: The third reviewer didn't know his polliwog from his golliwog — the first being an old-English name for a tadpole, and the latter a rag doll in the guise of a blackface character.]

Even at this very early stage in Stan's apprenticeship as a comedian, he was noting and retaining the lines and 'business' which got the big laughs, some of which he would use decades later, in the films of Laurel & Hardy. Here is one example from the pantomime:

In addressing the Queen, Stan (as the golliwog 'Ebenezer Snow') says: *"Please Mrs. Pankhouse – I mean Mrs. Queen, will you protect us?"* The humour here is caused by Stan addressing someone with far too much familiarity, but then, upon realising his lack of formality, immediately offers a more appropriate form of address. He was to use this format of word-play in the 1933 Laurel & Hardy film *Sons of the Desert*, wherein he address Hardy's wife, firstly with a too familiar form, and then immediately switches. So the line from the pantomime, recycled for the film, now goes: *"Hello Sugar ... er ... Mrs. Hardy."*

But there were two bits of business in *The Sleeping Beauty* which were to make a far greater contribution to Stan's film character – both of which came from the routines of professional double act 'Graham & Barron.' In the panto, Jack Graham played the part of 'Colonel Fearnought,' and Benny Barron that of 'Major Flashlight,' but they would have played all their scenes as a double-act – like the 'Chinese Policemen' in the pantomime *Aladdin*. It was an accepted tradition in pantomime, in that era, for professional acts to fill-in between scene changes, in front of tabs (curtains), with one or more bits of business from their known act. Graham & Barron's speciality was Benny doing a soft-shoe shuffle, while Jack crooned a song. However, in this instance, it would seem to be the case that the two elder pro's had taught the routine to the young amateurs, as this how the dance was introduced in the pantomime:

> SCENE 5: THE TOWER RUINS
> ENTER GOLLIWOGS:
> EBENEZER: I say, Julius Caesar, where has our young master gone?
> JULIUS: I'm sure I don't know. He seemed so surprised at all he saw.
> EBENEZER: That may be, but we must not lose him. We must not forget it was he who brought us to see all this fun.
> JULIUS: But Ebenezer, one gets a little tired of always being hooked on to a kid. Let us wait and amuse ourselves. He is sure to find us.
> EBENEZER: All right, let us have one of our old plantation songs and dances.

So there is the cue, right there: *"Let us have one of our old plantation songs and dances."* And, as Julius says: *"Let us wait and amuse ourselves,"* it must be the case that it was indeed the two blackface golliwogs who executed the said dance.

It was after doing this routine during the two-hundred-plus performances of *The Sleeping Beauty* that Stan was able to replicate it for inclusion in the 1931 Laurel & Hardy film *Pardon Us*. So fast-forward to 1931, where one can now quite imagine Stan Laurel sat around a table with other scriptwriters, during a script conference for the film *Pardon Us,* trying to work out some business for Stan and Ollie to do in the scene in the film where they are sitting around a camp fire, with the workers from the cotton plantation. Suddenly, a bell rings in Laurel's memory as to a song and dance he had done when he and a previous comedy partner were also in blackface make-up. Ding! And thus *"one of our old plantation songs and dances"* from the pantomime *The Sleeping Beauty* is revised for the film *Pardon Us*, with Hardy providing the song, *Lazy Moon*, and Laurel providing the soft-shoe shuffle. That's my theory, anyway.

GRAHAM & BARRON
Refined Comedians & Novelty Dancers

[AJM: For anyone who doubts the validity of this claim, let me recount to you a personal event. In 1990 I proudly hosted the *Stan Laurel Centenary Celebrations*, in Blackpool, England. Among my top-table guests were Lord Delfont and his colleague Billy Marsh – the two men who had booked every theatre and act on Laurel and Hardy's post-war stage tours of variety theatres in the United Kingdom. (See my book: *LAUREL & HARDY – The British Tours*.) Another guest was Billy Barron, son of the said Benny Barron. After the showing of the film *Pardon Us*, at the Sunday afternoon film show, Billy came back to my house for tea. He then said to me:

> "You know that song and dance, in the film? That was what my dad and Jack Graham used to do in their act. Before he retired, he taught it to me and my comedy partner, and we carried on doing it around the clubs and theatres."

Billy then proceeded to do the exact dance for me, while I observed him. So there you have it – irrefutable evidence.]

But there was another part of Jack and Benny's comedy business, which had an even more profound and lasting impact on Laurel, and more so on fans of Laurel & Hardy. But firstly, let us look at their bill matter: "Graham & Barron — Refined Comedians and Novelty Dancers." A review of one of their shows stated:

> Graham and Barron's dancing is appreciated

And a second gave us:

> Messrs. Graham and Barron are smart knockabout artistes,

In the latter we can gauge that the two of them indulged in some personal physical exchanges. It was again Benny's son, Billy, who enlightened me as to what that was. He told me:

> The facial expressions Stan adopted were exactly the ones my father used in his act, as he was the one who got everything wrong, and used to 'cry' when his partner knocked off his straw-boater.

I, for one, am more than happy to accept that Stan's "cry" originated from Benny Barron. All comedians, in their formative years, have a tendency to copy those comedians to whom they have regular exposure. After seeing Graham & Barron getting big laughs, at each of the two hundred pantomime performances, it would have taken a strong man to resist the temptation to try and duplicate those laughs. Stan is on quote as saying that he didn't like doing the cry; but, as it worked for him, he continued to do it — which would seem to back up this theory that it did not come from within his own persona, and was thus borrowed from someone else.

Just twelve days after *The Sleeping Beauty* had ended its nine-month run, Stan leap-frogged straight into the saddle of *The Gentleman Jockey,* in which he played the part of 'Tommy' – a stable boy.

In the review of the copyright performance of *The Gentleman Jockey* (below), on Friday, October 18, 1907, at St. Julian's, Guernsey, the part of 'Tommy' is nowhere to be found.

THE GENTLEMAN JOCKEY

On Friday, October 18, 1907, at the *St. Julian's*, Guernsey, was produced a musical play in three acts by Edward Marris entitled:-

The Gentleman Jockey

Sir Francis Granmere	Cecil W. Parker
David Grayson	Mr. Percy Maitland
Frank Snakeworth	Mr. Frank Gala
Archie Fitzherbert	Mr. C. E. King
P.C. Blodgers	Mr. George Brentwood
Uriah Grant	Mr. Fred Parker
P.S. Barrowby	Mr. Arthur Harries
Dr. Potter	Mr. James Green
Jenny Jarvis	Miss May Norris
Moore	Miss Violet Laurel
Bellamy	Miss Norah Palliser
Mary Grayson	Miss Dora Hargreaves
Lady Kitty	Miss Maisie Gerrard
Poppy Grayson	Miss Norah Melton

Act One - The Entrance Hall at Woodsorrel (Morning) Act Two - Grayson's Cottage (Afternoon of Next Day) Act Three - Woodsorrel again (Night)

This, the latest work from the pen of versatile Mr. Edward Marris, met with a good reception from a large and representative audience. The play reveals possibilities which might be exploited by fuller treatment, but it contains within itself all the elements which make for popularity. There is a strong dramatic theme, and the several "situations" are admirably designed. The comedy element is somewhat accentuated, but the humour is good, and in many cases shows distinct originality. Several catchy songs are introduced, the new songs and incidental music having been written by Mr. Marris's musical director, Mr. George Ess. The story of the play concerns the fate and fortunes of Sir Francis Granmere, a riding-owner. At the outset the financial position of this gentleman is scarcely to be described as flourishing, and the victory of his horse 'Poppy', in a forthcoming race, is depended on to retrieve his fortunes. The victory, however, with the combination of horse and rider, is deemed to be a certainty, and in act one we find Sir Francis proposing for the hand of Poppy Grayson, his trainer's charming daughter. We also learn that Poppy has a sister, who has been decoyed away and ruined by some villain, whose identity she has not divulged. Poppy expresses to her lover a strong dislike for Frank Snakeworth who, she says, has insulted her. Sir Francis orders Snakeworth from the house, but the latter refuses to go till certain of Sir Francis' I.O.U's are met. At this juncture a county court bailiff enters with a writ for Sir Francis, which he serves on Snakeworth. The latter explains that this is a mistake, and the writ is then served on Francis. The audience, however, learns that this is the third, or contempt of court, writ, taken out in certain proceedings. The first two have been kept back by Snakeworth, and Sir Francis is therefore not aware that non-compliance with the writ actually served on him renders him liable to arrest. Towards the end of the act there is merrymaking over the engagement of Sir Francis and Poppy. In the midst of the rejoicing, Snakeworth steals in furtively and conceals himself. A moment later Mary Grayson rushes in declaring that she has just seen her betrayer enter the house, and on this scene the curtain falls.

Act Two opens on the day of the great race. Snakeworth, who already has a heavy book with Sir Francis, and is determined that his horse shall be prevented from winning, by foul means if necessary, induces the 'gentleman jockey' largely to increase the stakes. Sir Francis agrees, though he is obliged to pledge the family diamonds. Then, as he is about to leave for the starting post, he is arrested on a warrant issued in connection with the writ. Shortly before this, Snakeworth has received from Mary Grayson a compromising letter, in which she declared her intention of coming to the house, as she had heard that Snakeworth was making love to her sister. On the arrest of Sir Francis, Snakeworth sees an opportunity of making use of this letter. He induces Sir Francis to write a note to Grayson asking for assistance. This note he undertakes to deliver, but he contrives to substitute the compromising letter for the note. The old trainer at once comes to the conclusion that Sir Francis is the villain who has ruined his daughter Mary, and a scene ensues. Actuated by a sense of duty, Grayson agrees to ride Sir Francis' horse, and to ride to win, but declares that, afterwards, there must be a reckoning.

The last act finds Snakeworth non-plussed. Sir Francis' horse, cleverly ridden by Grayson, has won the race. After the race, Grayson disappears, but presently returns with his daughter Mary, having discovered who the villain really is. As a last desperate venture, Snakeworth attempts to steal the Granmere diamonds. He is discovered in the act; retribution follows hard on the heels of injustice; the position of Sir Francis is retrieved, and Poppy and he "live happily ever afterwards."

The play itself is somewhat short for presentation without a *lever du ride* [curtain raiser]. The performance, however, is somewhat lengthened by the inclusion of several songs and dances, and a brief variety entertainment in the last act. The music, written by Mr. George Ess is bright and tuneful, and the singing was good. The play was admirably mounted, and the dressing particularly good.

Mr. Cecil W. Parker was well-suited as Sir Francis Granmere, and acted with conspicuous ability. His most successful song was "My Fair Lady," a new song by Mr. George Ess. Mr. Percy Maitland made a manly David Grayson, and gave a robust interpretation of an excellent *rôle*. Mr. Frank Gala made Frank Snakeworth sufficiently villainous. Mr. C. E. King as 'Archie Fitzherbert' was also distinctly good, and introduced some light humour which added appreciably to the swing of the performance. Mr. George Brentwood was in his element as 'P. C. Blodgers', the village policeman. Mr. Brentwood introduced some clever buffoonery and kept the audience amused when he was on the stage. Miss Norah Melton made an altogether charming 'Poppy', and acted and sang with taste. Particularly good was the duet "When You and I were Children," sung with Mr. Parker. Miss Maisie Gerrard gave a vivacious performance as 'Lady Kitty'. Her songs, "No Fellow Should Be Without a Sweetheart," and "Don't Forget Mignonette," were excellently given. Miss May Norris made a decided hit as 'Jenny Jarvis'. The remaining minor *rôles* were all in safe hands. In the variety portion, Miss Norah Melton contributed a bright sabot song with dance [clog dance]; Mr. C. E. King, Miss May Norris, Mr. Brentwood, Miss Maisie Gerrard, and Misses Violet Laurel and Norah Palliser also contributed.

(*The Stage*)

Maybe in response to the reviewer's comment: *"The play itself is somewhat short for presentation ...,"* the part of 'Tommy' was later written in, so as to create an additional scene or scenes. If so, then Master Jefferson must be given extra praise for making the role so affective — although it wasn't *always* effective, as he tells here:

> It was a racing drama, and I was a stable lad. In the big scene, the villain was plotting to open the stable and steal the horse. At the climax I had to put my head over the top of the door and declaim: "Ah, Sir Reginald, you can't get in—I have the key!" On the first night, as I waved the key triumphantly in the air, it slipped from my perspiring fingers and fell right at the villain's feet. He stared at it for a moment, not knowing what to do. Then, instead of ignoring it, he lost his head, picked up the key, and solemnly handed it back to me. How the audience yelled!

(*Tit-Bits* — October 31, 1936)

GLASGOW - King's
THE GENTLEMAN JOCKEY

Mr. Edward Marris's company present *The Gentleman Jockey* here. 'Sir Francis Granmere' is played with befitting dash by Mr. C. W. Parker. Mr. Leonard Dalrymple is excellent as 'Archie Fitzherbert.' Mr. Walter B. Nugent gives a most effective portrayal of 'Frank Snakeworth.' As 'P.C. Blodgers,' Mr. George Brentwood is irresistibly comic. A splendid character study is given by Mr. Helier Le Maistre as 'David Grayson.' Mr. Victor Rowland is good as 'Grant,' as too is Mr. Henry Wood in the part of 'Mitchell.' Mr. Stanley Jefferson as 'Tommy' is very humorous. Miss Ethel Ward is a charming 'Poppy Grayson,' and sings pleasingly. Miss Lillian Drake is capital as 'Kitty Granmere,' and her musical numbers are greatly appreciated. Miss Gertie Reid is an amusing 'Jenny Jarvis.' Some pretty dancing is contributed by the Lottie Stone Quartet.

YORK - Royal
THE GENTLEMAN JOCKEY

The Gentleman Jockey proves a lively and entertaining attraction. The company are clever throughout. The effective mounting is commendable. Amongst an excellent array of artists, Mr. C. W. Parker, Miss Ethel Ward, Mr. L. Dalrymple, and Miss Lillian Drake work hard to give pleasure in their various characterisations. A highly entertaining impersonation of the policeman is given by Mr. George Brentwood. Other good parts are well represented by Messrs. H. le Maistre, W.B. Nugent, S. Jefferson, and Miss Gertie Reid.

-----0-----

THE GENTLEMAN JOCKEY
Edward Marris Company

1908

June 01	Cheshire	CREWE, Lyceum	
June 08	Manchester	BROUGHTON, Victoria	
June 15	Scotland	EDINBURGH, Royal Lyceum	[rehearsal?]
June 22	Northumberland	NEWCASTLE, Tyne and Opera House	[Stan joins here.]
June 29	Scotland	GLASGOW, King's	
July 06	Yorkshire	YORK, Royal	
July 13	Hampshire	SOUTHAMPTON, Grand	
July 20	Dorset	BOURNEMOUTH, Royal	[Tour ends here.]

-----0-----

As can be seen in the above list of tour dates, *The Gentleman Jockey* had only a very short run. [You can insert your own pun here.] For Master Jefferson, it may have been even shorter, as he references his debut being at Newcastle. However, he may firstly have had to learn and rehearse his part during the Edinburgh run, before taking over the role proper.

Because Stan's part was so small (which is good for a jockey, but not for an actor), and the number of performances was so few, Stan seems not to have recalled much about this play in later life. So we must remain grateful for the newspaper reviews which provide information that would otherwise have been unknown to us.

The Gentleman Jockey	
Sir Francis Granmere	Cecil W. Parker
David Grayson	Mr. Helier Le Maistre
Frank Snakeworth	Mr. Walter B. Nugent
Archie Fitzherbert	Leonard Dalrymple
P.C. Blodgers	Mr. George Brentwood
Uriah Grant	Mr. Victor Rowland
Jenny Jarvis	Miss Gertie Reid
Lady Kitty Granmere	Miss Lillian Drake
Poppy Grayson	Miss Ethel Ward
Mitchell	Henry Wood
Tommy	Mr. Stanley Jefferson

With *The Gentleman Jockey* scheduled to end its run on July 25, 1908, Stan took out an advert in *The Stage* show business paper of July 16, 1908, announcing he was available for engagements after that date.

MR. STANLEY JEFFERSON, Climbing the "comedy ladder." Boys' Parts, Dance, Drama, Burlesque, Panto. Combine Assistant Stage or Acting-Management if required. Aged 18; height, 5 ft. 2 in. Concluded 9 months with Messrs. Levy and Cardwell's Juv. Panto. Co. Engaged by Edward Marris, Esq., as Tommy, the Stable-boy, in *Gentleman Jockey*. At Lib. (term. of Summer Tour) end of July. Offers invited. This, Grand, Southampton; next, Bournemouth. Permanent, Metropole, Glasgow.

But it was an agent a bit closer to home who was to give Mr. Stanley Jefferson his next engagement.

CHAPTER 4

HOME FROM HOME

It would appear that the young Jefferson's talent for scriptwriting had surfaced this early in his career as, on April 16, 1908, *The Stage* advertised:

> **ARTHUR JEFFERSON AND SON'S SKETCHES**
> "For His Sake," "Home From the Honeymoon,"
> "Her Convict Lover," "Amateur Fire Brigade,"
> "An Unwilling Burglar."
> Others in preparation
>
> -----------
>
> Managers and Agents requested to witness
> Home from the Honeymoon
> Opens Moss and Stoll Tour May 1st, Hackney.
>
> -----------

So when Stan's next engagement in 1908 happened to be with the Arthur Jefferson Company, touring with *Home From the Honeymoon*, it was through merit, and not nepotism, that he got the position. [Yes, I know "nepotism" means showing favour to a nephew. Thank you.]

Home From the Honeymoon had started its run on May 18, but part-way through the tour a position became available – thought to be that of assistant stage and/or assistant tour manager. Stan *could have* joined the company at Birmingham, straight from finishing the run of *The Gentleman Jockey*, if not, then the following week at Newcastle would be a good option.

1908

[July 25		Stan leaves *The Gentleman Jockey* at the end of its run.]
July 27	Worcestershire	BIRMINGHAM, Empire
August 03	Northumberland	NEWCASTLE, Empire
August 10	Durham	SUNDERLAND, Empire
August 17	Scotland	DUNDEE, Palace
August 24	Scotland	EDINBURGH, Empire
August 31	Scotland	GLASGOW, Empire
September 07	Scotland	GREENOCK, Alexandra
September 14	Scotland	PAISLEY, Hippodrome
September 21	Liverpool	LIVERPOOL, Empire
September 28	Manchester	MANCHESTER, Hippodrome
October 05	Yorkshire	BRADFORD, Empire
October 12	Yorkshire	LEEDS, Empire Palace
October 19	Yorkshire	HULL, Palace
October 26		vacant
November 02	Yorkshire	SHEFFIELD, Empire
November 09	Nottinghamshire	NOTTINGHAM, Empire
[November 14		Stan leaves *Home From The Honeymoon* at the end of its run.]

-----0-----

Previous biographers have referred to *Home from the Honeymoon* as if it were a play, and thus provided the whole evening's entertainment at a drama theatre. But that isn't so. It was a comedy sketch, and occupied less than twenty minutes on a music-hall bill. Its first airing was the copyright performance on October 7, 1905 at the Metropole Theatre, Glasgow, for one night only, as a "house production" (meaning that it was not put on by a travelling company, but by the Metropole's own band of players). One can guarantee that Arthur Jefferson Snr. AND Jnr. were present on the night. Moreover, there is a distinct probability that one or both took part it.

Most Laurel & Hardy scholars will readily tell you that the premise of *Home From the Honeymoon* forms the basis of the 1927 Laurel & Hardy silent film *Duck Soup*, plus the 1930 sound remake *Another Fine Mess*, although few, if any, have ever produced, or even seen, any evidence to support this. Ace researcher and whimsical author Simon Louvish is the exception, and actually sought out the original script of "Honeymoon." However, rather than print the script here, this newspaper review I unearthed will suffice in providing the comparison in plots we are seeking. It has been taken for granted that you already know the premise of the films in question, so only the plot for the stage play is supplied here.

> **SOUTH SHIELDS** - Empire Palace
> The principal item in an excellent programme is a smartly written farcical comedy sketch in two acts, by Arthur Jefferson, entitled *Home From the Honeymoon*. 'Colonel Pepper's house, which has been advertised to let furnished, is broken into by burglars, who discover a letter which informs them that the servant left in charge is out for the evening. Being surprised by a ring at the door, they rig themselves out in the clothes of the 'Colonel' and his maidservant, and receive the visitor, 'the Hon. Percy Fitzhuggins' who, returning from his honeymoon and finding the drainage of his own house is defective, rents the Colonel's house, and pays three months' rent in advance. The burglar, disguised as a maidservant, acquaints his accomplice of the unexpected return of the Colonel. Before the Colonel enters the apartment it is explained to Fitzhuggins that the newcomer is a madman, whose hallucination is that he is the Colonel, and owner of the house. The burglar persists in addressing him as Hunnable, who has escaped from the asylum (this allusion to the Jarrow election caused much merriment). A pugilist cabman is brought in to help turn the Colonel out, but, taking a revolver from the sideboard drawer, he is the master of the situation. At the height of the hubbub Fitzhuggins's wife, who had been telephoned to on the renting being agreed on, enters. She turns out to be the Colonel's niece, and a reconciliation ensues. The police enter and secure the burglar. The sketch is well mounted and enthusiastically received. Mr. T. G. Warry gives an exceedingly clever representation of Colonel Pepper. Mr. Wm. Compton is excellent as 'Percy Fitzhuggins'. 'Flash Harry,' the burglar, is admirably portrayed by Mr. F. Mounell. Mr. C. Lyle ably sustains the comedy part of 'Lightfoot Jim,' and Miss Miriam Holt gives adequate support as 'Lydia, the Hon. Mrs. Percy Fitzhuggins.' Other much appreciated items are by Horace White (ventriloquist), Ross and Lewis, Horsley Bros., Dolly Denton, Dan Leno jun., Barnard's Mannikins and also the Bioscope.

(The Stage – July 11, 1907)

The following two reviews are from shows played just before Stan joined the company:

NEW CROSS (London), Empire

Arthur Jefferson's farcical absurdity *Home From the Honeymoon* contains much fun, and the persevering efforts of the company, Charles Lloyd, Chris Fenton, Wilfred Compton, Fowler Thatcher, George Elliston, Frank Steadman, and Miriam Holt are liberally rewarded.

(The Stage – June 1, 1908)

A second review, from the Leicester Palace, ran:

> Good comedy sketches are always acceptable, and that introduced by Mr. Arthur Jefferson's Company, *Home From the Honeymoon*, is excellent. It is smartly written, and last night's audiences thoroughly enjoyed the many comical situations in which the sketch abounds.

(Leicester Daily Mercury – July 21, 1908)

Even though it was his father's company, and he had contributed to the script, the young Jefferson took only one of the smaller roles. Transferring the plot of this sketch to the screen, in 1927, was to do wonders in establishing Laurel's credibility as a film-maker both in front of, and behind, the camera –

even though proper credit for the original storyline *was* given to his father. But, here in 1908, it had a more immediate effect. Instantaneously, it promoted Stan to working the number-one circuit of theatres in the country – the Moss Empires. In these, he would not be surrounded by drunken louts who would as soon pillory him as applaud, but would be able to perform to nice people, who had paid good money to sit in comfort and be entertained.

Secondly, this is where he would have first begun to feel exactly what kind of performer he wished to become. Not here was our apprentice actor trained as to the use of the risqué joke, and the bawdy song, but to observe and practise the art of the comedy character – his true forte. An audience of several hundred listening to every word, and reacting to every expression of the players on stage, could not fail to both inspire and inflate the ego of one so impressionable. Once having experienced the stimulation it was possible to achieve under such favourable conditions, Stan would have been unwilling to return to the lower medium he had so recently worked in.

But then, just as Stan seemed to be achieving a happy status, he was dealt a resounding blow by the death of his mother (December 1, 1908). She had been ill for quite a while; but, now she was gone, her absence in the home caused A.J's domestic standards to be seriously questioned. Being able to manage theatres is one thing, but being able to run a household and bring up children is quite another. So, after the funeral, it was felt best that Stan's younger brother, Teddy, be removed from the Jeffersons' latest home at 17, Craigmillar Road, Glasgow, and be looked after by his Aunty Nant and Uncle John Shaw, in Batley, Yorkshire – where the Shaws had moved in 1906, from Ulverston.

Coinciding with the Shaws' move, Madge's parents too – George & Sarah Metcalfe – had left Ulverston and set up home opposite them. In 1907 the two families then merged to live as one twelve-strong family in a large house at South View, Soothill. Needing a bigger house they all moved, later in 1908, to 85 Warwick Road. No matter where they were, Stan always found time to visit – thus they were able to stay such a close family.

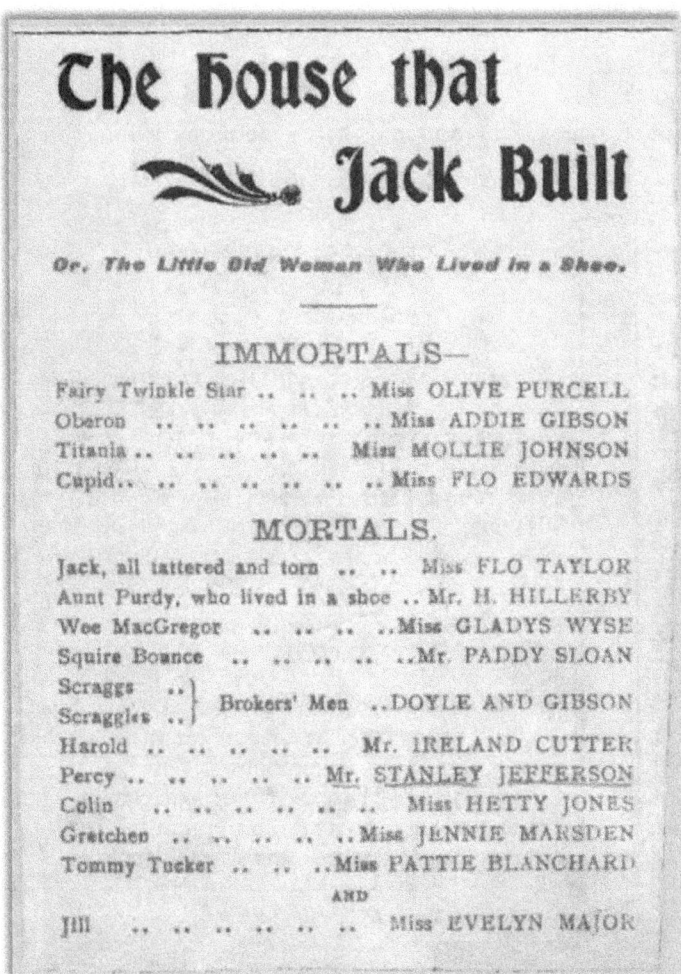

Immediately after his mother's funeral Stan had to hide his grief, when he went into rehearsals with the 'Levy & Cardwell Company' for their 1908 Christmas pantomime, *The House that Jack Built* — based on the children's nursery rhyme *The Old Woman Who Lived in a Shoe*.

From Stan Laurel's personal scrapbook. Stan, himself, has underlined his name.

The House that Jack Built ran from December 7, 1908 to April 11, 1909 — which, at eighteen weeks long, is only half the length of the run of *The Sleeping Beauty*, the previous year, but is still a considerable number of performances, for what is traditionally regarded as Christmas-time entertainment.

LAUREL — Stage by Stage

THE HOUSE THAT JACK BUILT

Levy & Cardwell Juvenile Pantomime Company

1908

[November 14		Stan leaves *Home From the Honeymoon* at the end of its run.]	
[November 16		disengaged]	
November 23	Staffordshire	STAFFORD, Lyceum	[Stan starts here.]
November 30	Cheshire	HYDE, Royal	
December 07	Lancashire	TYLDESLEY, Royal	
December 14	Yorkshire	CASTLEFORD, Royal	
December 25	Worcestershire	DUDLEY, Royal Opera House	[opens on Christmas Day]
December 28	Worcestershire	DUDLEY, Royal Opera House	

1909

January 04	Worcestershire	DUDLEY, Royal Opera House	
January 11	Wiltshire	SWINDON, Empire	
January 18	Lancashire	DARWEN, Royal	
January 25	Manchester	SALFORD, Regent	
February 01	Durham	BLYTH, New Royal	
February 08	Durham	CONSETT, New Royal	
February 15	Durham	JARROW, New Royal	
February 22	Durham	SEAHAM HARBOUR, New Royal	
March 01	Northumberland	NEWCASTLE, Palace	
March 08	Scotland	DUNFERMLINE, Opera House	
March 15	Scotland	KILMARNOCK, King's	
March 22	Scotland	KIRKCALDY, King's	
March 29	Scotland	DUMFRIES, Royal	
April 05	Durham	WEST STANLEY, Royal	[tour ends here – Saturday 10th.]

DARWEN - THEATRE ROYAL.
Lessees, The Animated Pictorial Enterprises, Ltd.
Manager Mr. J. A. Whitehouse. This week:-
Mr. and Mrs. H. B. Levy and Mr. J. E. Cardwell's juvenile pantomime company in *The House That Jack Built* is playing to packed houses. The role of "Jack" is filled by Miss Florrie Taylor with much success, and Miss Evelyn Major is a most pleasing "Jill"; Miss Olive Purcell, a charming "Fairy Twinkle Star", and Miss Hetty Jones a favourite as "Colin", "Gretchen" being a pleasing character in the hands of Miss J.Marsden.

Miss Gladys Wyse scores heavily as "Wee M'Gregor"; Mr. H. Hillerby is greatly amusing as "Aunt Purdy"; and Mr. Paddy Sloan makes the most of "Squire Bounce". Messrs. Doyle and Gibson as "Scragg" and "Scraggles", and Mr Stanley Jefferson and Mr Ireland Cutter as the Motor Tourists create much laughter. The Forget-me-Not Quartette provide some fine speciality dancing.

SEAHAM HARBOUR
NEW THEATRE ROYAL
Proprietor: Mr. A. C. Harrison
Manager: Mr. Wallace Childs
The House That Jack Built is being presented this week by Mr. and Mrs. H. B. Levy and Mr. J. E. Cardwell's company. The pantomime is exceedingly pretty and tuneful, and abounds in clever comedy. Miss Florence Taylor as "Jack" and Miss Evelyn Major as "Jill" earn great praise. Their singing as well as that of Miss Olive Purcell (the Fairy) is a feature. Doyle and Gibson as "Scraggs and Scraggles" are immensely funny and clever dancers. Mr. H. Hillerby is a comical "Dame Purdy"; as "Harold" and "Percy", Mr. Paddy Sloan and Mr. Stanley Jefferson keep the fun going; Miss Gladys Wyse as "Wee M'Gregor" contributes to the humour with Scotch delineations.

Specialities are given by Doyle and Gibson, the Forget-me-Not Quartette of dancers, Horace Hillerby, Florrie Edwards, and Wee Gladys Wyse.

-----0-----

Home From Home

THE HOUSE THAT JACK BUILT

A pantomime in one act by H.B. Levy

To be produced at the Colosseum Theatre, Oldham, December 21st 1907.

Harvest home, Villagers sing -

> In golden sunshine and fresh air,
> Why need we fear doubt or care,
> With hearts so light and visage gay,
> We must enjoy our holiday.
> Come lads and lasses all,
> Answer the welcome call.
> With laughter we care dispel,
> On holiday in sunny dell.

Ballet of Dairymaids, Postmen, Farmers, Laundrymaids, Cooks and Policemen.

Motor comes on stage, crash, enter police and Sergeant -

Sergeant: Hello, what's the matter here? Case of furious driving?

Motormen ogling girls in Hotel Metropole Buffet -

(enter Barmaid in bar)

1st Motorist: I say Percy, this is a dismal place. Nothing whatever to do I declare it gives me the pip.

2nd Motorist: Ha, jolly fine girl, about the best thing we've seen in the village.

1st Motorist: Bai Jove, Yes dontcher know, I think I'll mash her. Good evening Miss.

Barmaid: Good evening, sir.

1st Motorist: What can you recommend for a teetotaller, you know something cool.

Barmaid: A soda Sir.

1st Motorist: No, too tasteless.

Barmaid: Stone ginger Sir.

1st Motorist: No, too firey.

Barmaid: Lager, sir.

1st Motorist: No, I think I'll have the horse's neck.

Barmaid: You'll excuse me Sir, but this is an hotel and not a cat's meat shop.

1st Motorist: Oh I see you don't understand. A horse's neck is a ginger beer, with a slice of lemon in it, it's an American drink.

Barmaid: Oh I see Sir.

1st Motorist: I say old boy what are you going to have?

2nd Motorist: I think I'll have a B and S.

1st Motorist: Now my dear, how much.

Barmaid: Five shillings please.

1st Motorist: Your prices are high for a ginger beer with a slice of lemon, and a brandy and soda.

Barmaid: You did not ask for that, you asked for a horse's neck and a B and S. If you will have American drinks, you must pay American prices.

BUSINESS WITH MOVING COUNTER. MOTORMEN'S SPECIALTY.

Facsimile of the working script, highlighting Stan Jefferson's role of 'Percy – The Motorist.'

(Abridged and edited.)

A third review reiterated:

> Mr Paddy Sloan and Mr Stanley Jefferson (equally entertaining in the character of motorists), and Mr Ireland Cutter (as Sgt. McGinty), are all established in the favour of their audiences.

And *The Stage* backed them up:

> Levy and Cardwell's Company are proving a good attraction at the Royal Theatre, Castleford. The company give an excellent all round performance and the piece is well mounted. ... Mr Stanley Jefferson and Mr Ireland Cutter as Harold and Percy contribute greatly to the fun.

But then *The Performer* became the "Informer" when it told us of another part Stan played:

> The company contains some most charming and accomplished children, who have been trained to a high standard of achievement, and the pantomime is one which, from its all-round merit, is sure to gain success.
>
> Messrs. Jefferson, Adams, and Cutter, are excellent in animal studies.

Just what "animal studies" was comprised of will have to remain a mystery.

When the pantomime ended its run in April 1909, Stan returned to the Metropole Theatre, Glasgow, to take up the rather less glamorous roles of working in the box-office, and being a gofer for his dad. But then, in August 1909, he began what looked like a promising tour with the Percy Williams Company, in *Alone in the World*.

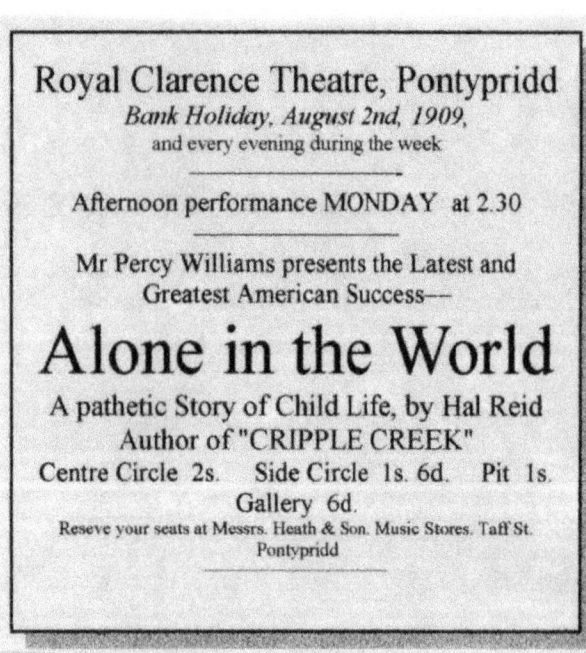

The story is about a New York newsboy who was abandoned by his mother as a child. After her second marriage, to a bank manager, the mother takes an absorbing interest in waifs in the hope of finding her child.

Stan's own memories of his involvement in this company, were published in the *Tit-Bits* – November 7, 1936 issue.

> The opening scene was set "Way Down South," with darkies singing "Swanee River" off stage, but the back-cloth behind me depicted a view of Brooklyn Bridge, New York. However, I didn't know it at the time, and neither did our audience, so everybody was happy.

Here, with his back to the audience, Stan was seen to be fishing – of which he further revealed:

> The character I played was that of an American 'hobo', if you please. Speaking through my nose, with a broad Lancashire accent, I fondly imagined I was giving a perfect impersonation of a true son of Uncle Sam. After a suitable length of time, I had to put down my fishing rod and say: "Wal, I guess 'n' calculate I can't catch no fish with that tarnation mob a-singin'. (Pause) Gee whiz."
>
> I did a lot of "guessin' and calculatin'" in the part, but I'm sure the audience had to do a great deal more [guessin' and calculatin'] to discover what I was talking about.

In remembering his role of the hobo in the opening scene, and little else about the rest of the play, Stan did himself a disservice, for the *Todmorden Herald* revealed a second role he had — one for which he received high praise:

> Mr. Stanley Jefferson, as 'P.C. Stoney Broke', is a first-rate comedian and dancer, and his eccentricities create roars of laughter.

A second review from Todmorden also cedited Stan:

> Other parts are in capable hands, the necessary touches of humour being well introduced by Mr. Stanley Jefferson, Mr. H.M. Vernon, and Miss Blanche Huber.

And from the Ashington Miners' Theatre came:

> Mr. Stanley Jefferson as 'Stoney Broke,' and Miss Blanche Huber are responsible for the comedy.

And of the audience reaction to the on-stage shortcomings, Stan told the story:

> Our final scene was the Great Bank Failure, with an angry mob storming into the building and threatening to lynch the cashier. At least, it was supposed to be a mob, according to the lurid posters outside, but in actual fact it consisted of five people, supplemented by "noises off."
>
> One night, as we dashed in and shouted: "We want our money back!" a wag in the gallery shouted back, "So do we!" There was such an outburst of ironical laughter and cat-calls that we had to ring down the curtain.

Stan's description of the bank scene, as given to biographer John McCabe, was: "*... a tiny box-set, a rickety table, a kitchen chair, and a safe – made of cardboard.*" But the reviews, and adverts for the set totally contradict Stan:

> PERCY WILLIAMS' COMPANIES.
> **ALONE IN THE WORLD**
> Huge success on production at the
> CLARENCE THEATRE, PONTYPRIDD
> Read the following from Mr Charles Tranchard Esq.
> Dear Mr Williams - Allow me to congratulate you on an excellent production of *Alone in the World*. Your most efficient company and staging command every success, which leaves little doubt in my mind you have already attained. I am certain in *Alone in the World* you have a sure winner. I shall look forward with no small amount of pleasure to your return visit. Wishing you every success which the play deserves. -
> Yours faithfully, Charles Trenchard.
> "ALONE IN THE WORLD," A Pathetic Life Story of Child Life, brimful of Human Interest, and altogether something new in Modern Drama.
> Over 3 tons of Scenery carried.
> Strong Dramatic Company of fourteen.
> Bookings include: All Mr Broadhead's Theatres; Theatre Royal, Leeds; Prince's, Bradford; Opera House, Wakefield; Palace, Newcastle; Scarboro'; West Stanley. &c &c.
> Wanted, Oct. 4, 16, Nov. 8 and on.
> Now Booking Spring, 1910.

> w/c August 9, 1909
> MANCHESTER, Metropole
> Mr Percy Williams' Company are here with *Alone in the World*, which is arranged in six scenes to suit the two houses nightly. The sensational episodes are ably sustained, and the company work well and win success. Excellent scenery is carried.

Note the comment, left:

> "Over 3 tons of Scenery carried."

And above:

> "Excellent Scenery is carried."

A comment from a third review reads:

> "Excellently mounted; efficiently staged."

To explain away the conflicting reports, I can only think it must have been the props used during rehearsals which Stan remembered.

Despite such excellent reviews for Stan, and for the play itself" – this inauspicious light drama soon hit trouble. Booked on the prestigious Broadhead Circuit of North West theatres, the play was withdrawn after just four weeks of scheduled engagements, and scratch bookings had to be taken at short notice.

-----0-----

LAUREL — Stage by Stage

ALONE IN THE WORLD
Percy Williams' Company

[Apr 10		[end of Stan's run in *The House That Jack Built*.]	
[Apr 12 till Jul 25		disengaged]	
Aug 02	Wales	PONTPRIDD, Royal Clarence	
Aug 09	Manchester	MANCHESTER, Metropole	
Aug 16	Yorkshire	WAKEFIELD, Opera House	
Aug 23	Manchester	QUEEN'S PARK, Hippodrome	[pulled out]
Aug 23	Yorkshire	BRADFORD, Prince's	
Aug 30	Yorkshire	LEEDS, Royal	
Sep 06	Manchester	SALFORD, Hippodrome	[pulled out]
Sep 06	East Riding	HULL, Alexandra	
Sep 13	Yorkshire	TODMORDEN, Hippodrome	
Sep 20	Manchester	LONGSIGHT, King's	[pulled out]
Sep 20	Lancashire	HORWICH, Prince's	
Sep 27	Worcestershire	KIDDERMINSTER, Opera House	[pulled out]
Sep 27		vacant date	
Oct 04	Northumberland	ASHINGTON, Miners'	[tour ends prematurely here]
	Northumberland	NEWCASTLE, Empire Palace	[cancelled]
	Yorkshire	SCARBOROUGH, Royal	[cancelled]
	Durham	WEST STANLEY, Royal	[cancelled]
[Oct 11		Stan disengaged]	

-----0-----

The efforts to keep it afloat, however, soon proved too much and, with scheduled bookings being pulled out quicker than new ones could be obtained, this "Beautiful and Pathetic Play" soon sank beneath the waves. To add insult to injury, the manager skipped with what small box-office receipts had been generated, leaving Stan living out his role of "Stoney Broke" and "Alone in the World."

Stan tells us what happened next:

> When that tour ended abruptly in, at Ashington, Northumberland, I found myself without even sufficient money to pay my fare home. Not that I wanted to go home: I was far too proud to let my father know that my resolution to earn my own living was not working out so well as I had anticipated. At one time I was on the point of writing home: "Dear Dad, I am making a huge success—please send me ten shillings," but I realised that a letter of that sort would only give me away. So, instead, I banked upon my initial success as a boy comedian and set out to try my luck on the music-halls.

(*Tit-Bits* – November 7, 1936)

So, in the winter of 1909, Stan set as a solo comedian; touring the music halls billed as: "Young Stanley Jefferson — He of the Funny Ways."

In later life, though, he was to confess:

> My act was an unashamed imitation of the great Harry Randall – make-up, songs, patter and all – but as most of the audiences in the cheaper halls I was working had never seen the original, I was never accused of plagiarism.

THE GREAT – Harry Randall

MR. HARRY RANDALL, THE COMEDIAN, AND HIS FACES

Stan is on record as saying that, when he lived in North Shields, he would regularly go to the Newcastle Empire to watch the acts, with his boyhood pal, George Black Jnr. Harry Randall would almost certainly have been one of the acts he saw there.

-----0-----

Stan's summation of his solo act continued:

> I wasn't too successful. I had no experience and no material [of my own]. I hadn't 'found myself'. I just didn't know what kind of comedian I was. All I know is that I enjoyed being in front of the footlights. I guess I was at an awkward age.

The phrase "awkward age" sums up exactly what was wrong with Stan's act. Although at that time a few boy-comedians were popular, the trend has never continued. Audiences are not willing to take from adolescents what they will accept from an adult. Also, a boy-comedian is automatically limited as to what material he can put over — sex, wives, mothers-in-law, drink, etc. are obviously excluded from his repertoire. What remains, almost always emerges with the little fellow sounding smug – and nobody likes a smart aleck. One critic was to say of Wee Georgie Wood: "He's so clever, I could smack his face."

Comedians need time to mature, and are normally at their best around forty, at which age they can relate to both ends of the age spectrum without talking up, or talking down, to either. So Stan Jefferson was pursuing the right course; for, through his trials, he ensured that when he attained forty he was indeed the master of his trade.

Some of his experiences he could laugh off in later years but, at the time, tears were the probable outlet. Before starting on a life of touring, Stan had always had his family around him. Now he was forced by circumstance to live with people whose company he hadn't chosen – i.e. the other acts in the shows. Many of these artistes were foreign speaking, and those who could speak English weren't always willing to console a kid who was still wet behind the ears. Consequently Stan spent many a lonely and uncomfortable hour in his quest for stardom. One story he narrated about these times, went as follows:

> I was staying in digs in Manchester, and money was so tight we had to sleep four to a room. I was only a small boy and the other three were all fat, and very smelly, as they had a seal act. The seal slept in a basket at the bottom of the bed, and made a terrible noise all night. I paid the landlady an extra 2s 6d to put me in another room. I didn't fare much better here. Although I only had to share with one man, the room was much smaller. He was a trick cyclist, and had six bikes which took up most of the room. Every time I got up to go to the toilet, which was outside in the yard, I tripped over the damn things.

[AJM: Despite many an hour scouring scores of newspapers, I could find not one single solitary booking for Stan Jefferson, even in places he had named as playing, such as Manchester, Bristol and Brighton. One would have to conclude that Stan was playing the lower-class venues, those which didn't even choose to advertise. But learning the comedy trade the hard way is nearly always a good thing. If you can survive the worst venues, then you will appreciate the nicer ones — and the nicer ones will appreciate you.

Realising that going on stage as a solo comic performer is tantamount to playing Russian Roulette, but with *most* of the chambers loaded, Stan next placed his comedic talents in a return to pantomime, a medium he felt at home in. On November 29, 1909, the King's Theatre, Sunderland, announced that the comedy role of 'The Page' in their Christmas pantomime, *Dick Whittington*, was to be Master Stanley Jefferson. For Stan, this would have been an automatic promotion from playing in a juvenile company, to a full-blown professional cast and company, and — in a mainstream theatre.

But, before the curtain rose on the Sunderland pantomime, 'the page' had turned. Stan Jefferson had skipped town, and gone to join the greatest troupe of comedians in the land — "The Fred Karno Company."

Chapter 5

TWO LOAVES AND SOMETHING FISHY

In December 1909, nineteen year-old Arthur Stanley Jefferson was assisting his father Arthur Jefferson, and older brother Gordon, with the running of the Metropole Theatre, in Glasgow. Meanwhile, comedy company entrepreneur Fred Karno was producing the Christmas pantomime *Mother Goose* over at the nearby Glasgow Grand Theatre, where the younger Jefferson went to meet him. Stanley himself tells of just why:

> I presented my card with a request for an interview, and was promptly ushered onto the stage where a gentle-voiced little man came forward to meet me. "Well, Mr Jefferson Junior," he said, "What can I do for you?" I told him I wanted to see Mr. Karno. "You're seeing him now," he replied quietly. It was quite a shock and such a relief to find him such a pleasant, friendly man. Briefly I explained that I wanted a job as a comedian. "Are you funny?" he asked. I told him of my youthful experience. He nodded. "Very well," he said, "I'll try you out at two pounds a week. Report to Frank O'Neil, who is running my *Mumming Birds* company in Manchester. Push yourself forward, and I'll see you in London in a few weeks' time."
>
> Bewildered at the suddenness of it all, I blurted out my thanks and staggered into the street in a daze. I had achieved the height of every budding comedian's ambition - I was one of Fred Karno's Comedians.
>
> (*Tit-Bits* – November 14, 1936)

Almost two decades later Stan gave a more insightful peek into this meeting with Fred Karno, in a letter to Karno's son, Freddie — of whom more, later:

```
                                                  March 21st.'59.

Dear Freddie:

I remember very well the incident you mention of my first meeting
your Dad - you sure have a good memory - this happened at the
Theatre Royal in Glasgow, I think in 1909, he was producing a Panto,
featuring two comics 'Burley & Burley', Harry Morgan was stage
manager. The first part of the story you tell is wrong. I first met
Morgan (the rehearsal was in full swing). He read my letter, then
took me over to meet your Dad - after he read the letter he got up &
took me by the hand & tip-toed with me behind some Flats leaning
against the wall - he did'nt want the people to know what he was
going to ask me & before he asked me, he looked out again from back
of the scenery to be sure no one was listening - it scared the hell
out of me, he was so mysterious - He finally said 'How much do you
want'? I blurted out loud £2.a week. he put his finger to his lips &
said Sh! do'nt let anybody know - then he said 'Can you take the
NAP'?' & made a pass at me - I did'nt know what he was talking about
& stood there confused. He took me by the hand again & tip-toed me
among all the people over to Morgan & whispered in his ear.
Everybody was wondering what had happened & were all staring at me,
trying to figure out who this stupid looking guy was.! Morgan then
came over to me & said you leave for Manchester tonight to join the
troupe at the Hippodrome Hulme - I'll notify the Manager right away
(Frank O'Neil). Needless to tell you how happy I was.
```

[AJM: Just to explain a few phrases in the last account: Firstly, Karno was at the Grand Theatre, Glasgow, NOT the Royal. Rehearsals started w/c November 29, 1909, so Stan could have gone there any day between Monday and Saturday. (Theatres were usually closed on Sundays). The letter Stan first proffered to the stage manager would have been a letter of introduction from his father. Both Morgan and Karno would have known of Arthur Jefferson who, by then, was an extremely prominent man in theatrical circles, so the decision to employ his son would have been made that much easier.

"Taking the nap" refers to the stage technique of reacting when someone punches you in the face. Obviously, the punch is only a pretend one. The effect is made to appear more realistic by someone in the wings clapping their hands to replicate the sound of the punch making connection. When Stan says that Karno made a pass at him," he was referring to Karno throwing a fake punch at him. [If you thought it meant something else, have a word with yourself!]

-----0-----

FRED KARNO — business card circa 1905   Later portrait of "The Guv'nor"

Karno was a former gymnast who, around 1895, had turned his hand to devising and producing comic sketches. In the fourteen years since then he had become a promoter and showman of legendary proportions. He also had a brilliant mind for comic invention. Although he could never adequately put his ideas down on paper, his personal coaching ensured the crafting of hilarious sketches. These sketches filled the halls throughout Britain for three decades; but it was *his* name on billboards, rather than those of the players, which led to full theatres. When theatre managers asked of Karno: "Who's your star name?" he would reply: "My name's up there, and that's good enough." And how right he was! Whereas today Andrew Lloyd Webber and Cameron MacKintosh are synonymous with staging musicals, Karno, in his era, eclipsed all their achievements in the field of stage productions. In 1909 alone, Karno had seventeen different troupes touring the UK, consisting of up to sixty cast members, and still managed to end the year with long-running spectacular pantomimes.

Stanley Jefferson, made his debut with the Karno Company on December 6, 1909, at the Hippodrome & Floral Hall, Hulme, Manchester, in one of two companies touring with *Mumming Birds* This sketch was to play such a huge part in the history of Stan's stage-work that it is worth taking time out to familiarise ourselves with it: *Mumming Birds* ran on-and-off, with numerous cast changes and in various forms, for forty-five years. Whether or not "Don't say a Mumming Bird" ever entered Cockney rhyming-slang for "Don't say a word" I don't know, but it certainly deserves to. 'Mumming' comes from the French verb "momer" – meaning "to mime." As late as 1903 the Karno companies had been billed as "Karno's Speechless Comedians," which was not so much a proud boast but, one must surmise, a very clever ruse by Karno to avoid having to submit his scripts to the Lord Chamberlain's office – where they would have been open to censorship laws.

The premise of *Mumming Birds* is the representation of a musical hall performance, as viewed by a "stage audience," and the humour depends on the frequent interruptions and interferences of that audience. The performers who appear are: the audience members; the artists; and the stage attendants. The principal characters, amongst the audience, are a boy dressed in an Eton suit, and his guardian, 'Uncle Charlie.' These two sit in the bottom box on the left. Bottom box on the right sits the 'swell,' in a state of intoxication, dressed in evening suit.

The various 'turns' are announced by a numbered card being placed in a frame immediately prior to the start of the act. A representative bill, of many, is:

1. The Topical Vocalist [male] — recites "*The Trail of the Yukon*"
2. The Swiss Nightingale [lady vocalist] — sings "*Come Birdie Come, and Live with me.*"
3. The Prestidigitateur [Magician/Conjurer]
4. The Rustic Glee Party [quartet of singers]
5. The Saucy Serio [soubrette] — sings "*Naughty, Naughty Men*"
6. 'The Terrible Turkey' [Wrestler] — 'Marconi Ali'

-----0-----

BILLIE REEVES
The original drunk from the 1904 debut version of *Mumming Birds*.

As the curtain rises another stage is discovered, with a proscenium, curtain, etc., and boxes on either side, the occupants of which treat the various artists who appear with a comic lack of courtesy. The mischievous Eton boy pelts the acts with missiles he has to hand; and much fun is provoked by an inebriated "masher/drunk/swell" whose persistent efforts to 'go behind' are most forcibly opposed by a stalwart attendant. The various performers, as listed above, meet with more and more opposition as the show progresses — especially from the drunk, who shows his dis-satisfaction with all the acts in the form of heckling, and/or chasing them off. The wrestler gets beaten up by the drunk, after refusing to pay the sum he loses in the bout with him; and the scene closes upon a laughable mêlée involving all the cast.

The boxes left and right are part of the set. [Photo taken pre 1909.]
As the various 'turns' are announced, a numbered card is placed in a frame immediately prior to the start of the act.
[AJM: You can just make out the No. 8 card, between the head and raised arm of the lady at right.]

The piece is acted mainly in pantomime, and the 'fun' consists in the incompetence of the performers; the disgust of the [stage] audience; the pranks of the boy who shoots peas or throws buns at the artistes and members of the audience; and especially the drunk, who heckles the speaking and singing acts; has some bye-play between the soubrette, and then a female programme attendant; spoils the magician's conjuring tricks, and then starts the free-for-all after besting the wrestler.

Other business performed in *Mumming Birds* can be found in the newspaper clippings illustrated in the pages which follow. Additional snippets will be gained as the story progresses. Meanwhile, here are a couple of bits of interesting trivia:

The finalé of the sketch was the spoof wrestling bout with a 'Champion' wrestler who would challenge all-comers to a bout of wrestling. A good spoof has to be based on an act the audience are familiar with. In this instance the wrestler was based on Ahmed Madrali – the Turkish wrestling champion – whose bill matter between 1903 and 1906 varyingly included the lines: 'The Terrible Turk'; 'The Sultan of Turkey's Chief Wrestler'; and 'The World's Champion Catch-as-Catch-Can Wrestler.'

So good a fighter was Ahmed that, during his act, the challenge "£25 to anyone who can throw him within fifteen minutes" would be issued. In May 1904, only a few weeks after the debut of *Mumming Birds*, he took part in the 'World's Catch-as Catch-Can championship for £400' at the London Alhambra. Meanwhile in the *Mumming Birds* sketch he was being parodied under the thinly disguised name of 'Marconi Ali – The Terrible Turkey.' The poor man. Here he was, trying to make a living as a serious wrestler, but was never able to be taken seriously by any audience who had seen *Mumming Birds* prior to his appearance.

Other characters in *Mumming Birds* whose names had comic value were: 'The Sisters Lymjus' [pronounced "lime juice"]; Zbiscuit, Champion of Nantypolonia [as in: 'Take zee biscuit.']; The Inharmonious Blacksmiths; Hermoniki, the Perishing Prestidigitator ['Harmonica' or 'Her Monarchy'??]; and "many other star (and garter) turns."

-----0-----

Although Stan was now employed by Karno, he continued to advertise himself with a series of business card-like entries in *The Stage*. These were to run weekly, right through until June 1910, with the only change being that, in May, his act went from being described as "Comedian and Dancer" to just "Comedian." What working benefits these adverts gave him is questionable. Maybe he was just showing off.

Stan with MIKE ASHER, who played the 'Naughty Boy' in *Mumming Birds* (but without the pipe.)

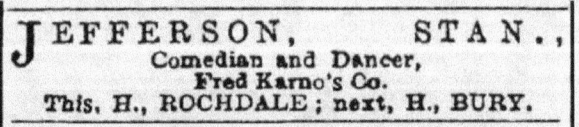

ABOVE: One of Stan's weekly adverts in *The Stage*, letting readers know he was in the Karno Company, and at which theatres they could go and see him.

RIGHT: Stan Jefferson's business card. At the end of the dotted line are the three figures "191." This is so that Stan could write in the last digit to correspond with whatever year it was. i.e. 1910, 1911, right through to 1919. Mind you, the photo would soon look to out-of-date.]

MUMMING BIRDS.

Cast.

Inebriated Swell.
Eton Boy
Uncle.
Usherette
Number Man.

Acts.

No.1 Can Can Girls
No.2 Double Act - 2 men Comedy.
No.3 Lady Vocalist (Comedy)
No.4 Actor - Recitation
No.5 Quartette. Comedy.
No.6 Soubrette.
No.7 Announcer introduces "Marconi Ali" the Terrible Turk" Comedy Wrestling Bout.
No.8 Girl Singer - Olde Tyme Songs.

- MUSIC -

Opening - "Lets all go to the Music Hall". Double ff.
Segue into Waltz.
Usherette shows Boy and Uncle into Box then brings
Drunk into his Box (Bus to be arranged).
Number man puts No.1 card in bracket (cue for Can
Can music) Girls enter and go straight into Dance.

No.2. Two Comics — Song, Dance and Patter - Song a la "Harry Champion's Tempo. (Interruptions from Boy and Drunk to be arranged).

No.3. (Lady Vocalist Comedy) Song "Come Birdie Come and Live with Me" (Interruptions from Boy & Drunk)

No.4. Cord on for Actors entrance. Recites "The Track of the Yukon" (Boy and Drunk interfere again).

No.5. Sustained Cord for Quartette. Comedy bus. to be explained. Drunk gets out of Box and gets them off.

No. 6. Soubrette. Song & Dance "You naughty, naughty Man" (bus from Boy & Drunk).

No. 7. Girl Singer - "Medley of Old Tyme Songs".

No. 8. Announcer enters to introduce Wrestling Bout.

1.

2.

"Ladies & Gents" (bus with Boy & Drunk) eventually
"Plant" in audience accepts challenge. Then Announcer
gives direct for music (Waltz — very Piano) and calls
for mat to be brought on.

Boy gets out of Box and has (bus.) with "Marconi Ali"
and is chased back to Box by Announcer.

Enter Plant, takes his coat off and lays it on Drunk's
Box. (bus with Drunk).

Announcer starts Bout (bus with "Marconi Ali" and Plant
to be arranged, finally Marconi throws Plant.

Announcer: Anyone also care for a bout with Marconi.
Drunk gets out of box and goes after Marconi — bus to
be arranged - finally Drunk gets Marconi on his back and
wins bout - is presented with prize money; and
congratulations.

Announcer. And what would you like now Sir?

Drunk. First bring on the Girls. Everybody on for
Finale, with number to be arranged.

PROPS.

Prop Oranges and Bananas.
Pea Shooter - Buns - Buckram, Bouquet, Trumpet, Pie.

Number Boards 1 to 8.
Small mattress for Drunks Box. Wine Glass, Champagne
Bottle, Cushion, Opera Glasses, Ash Tray, Wrestling Mat,
Nap Sticks.

Reproduction of an original script for a later version of *Mumming Birds*, typed by Fred Karno Jnr.

(Courtesy of the late- Olive Karno.)

After the Christmas holiday Stan played the Wakefield Empire, where he learned a second sketch – *Skating*. Sydney Chaplin was not only the principal comic in *Skating*, but had also co-written it, along with legendary writer J. Hickory Wood. *Skating* had made its debut in May 1909 and played continuously until the end of August. It was then revived and played for two weeks, commencing December 20, 1909, as a "Gigantic Christmas Production" at the Manchester Palace Theatre.

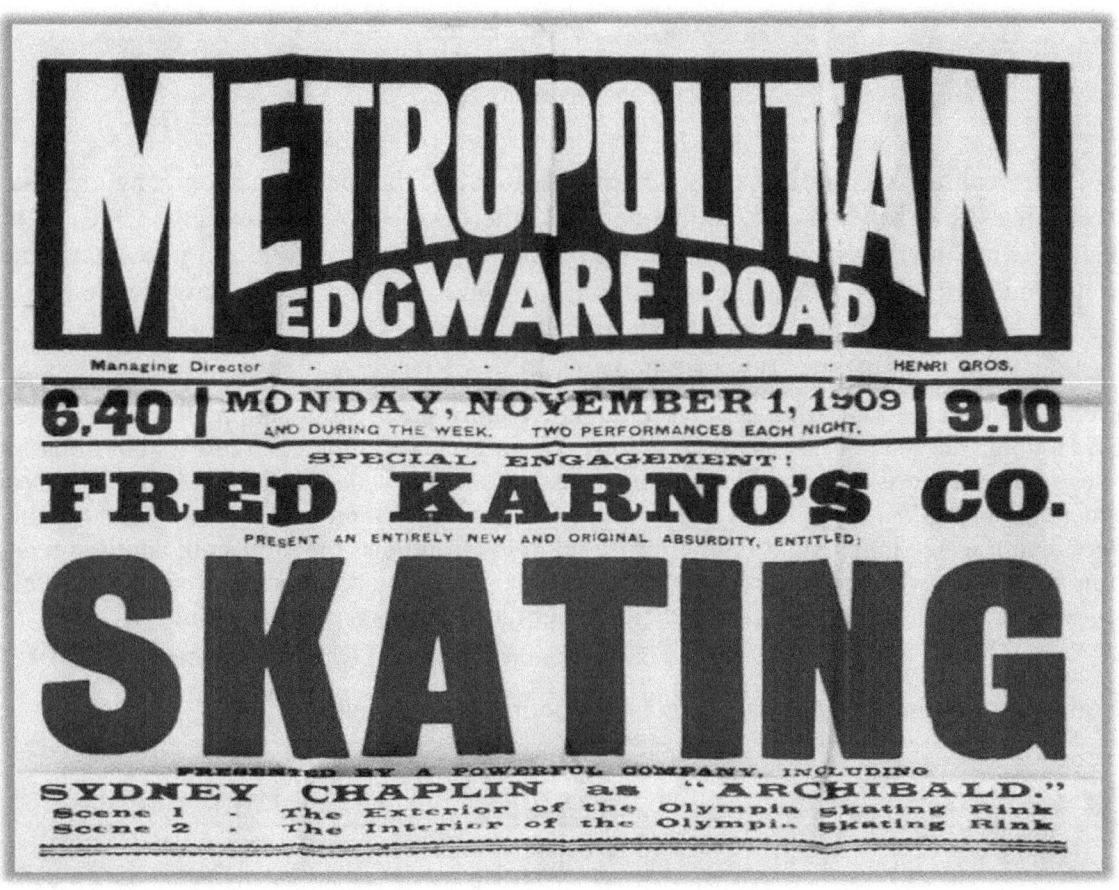

The main character in *Skating* was 'Archibald Binks' – a name which was to be used in other Karno sketches for the character billed under the various soubriquets of 'the inebriate,' 'the drunk' or the 'drunken swell' and, in North America, 'the souse.' The supporting role was 'Zena Flapper' played by Jimmy Russell – in drag. There were, however, "real" ladies in the company, one of whom was billed as Minnie Chaplin. But the surname "Chaplin" was being used as a name of convenience, as Syd and Minnie Constance had not yet tied the knot.

The following week the company travelled the short distance to Liverpool where, at the New Pavilion Theatre, Stan was back to playing a bit-part in *Mumming Birds*; of which he recounted:

> In due course I was given a small part to play, but before I could make my first big appearance, I received a setback. The wardrobe mistress told me, 'There's a new comedian just joined us from one of the other companies. He's taking over Mr [Frank] O'Neill's part as 'the drunken swell'. I haven't a suit to fit him, except the one you are wearing, so I'm afraid you will have to take that off and hand it over.'
>
> Reluctantly, I removed the suit and took it along to the new comedian's dressing room. I found him to be a pleasant little fellow with dark, curly hair, blue eyes, very white teeth, and a friendly smile. I took to him right away, and in the course of time we became close friends, sharing rooms together on tour. You are quite right; his name was Charlie Chaplin.
>
> (*Tit-Bits* – November 14, 1936)

It might seem that the odds of these two great English comedians coming together, in the same company, are massive, when in actual fact they are remarkably short – by the same reasoning that the best two footballers in the Football League, at any one time, are often playing for the best club.

Who could have possibly forseen that these two handsome young men, one just nineteen, and the other only twenty, would come together by chance, go to America, and become the two funniest men film-world has ever seen?

During their week in Liverpool, Messrs. Chaplin, Laurel and the rest of the company must have held further rehearsals for *Skating* as, the following week, there were two different companies playing this very sketch. One company headed south to play London boroughs, while the one Charlie and Stan were in headed north. After weeks in Lancashire, Yorkshire, and one in Glasgow, they came down to Birmingham, with Charlie continuing in the lead part.

BIRMINGHAM HIPPODROME – (w/c February 21, 1910)

Fred Karno presents an original and screamingly funny sketch at the Hippodrome this week, based upon the latest craze - roller-skating. It is a clever and remarkably humorous but exaggerated representation of how others see us on the rink. Johnny Doyle, as "Zena Flapper", and Charles Chaplin, as "Archibald", present themselves with other strange people at the 'Olympia Rink', and after initial noisy trouble at the door gain admission and join with those who can skate inside to create one continuous outburst of fun. Incidentally some smart skating is introduced, and altogether the sketch is highly diverting.

(*Birmingham Evening Despatch* — February 22, 1910)

And from the following week at Barrasford's Hippodrome, Sheffield, we get:

(w/c February 28, 1910)
BARRASFORD'S HIPPODROME SHEFFIELD
TO-NIGHT 6.45 and 9. LAST NIGHT of
LITTLE TICH

Next Week:-
FRED KARNO'S Pantomimical Absurdity,
SKATING
Including JOHNNY DOYLE as "Zena Flapper"
CHARLIE CHAPLIN as "Archibald"

BARRASFORD'S HIPPODROME
Fred Karno's sketches always appeal to the frequenters of the *Hippodrome*, and last night's *Skating* - an entirely new and original pantomimical absurdity was typical of all Fred Karno's sketches, with its broad rollicking fun. The large house was kept in continuous laughter from start to finish, and the skating scene in the second act included a clever Quadrille dance. **Charlie Chaplin**, as "Archibald" was in great form, his tumbling and foolery being extremely funny. With Johnny Doyle as 'Zena Flapper', he was particularly nimble on his skates, and fell with a ludicrous freedom that all learners must have envied. About thirty artistes were included in the cast, the "ladies" providing not the least entertainment.

(w/c February 28, 1910)
SKATING AT THE HIPPODROME
You must see "Archibald" at Barrasford's *Hippodrome* this week. He is a prominent figure in Karno's latest absurdity *Skating*, which last night made the audience laugh until they cried.

There are two scenes, the exterior and interior of a skating rink, and the fun is fast and furious. Inside the rink 'Archibald' and 'lady' friends provide any amount of good comedy - it is really remarkable how they seem to fall so naturally - and there is also some first-class skating by a talented company. The sketch is staged in Fred Karno's best style, and promises to be one of the most popular of his productions.

(w/c February 28, 1910)
HIPPODROME
Fred Karno's sketches are always amusing and the latest production, *Skating* - which is taking so well at the Hippodrome, this week, is one of the funniest ever staged. Not only are the crowded audiences kept in a continuous roar of laughter, but the members of the troupe - including Johnny Doyle as "Zena Flapper", and **Charlie Chaplin**, as "Archibald" - sandwich some excellent fancy skating in with their burlesque performance. The scenery is excellent, particularly the interior of the rink.

These Karno boys were certainly fit athletes. Not only did they perform up to thirteen shows over a six day week, but also voluntarily played a full-on game of roller-hockey at a local rink on several occasions, during the run of *Skating*. And because it was a proper match against a proper team, the boys would go to the rink on pre-match days, to practise. That's one heck of a weekly workout.

IF IT'S HOCKEY WITH YOU — IT'S HOCKEY WITH ME

The Karno Roller-Hockey Team at a Rink in Liverpool

Taken March 12, 1910, on the Saturday of the week at the Royal Hippodrome, Liverpool.

Standing back left: Stan Jefferson (substitute). Seated Front Left: Ted Banks, Charles Chaplin. The 3 players forming the right-side triangle are thought to be: Ernie Stone, Jimmy Beresford, and Fred Gordon.

Note in the review from Bury, below, that Chaplin was in this, their first-ever match. Maybe he had learned from Harry Weldon — whom he played opposite in Karno's *The Football Match* — that, to become popular with "the people" you needed to do more than just turn in a good stage performance, you also had to turn out.

TRAFALGAR RINK
LORD STREET, BURY
THE HOCKEY MATCH OF THE SEASON
THIS (SATURDAY) AFTERNOON
FRED KARNO'S FAMOUS SKATERS
v TRAFALGAR H.C. MIXED TEAM
(two Ladies and three Gents either side)
Bully-off 3-30 p.m. Admission 3d.
Skating before and after as usual.
Don't fail to miss this match.

RINK HOCKEY
TRAFALGAR v FRED KARNO'S COMPANY
The match between members of Mr Fred Karno's Company of artistes, at the *Trafalgar Rink*, on Saturday afternoon, and members of the Ladies and Gentlemen's Hockey Club, proved a great attraction, there being a crowded attendance. The teams were:-
Fred Karno's Co.:- Ernie Stone, goal; Miss M. Schofield, full-back; Gertie Jackson, half-back; Ted Banks and James Beresford, forwards.
Trafalgar:- W.Holt, goal; J.Boardman, full-back; F.Taylor, half-back; Miss S.Lucas and Schofield, forwards.
  Trafalgar .... 3 goals
  Karno's Co. .... 1 goal
The Trafalgar team deserved their victory, but the visitors ought not to be downhearted. It was the first hockey match they had taken part in and, in view of their performance, was a good one. The Karno contingent, Banks and Beresford got in some effective work against a smart defence. A better knowledge of the game and more practice should ensure a good team being made up by the talent to be found among the visitors.

(Wednesday 26 January 1910)
COMEDIANS IN HOCKEY MATCH
On Wednesday afternoon, Fred Karno's Comedians from the Hippodrome played a rolling skating match with the King Street Skating Rink team. The King Street Rockets were far the superior team, but the comedians gave a good display considering it was only their second match. The result was 3—1 for the Rink team, the scorers for the Rink team being Smith 4, Cubby 2, Topping 1, and Little 1. C. Chaplin scored for the comedians. The teams were as follows: Rink: J. Connor; J. E. Little; J. Topping; J. Smith, and J. Cubby. Comedians: E. Stone, goal; F. Gordon, full-back; C. Chaplin half-back; and Ted Banks (captain), Jimmy Beresford, and J. Doyle, forwards. There was a good attendance of spectators.

ABOVE: *Wigan Examiner*
February 10, 1910

LEFT: *Bury Times*
– January 29, 1910

(August 8, 1910)
RINK HOCKEY AT NEWINGTON
An enjoyable afternoon was spent at the Newington Rink, Anlaby-road, West Hull, on Saturday, the attraction being a hockey match, Newington v. Fred Karno's "Jimmy the Fearless" Co., from the Hull Palace Theatre. Rink hockey has certainly caught on at Newington, the rink being patronised by a large number of spectators and skaters. The teams were: Newington: . Harrison (captain), C. Cox, F. Gilby, T. Wheatley, and S. Bonewell. Fred Karno's Co. : T. Banks (captain), M. Asher, S. Jefferson, F. Jordan, and T. Rudd. Result : Newington, 3 goals : Fred Karno's Co., 1 goal. Banks scored for Karno's.

The above match was played during the run of another Karno sketch: *Jimmy the Fearless*. Note that Jefferson has replaced Chaplin in the team. This wasn't the first occasion Stan had replaced Charlie, of which more, soon.

Newington, Hull – August 8, 1910

There is no question that Chaplin's 1916 film *The Rink* is based upon *Skating*; but only the ... er ... skating scenes. What you don't see, or rather 'hear' in the film, is the two pages of cross-patter between Chaplin and the Attendant before Chaplin is eventually allowed in.

```
                    Fred Karno's Company in

                            SKATING

          Cast:
          Attendant - (doorkeeper of rink)
          Archibald - (a broken down swell)
          Percy - (a young swell)
          Aunty - Percy's aunt
          Herr Polka - (Champion skater)
          Miss Flapper - (lady skater)
          Lord Dundreary -
          Telegraph boys, messengers, etc.
1st scene: Exterior of Olympia Skating Rink
AFTER HERR POLKA HAS LEFT, ENTER ARCHIBALD FROM P.S.
Archie:     Has the last train gone for Waterloo?
Attendant:  What! Do you take this for - a station?
Archie:     What is it?
Attendant:  Skating Rink.
Archie:     Can you put me up for the night?
Attendant:  Certainly not, I don't know you.
Archie:     Don't you remember Archibald?
Attendant:  Archibald!
Archie:     Look at me!
Attendant:  Why, it's the Captain, my dear old Captain. Why,
            I haven't seen you since we were in the army
            together.
Archie:     The dear old Salvation Army.
Attendant:  Do you remember when we were in the Sudan
            surrounded by the enemy on every side?
Archie:     Every side, left side, right side, front side,
            and - all around us.
Attendant:  There we stood with our retreat cut off.
Archie:     Our what cut off?
Attendant:  Retreat cut off.
Archie:     Oh! Reggie.
Attendant:  Do you remember those 3 days and nights without
            food or water, think of it, not a drain of water,
            but what did we do?
Archie:     Drink it neat.
Attendant:  Well, how's the world been using you?
Archie:     Now and then.
Attendant:  Where are you working?
Archie:     Here and there.
Attendant:  What do you work at?
Archie:     This and that.
Attendant:  Do you have to work hard?
Archie:     On and off.
                     ......................../ cont....
```

(Reproduction of Page 1 of the original script. With thanks to Simon Louvish.)

[INSET: Chaplin as 'Archibald']

In March, Syd Chaplin transferred from the No.1 '*Skating*' company, and took over the lead in Charlie and Stan's company, where he could train the new actors brought in to fill the gap shortly to be left by the out-going Charlie and Stan. When they did leave – after the week at the Hackney Empire, April 9, 1910 – Syd continued in *Skating,* while Charlie and Stan went into a brand new sketch, *Jimmy the Fearless*. The lead role in this may have been Karno's twenty-first birthday present to Charlie. If so, it turned out to be an unwanted gift, as Stan explains:

> Presently we started rehearsals for a new sketch called *Jimmy the Fearless*, in which Charlie was naturally cast for the leading part, while I was just one of the cowboys in the background. Then, one day, Fred Karno himself dropped in to see how things were shaping and, to tell the truth, said he didn't like Charlie's interpretation of the comedy role. Thereupon Charlie replied that he didn't like the part anyway, and said that he would rather not play it.
>
> (*Tit-Bits* – November 14, 1936)

To Stan's amazement, Frank O'Neill immediately put him up for the part, and Karno nodded his assent. On the opening night the company were appearing at two theatres – Willesden and Ealing – and had to travel between them by one of Karno's private buses. Stan Laurel:

> The show was a terrific hit. I had to take five curtain calls. You can imagine how I felt. I was a 'star' comedian, at last, and a Karno one at that!

Such an enthusiastic response was too much to bear for Chaplin who, after watching the sketch, stated he liked the 'potential' of the part, and decided he would do it after all. Others might prefer to say he took the part after witnessing *Stan's* potential. Stan, however, was more than happy to give praise where praise was due. To biographer John McCabe he opined:

> I never quite understood why Charlie didn't take the part in *Jimmy the Fearless*. I thought it was a wonderful sketch, so I jumped at the chance to play 'Jimmy.'
>
> Charlie was out front the opening night and right after the show he told Karno he had made a mistake. He wanted to play Jimmy. And he did. I didn't feel bitter about it. For me, Charlie was, is, and always will be, the greatest comedian in the world. I thought he should have had the part to begin with. But after that I used to kid him – always very proudly – that for once in my life Charlie Chaplin was my replacement.

Well Stan may have been kidding, but Chaplin wasn't going to risk anyone else saying that Stan Laurel had bested him, and so omitted the whole of his involvement with this long-running sketch from his memoirs. So the mystery remains: "Just why did Chaplin turn down the part of 'Jimmy'?" Stan did not know, and Chaplin chose not to enlighten us, but I believe it stemmed from his losing face in the Fred Karno sketch *The Football Match*, during the third tour of which, he had attempted to take over the lead role of 'Stiffy – the Goalkeeper,' played by the comic legend Harry Weldon. In his autobiography, Chaplin confessed:

> Great as my disappointment was about *The Football Match*, I tried not to dwell on it. But I was haunted by a thought that perhaps I was not equal to taking Weldon's place. As I had had not fully retrieved my confidence, every new sketch in which I played the leading comedy part was a trial of fear.

But Chaplin had adapted magnificently to the role of every character to date whose shoes he had stepped into. And there, I believe is the kernel of the matter. From 'Billy – the Page' in *Sherlock Holmes*, to Walford Bodie, and Dick Turpin in *Casey's Circus*, and through all the parts he had played in the Karno sketches, Charlie had never had to invent a character. Chaplin's gift was for mimicry and, in every case so far, he had seen the actual person he was about to impersonate, or had seen the role being played by an actor whose place he was about to take. But 'Jimmy' was a completely new character, a character that he would have to find, to develop, to make likeable, and to make funny. And that, I believe, is what frightened the hell out of him.

However, once Chaplin had seen Laurel as 'Jimmy,' all the unknown elements had been revealed. Laurel had created the character, made him likeable and, most importantly of all, had shown Chaplin how to translate the action from the written word, and make it funny – ON STAGE. Now Chaplin had nothing to fear. All he needed do was mimic the character that Stan Jefferson had brought to life.

So, with Chaplin in the eponymous role of 'The Boy 'Ero,' and Jefferson back to being a lowly cowboy, *Jimmy the Fearless* toured the U.K. In omitting 'Jimmy' from his memoirs Chaplin denied himself the opportunity to reveal some flattering reviews; reviews which actually give more praise to Chaplin than to the sketch itself, which is a considerable achievement considering the reputation attached to Karno productions. The review at the Stratford Empire ran:

> As it stands at present, *Jimmy the Fearless*, is hardly likely to emulate the success of its predecessors. The best work is done by Chas. Chaplin in the name part.
>
> (April 25, 1910)

And from the Swansea Empire review:

> Fred Karno's latest production causes much laughter. The name part is cleverly acted by Charles Chaplin.
>
> (July 11, 1910)

For his appearance at Leeds Empire, Chaplin was singled out for high praise indeed:

> To assume roles made famous by Fred Kitchen is no small task for a stripling of twenty-one, yet Mr. Chas. Chaplin, who has caused so much laughter this week as "Jimmy the Fearless," has done so with vast credit to himself. Mr. Chaplin has not been more than three years with Mr. Karno, yet he has played all the principal parts, and he fully realizes the responsibility of following so consummate an artiste as Fred Kitchen. He is ambitious and painstaking, and is bound to get on. Young as he is, he has done some good work on the stage, and his entrance alone in "Jimmy the Fearless" sets the house in a roar and stamps him as a born comedian.
>
> (*Yorkshire Evening Post* – July 23, 1910)

A fourth, from the Ardwick Green Empire read:

> Somehow the performance is not so amusing as it ought to be, but the swank of the invincible hero makes one laugh fitfully.
>
> (August 15, 1910)

The *Jimmy the Fearless* company leaving a London railway station to go "up North."

And here are the ten known company members: Chas. Chaplin, Bert Williams, Arthur Dandoe, Mike Asher, Stan Jefferson, Emily Seaman, Ernest Stone, Albert Austin, Harry Daniels, Mrs. Bert Williams, plus Manager Frank O'Neil (although not in order of the above, of which there are fifteen – plus the children.)

-----0-----

> "JIMMY THE FEARLESS"
>
> Written by:- Fred Karno and - Charles Baldwin
>
> SCENE 2. ENTER JIMMY.
> Hands up. I've got the drop on yer.
> Business - Ike put hands up.
>   (Omnes) ------ the Fearless
> Ay - Jimmy the Fearless. So, Ike, you thought when you shot
> my mustang and I fell over the cliff - that you had done for
> me. Now go.
>   ----- did you escape?
> When I went over the cliff - I dropped on to a grissly -
> that broke my fall - hastily I mounted a buffalo and
> followed your tracks and got here in time to save you.
>   ----- brave of you.
> It's nothing. But you must rest. Go into yonder room while I
> catch a couple of bronchos. We must leave this place by
> daybreak. Good night dear one. One chaste salute. (kisses
> her and sees her off - business)
> So Alkali Ike has crossed my path again.
> Indian mouth rattle heard off.
> 'Tis Wampum na Washti the Indian Chief.
> Does Indian mouth rattle.
> ENTER - Wampum na Washti a typical Red Indian
> in War paint - feathers etc.
>   ----- is sad.
> Ay - I am not myself to-night.
>   ----- fourteen of his enemies.
> Yes - curse it - but my greatest enemy has again escaped me.
> Umpuni na Umpini sackety way long.
>   ------ Nerper na muni no.
> Nanty munjari sculpa thi letty.
>   ------ Uti language fluently.
> Does Man-afraid-of-soap imagine that Jimmy the Fearless has
> spent years on the Prairie without keeping his lugs open.
> I long for the day when I shall meet my enemy
>
>   ..../ cont....

(Associated Chaplin)

Anyone reading the above script will immediately realise just why Chaplin turned down the part of 'Jimmy.' There just doesn't seem to be anything in it which sounds even the remotest bit funny. But then it has already been said of Karno: "*Although he could never adequately put his ideas down on paper, his personal coaching ensured the crafting of hilarious sketches.*" The man must have been a miracle-worker.

THE STAGE   28 APRIL 1910

THE STRATFORD EMPIRE

On Monday 25 April, was produced here a sketch, in four scenes, entitled:-

'Jimmy, the Fearless'

Jimmy	Mr. Chas. Chaplin
Alkali Ike	Mr. Bert Williams
Jimmy's Father	Mr. Arthur Dandoe
Mike	Mr. Mike Asher
Jimmy's Mother	Miss Emily Seaman
Bartender	Mr. Ernest Stone
Washti Wampa	Mr. Albert Austin
Chinaman	Mr. Harry Daniels
Gwendolen	Mrs. B. Williams

Scene 1: A Hearty Supper and its After-Effects - The Nightmare;
Scene 2: 'The Dog's Nose' Drinking Saloon, Deadman's Gulch.
Scene 3: The Rocky Mountains - The Attack - The Hand-to-Hand Fight - Saving the Girl - The Rescue - Jimmy Triumphs;
Scene 4: Then He Awoke!

The name of Fred Karno has so long been a household word in the music hall world, and the popularity of his enterprises so indisputable, that the success of a new production associated with his name is invariably looked upon as assured. It is therefore surprising that *Jimmy, the Fearless*, which is being presented here after a preliminary run at Willesden should prove such a feeble affair. Of course, one hardly looks for a plot in sketches of this class, but rather humorous situations and individual cleverness: these features, however, which often redeem a weak show from mediocrity, are strangely absent. In the 'big' scene there is a quite unnecessary display of six-shooters, and indiscriminate firing is maintained. This is neither skilful, funny, or necessary. The theme is somewhat reminiscent of *When Knights Were Bold*. Jimmy, the son of a raucous-voiced collier, has a penchant for blood-curdling literature. His parents naturally do not approve of this, and during supper Jimmy is treated to a dissertation on the manifold troubles that are bound to follow should he persist in ignoring their advice. Jimmy is not convinced, however, and, when his parents have retired, seats himself comfortably in front of the fire and voraciously devours his latest weekly - "The Boy Avenger of the Plains" in which the boy avenger comes up against 'Alkali Ike' - the bad man of Deadman's Gulch. This done, he sinks into the arms of Morpheus, and shortly (in his dream) finds himself at the Dog's Nose Drinking Saloon, Deadman's Gulch, where his 'tart' as he touchingly calls her, has been kidnapped by Alkali Ike. This worthy is drinking and making merry in company with a dozen mates to the accompaniment of deafening pistol reports when Jimmy, the Fearless, stalks in. He quickly clears the saloon, and flies to the Rocky Mountains where he engages in a fight with the notorious Ike. Next he confronts a pirate band, to whom he demonstrates his prowess with the cutlass, before returning home in triumph with his fairy princess and a hoard of treasure and gold coins, only to find his parents turned into the street for debt. This affords an opportunity for the introduction of the note of comedy-pathos, without which these shows would appear to be incomplete. Jim clears off the arrears and the family decide to enter the portals of the workhouse together. This marks the conclusion of the penultimate scene, and, incidentally, the dream. The next morning Jim's father, prior to starting his day's work, discovers his progeny noisily snoring in the kitchen armchair, gripping in his hand one of the banned tales. This is the last straw, and his anger rising he roughly pulls the unhappy Jim out of the chair. The last view we have of the Fearless one is as he is ignominiously chastised by his father. The performance calls for little comment. The best work is done by Chas. Chaplin in the name part, and Arthur Dandoe as Jimmy's father. As it stands at present, *Jimmy the Fearless*, is hardly likely to emulate the success of its predecessors. The scenery and dressing are adequate without being in any way pretentious. The show is produced by Fred Karno in conjunction with Charles Baldwin and Frank O'Neill.

Facsimile of a review for *Jimmy the Fearless*, at the Stratford Empire.

(Taken from different sources so as to include as much of the business as possible.)

Alf Reeves, Karno's top manager, remembered one outstanding bit of business which Charlie performed in the kitchen scene of *Jimmy the Fearless*:

> His father in the skit was ordering him to drop his novel and eat his supper. 'Get on with it now, m'lad,' and jabbing a loaf of bread at him. Charlie, I noticed, cut the bread without once taking his eyes off his [comic] book. But what particularly attracted my attention was that while he absentmindedly kept cutting the bread, he held the knife in his left hand. Charlie's left-handed, but I didn't know it then. The next thing I knew, he had carved that loaf into the shape of a concertina.
>
> (Photoplay – August 1934)

But Stan Laurel also wrote a later account of the origin of the concertina loaf, from a performance which had preceded Chaplin's.

> It was winter and, according to custom, the principals sat inside [the Karno buses] and the lesser lights sat on top. Not yet having earned my spurs, I had an outside seat and, as usual, carried a hot potato to keep my hands warm, as well as to provide a little supper after the show.
>
> But my hands were warm enough that night. In fact, I was hot all over. One of my bits of business was to cut myself a slice of bread, but I was so nervous that I cut the loaf into a sort of spiral. To cover my embarrassment I picked up the loaf and pulled it in and out, as if it were a concertina. That made the audience laugh, and gave me confidence.
>
> (Tit-Bits – November 14, 1936)

Laurel tagged onto his reminiscences:

> Jimmy, and the memory of that role and of that production stayed with him [Charlie] all his life, I think. You can see *Jimmy the Fearless* all over some of his pictures—dream sequences for instance. He was fond of them, especially in his early pictures. And when it comes right down to it, I've always thought that poor, brave, dreamy Jimmy one day grew up to be Charlie the Tramp.

Charlie and Stan toured in *Jimmy the Fearless* till the end of August, then switched to a brand new sketch entitled *The Wow-Wows*, a sketch satirising an initiation into a secret society. After playing this sketch in London for just two weeks, they moved slightly farther afield — America.

Chapter 6

VARIETY TO VAUDEVILLE

The full Karno company setting off to play New York was: Alfred Reeves, Amy Minister, Charles Chaplin, Albert Austin, Albert Williams, George Henry Seaman, Emily Seaman, Frank Melroyd, Freddie Westcott (aka: Fred Karno Jnr.), Stanley Jefferson, Arthur Dandoe, Fred Palmer, Muriel Palmer, Mike Asher, and Charlie Griffiths – totalling twelve men and three women.

After missing the *SS Lusitania*, which left Liverpool on September 17, our intrepid travellers ended up on the British steamer the *Cairnrona*. This had two major drawbacks: the majority of passengers were farmers emigrating to Canada, many taking their cattle with them; and secondly, it wasn't going to New York, but to Montreal, Canada. How they were to rue missing the *Lusitania*, and the comfort it would have afforded them. From leaving Southampton on September 22, 1910, the passengers on the *Cairnrona* had to endure bad weather and rough seas. This not only incapacitated the passengers but also the ship, for which there was a three-day delay while the broken rudder was repaired. Consequently, during the eleven days between departure and arrival, rehearsals were infrequent.

The Karno Company aboard the *SS Cairnrona*, bound for Quebec, September 22, 1910.

Back Row: Charles Chaplin, Albert Austin, Fred Palmer, Bert Williams, Frank Melroyd
Middle Row: Fred Karno Jnr. (Westcott), Arthur Dandoe, Alf Reeves
Front Row: Stan Jefferson, Muriel Palmer, Mike Asher, Amy Minister, Captain C. J. Slooke
(Missing from picture: George Seaman, Emily Seaman, Charles Griffiths)

After finally disembarking on Sunday October 2nd, and taking a train ride via Toronto, the weary and travel-stained company arrived with a little over twenty-four hours to spare before the opening curtain at the Colonial Theatre, New York.

A less-formal pose of the male section of the Karno Company on board the *Cairnrona*

Fred Karno Jnr., Charlie Chaplin, Arthur Dandoe, Fred Palmer (on steps), Frank Melroyd, Albert Austin, Stan Jefferson

Walking around in daylight hours, Chaplin found the city to be bewildering, and a little frightening. Of his inner feelings he said he felt 'inadequate;' 'uncomfortable;' 'lone;' and 'isolated'. However, in the evening, the city took on a new dimension, for which Chaplin had more of an affinity:

> As I walked along Broadway with the crowd dressed in their summer clothes, I became reassured. We had left England in the middle of a bitter cold September and arrived in New York in an Indian summer with a temperature of eighty degrees; and as I walked along Broadway it began to light up with myriads of coloured electric bulbs and sparkled like a brilliant jewel. And in the warm night my attitude changed and the meaning of America came to me: the tall skyscrapers, the brilliant gay lights, the thrilling display of advertisements stirred me with hope and a sense of adventure. "This is it!" I said to myself. "This is where I belong!"

Sad to say, this feeling of belonging was to last less then twenty-four hours — to be exact, until the review for the first evening's show came out. The chosen sketch was the one they had most recently played back in London – *The Wow-Wows* (subtitled: *A Night in a London Secret Society*). Karno thought that America was full of secret societies, and so a burlesque on them would be a great success. Stan Laurel said of this:

> Karno was dead wrong. *The Wow-Wows* was awful. Everybody in the company said so during all those dreary days of rehearsal [back in England].

> (*Charlie Chaplin*, John McCabe)

Chaplin too thought it a bad choice:

> Reeves and I thought the show silly, fatuous, and without merit.
> ..... and I had advised Karno not to open with it.

> (*My Autobiography*, Charles Chaplin – 1964)

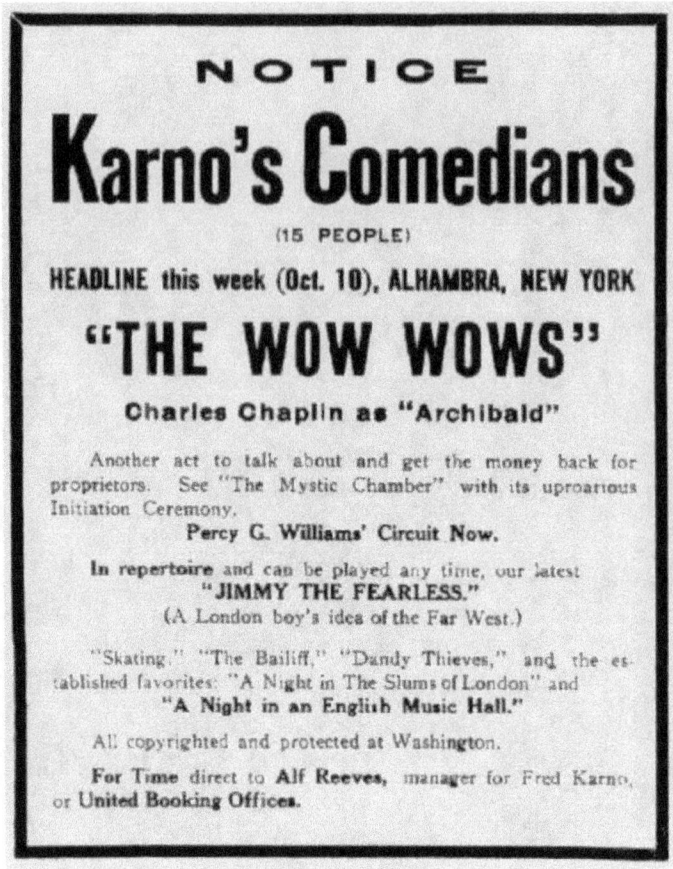

The fears the latter two had held were to be borne out in the review printed in the show business newspaper *Variety*:

(w/c Monday October 3, 1910)

NEW YORK, Colonial Theater

A Karno company that talks seemed to hit the Colonial audience as a bit queer. Having seen the 'Music Hall,' 'Slums' and 'Dandy Thieves' [performed by previous companies], it is but natural that American audiences should expect only pantomime from a Karno group. Anyone familiar with London music halls at all will not be surprised, for most of the Karno productions over there depend to some extent upon dialog. *The Wow Wows* is the real English type of Karno act, with the red nose comic in the fore, and the proceedings built around him.

Laid in three scenes, the act consists merely of a burlesque on a secret society initiation. To 'get even' on the 'tightwad' of a summer camp, the rest of the bunch frame up a phony secret society into which they initiate M. Neverloosen *[1].

Charles Chaplin is the 'mark' and chief comedian. Chaplin is typically English, the sort of comedian that the American audiences seem to like, although unaccustomed to. His manner is quiet and easy and he goes about his work in a devil-may-care manner, in direct contrast to the twenty-minutes-from-a-cemetery make-up he employs.

The make-up and the manner in themselves are funny. That is what will have to carry *The Wow-Wows* over, if it goes that way. Chaplin will do all right for America, but it is too bad that he didn't first appear in New York with something more in it than this piece. The company amounts to little, because there is little for them to do. Dialog in the opening doesn't amount to anything and at intervals during the piece there are talky places which drags the time when Chaplin does not occupy the center *[2] of the stage.

In the last scene—initiating chamber—there are one or two funny bits of business. Three women in the act are not needed. One has a scene with the comedian; the others simply

---

*[1] Chaplin's role was 'Archibald Binks' – 'M. Neverloosen' is merely a term to reflect that he was a 'tightwad.'

*[2] U.S. variant spellings have been left in, in all reviews quoted from American newspaper sources.

walk on and off a couple of times. The genuine fun in *The Wow-Wows* is not quite enough to stand off the half-hour of running time. The act can be fixed by interjecting more speed, and cutting the unnecessary talk.

The Colonial audience laughed at the show Monday night, but not enough. An act of this sort, erected solely for comedy, should register a bigger percentage of laughs.

(Variety – October 8, 1910)

The Wow-Wows, written by Herbert Sydney, owes much of its premise to the sketch *A Night in a Chamber of Horrors,* which Charles Baldwin produced in November 1909. In the latter, a group of wags make one of their members spend a night alone in the Chamber of Horrors in 'Baxter's Famous Waxworks,' as part of an initiation ceremony. Some time between then and August 1910 the idea had been "borrowed" by Karno, and the setting moved to that of a campsite by the river. I would surmise that Herbert Sydney didn't write the additional scene, as it differed greatly from his usual style of work. Sydney wrote 'business' (a term for physical/visual gags) not verbal humour. He was to write at least three subsequent sketches for Karno, but let it be put on record that his greatest creation was *Mumming Birds*, which relies little, if at all, on verbal dexterities. The first scene of *The Wow-Wows*, however, is just a succession of terrible puns, enough to make even the most receptive of audiences groan. Consider having to endure the following:

Jimmy: There's two eggs for you, but they're both rotten.

Archie: What, that one bad and that one bad?

Jimmy: Yes.

Archie: Oh that's too bad. I am a devil when I crack these little jokes.

Lydia: Oh, how dreadful, I say dear, have you been in for your morning dip?

Archie: Yes, I've had my usual river plunge.

Lydia: And was the water up to your expectations?

Archie: No, only up to my knees.

If you can stand any more of this, read the extract from the script reproduced on the next page. The audience certainly couldn't. At the following week's venue, the Alhambra on 7th Avenue, the reviewer for *New York Clipper* branded the cast: "… a collection of blithering, blathering Englishmen," and with material like the above, who could question him?

(w/c Monday October 10, 1910)

A Night in a Secret Society

Now, in Charles Chaplin, is so arriving a comedian that Mr Karno will be forgiven for whatever else the act may lack. The most enthusiastic Karno-ite will surely admit, too, the act lacks a great deal that might help to make it vastly more entertaining. Still, Mr. Chaplin heads the cast, so the people laughed and were content.

He plays Archibald, a chappie with one end of his moustache turned up and the other turned down, a chappie with spots on his face betokening many a bad night, a chappie who declared himself in on everything though never paying his or any share. [hence: 'Mr. Neverloosen'].

His first appearance is made from a tent, one of several occupied by a camping party. He looks more than seedy, despite his dress being immaculate.

'How are you, Archie?' inquires a woman visitor, decidedly attractive, and of whom Archie appears to be enamoured.

'Not well,' he responds. 'I just had a terrible dream.'

'Very terrible?' she asks solicitously.

'Oh, frightful!' says Archie. 'I dreamed I was being chased by a caterpillar.'

Archie makes such remarks as this in an exceedingly droll, ludicrous fashion. Outside Archie the company is composed of the most remarkable collection of blithering, blathering Englishmen New York has seen in many a day.

(New York Clipper – October 1910)

THE WOW WOWS

A Farcical Sketch in 3 Scenes.
Scene 1 - Up the River
Scene 2 - Corridor at Brown's Club House
Scene 3 - the "Lodge" at Brown's

<u>Characters:</u>
Hon. Archibald Binks   Who won't pay his share
Charlie Blazer
Jimmy Bottles
Freddy Brunton
Billie Brindle   His friends are determined to make him pay
Miss Lydia Flopp   Archie's sweetheart
Florrie & Vi   Up River girls

Tom. Dick. Harry. Alf. Charlie. Frank. Jack. Etc - Up River men on their holidays.

<u>Scene 1</u> - Blazer is shaving, Brunton on stool reading paper. Bottles cooking breakfast at table. Up river men cross left to right, with boat oars over shoulder. 2nd man knocks up against Blazer.
<u>Blazer:</u>   Confound you, man, can't you see I'm shaving.
<u>2nd Man:</u> Sorry old man, an accident.
<u>Blazer:</u>   Sorry, so am I. I'll have no face left shortly.
(more bus. with oars)
<u>Brunton:</u> Its going to be a glorious day, Blazer!
(talk about rain, and being tired of standing Archibald drinks without him ever paying.
<u>Archie enters</u>):
[<u>Archie:</u> Good morning Brunton. Do you mind giving me a little water?
<u>Brunton:</u> Certainly. What do you want if for?]
<u>Archie:</u>   I'm going to have a bath. I say, Jimmy, what have you for breakfast?
<u>Jimmy:</u>   There's two eggs for you, but they're both rotten.
<u>Archie:</u>   What, that one bad and that one bad?
<u>Jimmy:</u>   Yes.
<u>Archie:</u>   Oh that's too bad. I am a devil when I crack these little jokes. (to Blazer) I say, Blazer, where are you going tonight?
<u>Brunton:</u> Well I'll tell you, Archie, tonight we are going to Brown's Club House to have a lovely supper.
<u>Archie:</u>   Ha! That just reminds me, you might tell old Brown I can't come tonight.
<u>Brunton:</u> My dear old chap, you're not invited.
<u>Archie:</u>   No, that's why I can't come. (leaves)
<u>Brunton:</u> (rising): Blazer, he's impossible.
<u>Blazer:</u>   He's incorrigible.
<u>Jimmy:</u>   He's sickening...

(Reproduction of original script — courtesy of Associated Chaplin)

Karno had allowed the first three rules of comedy to be broken: "No puns; no puns; no puns." Also, in the programme notes, Scenes 2 and 3 are billed as the 'exterior' and 'interior of the Chamber of Horrors,' respectively, whereas it was merely a darkened room (in 'Brown's Lodge' on the campsite). Here, the level of expectancy turned into a total let-down, as the only 'horror' Archibald had to endure was sitting on an electrified magic-carpet. Oooo! – scary! No wonder the audiences were unimpressed.

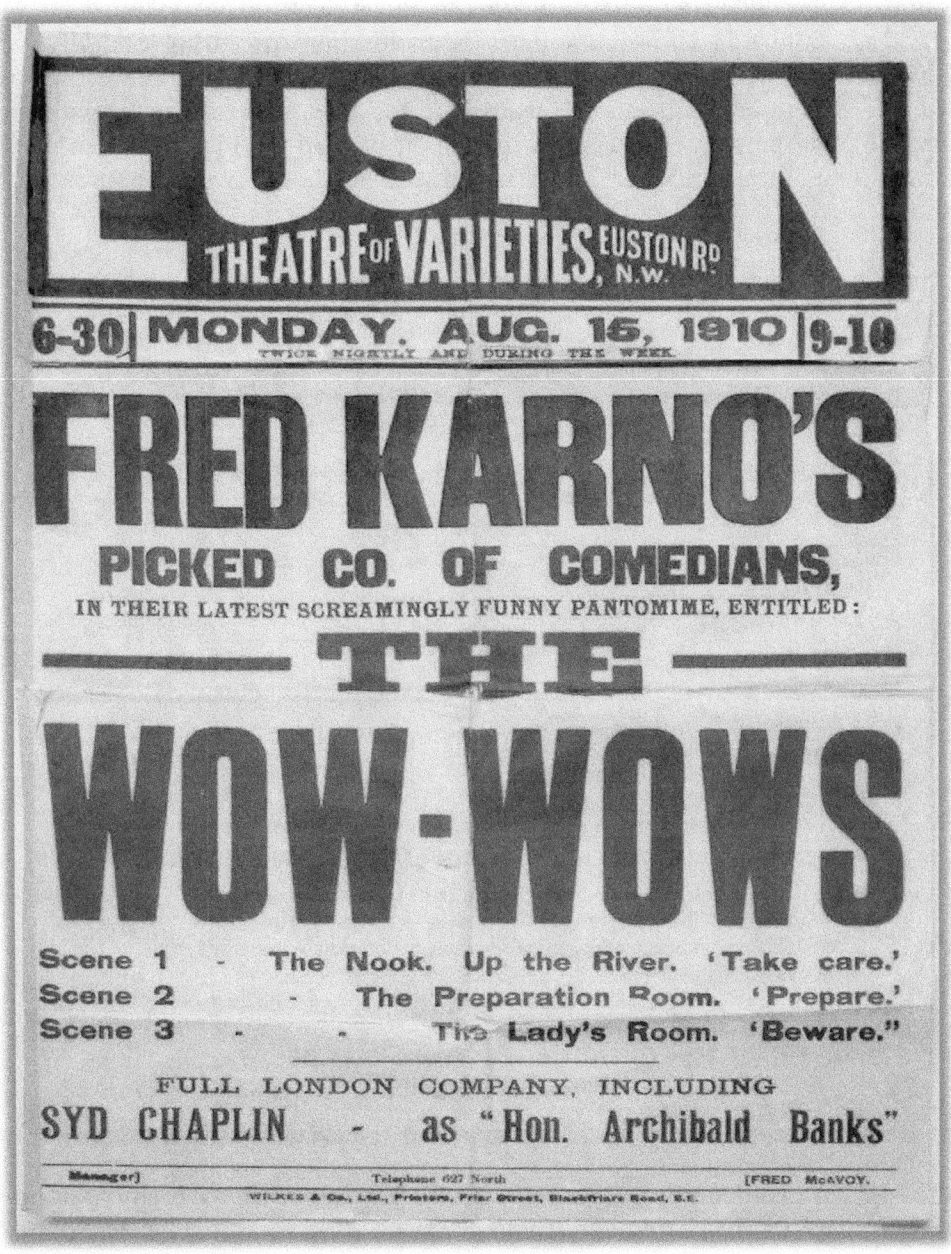

[AJM: Note that in the original version, the scene of Archie's Initiation into the secret society of the Wow-Wows takes place in what is termed 'The Preparation Room,' thus raising no expectations of a Chamber of Horrors.]
(Courtesy of Associated Chaplin)

Chaplin was particularly affected by the poor reception the sketch received. He had come to conquer America, not run home with his tail between his legs. He reflected:

> Although I hated the sketch, I naturally tried to make the best of it. I will not describe the nerves, agony and suspense that preceded my entrance the first night, or my embarrassment as the American artists stood in the wings watching us. My first joke was considered a big laugh in England and a barometer for how the rest of the comedy would go over. It was a camping scene. I entered from a tent with a cup of tea.

Archie (me):   Good morning Hudson. Do you mind giving me a little water?

Hudson: Certainly, what do you want it for?

Archie: I want to take a bath.

(A faint snicker, then cold silence from the audience.)

Hudson: How did you sleep last night, Archie?

Archie: Oh! Terribly. I dreamt I was being chased by a caterpillar.

Still deadly silence. And so we droned on, with faces of the Americans in the wings growing longer and longer. But they were gone before we had finished our act.

To say the least, failure in a foreign country is distressing. Appearing each night before a cold and silent audience as they listened to our effusive, jovial English comedy was a grim affair. We entered and exited from the theatre like fugitives. For six weeks we endured the ignominy. The other performers quarantined us as if we had the plague. When we gathered in the wings to go on, crushed and humiliated, it was as though we were about to be lined up and shot.

"A Night in a London Secret Society"

FRED KARNO presents his Latest and Greatest Laughable Production, entitled:

"THE WOW-WOWS"

In Three Scenes. The sign of the three flaps or Pom-tiddle-om-Pom-Pompom
Written by Fred Karno and Herbert Sydney

The Cast Includes

Chas. Chaplin, as	Archibald Binks
Arthur Dandoe, as	Charlie Blazer
Albert Williams, as	Fred Brunton
Frank Melroyd, as	Jack Denton
Mike Asher, as	Jimmie Bottles
Fred Palmer, as	Peroy
Muriel Palmer, as	Lady Binks
Amy Minister, as	Lydia Scotch

Albert Austin, Stan Jefferson, Fred Westcott, Geo. Seaman, etc.

Supported by the renowned Karno Troupe of picked London performers.

Scene I. "The Nook," Depicting River Life with its beauty and gayety.
  PREPARE: "What man hath joined together, let no man put asunder."
Scene II: Entrance to Secret Society's Chamber of Horrors. The password. "Kiss me. Good Night! "Nurse!" TAKE CARE.
Scene III. Interior of Chamber of Horrors. The Initiation. Archibald on the Magic Carpet. BEWARE.

Manager for Fred Karno's Company: ALF REEVES.

So just why had Karno decided not to tour the trusty *Mumming Birds* sketch (re-titled for American audiences: *A Night in an English Music Hall*)? One reason may be found in its earlier history in the U.S. Firstly, there were the incidents in 1906, when the actions of copycat companies had led to Karno disbanding his company. But then in the Autumn-Winter seasons of 1907, 1908, and 1909 Karno had again sent over companies to the States, all of which performed *Mumming Birds*. Now, come the 1910 tour, maybe Karno believed that *Mumming Birds* was too well-known to have any impact.

So with *The Wows-Wows* as the chosen sketch, the morale of the company began to sink lower and lower. But then, in week three, a little ray of hope shone through. Chaplin tells:

> By now we had resigned ourselves to pack up and return to England after six weeks. But the third week we played at the Fifth Avenue Theatre, to an audience composed largely of English butlers and valets. To my surprise on the opening Monday night we went over with a bang. They laughed at every joke. Everyone in the company was surprised, including myself, for I had expected the usual indifferent reception.
>
> (*My Autobiography*, Charles Chaplin – 1964)

> (w/c October 17, 1910)
> **BROOKLYN, Orpheum**
> Fifth Avenue, Brooklyn
> **Charles Chaplin**, leading comedian of Karno's Comedians, which are playing at the Orpheum Theatre, this week, is being extensively entertained by the British residents of Brooklyn. The members of the St. George Society and the Usonas are among those who have arranged affairs for Mr. Chaplin and his confrères.

The newspaper review, at left, sheds further light on just who the audience was composed of:

(*Brooklyn Eagle* – October 18, 1910)

[USONAS is an acronym for:
United States Overseas Nannys and Servants – I think!]

Next was the Bronx Theatre, at 149th Street and Bergen Avenue, in the suburb of New York City known as 'the Bronx.' The booking was obtained almost by chance, as this new 2,800-seater theatre had opened only the previous week. This is, and always has been, a tough area, but the audiences inside the theatre seem to have been remarkably kind:

(*Variety* – October 29, 1910)

> (w/c October 24, 1910)
> **BRONX, Bronx Theatre**
> Another act that made its first appearance over the Harlem River side was Karno's *Wow-Wows* replete with laughter provoking situation. **Charles Chaplin**, the star of the aggregation, received a wave of applause almost continually after he got started.
> (Fred)

Chaplin was also able to gain comfort from the quote in *Variety*: "*Chaplin will do all right for America*," And it was in America where Chaplin felt his future lay, but not necessarily in his present capacity, as he himself confirms:

> Paradoxically enough, as a result of our failure I began to feel light and unhampered. There were many other opportunities in America. Why should I stick to show business? I was not dedicated to art. Get into another racket! I began to regain confidence. Whatever happened I was determined to stay in America.
>
> (*My Autobiography*, Charles Chaplin – 1964)

The following week the troupe was at the Greenpoint Theatre – a theatre so far down the newspaper listings that it often fell off the page. New York theatres then shut their doors on the Karno Company, and they found themselves out-of-town in Fall River, Massachusetts.

> Karno's Company, presenting *A Night in a London Music Hall*, is to be the feature attraction of the Loew bill at the Savoy, Fall River (Mass.) next week. This is the inauguration of the full week policy at the house.
>
> (*Variety* – November 5, 1910)

Oct 03	New York	NEW YORK CITY, Colonial	*The Wow-Wows*
Oct 10	New York	NEW YORK CITY, Alhambra	*The Wow-Wows*
Oct 17	New York	BROOKLYN, Orpheum	*The Wow-Wows*
Oct 24	New York	BRONX, Bronx	*The Wow-Wows*
Oct 31	New York	BROOKLYN, Greenpoint	
Nov 07	Massachusetts	FALL RIVER, Savoy	*Music Hall*

Their initial six week run with the Percy Williams Agency had now finished, and was not about to be extended. The English entertainers had "come, been seen, and been conquered." It was time for Karno's London Comedians to pack up and go back to where they worked best — LONDON.

Chapter 7

THE ELEVENTH HOUR

At the eleventh hour, just as the Karno Company members were resigned to returning to England, they were given a reprieve. Marcus Loew – a major booker for numerous vaudeville houses in and around New York – offered to give them a try-out week at the National, but with the proviso that they play *A Night in an English Music Hall*. If that week were to prove successful, then Lowe would add on a three-week booking at the American Music Hall, also in New York City. The week they had just played in Fall River had given the company the opportunity to work-up "Music Hall." And so, on week seven, they duly played at the National:

> (w/c November 14, 1910)
> **BRONX - Loew's National Theatre**
> A play within a play is "A Night in a English Music Hall." now filling Marcus Loew's fine new National Theatre in the Bronx by its drawing powers as the head-liner. In this comedy skit it's the box-holders having fun with the actors that makes fun for the onlookers. On one side is the schoolboy with his stock of buns and "banawnas," some for eating, more for human target ammunition; on the other side is the real "toff" in a state of real spifflication, and between them the audience are kept in a state of laughable uproar. A burlesque wrestling match brings the act to a climax.

The change of sketch had obviously fixed the problem as, when the week at the National ended, came the announcement:

> November 28th the Karno act opens at the American, New York, in *The Wow-Wows*, remaining there three weeks, playing a different sketch each one. *Jimmy the Fearless*, and *The Music Hall* will be the other two.

(*Variety* – November 19, 1910)

Although it was Marcus Loew who had extended the Karno Company's stay in the U.S., it was their tour manager, Alf Reeves, who should be given the credit for negotiating the deal. His qualities have rarely, if ever, been acknowledged. He didn't just book the hotels and the transport; arrange rehearsals; get the company on and off stage, and on and off trains – he was far more than that. He was the man who had to 'sell' the company to the agencies. Whenever the FKC faced rejection, or had bad reviews written about them, he would go into the agency offices, disperse all the negative comments, and come out of the meeting with more bookings. The situation in 1910 was very delicate as the Karno Company had been placed on a blacklist, for breaking the rule which states that, when an act returns to the States within a year of leaving, they have to do so through the same agency which had last booked them. Somehow, Reeves had managed to get the Karno Company off the blacklist, after which they were allowed to continue touring the States again.

Reeves next secured an additional two weeks at the American Music Hall, making a total of five. This may not seem a lot, but it would at least ensure that Christmas was not spent aboard a ship bound for England. As Reeves well knew, it would also act as a great showcase. The terms of the extended engagement stipulated that the company play their full working repertoire of sketches. For some reason *Jimmy the Fearless* was sidelined, and so *A Night in an English Music Hall* played week one; *The Wow-Wows* – week two; *A Night in a London Club* – week three; *A Night in London Slums* – week four; and for week five *A Night in an English Music Hall* was to be repeated. If Reeves thought the cast members might baulk at this schedule, and demand to be allowed to keep *The Wow-Wows* throughout the run, he needn't have worried. To them, it was like being told to drop a piece of red-hot coal and pick up three cold ones. It may have been extra work, but it was certainly less painful.

The Eleventh Hour

SIXTH CONSECUTIVE XMAS IN NEW YORK   **SIXTH CONSECUTIVE XMAS IN NEW YORK**

Fred Karno's Comedians
ESTABLISHED HEADLINERS
"A NIGHT IN AN ENGLISH MUSIC HALL"
"SLUMS OF LONDON"   "DANDY THIEVES"   "WOW WOWS"   "NIGHT IN CLUB," Etc

The Company that is always working and always gets the money back for the proprietor

A Sure Draw   Always a Hit   Always a Great Big Act

Presented in the United States for the Sixth Consecutive Christmas by ALF. REEVES, to whom all communications should be addressed. (En route with the Show.)

COMPLIMENTS OF THE SEASON TO ALL   American Music Hall, New York, Next Week (Dec. 12)

The company's fortunes now appeared to be turning. The earlier booking at Fall River had materialised because the theatre had changed its policy to staying open for the full week, thus causing an unforeseen last-minute demand for acts. For the week commencing November 21, 1910 they were also asked to fill a vacuum. The Nixon-Nirdlinger Agency, who ran a rapidly expanding circuit of theatres, was opening a brand new venue in Philadelphia; simply named 'The Nixon,' and hired the Karno Company for its first week.

Having broken-in "Music Hall" out-of-town, the act was now ready to start its run at the American Music Hall, New York City. The first two weeks passed off with little press attention:

AMERICAN MUSIC HALL (Hammerstein's) – (w/c Monday December 5, 1910)

The Karno Comedians, for their second week here, are offering *The Wow-Wows*. The act has been changed for the better since seen in the United houses, and scored a laughing hit.

(*Variety* – December 10, 1910)

But then, in week three, came a review which Chaplin would not have been at all pleased with; and it had nothing to do with the bad reception many of the acts were given – far from it:

AMERICAN MUSIC HALL – (w/c Monday December 12, 1910)

The show on the stage at the American this week could not have been recognized from the program Monday evening. The bill was all chopped up, many names listed in the billing not appearing on the indicators. The show started rapidly because they died fast. They were dying all evening. But a few successes came out of the eighteen acts. The faster they died the better the show seemed, for that gave speed through speedy exits.

(*Variety* – December 17, 1910)

The rest of the review, plus a second one, comes courtesy of two cuttings from Laurel's scrapbook:

In the second part Karno's Company in "A Night in a London Club," a revival over here, made the laughing hit of the bill. Though full of rough slapstick, and the usual Karno ingredients, it looks like the best of all the Karno acts, not excepting "The Music Hall." The hit with S. Jefferson as the dude was really very funny. Mr. Jefferson, Chas. Chaplin, Arthur Dandee, Muriel Palmer and Frank Melroyd all did famously.

Fred Karno's London Comedians, in "A Night in a London Club."

"A Night in a London Club" was revived by Fred Karno's London Comedians at the American last week, and it proved one of the biggest laugh getters of any pantomimic farce shown there in an age. Chas. Chaplin was Binks, the inebriate, and as he is beyond question a past master in dumb show mimicry, it may readily be understood that he was a howling success in the part. S. Jefferson, as Percy Swoffles, a dude, was exceptionally clever, and Arthur Dandee, Muriel Palmer, Albert Williams, Amy Minister and Emily Seaman gave capital aid in other principal roles.

The funny stunts in the club, which include an amateur entertainment, were all arranged with a good eye to their laugh-provoking possibilities, and they carried across with great results. About twenty-five minutes were taken up, on the full stage.

Ho! Ho! – *"The hit with S. Jefferson as 'the dude' was really very funny."* That's not what Chaplin wanted to hear. In Philadelphia, when Alf Reeves had been credited as keeping the large audience in "paroxisms" of laughter, that was a mistake, but this wasn't. The reviewer genuinely felt that Stan Jefferson as 'Percy Swoffles – the Dude' was the funniest thing in the sketch.

Chaplin now had two courses of action to choose from: he could suppress Stan's role, or he could improve his own performance. Having seen the reviews to come, I can happily inform you that he chose the latter.

Stan Jefferson as 'Percy Swoffles – the Dude'

For week four the company were to play *A Night in the Slums*, which both Stan and Charlie had played back in England, at Rochdale and Bury, in January 1910, under its then title – *Early Birds*. Six of the rest of the current company had also played *A Night in the Slums* in January 1910, but they had performed it in Winnipeg, amongst other places. So with at least eight company members reprising their roles, *A Night in the Slums* was able to be staged without having to take time out, or work ungodly hours, to rehearse.

> **THE DOMINION**
>
> As a curiosity, and is without precedent in this city, and many other cities, the full cast is here printed of Fred Karno's London Pantomime company, which presents during the second week of its engagement at the Dominion theatre "A Night in the Slums of London."
>
> It is an organization of fourteen people, and can therefore, only be played in the leading vaudeville houses throughout the country as it is an expensive attraction, carrying its own scenery. This section of Karno's enterprises is under the management of Alf. Reeves.
>
> Scene 1—A street in Whitechapel.
> Scene 2—The lodging house
>
> The street scene is merely a knockabout medley of incidents rushed together in burlesqued form, to get laughs from those who desire fun in its broadest form. The incidents in the slum lodging house must be taken more seriously, for the notice hung up on the wall offers a reward for the capture of the criminal. Who knows whether that much sought after person is not present in the room.
>
> A lot of comit business is introduced by a Jew, who has a little money saved up in a handkerchief, and creates lots of merriment among the audience in trying to keep it from the clutches of the other sleeping, or waking occupants of the beds. The entrance of a policeman silences the grotesquely played incidents for a time, but soon breaks out again and goes on until the curtain falls.

Winnipeg — January 25, 1910

And this earlier review from the Winnipeg show (above) will provide us nicely with some additional details of the sketch. For the current show, however, the burden in reviving this sketch was made easier by their having to perform only the second scene: "The Lodging House."

(w/c December 19, 1910)

AMERICAN MUSIC HALL

The Karno Company, for the fourth week, presented the last half of *A Night in the Slums*, and scored easily.

(*Variety* – December 24)

For week five at the American Theatre, commencing Boxing Day, 1910, the company repeated *A Night in an English Music Hall*. On the same bill was the sketch '*Harlequinade* – an old fashioned English pantomime.' The latter term might make one think of such pantomimes as *Cinderella*; *Puss in Boots*; or *Aladdin*; but this one was a 'shadow mime,' i.e. a playlet performed behind a back-lit white screen.

The Eleventh Hour

(w/c December 26, 1910)

AMERICAN MUSIC HALL

"A Harlequinade in Black and White" – Shadowgraph Pantomime

> The entire action takes place behind the moving-picture sheet. The characters are Clown, Pantaloon, Harlequin, Columbine, Policeman, Nursemaid, and Strolling Musician. The figures are shadowed onto the sheet by means of light placed upon the stage, the entire effect being a motion picture in black and white. The finish, the illusion of the artists leaping out over the heads of the audience, received quite a bit of laughter. It is an expensive little novelty that just filled the mood of the holiday theatregoers and was applauded. As a good filler in at the holiday period it answers.
>
> (*Variety* – December 31, 1910)

Chaplin was very taken by this sketch, and saved the following contemporary newspaper review, in which more of the business was revealed:

> It brought forth our old friends: Clown, Pantaloon, Harlequin, Columbine. The pantomime was much more interesting than one would imagine it to be by merely hearing about it, for the pantomimists were funny in their extravagant make-up and actions. There was plenty of action to it, a diversity of ideas shown, and much pleasure derived by the audience, judging by the way they received it.
>
> First the characters indulged in a little general knockabout fooling, then they had fun with a stolen bottle, after which the policeman was relieved of his clothes, and another 'cop' was knocked out and laid upon a table to be dissected, his internal organs being brought forth one-by-one. The baby was stolen from the carriage of the nurse-maid, and all the characters had a 'rough-house' experience while seeking lodgings. A droll duel brought forth two characters who grew and diminished in size rapidly as they fought, the phantom army appeared and paraded, and all the characters leaped 'up to the moon,' the silhouettes showing them apparently jumping up into the air and out of sight. They all jumped back again, and the act closed. It was quite a happy little idea for the holiday season, occupying about eleven minutes.
>
> (Cutting found by David Robinson in the Chaplin Archives – original source unidentified)

-----0-----

The advanced publicity proclaimed *Harlequinade* as, "Especially for the Children" and that: "… it will have the important place on the program." So just why was Chaplin smitten by this presentation? Well, the surprising answer is that *A Harlequinade in Black and White* was actually performed by the Karno Company. So where had this previously unknown-of sketch suddenly sprung from – fully formed? It could not have been a new act, as why would the Karno Company feel a need to devise a new act, when they still had other sketches in their repertoire? Then there was the time factor. In the last five weeks the Karno members had been performing '3 Shows Daily.' They had also staged *four* different sketches, which meant that all spare time must have been spent in run-throughs to refresh the memories of the members who had played them back in England, and to break-in those members who hadn't. This left little or no time at all for devising and rehearsing a new sketch.

Thirdly, *Harlequinade* ran for ten to eleven minutes which, taking in the breath-taking speed at which it was played; the split-second timing; and the performance skills involved; would have taken weeks to perfect. Fifth drawback was how would they have acquired or had made, in such a short time, all the necessary equipment, props and costumes needed to stage it? And, lastly, from where had Chaplin learned and developed the knowledge and techniques needed to stage a back-lit projection presentation? He makes no mention of any previous performance of this art. And it was then, whilst I was pondering this question, that something led me back to my notes on *London Suburbia*. There, in one review, I found the following mention:

> The second scene reveals the backs of the same three houses. ... The inhabitants at length go to bed, affording an opportunity for shadow displays on the various blinds.
>
> (*Blackburn Times* – April 14, 1908)

Further searching in my records revealed that, from among the Karno players on the current U.S. tour, Bert Williams, Fred Westcott, George Seaman, Muriel Palmer, Amy Minister, Frank Melroyd, and Chaplin himself, had all played in *London Suburbia* back in England. So here then were the players with the experience, the knowledge, the skill, and the timing to execute *Harlequinade*.

FRED KARNO'S COMEDIANS

"A NIGHT IN THE SLUMS OF LONDON"

A Pantomimic Comedy, in Two Scenes

Scene I: A Street in Whitechapel   Scene II: The Lodging House

CAST:

Bill, an East Side bully	Charles Chaplin
Bobbie, a newspaper boy	Arthur Dandoe
Dennie, a bootblack	Albert Williams
Jack Manly, a sailor ashore	Fred Palmer
Bung, landlord of "Seven Dials Saloon"	Stanley Jefferson
Sergeant A.Z., a London policeman	Mike Asher
Blowhard, a wondering musician	Charles Griffiths
McBooser, his companion	Frank Melroyd
Jane Makebread, a police nuisance	Emily Seaman
Furpence, keeper of lodging house	Fred Westcott
Harold Hardup, a broken-down swell	Fred Westcott
Piecan, lunch wagon proprietor	Albert Austin
Isaacstein, a glazier	Will Stanley
Nancy, an East End Belle	Maude Crewe
'Liza, her pal	Muriel Palmer
Virginia, a flower girl	Amy Minister

Produced under the direction of Alf Reeves, manager Fred Karno's Companies in the United States

---

A quick look at the cast list reveals two extra players, Will Stanley and Maude Crewe, both of whom had also played "Slums" before. These two were probably called in to supplement the number of cast members needed to perform all of the sketches being played during the run at the American Music Hall. Maybe there was dual purpose for them being brought over from England at late notice, as they may have supervised the shipping of the props and costumes needed to stage *A Harlequinade in Black & White*? It's a theory.

So now we know the source of the sketch, and how it may have been possible to produce it at such short notice, but the question still remains as to why they went to all that time, trouble, and expense to put on *Harlequinade*, when they could have simply inserted another working sketch. For instance, *Jimmy the Fearless* was on their repertoire of sketches available for bookings. Surely, "Jimmy" would have gone down well with the children in the Christmas audiences — with its Wild West and swashing-buckling pirates themes featuring a "Boy 'Ero."

For the first show of the New Year the company moved over to the Plaza, on 59th Street and Madison Avenue. Here they reverted to playing *The Wow-Wows*, but retained *Harlequinade*.

(w/c Monday January 2, 1911)

NEW YORK, Plaza

The Karno Company gave two shows, *The Wow-Wows* and the shadowgraph thing [*sic*]. *The Wow-Wows* closing the interval was a big laughing success. The act has been cut some since first shown at the Colonial, and is now a fast moving laughing number of the best sort. The Shadowgraph was interesting and amusing and should be a corking number for the matinee audiences.

(*Variety* – January 7, 1911)

Chaplin intimates that they played *A Harlequinade in Black and White* for six weeks at the American Music Hall, New York, but I can assure you that it was performed there solely during the fifth of their *five* weeks there, and for just one week more, here at the Plaza. After that, there is no sign of it being staged again.

The bookings so far:

Oct 03	New York	NEW YORK CITY, Colonial	*The Wow-Wows*
Oct 10	New York	NEW YORK CITY, Alhambra	*The Wow-Wows*
Oct 17	New York	BROOKLYN, Orpheum	*The Wow-Wows*
Oct 24	New York	BRONX, Bronx	*The Wow-Wows*
Oct 31	New York	BROOKLYN, Greenpoint	
Nov 07	Massachusetts	FALL RIVER, Savoy	*Music Hall*
Nov 14	New York	NEW YORK CITY, National	
Nov 21	Pennsylvania	PHILADELPHIA, Nixon	*Music Hall*
Nov 28	New York	NY CITY, American Music Hall	*Music Hall*
Dec 05	New York	NY CITY, American Music Hall	*The Wow-Wows*
Dec 12	New York	NY CITY, American Music Hall	*London Club*
Dec 19	New York	NY CITY, American Music Hall	*A Night in the Slums*
Dec 26	New York	NY CITY, American Music Hall	*Harlequinade in Black & White*
Dec 26	New York	NY CITY, American Music Hall	*Music Hall*
1911			
Jan 02	New York	NEW YORK CITY, Plaza	*The Wow-Wows* plus *A Harlequinade in Black & White*

-----0-----

This run at the New York American Music Hall did, as had been hoped for, prove to be a great showcase. Chaplin tells that Mack Sennett saw him there one night and said: "*If ever I become a big shot, there's a guy I'll sign up.*" At the time, Sennett was working as an actor and part-time director of comedies for D. W. Griffith, at the Biograph Company, based in Manhattan. It would be two more years before he went on to help form the Keystone Film Company. There are several versions of Sennett's sighting of Chaplin, with various theatres and years being offered, but if these accounts do not cite one of the theatres the Karno company played between October 3, 1910 and January 7, 1911, then they can be dismissed; for when Chaplin left New York at the end of this period he never played New York again.

With bookings at New York venues now spent, the company moved on to Philadelphia, for a three-week engagement at Nixon-Nirdlinger theatres – commencing January 9, 1911. For the first two weeks they were at the Park Theater and then, for the third, returned to the 'Nixon' – the theatre they had appeared at on its opening week back in November. The sketches played were: *A Night in a London Club, A Night in an English Music Hall,* and *The Wow-Wows* – in successive weeks.

Nixon-Nirdlinger Circuit

Jan 09	Pennsylvania	PHILADELPHIA, Nixon	*London Club*
Jan 12 (1 night)	Pennsylvania	PHILADELPHIA, Academy	*London Club*
Jan 16	Pennsylvania	PHILADELPHIA, Park	*Music Hall*
Jan 23	Pennsylvania	PHILADELPHIA, Nixon	*The Wow-Wows*

-----0-----

And that should have been the end of the Karno Company's stay of execution; but then, thanks to their fantastic success of the December run in New York, they had secured a twenty-six week booking on the Sullivan-Considine circuit. The tour was to run from January 30 to August 4, 1911, travelling east to west. Everything was on the up-and-up.

CHAPTER 8

THE AWAKENING

First stop-over on the Sullivan-Considine circuit was in Chicago, for three weeks at the American Music Hall, where they had a similar arrangement to the one in Philadelphia.

CHICAGO, American Music Hall — (w/c January 30, 1911)

Fred Karno's London Comedians began a three weeks' stay at the Music Hall with *A Night in a London Club*, or: *The Amateur Entertainers*. The plan is to produce a different farce each week. There are ten men and three women in the company*[1]. The caricatures of the individual members of the club are with a graveness that makes the comedy stand out. The comedy is rough, but the characters are well drawn.

Various members of the Club are called upon to entertain. There is a woman singer who gets her key repeatedly, but cannot strike it when she begins to sing, a precocious daughter of one of them, who offers a childish selection to the plaudits of admiring friends, and among others an ambitious tragedian who, after reminding the Master of Ceremonies several times, is at length permitted to start a scene of a play, only to be interrupted by 'the drunk' (played by Charles Chaplin) which has come to be recognized as the leading comedy character of the Karno offerings. As seen Monday afternoon the only shortcoming of the farce was the lack of a big laugh at the finish.

(*Show World* — February 4, 1911)

A Night in a London Club is simply *The Smoking Concert*, under a new title. In the publicity for the U.S. tours, Karno was keen to reflect that this was an *English* company, playing sketches containing *English* humour: Hence we get "Karno's *London* Comedians;" "A Night in an *English* Music Hall;" "A Night in a *London* Club;" "A Night in *London* Slums;" and "A Night in a *London* Secret Society," replacing the titles the sketches were known by over in the U.K.

As can be seen, the premise of "London Club/Smoking Concert" was very similar to "Music Hall" in that it was a succession of bad 'turns' being abused by the drunk. *The Smoking Concert*, had made its debut in England, in 1906, and was usually played when two Karno sketches were on the same bill. Charlie and his brother Syd had toured with *The Smoking Concert* between July and October 1908, over in the U.K.; but the last time it had been staged was July 1909. One has to wonder how many others in the U.S. company, if any, had previously performed in it, and just why it was chosen above others in their repertoire. My guess would be it was because it was another vehicle for 'the drunk,' a character which vaudeville patrons had really taken to. But the most puzzling aspect is just how and when did the current US company get together to rehearse it?

There were good reasons why "London Club" was often staged in preference to "Music Hall." The first was as a change of programme when the FKC stayed more than one week at the same venue, or split a six-day week into two threes. The second was as a change of programme when they went back to a particular venue. The third is that some venues simply didn't have enough headroom to install the massive two-storey theatre boxes used in "Music Hall" — whereas the "London Club" set, which was basically a layout of tables and chairs, could easily be accommodated.

The volume of props and scenery carried by the FKC necessitated them having their own railway box-car to transport it from town-to-town. It would then be parked-up on a siding, ready to be on- and off-loaded for the next move. There is no such thing as "Fred Karno's Circus," but the way the company set up and broke, at each and every short stayover, is as near as one could get to a travelling circus.

---

*[1] There were still the original *twelve* men in the company, if one includes Alf Reeves. See cast list on next page. Plus, late-additions Will Stanley and Maude Crewe may have to be added to this number.

The Awakening

THE KARNO BOX-CAR

Amy Minister, Emily Seaman, Muriel Palmer — Albert Austin, Fred Westcott, Bert Williams, Charlie Chaplin
George Seaman

ALF REEVES Presen's

Fred Karno's London Comedians

In a New Pantomime Farce

"A NIGHT IN A LONDON CLUB;" Or,

"The Amateur Entertainers"

CHARACTERS

Archibald Binks (Inebriated)	Chas. Chaplin
Mr. Meek (Henpecked)	Arthur Dandoe
Mrs. Meek (The Pecker)	Muriel Palmer
Martin Harvey Dustbin (An Actor)	Albert Williams
Percy Swoffles (A Dude)	S. Jefferson
Miss Taylor (A Guest)	Amy Minister
Agnes (The Infant Prodigy)	Emily Seaman
Mr. Taylor ⎫ Members ⎧	M. Asher
Mr. Clark ⎬ of ⎨	A. Austin
Mr. Jenkins ⎬ the ⎨	C. Griffiths
Mr. Wilkins ⎭ Club ⎩	A. Seaman
Mr. Lothario (At the Piano)	F. Westcott
The Steward ⎱ Of the ⎰	Fred Palmer
The Chairman ⎰ Club ⎱	Frank Melroyd

Manager for Fred. Karno's Company: Alf. Reeves. Repertoire: "Night in London Music Hall," "Night in Slums," "Wow-Wows," etc

ABOVE: actual cutting from a programme, kept in the Stan Laurel Archive.

In the newspaper advert, at left, Chaplin is depicted as a gent in evening suit and topper — but in reality, the character is *less* toff and *more* tramp.

67

A NIGHT IN A LONDON CLUB

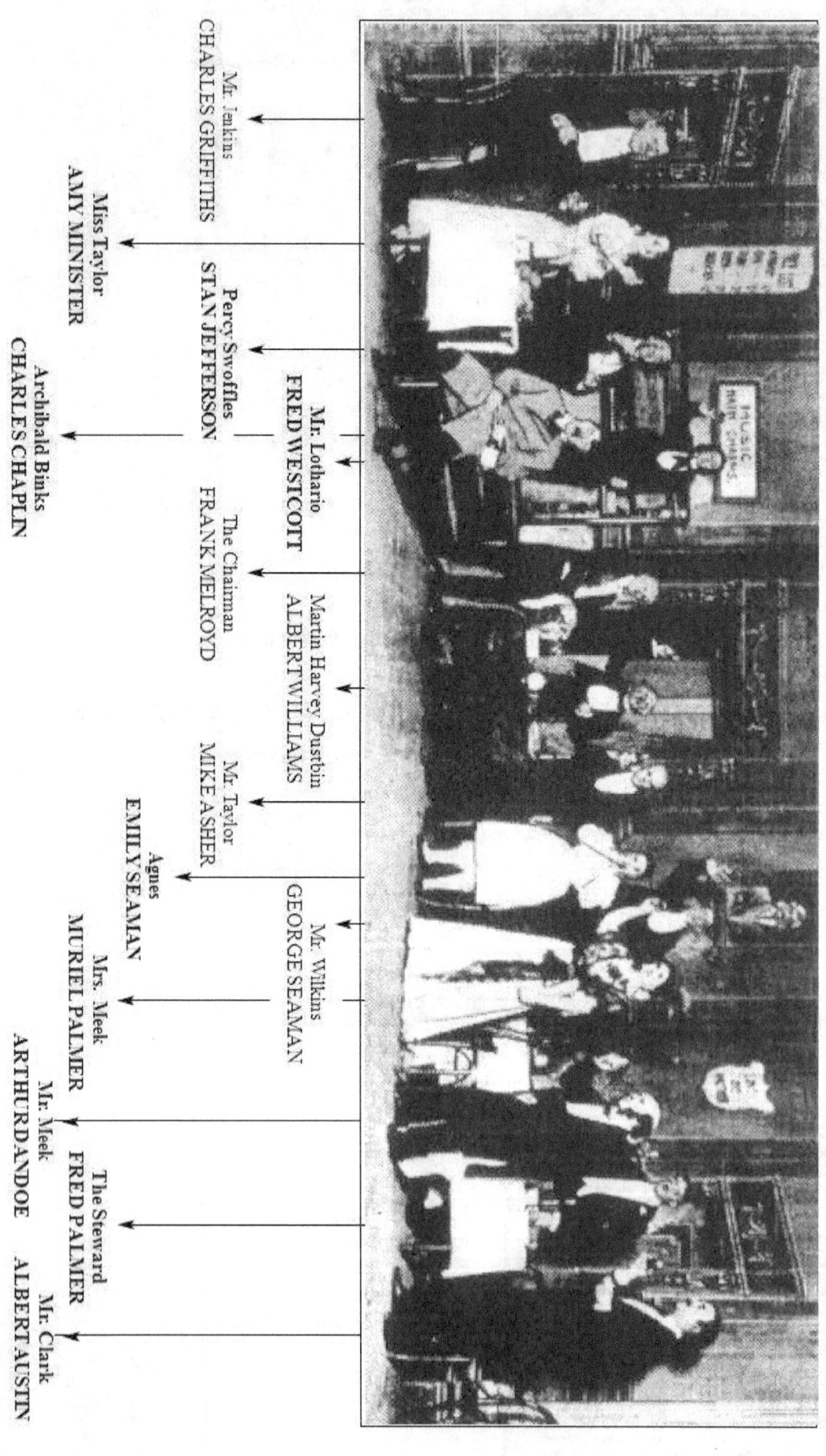

- Mr. Jenkins — CHARLES GRIFFITHS
- Miss Taylor — AMY MINISTER
- Percy Swoffles — STAN JEFFERSON
- Mr. Lothario — FRED WESTCOTT
- The Chairman — FRANK MELROYD
- Martin Harvey Dustbin — ALBERT WILLIAMS
- Mr. Taylor — MIKE ASHER
- Agnes — EMILY SEAMAN
- Mr. Wilkins — GEORGE SEAMAN
- Mrs. Meek — MURIEL PALMER
- Mr. Meek — ARTHUR DANDOE
- The Steward — FRED PALMER
- Mr. Clark — ALBERT AUSTIN
- Archibald Binks — CHARLES CHAPLIN

Unique and previously unpublished photograph showing the cast and the set of "**A Night in a London Club**" – (Names in **BOLD** are confirmed).

"CLUB NIGHT".

Scene. CONCERT ROOM - CHAIRMAN'S TABLE, GUESTS TABLE. SMALL ROSTRUM WITH PIANO.

Cast.

    CHAIRMAN

    STEWARD

    ARCHIE BINKS (Semi-intoxicated)

    MRS. MEEK

    MR. MEEK.

    PERCY SWOOFLES

    LITTLE AGGIE

    PIANIST

    HERBERT TAYLOR

    HARRY CLARK

    MR. BASIL KEENE (ACTOR)

    MISS PARKER etc (GUESTS)

The idea of the sketch is that the members of the Club have got together on this special occasion to receive their prizes which they won at their "ANNUAL SPORTS" and followed by a Concert given by members of the Club.

The Scene opens - Everyone standing with raised glasses toasting the "Chairman" and singing "For his a Jolly Good Fellow".

Chairman raps on table and everyone takes their seats.

Chairman - Now Ladies & Gents you all know why we are here this evening - it is to present the prizes that were won at our "Annual Sports" which we held last Saturday, so while the Steward is putting things in order "Liberty All" (Chairman moves among Members and Guests introducing one to the other). While this is going on Waltz is being played (<u>very piano</u>) then a special introduction is

2.

given to Archie Binks and Mrs. Meek (comedy business) with Binks eventually finishing with his arms around Mrs. Meek. Mr. Meek in the back ground very much annoyed with this and starts to take off his coat to fight Binks.
<u>Chairman</u> brings things to order goes back to his table and then starts to present the prizes.
Now, the first prize was won for the Hurdle race by Mr. Harry Clark. (Everybody applauds - Bravo Clarkie).
Clark gets up and goes to Chairman's table to receive prize.
Chairman: Now Mr. Clark it gives me great pleasure to present you with this very handsome alarm clock and I hopes as how it will be always like you - <u>Keep good time</u> and <u>never go</u> on strike.
Chairman takes a bow for his own joke and Clark gets a hand from the members.
<u>Clark</u> takes the alarm clock and goes back to his seat where Archie Binks has dosed off while these proceedings are going on.
Clark wakes Archie, then holding clock for Archie to see, says "Look Archie, see what I've won".
Archie looks at clock then knocks it out of his hand causing angry comments, from all present.
Chairman finally gets order, raps table and starts to present the next prize.
"Now Ladies & Gents! the next prize was won for the 100 yards sprint by Mr. Herbert Taylor"(applause from members). Taylor struggles to get up, being a victim of rheumatism and just about makes it to the Chairman's table.
<u>Chairman:</u> Now Mr. Taylor it gives me great pleasure to present you with these Handsome pair of Vases which you so nobly won for the 100 yards sprint and I hopes as how you will live long to wear 'em.
Taylor accepts prize amid applause from members and finally returns to his table where Archie is fast asleep.
Chairman. Now! last but not least is this very useful Cigar Case which was won by Mr. Archie Binks for the Egg & Spoon Race - applause.- then business with Taylor & Clark trying to get Archie to his feet to go and receive his prize.
Archie staggers to Chairman's table and immediately picks up Chairman's drink.
Chairman, just sees him in time - takes glass from Archie and puts it back on table.
<u>Chairman.</u> Now Mr. Binks it is with great pleasure that I present you with this beautiful Cigar Case, which contains 5 cigars - as for the brand of them I can't speak - but when you smoke them they will speak for themselves. Archie snatches Cigar Case out of Chairman's hand and starts back to his table - takes Cigar out of case - Clark lights it for him and they start to settle down.
<u>Chairman.</u> Raps on table - Now Ladies & Gents the time has arrived to start our little Concert - so it gives me great pleasure to call on Mrs. Meek for the first song.

(Author's collection – courtesy of the late- Olive Karno)

The second and third weeks in Chicago, during which they played their other two sketches, seemed to have hit a happy-medium, and nothing more:

CHICAGO, American Music Hall — (w/c February 6, 1911)

Before intermission very little of moment happened, save the appearance of the Karnos in *The Wow-Wows*. Chas. Chaplin, as Archie, won a personal success, to which the others contributed as support.

(*Variety* – February 11, 1911)

CHICAGO, American Music Hall (w/c February 13, 1911)

"A Night in An English Music Hall" ended the show joyfully

(*Variety* – February 18, 1911)

Chaplin was well aware of the lack of impact the company were making:

Although on that Sullivan and Considine first tour we were not a roaring success, we passed muster by comparison with the other acts.

Of Chicago, itself, he revealed:

We lived up-town on Wabash Avenue in a small hotel; although grim and seedy, it had romantic appeal, for most of the burlesque girls lived there. In each town we always made a bee-line for the hotel where the show girls stayed, with a libidinous hope that never materialised. The elevated trains swept by at night and flickered on my bedroom wall like an old-fashioned bioscope. Yet I loved that hotel, though nothing adventurous ever happened there.

After Chicago, the company switched to presenting "Music Hall," playing in the mid-west for several weeks — firstly Milwaukee, then Minneapolis:

MINNEAPOLIS, Unique Theater (w/c March 20, 1911)

Broad English humor is very broad indeed. It smacks even more of the slapstick than our old friend, the burlesque comedian. Yet there are always moments of unexpectedness. Where the American would do the obvious thing, the Englishman does the unusual. Fred Karno's *Night in an English Music Hall*, now headlining at the Unique, is one of the funniest of all the skits. It is elaborately staged, showing several boxes and a miniature stage, with all the habitues of that place of entertainment. There is the inebriated swell, the fresh young chap from Eton, his dignified uncle, and then the typical turns - the topical extemporist, the ballad vocalist, the magician, the village choir singers, the saucy soubrette, and, finally, 'The Terrible Turk', the whole ending with a wild rough-and-tumble burlesque wrestling match. There is just enough of truth in the whole to make it entertaining, despite some far-fetched comedy and the fact that the company is not especially strong.

(*Minneapolis* — March 21, 1911)

DULUTH, Empress — (w/c Sunday March 26, 1911)

Featured by Karno's Pantomime company presenting *A Night in an English Music Hall,* the new vaudeville bill which began yesterday at the Empress theater is thoroughly up to the standard set by the Empress management. The sketch by sixteen people is a combination of farce, caricature, and comedy. Perhaps that latter virtue—for comedy is a virtue in vaudeville—predominates.

It is a play within a play and it gets safely across two sets of footlights easily and naturally.

The reception of some of the performers by the "Lunnon" audience is not the most polite. They "kid" some of the actors and others are dealt with more roughly, while the Duluth audience applauds.

The spectators—the London ones—come to the theater loaded with ammunition and they do not hesitate to show their likes and dislikes. Those who try to please the London music hall audiences take an awful chance, apparently.

The act provides music for everybody, however, and as a mirth provoker *A Night in an English Music Hall* has the average act beaten by a logging road mile.

(*Duluth Herald* — March 27, 1911)

The troupe then headed north, and crossed the border into Canada, to spend a week in Winnipeg:

WINNIPEG, Empress (w/c April 3, 1911)

A more delightful audience than was found at the conclusion of yesterday's bill at the Empress would be indeed hard to find, and they had good reason to be satisfied for the bill was unquestionably one of the best that has been seen in this theatre this year. It is headed by the Karno Company in their burlesque *A Night In An English Music Hall*. It is purely slapstick, but very funny slapstick. Charlie Chaplin, the drunken swell, is decidedly clever, and supplies the greater part of the fun throughout the entire act, which is exceptionally well-staged.

Newspaper advertisement from the *Winnipeg Telegram* — w/c April 3, 1911

Showing the giant set for
A NIGHT IN AN ENGLISH MUSIC HALL
In the bottom L/H box is the 'Eton Boy' with his 'Uncle Charlie'
In the bottom R/H box is 'the souse' (Chaplin)
The top two boxes are filled by other members of the cast, when they are not performing as an act.

Mar 12	Wisconsin	MILWAUKEE, Empress	*Music Hall*
Mar 20	Minnesota	MINNEAPOLIS, Unique	*Music Hall*
Mar 26-Apr 02	Minnesota	DULUTH, Empress	*Music Hall*
Apr 03-08	Manitoba	WINNIPEG, Empress	*Music Hall*
[Apr 10-14	no trace	possibly: Billings – Montana, or Miles City, or both]	
Apr 15-21	Montana	BUTTE, Majestic	*Music Hall*

The Awakening

A few years earlier, the extensive tour the Karno Company were engaged upon would not have been possible. The railway had developed in the form of a squid, with New York at its head, and the tentacles spreading westwards, but only for a few hundred miles. Now, in 1911 the lines reached coast to coast, and North to South, although not *every* town was easily accessible. Still, the "Golden Age of Railways" had spawned the "Golden Age of Vaudeville."

From Winnipeg the troupe would have most likely broken their journey, for a couple of nights each in Miles City and Billings (or both) before moving on to the major town of Butte.

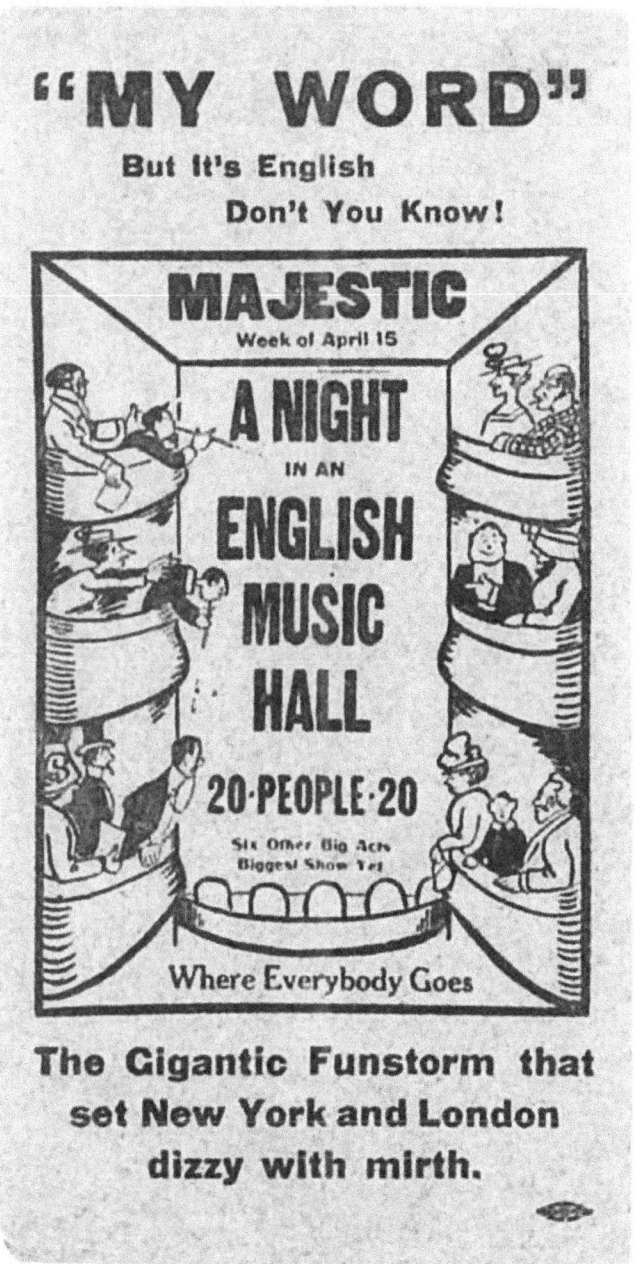

BUTTE, Majestic

(w/c Saturday April 15, 1911)

The art of pantomime is recognized in theaterdom as one of the most difficult known to the profession. It means that the actor must make known his intentions solely by signs and his general actions.

The great act known as Fred Karno's *A Night in an English Music Hall* is in considerable part pantomime, and it therefore is essential that each member of the cast should be a pantomime artist of much ability.

The act shows the stage and the boxes of an English music hall. Seated in one of the music boxes is a decidedly hilarious person who evidently is suffering from too many exciting libations and consequently he insists on participating in each and every act in a manner that is so funny that the audience out front can't help laughing enthusiastically. He scarcely says more than three words during the entire course of the act, yet so funny are his actions that he proves himself one of the best pantomime artists ever seen here.

There are many others in the cast who provide all manner of fun, and the act from start to finish is one of the greatest novelties as well as thoroughly entertaining creations ever brought to this part of the country. Not only are various members of the cast excellent pantomime artists, but they are high class athletes and acrobats as well, for they have to take many falls and go through various stunts that only well qualified athletes could hope to successfully attempt.

The act has become the talk of Butte. Everywhere the great importation is spoken of and those who have seen it are urging their friends to see it before it concludes its Butte engagement.

Twenty people are required for its presentation and much special scenery. The act is one of the biggest sent on tour this season and testifies to the enterprise and up-to-date methods of the Sullivan and Considine organisation.

(*Butte Inter Mountain* – April 18, 1911)

THE GREAT DIVIDE
Butte, Montana

Photos taken during the week in Butte, Montana, w/c April 15, 1911.

LEFT: About to leave their cheap hotel.

STANDING:
[Charlie Griffiths], Albert Austin,
Bert Williams
Mike Asher (with cane)
SEATED
George Seaman – Stan Jefferson
Fred Westcott (with dog)

Six miles out of town, the boys visit the Continental Divide.

STANDING:
Austin, Frank Melroyd,
Williams, Dandoe
SEATED
Chaplin, Asher, Jefferson

As the day got hotter, the jackets came off.

LEFT: Asher, Jefferson, Chaplin, Dandoe, Westcott (seated)

Asher, Chaplin
Dandoe, Jefferson, Westcott

Both photos taken on the scree slope, below the 'Divide' sign.

BELOW: On the porch of the warden's hut, seen top right, next to ranchhouse.

The writing on the stones is advertising:
"The Red Boot Shoe Co. 36 N. Main St."

[AJM: The western slope of Colorado's Rocky Mountains begins at the Continental Divide, the apex of the high peaks. Rivers east of the divide flow eastward to the Gulf of Mexico and the Atlantic Ocean, while rivers west of the divide flow into the Pacific Ocean.]

Melroyd, Williams, Dandoe, Jefferson. Taken around the same time as the Continental Divide photos, but note that Stan is wearing a bow-tie in this one, and Williams has a cravat.

RIGHT: Chaplin was so pleased with this review that he kept a copy in his scrapbook:

THE BUTTE INTER MOUNTAIN.

TUESDAY, APRIL 18, 1911.

PANTOMIME STAR AT THE MAJESTIC

"A NIGHT IN AN ENGLISH MUSIC HALL" IS CHIEF THEME OF SHOW WEEK

The art of pantomime is recognized in theaterdom as one of the most difficult known to the profession. It means that the actor must make known his intentions solely by signs and his general actions.

The great act known as Fred Karno's *A Night in an English Music Hall*, is in considerable part pantomime and it therefore is essential that each member of the cast should be a pantomime artists of much ability.

The act shows the stage and the boxes of an English music hall. Seated in one of the music boxes is a decidedly hilarious person who evidently is suffering from too many exciting libations and consequently he insists on participating in each and every act in a manner that is so funny that the audience out front can't help laughing enthusiastically. He scarcely says more than three words during the entire course of the act, yet so funny are his actions that he proves himself one of the best pantomime artists ever seen here.

There are many others in the cast who provide all manner of fun, and the act from start to finish is one of the greatest novelties as well as thoroughly entertaining creations ever brought to this part of the country.

Not only are various members of the cast excellent pantomime artists, but they are high class athletes and acrobats as well, for they have to take many falls and go through various stunts that only well qualified athletes could hope to successfully attempt.

The act has become the talk of Butte. Everywhere the great importation is spoken of and those who have seen it are urging their friends to see it before it concludes its Butte engagement.

Twenty people are required for its presentation and much special scenery.

The act is one of the biggest sent on tour this season and testifies to the enterprise and up-to-date methods of the Sullivan and Considine organisation.

It enjoyed a remarkably long run in London and New York, and after much persuasion its proprietors agreed to send it on tour to the Northwest.

The great success with which it is meeting here doubtless will be a factor in its continued success in future.

Inside the Butte Majestic Theatre the audiences were civilised and friendly but, outside, the townsfolk seemed a little different. Chaplin:

> In 1910 Butte, Montana, was still a 'Nick Carter' town, with miners wearing top-boots and two-gallon hats and red neckerchiefs. I actually saw gun-play in the street, a fat old sheriff shooting at the heels of an escaped prisoner, who was eventually cornered in a blind alley, without harm, fortunately.

Chaplin also painted a picture of the more colourful part of town:

> The red-light district consisted of a long street and several by-streets containing a hundred cribs in which young girls were installed ranging in age from sixteen up, for one dollar. Butte boasted having the prettiest women of any red-light district in the Middle-West, and it was true.

He also confessed:

> We made friends with the members of other vaudeville companies. In each town we would get together in the red-light district, six or more of us. Sometimes we won the affection of the madam of a bordel [sic] and she would close up the 'joint' for the night and we would take over.

Boy! Had he had some sexual awakening! Just eleven weeks earlier Chaplin had been staying in a hotel in Chicago where the show girls stayed, holding, in his own words, "a libidinous hope that never materialised," and at a hotel where "nothing adventurous ever happened." Now he was taking over bordellos for a whole night. That thin air at high altitude might well make you a bit dizzy in the head, but it sure compensates in other areas.

CHAPTER 9

WAY OUT WEST

In the next state, Washington, the Karno Company first spent a week in Spokane, where Chaplin was delighted to pose in front of a billboard poster advertising *A Night in an English Music Hall*, at the Washington Theatre — w/c Sunday April 23rd.

To think that, only a couple of months earlier, it had been difficult to spot the
Karno Company on the bill, and/or in newspaper adverts.

Then it was on to Seattle, in the Pacific Northwest.

SEATTLE, Majestic – (w/c Monday May 1, 1911)

No act that has ever played the Sullivan & Considine circuit has made the hit that has been made this week by Fred Karno's Comedians in *A Night in an English Music Hall*. For a matter of fact, it is the biggest comedy act that has ever come into Northwestern vaudeville. The act is all comedy, every minute, but the biggest fun in it centers in the intoxicated chappie who sits in one of the stage boxes and makes evident his poor opinion of the numerous turns that are brought on.

(*Seattle Post Intelligencer* – May 6, 1911)

Armed with the above review, Alf Reeves went along to the Sullivan-Considine Building in Seattle to start negotiations for a second tour, as the current tour was scheduled to end in eight weeks' time. By luck, or arrangement, John W. Considine was visiting there that week, so Reeves had no middleman to go through. He again proved himself to be the man for the job, and came away with a twenty-week second tour. There was one proviso, however, which was that "Music Hall" be replaced by *A Night in a London Club*. This is rather a surprising requirement especially considering that the reviewer for the current show had opined: "*A Night in an English Music Hall* is the biggest comedy act that has ever come into Northwestern vaudeville." However, Reeves was up for it, and immediately commissioned new scenery to be made in readiness for the run of *A Night in a London Club*, to begin in August.

Of the eight weeks left on this tour, the next one was to be spent in Vancouver, British Columbia:

VANCOUVER, Orpheum – (w/c Monday May 8, 1911)

The much-heralded *A Night in an English Music Hall* was the reason of the crowded houses at the Orpheum Theatre yesterday. The chief cause of their amusement, and the one to whom all the honors go, is Charles Champlin*[1] [*sic*] who plays the part of the inebriated swell. During the whole action he does not say a single word, but expresses himself in pantomime. His gestures, his facial expression as the various artistes appeared in their turns, and his approval or disapproval of the same, all are inimitable, and evokes roars and roars of laughter. The wrestling bout at the finish, in which he bests the "Terrible Turk," is the best of all, and he brings the offering to an enjoyable conclusion. Mike Asher, as the "bad boy", is also very clever, and he causes a lot of fun also. The English music hall turns are, of course, all caricatured and of the comedy kind, and the artistes who take part are all excellent. *A Night in an English Music Hall* is an act that should be seen by everyone. All attendance records will undoubtedly be broken this week.

(*Vancouver Daily News Advertiser* – May 9, 1911)

Interesting to note the line: "The wrestling bout at the finish, in which he bests the 'Terrible Turk,' is the best of all." Just where did Chaplin get his ideas from for the wrestling match? Well obviously from the business Karno, Syd Chaplin, and other previous 'drunks' who had played the part, had passed on. But an event which happened when Chaplin was with Wal Pink's company in 1906 would also have helped:

BELFAST, Palace — (April 16, 1906)

A funny turn was that supplied by "Wal Pink's Workmen," who appear in an amusing rough and tumble acrobatic sketch entitled *Repairs*. The production is well set, and evoked hearty laughter from crowded audiences at both performances.

Ahmed Madrali, the terrible Turk, is appearing with a troupe of three exponents of the "catch-as-catch-can" style. This will be his last appearance before his meeting with Hackenschmidt at the Olympia, London, 28 April. Madrali fights two of his own troupe, then a volunteer for £25.

(*Belfast Morning News* – April 17, 1906)

---

*[1] There was actually an American entertainer working the vaudeville stage, by the name of CHARLES K. CHAMPLIN, so it would appear that the reviewer had reverted to the name more familiar to him, instead of being able to accept there were two individuals with similar names. This was not to be the last time this would happened.

The first-known picture of the Karno Company captured live on stage, showing the climax of the wrestling bout.
New Nixon Theatre, Philadelphia
w/c January 16, 1911

L-R: The Stage Manager (Fred Palmer), Mary - the Attendant (Emily Seaman), Bad Boy (Mike Asher), Uncle Charley (Chas. Griffiths), Inebriated Swell (Chas. Chaplin), Bunco the Magician [Arthur Dandoe] The Terrible Turk (Albert Williams)

-----o-----

FRED KARNO'S Original London Pantomime Company

Presenting "A NIGHT IN AN ENGLISH MUSIC HALL"

CAST:

The Inebriated Swell	Chas. Chaplin)	
The Bad Boy	Mike Asher)	In the Boxes
Uncle Charley	Chas. Griffiths)	

The Turns

1	The Topical Extemporist	Frank Melroyd
2	The Ballad Vocalist	Muriel Palmer
3	Bunco the Magician	Arthur Dandoe
4	The Village Choir Singers	J. Westcott, A. Austin, S. Jefferson, and G. Seaman
5	The Saucy Soubrette	Amy Minister
6	The Terrible Turk	Albert Williams
7	The Stage Manager	Fred Palmer
8	Mary the Attendant	Emily Seaman

Manager for Fred Karno, Alf Reeves

The Comany's repertoire includes: "Wow Wows," "A Night in the Slums of London," "Early Birds" and "Dandy Thieves," all of which will be seen on the Sullivan & Considine Tour and at this Theatre at dates to be announced later. All productions under copyright in London, England.

At this moment in time, it was impossible to ascertain if the Karno Company had recruited additional members, as newspaper reviews and adverts claimed conflicting numbers — from 12 to 25:

MILWAUKEE, Empress — (w/c March 12, 1911)

A laughing success entitled *A Night in an English Music Hall*, presented by Fred Karno's English Pantomime company, with a cast of **fourteen artists**, is the featured attraction on the bill at the Empress.

-----0-----

DULUTH, Empress — (w/c Sunday March 26, 1911)

Featured by Karno's Pantomime company presenting *A Night in an English Music Hall,* the new vaudeville bill which began yesterday at the Empress theater is thoroughly up to the standard set by the Empress management. The sketch by **sixteen people** is a combination of farce, caricature, and comedy.

-----0-----

BUTTE, Majestic — (w/c Saturday April 15, 1911)

"A Night in an English Music Hall" won unqualified praise during its lengthy London run and it could have remained there indefinitely had not the enterprising American vaudeville purveyors, Sullivan and Considine persuaded the proprietors of the act to send it to this country. It requires **a cast of 20 artists** and a carload of special scenery.

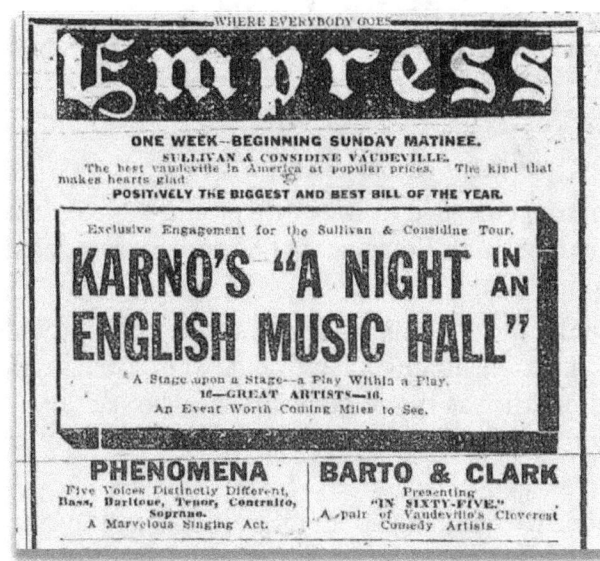

Duluth Herald — March 25, 1911   *Tacoma Times* — May 13, 1911

-----0-----

PORTLAND, Grand — (w/c May 22, 1911)

The headline act is considered by East and West as the greatest comedy act in the world of vaudeville. This is *A Night in a London Music Hall.* It will be presented by Fred Karno's original London pantomime company. Karno's comedians are world-famous. There are **20 English players** in this act, the salary bill of which is greater than is paid in some theaters for an entire bill.

-----0-----

PORTLAND, Grand — (w/c May 22, 1911)

A Night in a London Music Hall, as given by Fred Karno's London Pantomime Company at the Grand, is a scream. It is one of the funniest of knockabout acts seen in this city. The fun is rough and slapsticky, but it sets the audience in convulsions. The act shows the stage and stage boxes of a music hall, and the fun is caused by what happens between the "artists" and the patrons in the boxes. An inebriated swell and a bad boy break up the show.

Charles Chaplin is the man with the package, and his silent waving away of the performers after he has given them start is eloquent. With the bad boy throwing lunch and fruit at the performers, and the swell falling in and out of his stage box and the artists entering into a general scramble, the "Night in an English Music Hall" is a continuous howl of fun. There **are a dozen people** in the act.

-----0-----

Denver Post — July 16, 1911   *Duluth Herald* — August 8, 1911

(w/c Monday May 15, 1911)
At the Majestic
"A Night in an English Music Hall" presented by the London Pantomime Company at the Majestic, is one of the best entertainments recently shown in vaudeville in Tacoma. It is a laugh from beginning to finish. One feature of the play is a realistic stage-upon-the-stage, with Charles Chaplin as the inebriated swell, in one of the boxes affording unending fun. Mike Asher, as the bad boy, and Charles Griffiths as 'Uncle Charlie' play their parts cleverly and keep the audience in a spasm of laughter. The Village Choir is a comedy by itself, sure cure for the blues. The Terrible Turk and the Saucy Soubret are side-achers. The play is well-staged with a company of 11 merry-makers. The cast includes the following:

IN THE BOXES
The Inebriated Swell . Charles Chaplin
The Bad Boy .... Mike Asher
Uncle Charlie .... Charles Griffiths
THE TURNS
Topical Extemporist .... Frank Melroyd
The Ballad Vocalist ...... Muriel Palmer
Bunco, the Magician.... Arthur Dandoe
The Village Choir Singers ....
  A. Austin, S. Jefferson, J. Westcott,
  G. Seaman
The Saucy Soubret..........Amy Minister
The Terrible Turk ..... Albert Williams
The Stage Manager........... Fred Palmer
Mary, the attendant........Emily Seaman
Manager for Fred Karno ... Alf Reeves
  The company's repertoire includes *Wow Wows*, *A Night in the Slums of London*, *Early Birds*, *Dandy Thieves*, all of which will be seen here at a later date.
The bill closes with a good comedy film.

From Vancouver, the troupe headed back North, on the same railway line they had come down on from Spokane, but disembarked a couple of stops earlier in Tacoma.

Thankfully, the review in one Tacoma newspaper did provide accurate information as to just how many, and who, was in the company. As it turned out, it was the original fifteen who had started out on the tour. (See left!) Also, Will Stanley and Maude Crewe might still be with them.

One week later they headed south again, to hit Portland, just over the border, in Oregon:

PORTLAND, Grand – (w/c May 22, 1911)

Fun runs riot at the Grand this week when Fred Karno's "*A Night in a London Music Hall*" is presented by a company of good English comedians. The acting of Charlie Chaplin as the 'inebriated swell' and Mike Asher, the bad boy from Eton school, is especially praiseworthy, though all turn out a series of screamingly funny stunts.

(*Morning Oregonian* — May 23, 1911)

No venue was traced for the week following Portland, but then the trail picks up in San Francisco, of which Chaplin informs us:

At last California! – a paradise of sunshine, orange groves, vineyards and palm-trees stretching along the Pacific coast for a thousand miles. San Francisco, the gateway to the Orient, was a city of good food and cheap prices. We arrived in 1910, after the city had risen from the earthquake of 1906, or 'the fire,' as they prefer to call it. There were still one or two cracks in the hilly streets, but little remnant of damage was left. Everything was new and bright, including my small hotel.

We played at the Empress, owned by Sid Grauman and his father, friendly gregarious people. It was the first time I was featured alone on a poster with no mention of Karno.

Time to untangle a few more knots: The Karno Company arrived in June 1911, not 1910, but Chaplin does at least get the year of the earthquake correct. The quake stuck on April 18, 1906, and caused a fire which burned for four days. When Chaplin talks of the Karno poster, he again quotes the wrong date. His landmark event is yet five months away. Of the present show, Chaplin recalled:

> And the audience, what a delight! In spite of "The Wow-wows" being a dull show, there were packed houses every performance and screams of laughter. Grauman said enthusiastically: 'Any time you're through with the Karno outfit, come back here and we'll put on shows together.' This enthusiasm was new to me. In San Francisco one felt the spirit of optimism and enterprise.

The reviews confirm the laughter, but Chaplin is again pre-empting the next time they would visit San Francisco, and so he has named the wrong sketch. Here is the correct visit, and sketch:

SAN FRANCISCO, Empress — (w/c Sunday June 4, 1911)

> A crowded house enjoyed a splendid bill at the Empress yesterday afternoon. Beginning with the headliner, Fred Karno's *A Night in an English Music Hall* kept the audience in continual roars of laughter. This sketch is almost a whole show itself.
>
> (*San Francisco Chronicle* – June 5, 1911)

And a second:

> Without a doubt the week of 4 June was the record week at the Empress Theatre: even with three shows daily [4 shows, actually: 1.30 - 3.30 - 6.30 - 8.30] and a big capacity, turnaways were the rule at many of the performances. The big draw was Fred Karno's London Pantomime Company, in *A Night in an English Music Hall*, which was one continuous scream of laughter.
>
> (*Billboard* — June 24, 1911)

As to Chaplin's claim: "It was the first time I was featured alone on a poster with no mention of Karno," here are the very posters he is referring to. However, the date "November 5" can clearly be seen, which means that, once again, Chaplin is referencing what will be the Karno Company's second visit to San Francisco. For reasons which will become clear, I am including the pictorial evidence here.

BELOW: Chaplin is standing to the left of the Hotel Exeter.

RIGHT: He has moved along to where the rows become two-tiered. [The extra six posters were there, in case someone hadn't spotted the first four.] (San Francisco — November 5, 1911)

In Sacramento, the following week, a great photo was taken of the original members of the Karno Company outside the Grand Theatre, and a second with additional subjects. Fred Palmer is known to have bought a camera around this time but, as he appears in both photos, I cannot determine if it was indeed his camera that was employed:

FRED KARNO COMPANY — Sacramento — June 11, 1911
Arthur Dandoe, Stan Jefferson, George Seaman, Alf Reeves, Charlie Chaplin, Fred Karno Jnr., Albert Austin
Emily Seaman, Amy Minister, Muriel Palmer
Mike Asher, Fred Palmer
[Missing are: Chas. Griffiths, Frank Melroyd, and Bert Williams]

A PICTURE PUZZLE

This photo was snapped in the same place and time as the above, but the extra numbers are a puzzle. Are they additional members of the Karno Company (a few newspaper did carry adverts which stated there were 25 in the company)? Or, have the other acts on the bill at the theatre joined in? All I can do here is try to identify the ones who are known.

	man white trilby	lady featherhat		unknown	unknown		George Seaman	
Arthur Dandoe		lady whitehat	Emily Seaman	Lady white hat	unknown Karnoman		Frank Melroyd	Bert Williams
Charlie Griffiths	[Will Stanley]	[Maude Crewe]	Amy Minister	Alf Reeves	Muriel Palmer		Man in bowler
Stan Jefferson		Albert Austin		Mike Asher		Charles Chaplin	Fred Karno Jnr.	
			Fred Palmer					

If the unknown people are the other acts on the bill, then these are their names:
Barrows-Lancaster, Sadie Sherman, Lohse and Sterling, Jack Goldie, Professor Oleson.
Other Karno members may be Will Stanley and Maude Crewe.

Normally, *A Night in an English Music Hall* outshines every other act on the bill, but this reviewer felt it only held its own, and that Chaplin rescued it.

SACRAMENTO, Grand — (w/c Sunday June 11, 1911)

The much-heralded *A Night in an English Music Hall* is with us this week at the Grand. It is good and in every way acceptable, but does not outclass other things on the bill. The fact is that the show is made up, with a slight exception, of about as good material as the public has a right to demand from a vaudeville house.

There are a dozen or more characters and participants in the act, but its success depends entirely upon one man, Charles Chaplin, who enacts the role of the inebriated swell occupying a box at the music hall show. As a bit of character work his acting is perfect. He is the whole show. The act commends itself because it is different and is a success on account of Chaplin.

(*Sacramento Bee* – June 12, 1911)

However, one reviewer from around this time actually reserves his praise for an uncredited and unseen member of the company — [thought to be George Seaman]:

EMPRESS:— It might not be generally realized by those playgoers who witness *A Night in an English Music Hall* at the Empress this week, but one of the highest priced men with the company is the performer who stands off stage and operates the noise machine with which the illusions are carried out in the performance of the sketch. Charles Chaplin, who plays "the souse," is constantly thrashing around in his miniature stage box, that forms a portion of the scenic set in *A Night in an English Music Hall*, and every time he bumps his face or some other part of his head or tumbles backward into his box, the man in the wings, who operates the noise apparatus, must work the latter with a great deal of finesse.

(Cutting from Chaplin's personal scrapbook – undated.)

-----0-----

For their third week in California, the company moved on to Oakland:

OAKLAND, Bell

(w/c Sunday June 18, 1911)

A record-breaking week just concluded. The cleanest pantomime stunt that ever graced a vaudeville stage was given unanimous support and patronage this week at the Bell theater. Fred Karno's *A Night in an English Music Hall* was the pacemaker for fun and laughter.

(*Oakland Tribune* – June 25, 1911)

The fourth week was spent in Los Angeles, which Chaplin did not exactly find to be "The City of Angels."

Los Angeles was an ugly city, hot and oppressive, and the people looked sallow and anaemic. It was a much warmer climate but had not the freshness of San Francisco; nature has endowed the north of California with resources that will endure and flourish when Hollywood has disappeared into the prehistoric tar-pits of Wilshire Boulevard.

RIGHT: Los Angeles newspaper advert – June 26

Chaplin was probably grateful that the locals thought more of him, than he of them:

LAUREL – Stage by Stage

EMPRESS THEATER — (w/c Sunday June 25, 1911)

"A NIGHT IN AN ENGLISH MUSIC HALL"

One Charles Chaplin playing Billy Reeves' original role of the polite drunk, is the best member of the boisterous crew. Large laughs still result from these oft-done and well-remembered antics.

(*Los Angeles Times* — June 27, 1911)

Next on the tour was a trip south, almost to California's border with Mexico, to San Diego:

SAN DIEGO, Garrick — (July 3, 1911)

"Really, it's a shame; such a nice looking young fellow, too." That's what a woman, who had been at the Empress theater yesterday afternoon, said when she had got a glimpse after the show of the real Chaplin, who plays the inebriated swell in *A Night in an English Music Hall*. He was easily the star of the production, which is saying much, for every one of the twenty performers helped sustain the chorus of laughter that ran through the audience from the minute after the curtain went up. Chaplin is one of the most artistic inebriates that has ever appeared on any stage. He is loaded to the limit of capacity and yet there is no exuberance in the jag—no staggering, no horseplay. He is just simply soaked to the cracking of his skin; and it is this condition of being "soused" that makes more than half of the fun of the performance.

(*San Diego Union* – July 4, 1911)

The comparison between Chaplin's visage, in and out of character, was a constant source of fascination.
This later newspaper ad' even sought to highlight the makeover.

-----0-----

Of the next four weeks, no engagement was traced for week one. Week two was spent in Denver, Colorado; week three in Colorado Springs; and week four in Kansas City, Missouri; where the tour ended on Saturday August 3, 1911. However, thanks to the good business they had done, the troupe were about to start a new tour. Two of the current members though would not be going with them.

Although young Jefferson was grateful for the experience he was gaining with the Karno Company – experience which would prove invaluable to him in years to come – the lack of a decent wage seemed too high a price to pay. So here in Kansas, he, and like-minded fellow-comedian Arthur Dandoe, quit.

Here is a résumé of the tour dates covered in this chapter:
1911 (continued)

Apr 23-29	Washington	SPOKANE, Washington	*Music Hall*
May 01	Washington	SEATTLE, Majestic	*Music Hall*
May 08-13	British Columbia	VANCOUVER, Orpheum	*Music Hall*
May 15	Washington	TACOMA, Majestic	*Music Hall*
May 22	Oregon	PORTLAND, Grand	*Music Hall*
[May 29		no trace]	
Jun 04	California	SAN FRANCISCO, Empress	*Music Hall*
Jun 11-17	California	SACRAMENTO, Grand	*Music Hall*
Jun 18-24	California	OAKLAND, Bell	*Music Hall*
Jun 26	California	LOS ANGELES, Empress	*Music Hall*
Jul 05-11	California	SAN DIEGO, Empress	*Music Hall*
[Jul 10-13		no trace]	
Jul 15	Colorado	DENVER, Empress	*Music Hall*
Jul 22-28	Colorado	COLORADO SPRINGS, Majestic	*Music Hall*
Jul 29	Missouri	KANSAS CITY, Empress	*Music Hall*

August 4, 1911 – Sullivan & Considine tour ENDS HERE. Jefferson and Dandoe leave.

[Aug 07　　　　　　　　　　timeout, between turnaround]

-----0-----

But, in the following article, the dates and location vary from what I believe are the correct ones — above. If Stan and Arthur had indeed left the company in Philadelphia, which the FKC played back in January, then he could not have played Los Angeles, which he confirms in this article. It would be wrong to keep blaming Stan for these inaccuracies. Often it is the person taking notes who is at fault:

> I actually visited Los Angeles with the Karno Company. But I wasn't interested in films, and never thought of going to Hollywood. To tell the truth, my only desire was to get out of America. I was so sick of travelling from coast to coast and back again, so terribly anxious to get another glimpse of the old country, that I was scraping and saving every dollar I could to pay my fare home.
>
> Presently, I discovered that another member of our company, Arthur Dandoe, was just as homesick as myself. So we put our heads together and concocted a scheme. We would work out an act and put over a big bluff to the agents in England that we were a famous American Vaudeville turn. So we had some notepaper printed, "The Barto Brothers," with a list of all the theatres at which we had appeared "with enormous success" (carefully omitting to mention that we were with the Karno Company, of course), and sent letters to England offering to come over if a suitable engagement could be found.
>
> To our amazement, the trick worked. We received several offers at tip-top salaries. By this time I had £60 in the bank, so we left the company at Philadelphia, took the train to New York, and sailed as steerage passengers on board the *Lusitania*.

(*Tit-Bits* – November 14, 1936)

Is this story about "The Barto Bros." a flight of fantasy, a show business anecdote to appease a journalist, or did it really happen? To find out, we will leave the Karno Company in the USA, and follow Messrs. Jefferson and Dandoe back to Blighty.

POSTSCRIPT:

This photo was taken in Butte, during the second visit — w/c September 16, 1911. I include it here to emphasise that Stan Jefferson is NOT pictured – having returned to England six weeks earlier. But so many times I have seen it posted on the Internet, identifying the monocled man at the back as Stan.

I am fortunate to have been supplied with a copy of an original postcard bearing this photo, which was sent to a relative in England by Muriel Palmer. She has overwritten "me" on her dress and "Amy" on Amy Minister's dress. Over the man with the monocle she has drawn an "X," then on the back of the postcard she has identified him as her husband, Fred Palmer, and the man squatting down as Fred Karno Jnr. Here is the full list of names:

[George Seaman] Fred Palmer, Albert Austin
Charles Chaplin, Mike Asher, Muriel Palmer, Amy Minister, Bert Williams, Emily Seaman, Charles Griffiths
Fred Karno Jnr. (Westcott)
(Name in [brackets] is where there is some uncertainty.)

-----0-----

```
ALF REEVES Presents
FRED KARNO'S LONDON COMEDIANS
In a new Pantomime Farce
"A NIGHT IN A LONDON CLUB"
or "The Amateur Entertainers"
CHARACTERS:
Archibald Binks (Inebriated) .................... Chas. Chaplin
Mr. Meek (Henpecked) ............................ Mike Asher
Mrs. Meek (The Pecker) ......................... Muriel Palmer
Martin Harvey Dustbin (An Actor) ....... Albert Williams
Percy Swoffles (A Dude) ........................... Fred Palmer
Miss Taylor (A Guest) ............................... Amy Minster
Agnes (The Infant Prodigy) .................... Emily Seaman
Mr. Taylor (Member of the Club) ............. Tom Cardon
Mr. Clark (Member of the Club) .............. Albert Austin
Mr. Jenkins (Member of the Club) ....... Charles Griffiths
Mr. Wilkins (Member of the Club) ........ George Seaman
Mr. Lothario (At the Piano) ..................... Fred Westcott
The Steward of the Club ......................... Edward Banks
The Chairman of the Club ..................... Frank Melroyd
Manager for Fred Karno's Company: Alf Reeves.
```

Revised cast list, with Tom Cardon and Edward Banks brought in to replace
Dandoe and Jefferson (although not in the same roles).

CHAPTER 10

ROTTEN DAM

Arthur Dandoe (born Arthur George Webb – 1878) was twelve years older than Stan, and had a longer history as a stage performer. Confirmed sightings of him in 1901 show that he was touring with his then wife Ethel (nee Taylor) billed as 'DANDOE and NEAME' (Arthur and Majorie) "Eccentric Comedy Act." Part of the act was Arthur showing off a second talent of his, which was painting lightning-quick sketches in oils.

One of his engagements (w/c April 4, 1901) was at the Britannia Theatre, Glasgow — the very venue where Stan later did his first try-out as a comedian (though not as a professional, as in Dandoe's case).

Dandoe went on to form "Arthur Dandoe's Company," for which he is known to have advertised for singers and dancers, etc., but then, in 1906, capitulated and joined a company he couldn't possibly compete with — Fred Karno's. Unfortunately, this necessitated his being torn away from his wife and children to commence a three-month tour of America — sailing to New York September 1, 1906, along with, among others – Syd Chaplin. Dandoe did a second tour of America with different members of the Karno Company, commencing August 1907, before making the documented third trip, in 1910.

Following the curtailment of the 1910-11 tour of America, and upon Dandoe and Jefferson's return to London, it is believed that Stan went to stay at the Dandoe's family home in Vaughn Road, a stone's throw from the Fred Karno Fun Factory, in Camberwell. For work, Stan tells of the following:

> Arrived in England, Arthur Dandoe put on a broad-shouldered American suit and an equally broad American accent, stuck a cigar in one side of his mouth and some chewing gum in the other, and took me along to interview one of the agents. Of course, I let Arthur do all the talking, carefully keeping my mouth shut in case my Lancashire-cockney accent should give me away.
>
> The agent, duly impressed, offered us a booking on a big circuit, with a preliminary try-out at a smaller theatre at a purely nominal salary of £40 a week.
>
> Forty pounds! And we had been getting four pounds each until now! We almost tumbled over each other in our eagerness to sign on the dotted line.
>
> Hurrying home, we proceeded to build the scenery and props—which were supposed to be on their way from America! —and began to rehearse the new act, which at the moment, was hardly more than an idea.
>
> (*Tit-Bits* – November 14, 1936)

Dando and Jefferson ...   ... as 'The Barto Bros.'

> Our opening performance was definitely a success; bookings came pouring in. Then like a couple of silly school girls, Dandoe and I had a slight difference of opinion—and our partnership fizzled out like a seidlitz powder. After that, I was out of work for a whole year.
>
> (*Tit-Bits* – November 14, 1936)

Well that's Stan's story, and we're stuck with it — or maybe not. Let's check out the timeline:

If Messrs. Jefferson and Dandoe did indeed leave the Karno Company on August 4, 1911 (in Kansas) then the earliest they could have landed back in England would have been August 14 — give or take a day. But then, knowing as we do that Stan joined Charles Baldwin's sketch company, playing *The Wax-Works*, we find only a three-week gap before this 5-date run:

THE WAX-WORKS

1911

September 4	LIVERPOOL	LIVERPOOL, Pavilion
September 11	MANCHESTER	HULME, Hippodrome
September 18	LANCASHIRE	ASHTON, Empire Hippodrome
September 25	MANCHESTER	QUEEN'S PARK, Hippodrome
October 02		vacant
October 09	YORKSHIRE	KEIGHLEY, Hippodrome

The run of *The Waxworks* ends here — October 14, 1911

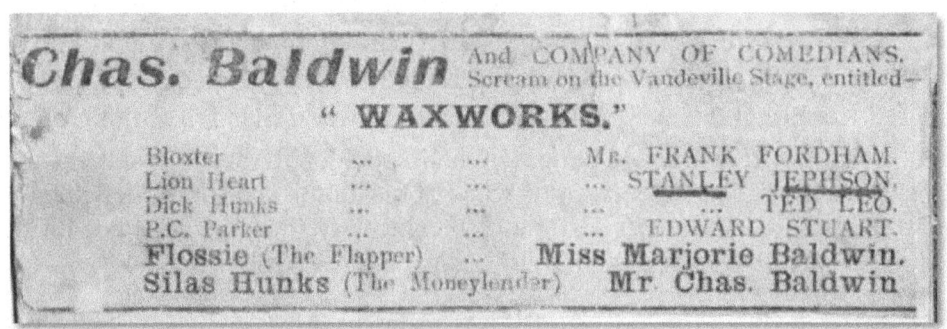

The Chas. Baldwin Company was given as '30' in number, so Stanley Jefferson did well to be billed in second place on the cast list – even though his name was mis-spelt. Following, are 'reviews' from *The Stage*:

LIVERPOOL, Pavilion Theatre,

The chief attraction here is by Chas. Baldwin and company in *The Waxworks*, which provides two scenes full of broad fun, which keeps the house in continuous laughter.

MANCHESTER, Hulme Hippodrome

A laughter-provoking sketch, *The Waxworks*, is capitally played by Chas. Baldwin and company.

KEIGHLEY, Hippodrome and Queen's

Charles Baldwin in sketch, *The Waxworks*, heads the bill.

Chas./Charlie Baldwin (*ibid*) was also a prolific sketch writer, one of the best in his field; even having written sketches produced by Fred Karno — *The Village Sports*, and *The Annual Sports of Duddington*, which were variations of each other, and went on to form the first part of *The Wow-Wows*.

As *The Wax-Works* was a top-of-the-bill act, and with not a bad review to be found, it is hard to understand why it was pulled off the circuit. My personal theory is that keeping a cast of thirty on the road was unsustainable, in that the fee did not cover the wages; and so although the wax-works, the acts didn't.

With his considerable Karno Company experience, Stan Jefferson would have had no trouble convincing Charles Baldwin to take him on. However, Stan would not have been able to walk in on Day 1 of the first show, so there must have been a period of at least one week before opening, when Stan was in rehearsals. Likewise, Stan and Dandoe would have needed at least a couple of weeks to write and work-up the new sketch, *The Rum 'Uns from Rome*, plus make all the props, plus generate bookings. It is probably safe to say, therefore, that any bookings of Stan Jefferson and Arthur Dandoe as 'The Barto Bros.' in *The Rum 'Uns from Rome*, came *after* the run of *The Wax-Works* had ended, on October 14. As for those bookings which Stan claims "… came pouring in," I couldn't find a single one — and, believe me, I LOOKED.

Having split from Dandoe, the young Jefferson had not only lost his working partner, but also lost the Dandoes' hospitality. Of his new accommodation arrangement, Stan tells us:

> If Mrs. Boon, who kept apartments for professionals in London, is still alive, will she please accept this little tribute from Stan Laurel, the comedian whom she mothered and befriended for nearly a year in the days when he was out of work? She was indeed a boon. When I told her that I had no money to pay her rent, she smiled and said: "Never mind, Son, you stay here. Pay me when your good luck comes along." That was many years ago, and when my luck changed I repaid her immediately. But I still owe her a debt of gratitude which I shall never be able to repay.
>
> (*Tit-Bits* – November 21, 1936)

[AJM: In a look through the adverts for "APARTMENTS" in *The Stage*, a Mrs. Boon is found to be renting rooms at 153 Stamford Street, Waterloo Road, London SE1 9NQ.]

Based on this cutting found in Stan's Scrapbook, he next made another attempt to launch himself as a solo comedian.

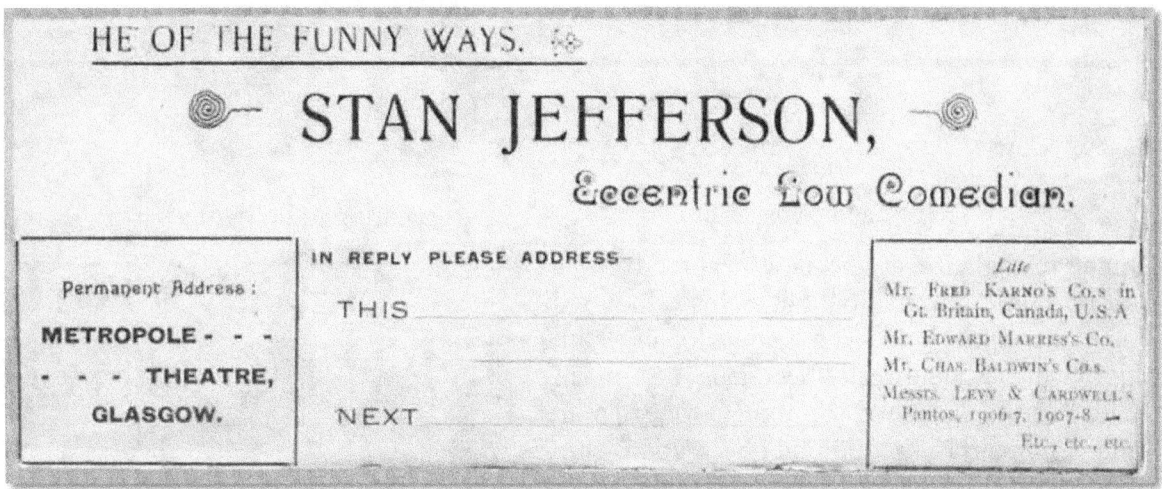

Although this business reply slip is not dated, in the right-hand box we can see that Stan has listed himself as 'late' of the Fred Karno Company in the USA; and also Chas. Baldwin's Company — which places it post-October 1911. As no other companies or acts are listed which come after this date, we can assume the item is contemporary with where we are currently at.

In hundreds of hours of looking, I have never once found a theatre entry naming Stan Jefferson as a solo comedian, which throws up another cutting which raises more questions than it answers. Again, it is to be found in Stan's Scrapbook.

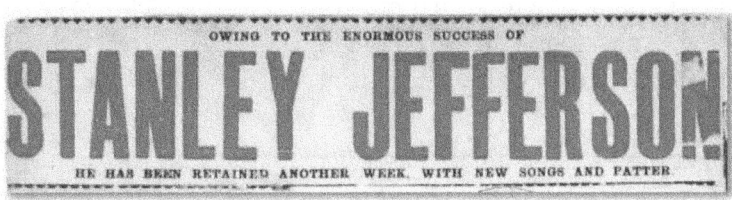

Mercifully, we do have a good idea of Stan's next move in the show business world:

> My spell of unemployment was brought to an end by a chance meeting with Ted Leo, better known as Teddy Desmond. When I poured all my trouble into his sympathetic ear he said, "Why shouldn't we put an act together?" His sister scraped together the sum of six pounds and we worked out a new variation of the old "Barto Brothers" sketch.
>
> (*Tit-Bits* – November 21, 1936)

Stan's "chance meeting" with Ted Leo came when both were in *The Waxworks* (*ibid*). And so, with new props and new Roman uniforms, our two gladiators set off for the Forum, to see if anything funny happened on the way.

Preparing to go on stage …   … preparing to do battle.

One might just glance at the newspaper advert, at right, and find little information, but a close study will reveal a whole mine lode. The Latin slogan "Nulli Secondus" (which should read "Secundus") — means "Second to None." Next we see the Barto Bros. are now "and Company" — and then a second entry confirming "IV PERSONS." From a second advert (shown later) the four persons are identified as: "Three Artistes and One Super." A super is a very small role, usually not much more than a walk-on part, which can virtually be performed by anyone. Often, the super was just recruited from among the stage crew. One would surmise that this super is part of the Company who, though he wouldn't be worth a week's wages for his stage work, would almost certainly be used in a menial capacity — including packing, loading, and transporting the props and scenery to and from theatres.

We cannot be certain that the first version of *The Rum Uns from Rome*, with Arthur Dandoe, was played as a foursome, but we do know how this four-act worked:

The two main parts, as played by Jefferson and Leo, are the: "Ridiculous Romans, and Grotesque Gladiators – 'Barmicuss and Sillicus'" — who at one part of the act are confronted by "Titus – the famous Banana-eating Lion." This part would have been played by either the third artiste or the super; and "Brutus – the Only Filleted Horse in Existence" by both, in a pantomime-horse skin. And here is how those twelve minutes ran:

The setting is a city square in ancient Rome. A wide 'stone' column, surrounded by a raised platform, stands centre-stage. A (pantomime) horse enters, pulling a chariot. Stan is riding the horse in full Roman costume — brass helmet, shield, and an axe. Leo appears to be riding in the chariot, but his feet can clearly be seen walking it across the stage. After dismounting from the chariot, Leo mounts the dais, unfurls a roll of parchment, and booms out the command: "Gather around!" Stan takes the instruction literally, and walks around the dais, until stopped in his tracks by a stern gaze from Ted.

With only a minimum of provocation, the two become involved in combat. Stan swings an axe at Ted, who then disappears from view behind the column. Stan is seen to swing his axe at the unseen figure, at which a dummy head, made up to look like Ted, immediately appears. [The head is initially secreted in a compartment in the column, out of view from the audience]. The head disappears and Leo reappears with a duplicate axe stuck in his head.

Stan removes the axe, and then ties an enormous bandage around Leo's head. Having nothing else to hand to secure the loose end of the bandage, he knocks a nail in it. Not put off by his near-mortal wound, Stan's adversary recommences the hand-to-hand battle (the "cod fight"). The fight is curtailed when a mangy lion enters the scene, and the two gladiators join forces to try and kill it. After a wrestling match, the lion finally succumbs to its fate after being fed a railroad sandwich, and the scene ends with them carrying off the lion, white-hunter style.

[AJM: Don't ask me how a railroad sandwich managed to turn up in ancient Roman times].

ABOVE: Clipping, from Stan's Scrapbook. [In a second advert, the horse was named as 'Brutus.']

Again, no bookings for the Barto Bros. could be found; but, from a letter later kept in Stan's Scrapbook, we know that by February 14, 1912 he was lodging at 25 Allendale Road, Camberwell, London SE. (which means that his "year" with Mrs. Boon could not have been more than six months).

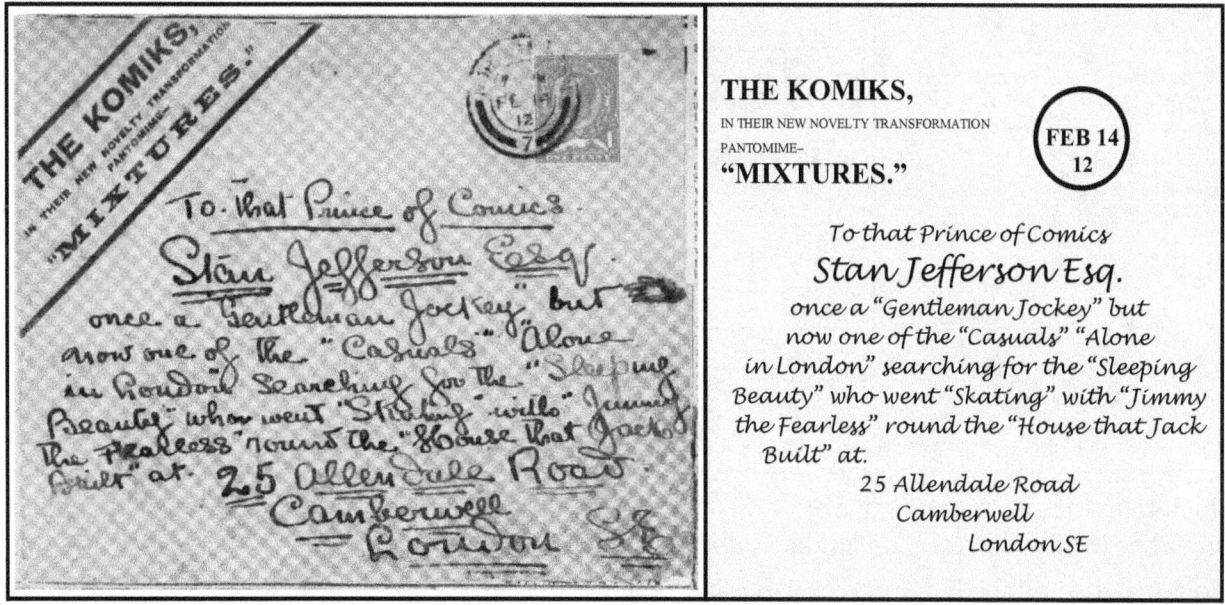

[AJM: Allendale Road, Camberwell, is now Allendale Close, Denmark Hill, London. SE5. Located just south of the north end of Coldharbour Lane, where it changes to Danehill Road. So Stan was again just a short distance from Karno's offices and The Fun Factory, but whether he ever plucked up the courage to call in, we will never know.]

In the main body of the envelope you will have clocked that the titles of some of the stage productions Stan had been in are used to tell a little story. The greater interest though lies with the logo of the addressee, top left. The reference to "The Komiks" seems to tie in with this one in the continuing *Tit-Bits* article:

> Along came a comedian called Bob Reed. "I've got a booking to open at the Circus of Variety, Rotterdam, next week, with a knockabout act called 'The Eight Komics'," he announced. "At the moment there are only four of us. Would you like to help make up the number?" A trip to a foreign country certainly appealed to us, so we agreed. The octet consisted of Bob Reed, his wife, son Jim, and daughter, Ted Leo, his wife, and myself, and the eighth member was a youth who had run away from home to go on the stage—but so far had never made a single public appearance.

The article continued:

> We opened in Rotterdam on a Monday and were well received. The next day it rained, and it was announced that there would be no show. The next day it rained again, and once more the show was cancelled. Rain continued throughout the week and we had a really good time seeing the sights. But when Bob went to collect our money the management pointed out that our contract distinctly stipulated "No play, no pay." So we received exactly one-sixth of a week's salary between us.

Confirmation of this show comes from the above cutting from Stan's scrapbook, but then a similar one reveals a second booking which Stan is not known to have ever mentioned. On both, Stan has written the opening dates — both of which are a Saturday, and not Monday, as he states:

Laurel's account, as given to author John McCabe, is that the Reed Company were about to play the sketch: "*Fun on the Tyrol.*" The nearest match my own research unearthed was a sketch called: "*On Tour in the Tyrol,*" being toured by the Reed-Oetzmann Troupe, and which had played dates six years earlier (March to August 1906) around England and Scotland. This is almost certainly the same sketch, but Mr. Oetzman has left the partnership.

The billing for The 8 Komiks reads: "*Pantomime: 'Het dolle Hotel'.*" Which translates as "*The Crazy Hotel.*" So 'The 8 Komiks are NOT playing *Fun on the Tyrol*, although it could be the same sketch, or similar, with just a name-change.

Note that also on the bill are "The 4 Barto's, English Eccentrics." This is undoubtedly Stan Jefferson and Ted Leo reprising "*The Rum 'Uns from Rome,*" with two of the Komiks assisting. This is yet another detail about the Rotterdam booking which Stan is not known to have mentioned at any time; and so, without these cuttings, the appearance of the Barto's would never have been documented.

Another problem stemming from Stan's account of being "rained out" at the Circus Variété is twofold. Firstly, we now know that the 8 Komiks were booked to appear there for *two* weeks, so it is most unlikely that it rained continuously for thirteen days straight, otherwise we would be writing about "The Great Flood of 1912." As the Circus Variété was built of a timber frame, covered with a tin roof, it was a common for shows to be cancelled during rainy weather, as the noise of the rainfall on the roof would only have drowned out any talk, or even music, being performed on stage. However, Dutchman and stalwart researcher Bram Reijnhoudt went that extra mile to test Stan's account, and checked the weather forecast for the relevant days, only to find clear skies and balmy days. Digging even deeper, Bram came up with theory that the Circus had been closed because it broke too many fire regulations. If rain was the reason for them being unable to play the Circus Variété, as per the original contract, why had the management not re-booked them during the subsequent weeks?

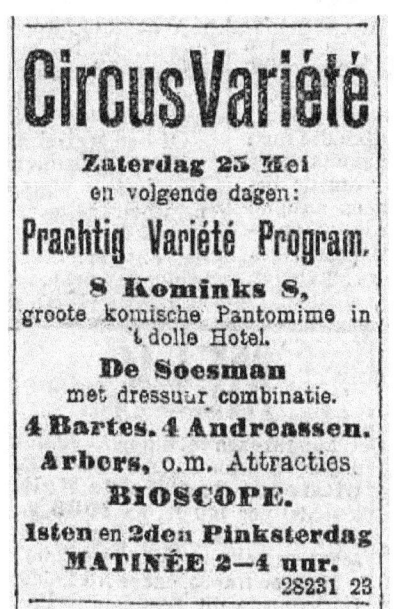

It was looking as though Bram Reijnhoudt is correct when he theorises that the building was shut down because of fire safety infringements. But then, I was suddenly hit by the most obvious answer possible. The reason the 8 Komiks didn't work during those two weeks was because THEY HADN'T BEEN BOOKED FOR TWO WEEKS. They had only been booked for two WEEKENDS. The opening days are both a Saturday, but the only mention of shows on any additional shows is "Zondagmiddag: Matinee" (on the two adverts on the previous page) — which translates as: "Sunday afternoon matinee." And on the newsclip, at left, "Zaterdag 25 Mei, en volgende dagen" which translates as: "Saturday 25 May and following days." But then, at the bottom of the advert the shows are listed as: "1st and 2nd [June] Pentecost. Matinee 2–4." So, again, only the Saturday and the Sunday is billed. So my personal theory now is that they worked the first weekend, (plus *maybe* the Pentecost Bank Holiday Monday), and it may have rained on the first Sunday (or Monday); then they had to kill time during the interim weekdays, but when the second weekend came, the building had been forced to close. You choose!

Whether the lack of work was caused by the threat of fire, or water, or both, or simply that one or more days on the two weekends had been cancelled, the end result was the same —the company were out of work, and out of pocket. Stan takes up the aftermath:

> There was no alternative but to pool the money and send the womenfolk home, leaving fortune to take care of the male members of the troupe. But fortune didn't favour us and, although we lived on the cheapest possible diet, our only meat being horseflesh, the money soon dwindled and we were unable to find work.

The agents who booked the Circus Variété were Franzis Pichler and G. A. Dekkers. Dekkers also owned a café, in Kruiskade [Cross Quay], above which were rooms which he rented out to visiting acts. The 8 Komiks stayed here during the dates of their contract, enjoying the luxuries of the inclusive free food in the café. However, when the contract expired, the rooms and food expired with it, and the troupe was forced to seek accommodation elsewhere, which they did in Helmerstraat. Now they had to pay for everything. Stan tells us:

> I did manage to get one temporary job. I walked into a café and asked if they would care to engage a comic waiter to amuse their patrons. The manager was not interested. But I pleaded to be allowed to give a free trial performance, and at last he consented. My turn consisted of falling all over the place with a tray of crockery—which was securely moored to it—and it did just succeed in raising a laugh. The manager asked me how much I wanted. "Give me food and I'll be satisfied," I said. He fell for that, and I continued to fall for him.
>
> (*Tit-Bits* – November 21, 1936)

[AJM: The said café may very well have been Dekkers.]

In the John McCabe interview, Stan confessed to even more drastic measures he went to, to obtain food, which was stealing bread off the trays of freshly baked loaves, being brought out of the bakery, opposite their accommodation But, as the biblical saying goes: "Man cannot live by bread alone," and so the now-depleted "8 Komiks' were going to have to find some paid work.

The cutting from Stan's scrapbook (at right) confirms what he said about the ladies being sent home, and the men staying on to find work, seeing as the former '8 Komiks' are now billed as just six. And there is that reference to "Mixtures" again, and not *Fun on the Tyrol*.

With things getting more and more desperate, a flicker of hope emerged. Tubby Reed had managed to get them a theatre engagement; but, to fulfil it, they would first have to find transportation to Liège, some two hundred and twenty miles south east, in Belgium. Food would have to wait.

CONTINENT.
1912.

THE KOMIKS,
KOMIKAL KOMEDY KROUD,
GROTESQUES, PANTOMIMISTS,
"IN MIXTURES."
6 ARTISTES, 6 PERFORMERS & 6 KNUTS.

The booking commenced Tuesday June 25, at the Palace Theatre, Liège. John McCabe (*ibid*) gave us this summation of what he purports Stan to have told him:

> The first performance began. As it progressed, it played superlatively and at furious pace. The sketch had an unusual ending, a clever sequence featuring a stilt-walking routine. All of the members of the troupe wore stilts of various length and walked about the stage wearing enormous papier-mache heads. The tallest walker wore a comic hat which he dropped on the stage. The smallest walker picked it up and passed it on to the next in height, he to the next, and thus on until it reached the tallest walker again. Stan was third from the end in this arrangement, and on opening night he became so overwrought with hunger pains that he fell against the man next to him. This man fell against the next, and within a few seconds the entire pack of cards came flipping down in a climax of disunion and dismay.

I'll go along with how the hat routine was worked, but I smell dramatic licence on McCabe's behalf when he writes that Stan: " … became so overwrought with hunger pains that he fell against the man next to him." There are two good reasons why you fall off stilts, and one of them isn't that you are dying of hunger. The first is that you accidently overbalance; the second is that you *deliberately* overbalance. As this was a comedy troupe, and they wanted a funny ending to the act, would it not seem that the second reason is the more likely? So many sketches (and later, films) end with a melee and/or tangle of bodies — the Karno sketches being prime examples.

Stan then tells of how, the following day, when the troupe went back to the theatre, they found all their props on the pavement outside, quite clearly indicating that their services were no longer needed. But I would question this, too. Despite meticulous searches by fellow-Laurel & Hardy fans Marc de Coninck, from Belgium, and Rene Riva, from the Netherlands, all that could be found was a very brief mention at the foot of a newspaper advert which said: "*Débuts le 25: Les 8 Komiks, pantomimistes*." The use here of the word "débuts" can be translated as: "the first of appearance of …" or " … introducing the 8 Komiks," or, similarly: "… presenting the 8 Komiks." But nowhere could be found a show, as such, with other acts on the bill; or any indication that the 8 Komiks were to appear there for more than just that one date. Until I am told differently, I would have to go along with the theory that the booking was for one night only. Maybe Bob Reed didn't tell the company members it was for just the one night, otherwise they may have been reluctant to travel all that way to do it.

Whatever the case, the outcome was the same: 'The Mixtures' just hadn't mixed, and the "Fun on the Tyrol" had become a progressive nightmare. It was time to split the mix. Moving on, though, is still a daunting task when you have no work, no money, and haven't eaten for three whole days. And when your next chosen venue is miles away, travelling by public transport isn't an option. Stan tells it thus:

Teddy Leo suggested that we should try our luck in Brussels, so we started out to walk there. The roads were hot and dusty, and the way was long. We went to the leading music hall to see if we could get an engagement. There was not a hope. Just as we were coming away, we noticed on the bill the name of the "Seven Jackley Wonders." So we went back and asked to see George Jackley. When he realized our plight he promptly gave us some money to pay our fare home.

(Tit-Bits – November 21, 1936)

Stan's description of the way to Brussels being "long" was a little understated — it is just under *one hundred miles* long. It is no wonder, therefore, that – following this trek to Brussels, almost immediately followed by his trip back to London – Stan arrived looking more like a tramp than a trouper. Calling on fraternal charity, he went to seek out his brother Gordon.

Whilst the younger Jefferson had been touring America, Gordon was still at the Metropole, in Glasgow; but then in December 1911 had transferred as acting-manager to the newly-built Prince's Theatre, in London. Upon setting eyes upon his wayworn brother, Gordon posed the question which every comedian has been asked at some stage of his career: "Why don't you get yourself a proper job?" Like most other comedians Stan's pride forbade him, and the belief that stardom was just around the corner led him to accept a stop-gap job at the Prince's – a small part in *Ben My Chree*.

Stan's part must have indeed been small, for in the programme he is not listed amongst the players. During the day, he earned extra money by typing out scripts. And he would certainly need to earn more money as his fee for being a 'super' in the play was just one shilling per night.

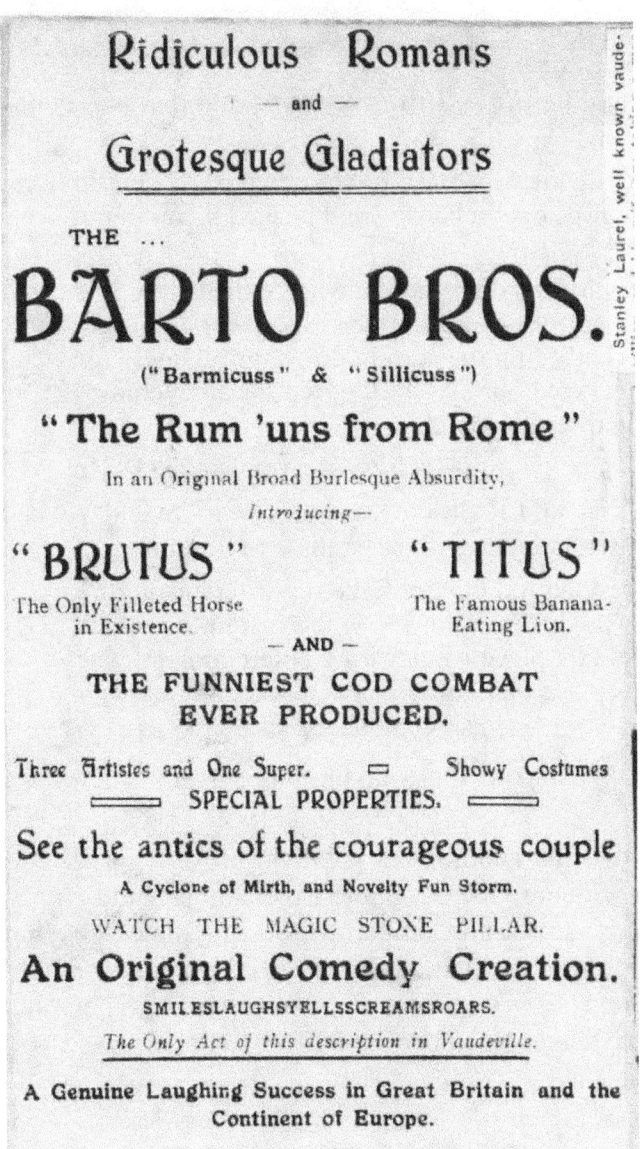

Ben My Chree (Manx for: *Girl of My Heart*), ran from July 1 to October 13, 1912 (or beyond), but Stan didn't stay throughout the full run, as he had ignored his brother's advice to "get a proper job," and gone on tour with another revised version of *The Rum 'Uns from Rome*.

Although no information accompanied this advert (from Stan's Scrapbook), the mention of "Continent of Europe" in the last line tells us that it was printed after the trip to Rotterdam. The advert also says a, "Genuine Laughing Success," but knowing what we know, we can ignore that line.

The phrases "Special Properties" and "Showy Costumes" are also telling. When Stan and Arthur Dandoe first arrived in England, they had made their own costumes and props. But here, for the 'Barto Bros. and Company' act, it would seem that the props and costumes had been upgraded, which suggests having been bought, or hired, from a prop and costume-maker.

With all the investment ploughed into it, the new act would need several weeks' paid bookings to get a return, after which they needed to make a living. I am still puzzled therefore why, after spending scores of hours searching, I turned up just ONE advertised booking — and even that featured in only a trade paper, and not the local Abertillery newspapers, where the sketch played.

> WANTED. Monday Next, various on, by The BARTO BROTHERS, Ridiculous Romans and Grotesque Gladiators in a screaming, broad Burlesque Absurdity introducing absolutely the Funniest Cod Gladiator Combat ever produced. Special Properties. Last week, Metropole, Abertillery (top). Wire for this Novelty Fun Storm, Flat 7, 3, Gloucester Street, London. W.C.

ABOVE: Advert from *The Stage*, dating the appearance in Abertillery as w/c September 9, 1912

RIGHT: I have never seen this photo accompanied by any information, but it does appear to be the third incarnation of *The Rum 'Uns from Rome*. Gone are the Roman helmets worn in the publicity pose with Dandoe; and both have completely different hairstyles to the ones in the second version, with Ted Leo. Also, in this one, Stan is sporting a beard which would sit well on the face of an archetypal Amish man, and a haircut which would be at home on the head of a Mohican. How this depicts a Roman character, I cannot comprehend.

As to Stan's partner, it may be Ted Leo, but it could just as easily be someone else. Not all the pieces to this puzzle have been found.

Stan did identify the location of just one appearance of the *Rum 'Uns from Rome*, but that was only a showcase:

> We were offered a one night try-out at the Royal Victoria Hall, now known as "The Old Vic," on the Waterloo Road, and we put all our props onto a barrow and pushed them all the way from Camberwell in the pouring rain.
>
> The lady who ran The Old Vic—I believe it was Miss Lilian Baylis, who controls it to this day [1936] — used to sit in a box and watch the performance with one eye on the audience. If she, or they, didn't like an act, she would promptly ring the curtain down. Fortunately for us, our turn went quite well, and we proudly pocketed our six-shilling fee for an evening's performance, and began to look around for further engagements.

(Tit-Bits – November 21, 1936)

It is strange that Stan should mention Lillian Bayliss as, up till late-September 1912, The Old Vic had been run by Emma Conns. This extract from the follow-on to her Obituary tells us a little more:

> The recent death of Miss Emma Cons is, we are glad to note, to make no difference to the activities of the Royal Victoria Hall, Waterloo Road (the "Old Vic"), the institution which the deceased lady founded thirty-two years ago as a place of elevating entertainment. The re-opening of the hall for the winter season takes place on Saturday next, September 28.

(The Stage — 26 September 1912)

So the evidence of the audition in front of Lillian Bayliss points to it taking place within a few days of the re-opening on September 28th.

Stan could have saved himself the time and worry of the audition, as it would prove to be a total waste of time. While taking a walk through Leicester Square, one day shortly thereafter, Stan bumped into Alf Reeves – now back in England with the rest of the Karno Company, following the completion of their tour of America and Canada. When Reeves enquired of Stan, *"What are you doing, nowadays? Starring in the West-end?"* Stan quickly replied, *"Starving in the West-end, more like it."* There and then Reeves offered him a pay-rise and, just a few days later (October 2, 1912) Stan Jefferson set sail for America once again.

CHAPTER 11

NEVER GO BACK

The members of the 1912 Karno Company sailing to America were: Alf Reeves, Amy Reeves (formerly 'Minister'*[1]), Charles Chaplin, Albert Westcott, George Seaman, Emily Seaman, and Stanley Jefferson; plus new members: Edward Banks, Edgar Hurley, Ethel Hurley, Amy Forrest, and 'Whimsical' Walker, who was listed as 'Tom' Walker — totalling eight men and four ladies.

This time the trip was from Southampton direct to New York; and, being on the British 'White Star' passenger ship the *Oceanic*, was a much more comfortable crossing than the one back in 1910. It took less time, too – Wednesday 2nd to Wednesday October 9th. This was a day longer than the trans-Atlantic record but, since the tragedy of her sister ship the *Titanic* just six months earlier, on that very route, the policy of "full-steam ahead and damn the consequences" had been revised.

The *Oceanic* was not the only improvement in conditions. This time they docked at New York itself, thus eliminating the train journey from Quebec. Also, the company members now had eleven days to go before opening night, and so had time off to explore the sights and sounds of New York, when not rehearsing.

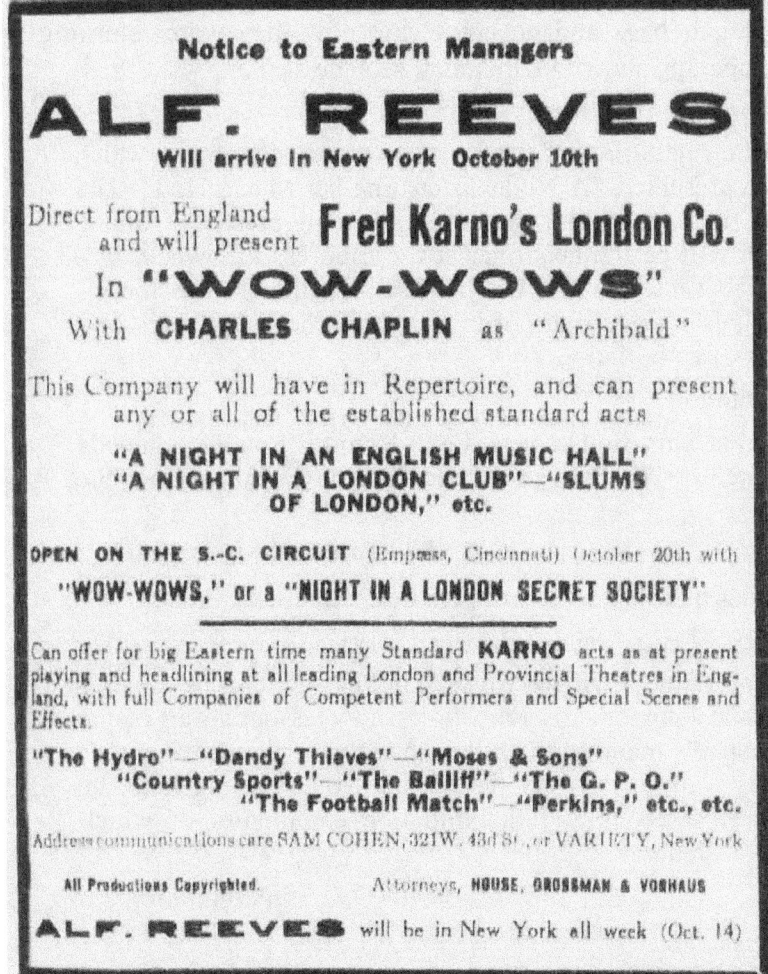

[AJM: When I first came across this advert in *Variety*, I thought Chaplin was having a private joke by giving his contact address as 'Sam Cohen,' as this was the name he himself had adopted when he did a one-night stand-up comedy act back in December 1907. (See my book: *CHAPLIN – Stage by Stage* for the full story.) But it turns out that this Sam Cohen was a 'real' person, who *did* work at the advertised agency.]

Chaplin recalled: "*This time I felt at home in the States—a foreigner among foreigners, allied with the rest.*" The company too would have felt more at ease. Upon their 1910 arrival they had been unrehearsed and unprepared but, for the latest tour, were familiar with the main sketch they were performing, and the audiences they would be performing to. Chaplin, however, wasn't happy with the contribution made by Whimsical Walker, of whom he gave the opinion:

We took a rehearsal room and had a week of rehearsing *The Wow-Wows*. In the cast was old Whimsical Walker, the famous Drury Lane clown. He was over seventy*[2], with a deep,

---

*[1] Amy Minister had married Alf Reeves on January 4, 1911, at the City Hall, New York.

*2 Walker was born April 1, 1856, making him fifty-six – which is somewhat short of Chaplin's placement of his being "over-seventy."

resonant voice, but had no diction, as we discovered at rehearsals, and he had the major part of explaining the plot. Such a line as: "The fun will be furious, ad libitum," he could not say and never did. The first night he spluttered 'ablib-blum,' and eventually it became 'ablibum,' but never the correct word.

(Chaplin's 1964 Autobiography)

Chaplin singling out this minor affliction as a major flaw was totally uncalled for. Walker himself had bigger worries than his stumbling over two Latin words, and astutely pointed out:

> We arrived at New York to find that New York had greatly altered. In fact it was a new America. I had been there eight previous times, but it was a new world to me, everybody and everything had altered so much.
>
> We found we were up against great opposition. The caterers for amusement had increased and multiplied since my previous visit. The taste had changed and novelties had been introduced to suit the jaded palates of the excitement-seeking Americans. We were on the Sullivan circuit and at each town we had opposition at the other theatres - Sarah Bernhardt at one theatre and Mrs [Lily] Langtry at the other - until we got right up to San Francisco.

(*From Sawdust to Windsor Castle*, by Whimsical Walker)

But for the Karno Company as a whole, returning to America was going to be a breeze. In 1910 they were on the brink of being told to pack their bags and go home, but now they were returning as conquering heroes. This preview for their opening show in Cincinnati sets the scene:

CINCINNATI, Empress — (w/c Sunday October 20, 1912)

> No act in vaudeville has attained the reputation of the Karno Comedy Company, which was a sensation last season when it presented "A Night in an English Music Hall." The theater was filled with laughter from first to last. This year the Karnos are presenting a new sketch called *The Wow-Wows*, which will be the headliner at the Empress this week. It is said to be even funnier than last year's sensation and Charles Chaplin, the "Polite Souse," still heads the array of funmakers. It is a sketch purporting to show the happenings in a fashionable London club on the night of an initiation.

So would they be able to follow their reputation?

> One of the best things ever seen at this house was Fred Karno's London Comedy Company in *The Wow-Wows*, presented by Alf Reeves. Charles Chaplin, who assumes the role of the souse, is exceedingly funny.

(*Billboard* — November 2, 1912)

So with a winning debut performance under their belts, the troupers trouped to Chicago:

CHICAGO, Empress — (w/c Monday October 28, 1912)

> Fred Karno's comedy company appearing in the "Kow-Wows" [*sic*] close the show. Charles Champlin [*sic*] as Archibald is fine and is practically the whole show, assuming all of the comedy parts and doing it in a very capable manner. His part is that of a "willie-boy" and he carries it out from the manner of his walk to the way he tips his "at," meaning hat. The whole thing is a burlesque on secret societies and the initiation ceremonies of which Archibald is the "goat" are extremely ridiculous.

(*Billboard* — November 9, 1912)

-----0-----

The advert for the Cincinnati Empress proclaimed that the Karno Company was fifteen-strong whilst, the following week, the advert for the Chicago Empress stated sixteen. Only twelve had come over on the *Oceanic*, so could these previews be wrong? Well, no! The cast list (on the next page) confirms that the company had been joined by Charles Griffiths, Charles Cardon, Fred Westcott, and Bert Howard. These additions could have come over on a later boat, or embarked on another boat at a different port – like Liverpool.

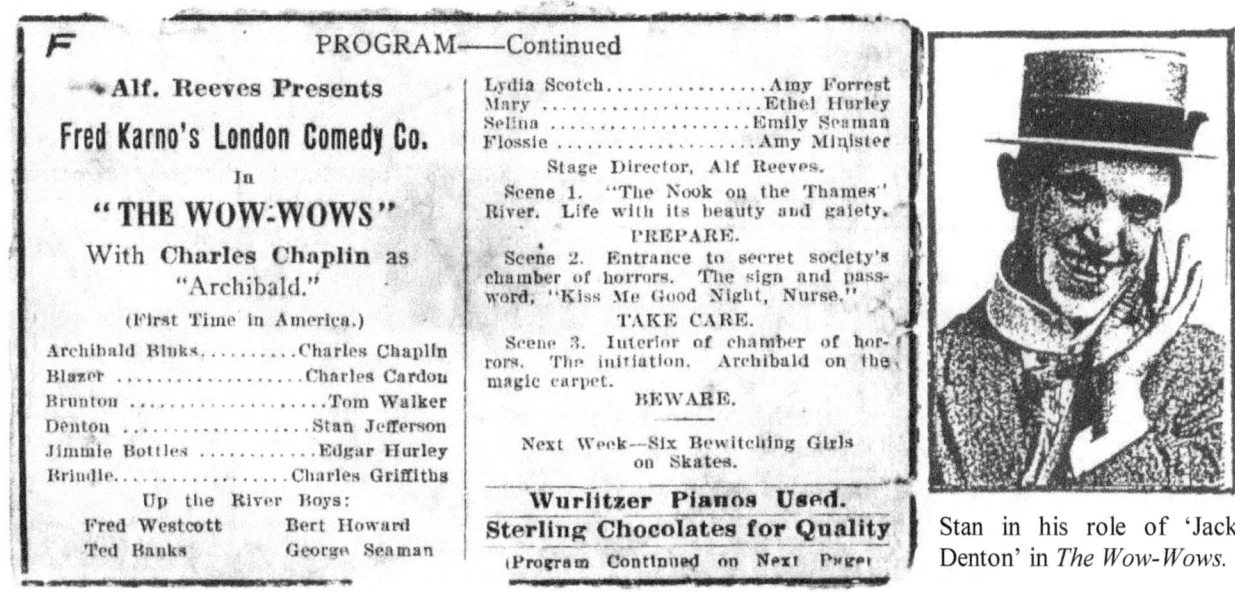

Stan in his role of 'Jack Denton' in *The Wow-Wows*.

[ABOVE: Actual cutting from the Stan Laurel Archive]

On the ship's manifest, which lists the Karno Company members boarding the *Oceanic*, is the following record:

Albert Westcott. Age: 27. Occupation: Actor. Nearest Relative: F. Westcott (Brother) 28 Vaughn Rd.

Other than being Fred Karno Senior's brother, there seems to be little documentary evidence about him. Another puzzling aspect is that it is Fred Karno's son (Fred Westcott) is named on the later cast lists, with no sign of Albert anywhere. Maybe he came over to help with the shipping of the scenery, and then rehearsals, before returning to Camberwell after the New York stay.

-----0-----

From Chicago, the sixteen-strong company then moved on through Milwaukee, Minneapolis and St. Paul, before arriving in Winnipeg:

WINNIPEG, Empress — (w/c November 25, 1912)

Every time Fred Karno's London Company of Comedians comes to Winnipeg it brings with it an act that taxes the house at every performance. This week on his third visit Charles Chaplin, in *The Wow-Wows*, keeps the audience in roars of laughter and the act promises to outdo his previous skits in popularity. In the leading part he takes the role of that peculiar type of English whose cheek and freshness is the source of great amusement. At all the performances yesterday the Empress was jammed to the doors to see the Englishmen in their new act.

(*Winnipeg Telegram* — November 26, 1912)

A second review gave us an insight into some of the players:

"The Wow-Wows" is based on the experiences of a camper, whose stingy propensities bring him into disfavor with his fellow campers. The latter, in revenge, induce him, by promise of many luxuries without cost, to join a secret society called "The Wow-Wows." He falls into the trap, and the subsequent proceedings are hilarious in the extreme.

Chaplin, as "Archibald Binks" is the victim. In this production he is seen in a totally different role, and has a speaking part. It must be admitted that the "drunk" impersonation which made him famous is more suited to his talents. This sounds like a veiled insinuation, so, to avoid a libel suit, and in justice to Chaplin, one hastens to add that he is a strict teetotaller. He doesn't know what it feels like to carry a skinful of fire water, but he can get the effect without the cause—which, by the way, is a scientific paradox. But with his remarkable ability as a comedian, it is impossible for him not to be funny, and he gets roars of laughter out of every line, out of every look, and out of every gesture.

Practically the same capable company is back again, with two or three notable additions, such as "Tom" Walker, better known as "Whimsical" Walker, who among other experiences was clown at Drury Lane theatre under Sir Augustus Harris; also Charles Cardon, who in England was partner in a double with Fred Kitchen (Kitchen now is probably the most popular comedian over there); and Charles Griffiths, a noted pantomimist, and clown for many years at the old Britannia theatre, Hoxton.

(*Winnipeg Tribune* — November 26, 1912)

After just a two-night play-over in Billings, and two in Miles City (unconfirmed) it was on to Butte, the mining town for which Chaplin had a fondness. The townspeople reciprocated the feeling:

EMPRESS THEATER
Direction of Sullivan & Considine. W. J. Swarts, Manager.
An Incomparable Laughing Attraction
Fred Karno's Big London Comedy Company Presents
"THE WOW WOWS"
With CHARLEY CHAPLIN and a Company
of 15 Comedians
One of the Most Enjoyable and Popular Laughing Attractions on the Stage, and
FIVE OTHER BIG ATTRACTIONS

BUTTE, Empress — (w/c Saturday December 7, 1912)

Archie is here. His coming to the Empress theater is a most interesting event for Archie's presence there means a thoroughly good time for all patrons, a good time made all the more so and in fact strongly emphasised by all other attractions on the delightful, sparkling bill.

'Archie' is really Charles Chaplin and he is the leading comedian in the big act produced by Fred Karno and known as *The Wow Wows*, or "*A Night in a Secret Society*." The latter part of the title begins to throw some light on Archie and what he does. Many patrons immediately will recall on reading it that Mr. Chaplin made a tremendous hit here as Archie in *A Night in a London Music Hall*, and Archie in *A Night in an English Club*. The way he used to fall out of the box in that London Music hall sketch and the funny pantomime work he did in the other production—well Archie certainly was one great big scream.

This time Mr. Chaplin has a new departure. Instead of pantomime work he has a speaking part as well and thus the question that often was asked as to what kind of a speaking actor he would be has been answered and most satisfactory at that.

As for the act, it is an elaborate affair in three big scenes with a big company of artists supporting Mr. Chaplin. The act is presented by Alf Reeves.

(*Butte Miner* — December 8, 1911)

Whimsical Walker, however, had totally different feelings, and memories, of the week in Butte:

We then went on to Butte, 2,000 feet above the sea, and when we arrived there we found out that the theatre at which we had arranged to appear had been burnt down[*3]. Ill-luck seemed bent upon pursuing us. However, our manager engaged a large hall and we opened. Most of the population were miners, diggers, etc., and a very rough lot too. It was the roughest place I have ever been into. The climate, the hard travelling and the living didn't suit any of us, and the company began to feel very bad. The ladies lost their voices - the gentlemen could hardly work, and some of them, including myself, began bleeding at the nose. This rather frightened some of us, and to make matters worse we could not get any quinine at the drug stores. Possibly we had influenza very badly. We were glad enough to be free from the town.

(*From Sawdust to Windsor Castle*, by Whimsical Walker)

[*3] In the week's newspapers for Butte, no account of a fire was to be found. The most-likely explanation is that the fire had been in Billings, or Miles City, immediately prior to the Butte engagement, for which no cuttings were forthcoming.

Chaplin's earlier criticism of "Old Whimmy" pales into insignificance when one considers the illness and discomfort that he, among other members of the troupe, was suffering. Just how the correct pronunciation of "ad libitum" would have alleviated all this begs to be questioned.

From Montana the troupe headed into Washington state. A week in Spokane was followed by a week in Seattle, where we pick up Whimsical Walker's account:

> We travelled on to Seattle, the starting point for the Klondyke region. It was a very long journey and raining hard all the while. I became so bad that I thought my time had come. I went up to my hotel, but could not sleep or rest a bit.
>
> (*From Sawdust to Windsor Castle*, by Whimsical Walker)

On Christmas Eve, Walker was sent to hospital, where he was diagnosed as having erysipelas – a streptococcal infectious disease of the skin, characterized by fever, headache, vomiting, and purplish raised lesions on the face. Poor chap! His hospitalisation lasted fully three months, after which he was happy to accept the advice that he would be better off going home, and went without waiting for a second opinion. Back in October 1912 an insert in *Variety* had proclaimed: "*One of England's greatest clown comedians, Whimsical Walker, has started on a tour round the world.*" Now, five months later, he was returning to England with his health, his finances, and his reputation all diminished.

Well, Stan.!
May your path
be a "rosy one."
Your Old Pal
Chas. Chaplin
Fred Karno Co.
Seattle
Wash. U.S.A.
Dec. 25th 1912

Chaplin drew this cartoon of himself as 'Archie' in *The Wow-Wows*. The phrase "rosy one" is in parenthesis and has a small arrow leading to his cheek. Obviously, a private joke.

-----0-----

I believe Arthur Dandoe then re-joined the company, as a replacement for Whimsical Walker. Walker's name does appear on a few further billings but, by his own account, he had left in Seattle. With a new narrator in place the troupe moved on to British Columbia, to ring in the New Year in Vancouver. Just how Stan Jefferson took to ringing out the old narrator, and ringing in the new one (considering the previous split of the Barto Bros.) we will never know. Let's hope Stan didn't try to stick an axe in Dandoe's head.

VANCOUVER, Orpheum — (w/c Monday December 30, 1912)

> The programme at the Orpheum Theatre this week has the correct expression when it announces the "welcome" return of Karno's Comedians, for this well-known company was given one of the heartiest of welcomes at the opening performance yesterday, and they deserved it too, for their offering this trip is even better than their last and it was considered excellent. These fourteen talented people offer a screamingly funny farce in three scenes, entitled *The Wow Wows*, and to say that it took the house by storm is putting it mildly indeed. The story concerns the efforts of a party of campers to get even with one of their number for various abuses by initiating him into a secret order and the situations can easily

be imagined. **Charles Chaplin, who has hitherto been a silent comedian, has a speaking part in this sketch and is very funny**. He is well supported by other members of the company

(*Daily News Advertiser* — December 31, 1912)

The above description: "*These fourteen talented people offer a screamingly funny farce*," is somewhat of a different turn of phrase to the one they had received back in New York in October 1910, when they were branded: "a collection of blithering, blathering Englishmen." *Then*, they were almost deported – *now*, they were "given one of the heartiest of welcomes." So what had brought about this complete turnaround? We do know that Chaplin was credited as having added more comic business to *The Wow-Wows*, most notably to his own role, by making Archie 'a souse,' but was Chaplin deserving of all the praise? Stan Laurel seemed to think so. He commented in later life: "The Wow-Wows *had been developed into a ruddy good show, which Charlie really built up out of nothing*." Even so, Chaplin had made a name for himself, last time around, as a drunk who barely spoke during the "Music Hall" and "London Club" sketches; so one has to have the utmost admiration for him, for returning to America with a *speaking* role, *and* in a sketch for which they had been lambasted — and then gambling everything on playing it AGAIN.

The first week of 1913 found the Karno Company back in Washington, this time in Tacoma.

TACOMA, Empress — (w/c January 6, 1913)

Chaplin has more to do than in previous sketches which is just what his audiences will like, for he is undeniably funny in everything he does and says.

(*Daily Ledger* — January 7, 1913)

And the following week in Portland, Oregon:

PORTLAND, Empress — (w/c January 13, 1913)

Charles Chaplin as Archibald Binks, at the Empress this week, makes "a hit" and incidentally is hit several times while being initiated into the order of "*The Wow Wows*." He is a clever chap and is supported by an excellent company, who present the little three-scene comedy depicting "A Night in an English Secret Society." The scenery is realistic, representing a camp on the Thames and, later, the interior of the clubroom of "The Wow Wows." Among those supporting Chaplin are Charles Cardon, Tom Walker, Stan Jefferson, Amy Forrest, Ethel Hurley and Charles Griffiths.

(*Morning Oregonian* — January 14, 1913)

[AJM: Another later inclusion in the cast was Billy Crackles, a veteran of the Karno Company, and a returnee to the U.S., and then Frank Williams.]

With the escalating success of *The Wow Wows*, and the sense of anticipation it instilled in audiences who couldn't wait to see it, the newspapers adverts went from being plain block letters, to high-class cartoon drawings. This less-classier "teaser" started it off, in which readers would be intrigued to find out who the four black-hooded figures are, behind the Chaplin character.

But then things really took off with the two stunning newspaper cartoon advertisements (See next page!)

Strangely, although we can see for ourselves the dress, and implications, of the characters of the garbed figures, not once in any review I found was mention made of them.

"THE WOW-WOWS"

I have two photographs of Chaplin, taken during live performances of *The Wow-Wows*, but neither one is of sufficient quality to reprint here. However, these two cartoons give us a good idea of some of the new business in this revised version of the sketch. When first aired, the 'Initiation Ceremony' consisted almost solely of 'Archie' being made to suffer electrical shocks from a "magic carpet." Here, though, we have a much more elaborate ceremony, with hooded figures leading 'Archie' through a decidedly darker ritual.

If the cartoon is a true depiction, then the Karno Company were either extremely brave or extremely foolish in their choice of costume, for it seems to be a direct satire on the Ku Klux Klan; but with blackface men in black garb, as opposed to white men in white garb,

(Good job they didn't play Georgia, I say).

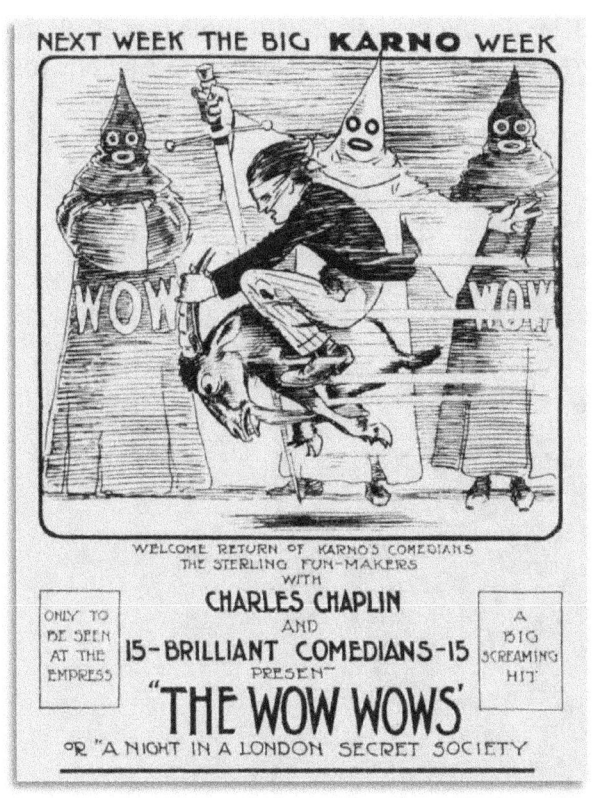

Little evidence exists as to the comedy business employed in the Initiation Ceremony in *The Wow-Wows*. The *San Diego Tribune* said of it only:

What his fellow members-to-be do to "Archibald" is said to furnish material for many humorous situations. Incidentally, some of the instruments of torture used in the initiation of new members into certain secret societies a decade ago will appear during the course of the performance.

The earlier review from Chicago did make mention of a goat: "...*a burlesque on secret societies and the initiation ceremonies of which Archibald is the 'goat'* ..." but no more than that.

I would not think that the sketch included a live goat, although they could have used a stuffed one; or maybe the cartoon is a literal translation of a mime in which Chaplin depicts he is riding a goat. In the absence of written evidence, it remains all I can offer.

Great cartoon though, isn't it?

-----0-----

Sullivan-Considine Tour starts here.

Oct 20	Ohio	CINCINNATI, Empress	*The Wow-Wows*
Oct 28	Illinois	CHICAGO, Empress	*The Wow-Wows*
Nov 03	Wisconsin	MILWAUKEE, Empress	*The Wow-Wows*
Nov 10-16	Minnesota	MINNEAPOLIS, Unique	*The Wow-Wows*
Nov 17	Minnesota	ST. PAUL, Empress	*The Wow-Wows*
Nov 25	Manitoba	WINNIPEG, Empress	*The Wow-Wows*
Dec 02-03		no trace	
Dec 04-05	Montana	BILLINGS, Babcock	*The Wow-Wows*
Dec 07-13	Montana	BUTTE, Empress	*The Wow-Wows*
Dec 15	Washington	SPOKANE, Empress	*The Wow Wows*
Dec 23-28	Washington	SEATTLE, Empress	*The Wow-Wows*
Dec 30-Jan 04	British Columbia	VANCOUVER, Orpheum	*The Wow-Wows*
1913			
Jan 06-11	Washington	TACOMA, Empress	*The Wow-Wows*
Jan 13-19	Oregon	PORTLAND, Empress	*The Wow-Wows*
Jan 20	California	OAKLAND, Empress	[unconfirmed]
Jan 26-Feb 01	California	SAN FRANCISCO, Empress	*The Wow-Wows*
Feb 02-08	California	SACRAMENTO, Empress	*The Wow-Wows*
Feb 10-15	California	LOS ANGELES, Empress	*The Wow-Wows*
Feb 17-22	California	SAN DIEGO, Empress	*The Wow-Wows*
Feb 23-25		no trace	
Feb 26-Mar 04	Utah	SALT LAKE CITY, Empress	*The Wow-Wows*
Mar 05-09		time out	
Mar 10	Colorado	DENVER, Empress	*The Wow-Wows*
Mar 17-18	Colorado	PUEBLO, Empress	*The Wow-Wows*
Mar 19-21	Colorado	COLORADO SPRINGS, Empress	*The Wow-Wows*
Mar 23-29	Missouri	KANSAS CITY, Empress	*The Wow-Wows*

Sullivan-Considine Circuit ends here.

You may have noticed a lack of mention of Stan Jefferson during the narrative for this tour. Well that is because Chaplin was out front in the spotlight, while Jefferson was still way back in a minor role. But here is photo to confirm he was still around.

No information is known about this previously unpublished photo, but my guess would be the company members are with the owners of the accommodation they were staying at.

2nd from Left: Ethel Hurley; 4th Amy Reeves, Alf Reeves (with what looks a wooden bowl on his head), Edgar Hurley, [George Seaman?], Stan Jefferson, Emily Seaman. [Amy Forrest?] The rest, I can't identify. (Missing are: Charles Cardon, Bert Howard, Ted Banks, and Freddie Karno).

-----0-----

From the state of Oregon the troupe took the train to California to play one week in San Francisco, one in Sacramento, and then one in Los Angeles — a city Chaplin had been disparaging about last time around.

LOS ANGELES, Empress — (w/c Monday February 10, 1913)

> One act on the bill which opened yesterday afternoon is worth double the price of admission if one compares the money paid out with the number of laughs received in return. And this happy state of affairs is all due to *The Wow Wows*—whatever they are. The act might just as well have been called by any other name, but it isn't the name that counts—it's the act itself. You snicker at the absurd costumes, you holler at the antics of the players, and you almost scream your head off when you hear them talk. If the old saying, "Laugh and grow fat," has a grain of truth in it, some six hundred or more persons at yesterday's matinee have taken on weight.
>
> (*Los Angeles Herald* — February 11, 1913)

A second review ran:

> "*The Wow Wows*" is composed of a small troupe of performers, featuring Charles Chaplin as Binks, an inebriate. Binks is one of a camping party. His companions decide to put him through the mysteries of "The Wow Wows," and the broad comedy and horseplay that takes place in the initiation scene is more than worth the money.
>
> (*Los Angeles Express* — February 11, 1913)

One more week in California found them in San Diego:

> SAN DIEGO, Empress — (w/c February 17, 1913)
>
> Charles Chaplin, who made a reputation as a comedian in "A Night in an English Music Hall," which appeared at the Empress two years ago, proved last night as much of a hit in his performance of the part of "Archibald Birke" in *The Wow Wows*. "The Wow Wows" is a burlesque secret society, and that the comedy consists mainly in action is indicated when it is said that the initiation of Archibald into the mysteries of the order furnishes the theme for most of the fun.
>
> Chaplin has an off-hand, indifferent way of "taking his medicine," which adds more to the comic effect by far than if he affected to undergo the most excruciating agonies. The company is a large one, but Chaplin, as always, outshines the rest.
>
> (*San Diego Union* — February 18, 1913)

San Diego was followed by a week in Salt Lake, Utah, from where they pushed on through Colorado, playing Denver, Pueblo, and Colorado Springs on the way, and ended the tour in Kansas City, Missouri. However, Reeves had secured them a twelve-week contract to tour part of the Nixon-Nirdlinger circuit, commencing in one week's time in Philadelphia. It wasn't something to celebrate, but it was work.

CHAPTER 12

BROTHERLY LOVE

The one-week break before commencing the next tour was very welcome, as the whole troupe was beginning to tire of the repetitiveness of their schedule. But for Chaplin, at least, there was one consolation. On March 6, 1913 he had entered into the third year of his three-year contract, which meant his pay had now been increased from £12 per week to £15 — the then equivalent of $75. This obviously gave him a feeling of affluence as, for one fleeting moment, he totally abandoned his usual thrifty ways, as he confesses to here:

> We had been working the 'sticks' continuously for five months and the weariness of it had left me discouraged, so that when we had a week's lay-off in Philadelphia, I welcomed it. I needed a change, another environment – to lose my identity and become someone else. I was fed up with the drab routine of tenth-rate vaudeville and decided that for one week I would indulge in the romance of graceful living. I had saved a considerable sum of money and, in sheer desperation, I decided to go on a spending spree. Now I would go to New York and shed myself of tenth-rate vaudeville and its whole drab existence.
>
> (Chaplin's 1964 Autobiography)

Chaplin then goes on to describe how he spent a whole week's wages on just a dressing-gown and a smart over-night case. The specification of the latter proved apt, as Chaplin's proposed week of indulgence in graceful living turned out to be for one night only. The experience of being fussed over by hotel staff in the New York Astor, and an uncontrollable bout of sobbing, brought about by watching *Tannhäuser* at the Metropolitan Opera House, had left him emotionally drained. It also affected his feelings towards his fellow man, as he himself disclosed:

> The following day I decided to return to Philadelphia. Although that one day had been the change I needed, it had been an emotional and a lonely one. Now I wanted company. I looked forward to our Monday morning performance and meeting members of the troupe. No matter how irksome it was returning to the old grind, that one day of graceful living had sufficed me.

Well there's an admission, "Charles Chaplin wanting company" — and not the company of writers, film stars, or state leaders, but his own teammates. Maybe it was being in 'The City of Brotherly Love' which had affected him.

Stan Laurel said of Chaplin:

> I was Charlie's roommate on that tour and he was fascinating to watch. People through the years have talked about how eccentric he became. He was very eccentric even then. He was very moody and often very shabby in appearance. Then suddenly he would astonish us all by getting dressed to kill. It seemed that every once in a while he would get an urge to look very smart. At these times he would wear a derby hat, an expensive one, gloves, smart suit, fancy vest, two-tone side-button shoes, and carry a cane.

[Note the stack heels on his shoes!]
(Photo by 'Sussman' Minneapolis (July 20, 1913)

The accuracy of Laurel's memories is, as usual, outstanding, and his accounts can be relied on about ninety per cent of the time; whereas Chaplin's come in at less than fifty per cent — and I feel I'm being generous at that figure. However, in this instance, Chaplin's version tallies: "I wore" he says, "my smart cut-away coat and derby hat and cane." However, he lets himself down badly when he claims: "As usual I lived alone." Why does Chaplin make this claim, when it so obviously isn't true? There is much documentation of the incidence of Stan and Charlie rooming together, stories that just wouldn't work had they not been sharing. The following two, from interviews Stan Laurel gave, should make the point:

Chaplin arriving at the Empress Theatre in San Francisco, carrying a small suitcase and a violin case in his left hand, and cello in his right hand – but no mandolin.
Photo taken by Karno comedian Fred Palmer – June 5, 1911.

It was on that tour that I shared rooms with Charlie Chaplin. To save spending money in restaurants we used to cook our food over the gas flame in our bedroom. One night, with my usual clumsiness, I tried to cook some tinned beans without first puncturing the lid. The tin bursts with a loud report and splattered its contents all over the wall. After that, the landlady issued a stern edict that cooking in the bedrooms was strictly forbidden. But I'm afraid we disregarded it.

One night while we were frying some chops, we heard her coming along the corridor. With characteristic resourcefulness, Charlie promptly snatched up his violin and played a lively air to drown the sound of the sizzling, whilst I snatched the chops from the gas jet and held the pan out of the window to get rid of the smell!

(*Tit-Bits* – November 21, 1936)

Stan had narrated this story some seven years earlier than the latter:

Charlie was the featured comedian in the troupe, while I was billed as second in importance and his understudy. He was earning twelve pounds a week, while I was only getting five – a mere pittance, in view of American costs – but we had fun in those days, with Charlie always the life and soul of the party.

Charlie and I lived together, sharing the same room, for more than two years, and many's the time we've cooked our dinners in our room. I fried the chops, while Charlie sat close to the door, playing his mandolin[1] *to keep the landlady from hearing the sizzling of the meat over the gas – which was put there for lighting purposes only and not with any idea of cooking!*

(*Film Weekly* – September 23, 1929)

[AJM: I cannot help but believe that the scene in the 1935 Laurel & Hardy film *Bonnie Scotland*, in which Stan and Ollie cook a fish in their lodging room, followed by improvising a makeshift table on which to eat it, owes at least some of its origins to Stan and Charlie's escapades in lodgings.]

To be fair to both Stan and Charlie, I believe it is highly probable that the two shared rooms on the first tour, but that on this, the second tour, Chaplin upgraded himself to hotel rooms, as befits the star of the show. Plus, he could afford it. Why rough it?

---

[1] The interviewer is probably at fault here. It should say "violin." He may have either misheard Stan, or couldn't read his own notes.

Stan added, in the *Film Weekly* article:

> Charlie was the ringleader in everything. Even then we all felt there was something in him which was different from other men. We didn't know what he was; we couldn't put our fingers on it; but it *was* there.

Two very telling additional comments are contained in the above. Firstly Stan says: "... *with Charlie always the life and soul of the party*," and then: "*Charlie was the ringleader in everything*." These give an entirely different picture to the one Charlie paints, wherein he is uncomfortable in the company of the rest of the troupe.

Fred Karno added his thoughts on Chaplin's social skills:

> He [Chaplin] could also be very unlikeable. I've known him to go whole weeks without saying a word to anyone in the company. Occasionally he would be quite chatty but, on the whole, he was dour and unsociable.

And there lies the ambivalence within Chaplin. He would join in fun and games with the company, but only if *he* were the leader. The best analogy I can think of to describe this relationship is to compare it with that between a sheepdog and a flock of sheep. The sheepdog will not run with the flock; nor will it socialise with the flock; nor lie down with it. The only time it spends time with the sheep is when it is controlling the action. Were it asked to relinquish its dominant role, and let one of the sheep have a turn, it would not acquiesce. When the fun is over the sheep stay together; whereas the sheepdog removes itself and becomes a solitary figure.

Upon his return to Philadelphia, following his one night sojourn, Chaplin found a telegram awaiting him. After reading the contents he was made to wish he had remained in New York. In his 1933 autobiography Chaplin relates:

> The wire read: 'Are you the man who played the drunk at the American Music Hall three years ago? If so, will you get in touch with Kessel and Bauman, Longacre Building, New York?'

> I hadn't the faintest idea who Kessel and Bauman were. Perhaps it was a firm of lawyers and some rich relative of mine had died and left me a fortune. I was a little let down when I discovered it was a motion picture concern, nevertheless I was elated.

So he immediately returned to New York, to see what they wanted:

> Mr. Kessel informed me that Mack Sennett had instructed him to get in touch with me. I remember how well I played my cards at that interview with Charlie Kessel; how I boosted my salary, I was getting seventy-five dollars a week at that time. I assured Kessel that my only interest in motion pictures was the consideration of my health. The work would be in the open air and the outdoor life appealed to me. It was for this reason only that I would consider pictures. Of course, I went on, I got two hundred and fifty dollars a week in vaudeville, but on account of the nature of the work, I would make a sacrifice.

> We eventually compromised for one hundred and fifty dollars, and I left the office firm in the belief that I was an embezzler.

The agreement was left open-ended, with Kessel and Baumann informing Chaplin that the final decision rested with Mr. Sennett. Chaplin was currently almost as far away from Sennett as it was possible to be within U.S. limits, as his studios were in Los Angeles, on the West coast. However, in five months' time the company was due in California, so Chaplin would be able to meet up with his potential new boss then.

As to why he had been summoned, Chaplin related:

> Mr. Charles Kessel*[2], one of the owners of the Keystone Comedy Film Company, said that Mr. Mack Sennett had seen me playing the drunk in the American Music Hall on Forty-second Street and if I were the same man he would like to engage me to take the place of Mr. Ford Sterling.

By Monday, Charlie was back in Philadelphia, ready for the evening's debut at the People's Theatre.

---

*[2] Kessel's first name was Adam. It was Baumann who was called Charles.

1913

Mar 31	Pennsylvania	PHILADELPHIA	[week out]

Nixon-Nirdlinger Circuit starts here

Apr 07	Pennsylvania	PHILADELPHIA, People's	
Apr 14	Pennsylvania	PHILADELPHIA, People's	
Apr 21	Pennsylvania	PHILADELPHIA, Nixon	*Music Hall*
Apr 28	Pennsylvania	PHILADELPHIA, Nixon	*London Club*
May 05-10	Pennsylvania	PHILADELPHIA, Nixon	*The Wow-Wows*
May 12	Pennsylvania	PHILADELPHIA, People's	
May 19	Pennsylvania	PHILADELPHIA, Metropolitan	*Music Hall*, and *London Club*
May 26	Maryland	BALTIMORE, Victoria	*Music Hall*
Jun 02	Maryland	BALTIMORE, Victoria	*London Club*
Jun 09	District of Columbia	WASHINGTON DC, Cosmos	*Music Hall*
Jun 16-21	District of Columbia	WASHINGTON DC, Cosmos	*London Club*

Nixon-Nirdlinger Circuit ends here

-----0-----

The first six weeks on the Nixon-Nirdlinger circuit were all at theatres in Philadelphia, so the company rotated three different sketches:

PHILADELPHIA, Nixon — (w/c April 21, 1913)

Karno's London Co. appeared in the uproariously funny sketch *A Night in a London Music Hall*, with Charles Chaplin enacting the part of the drunk. He was a scream.

-----0-----

PHILADELPHIA, Nixon — (w/c April 28, 1913)

Those lively and capable entertainers the Karno Comedians, created a furore of laughter in *A Night at the Club*, a satirical comedy playlet with many humorous incidents.

-----0-----

PHILADELPHIA, Nixon — (w/c May 5, 1913)

For the third week of their sparkling engagement at the Nixon, the Karno Komedy Company yesterday presented *The Wow-Wows*, a lively sketch, in which Chas. Chaplin made a decided hit as the silly bounder, who is the butt of much of the fun.

This was the first time on this tour that "Music Hall" was staged. Note some of the changes, below:

BELOW: Cutting from the Stan Laurel Collection

```
CHARLES CHAPLIN,
                    The Inebriated Swell
E. Hurley ................The Bad Boy
Charles Griffin ..........Uncle William
         THE VAUDEVILLE ACTS.
1. The Red Nose Comic, Stanley Jefferson
2. The Ballad Vocalists......Amy Forrest
3. Prof. Bunco, Musician....Chas. Gordon
4. The Village Glee Singers,
     Albert Austin, Fred Wescott, Bert
     Howard, Frank Williams.
5. The Saucy Soubrette....Amiee' Minster
6. The Terrible Turk.........Ted Banks
  Manager for Fred Karnos' Company in
America, Alf. Reeves.
```

FRED KARNO'S London Pantomime Company
Presenting "A NIGHT IN AN ENGLISH MUSIC HALL"
CAST:

CHARLES CHAPLIN	The Inebriated Swell
Edgar Hurley	The Bad Boy
Charles Griffiths	Uncle William

THE VAUDEVILLE ACTS

1	The Red Nose Comic	Stanley Jefferson
2	The Ballad Vocalist	Amy Forrest
3	Prof. Bunco, Magician	Chas. Cardon
4	The Village Glee Singers	Albert Austin, Fred Westcott, Bert Howard, Frank Williams.
5	The Saucy Soubrette	Amy Minister
6	The Terrible Turk	Ted Banks

Manager for Fred Karno's Company in America, Alf Reeves.

ABOVE: Correction of the six mistakes, at left.

New players: Chas. Cardon (*not* Gordon), Bert Howard, Frank Williams.

Stan is no longer one of the Glee Singers, but now has a solo spot as 'The Red Nose Comic.' His act would have been a succession of the worst jokes he knew, those guaranteed to get a groan from the audience, and heckling from the drunk.

-----0-----

LEFT
Stan Jefferson as "The Red-Nose Comic" — a new role written specially for him, and maybe even *by* him.

Edgar Hurley, who has replaced Mike Asher as "The Bad Boy."

For their sixth, and final, week in Philadelphia our unhappy band played the Metropolitan, formerly the home of opera, which had opened as a vaudeville venue just two weeks earlier. Here they changed the sketch in mid-week.

PHILADELPHIA, Metropolitan — w/c May 19, 1913

For the third week at the Metropolitan under the new management of Marcus Loew and Nixon-Nirdlinger, the headliner for the first half of the week will be Karno's Komedy Kompany in *A Night in a London Music Hall*, and, for the second half, *A Night at the Club*.

(*Philadelphia Inquirer* – Sunday May 18, 1913)

ABOVE, RIGHT: Rare, if not unique, newspaper photo of Alf Reeves (right) and Chaplin standing in front of an advertising poster for the show at the Metropolitan Opera House, Philadelphia.

-----0-----

From Philadelphia the troupe moved on for two two-week stays in Baltimore and Washington DC, where "Music Hall" was again presented the first week, and "London Club" the second.

"Music Hall" was played only four times on the 1912-1913 tour (April 21, 1913, in Philadelphia, to June 9, 1913, in Washington DC. Chaplin didn't know it then, but he had played his last ever performance in "Music Hall/Mumming Birds" — the sketch which had made his name in America and Canada.

June 21 in Winnipeg also signalled the end of the company's run on the Nixon-Nirdlinger circuit, which came as a relief to all involved. Working these second-rate, ten-cent theatres had taken its toll on them. Chaplin himself admitted:

> These cheap vaudeville circuits were bleak and depressing, and hopes about my future in America disappeared in the grind of doing three and sometimes four shows a day, seven days a week. Vaudeville in England was paradise by comparison. At least we only worked there six days a week and only gave two shows a night.
>
> (Chaplin's 1964 Autobiography)

The thrill of the chase had obviously run its course for Chaplin. The first challenge had been to become one of Fred Karno's Comedians; the second was to become the lead-comic; and the third – to become famous. Having passed all three challenges, there was nothing else within the Karno Company for Chaplin to achieve. All he had now was the tedium of returning to the same towns and venues, and repeating the same sketches.

'The Saucy Soubrette' sings "*You Naughty, Naughty Men*," whilst being leered at by Archie, from the box at right.

For the first six months of this tour they had played almost solely *The Wow-Wows*, and for the next five the only sketch would be *A Night in a London Club*. This must have been soul destroying. These players were masters of comedy. They thrived on comic invention and working-up new sketches but, on this tour, they were just going through the motions.

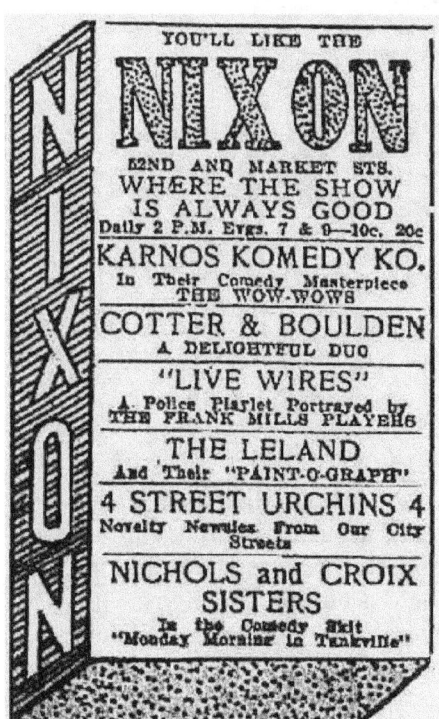

The newspaper adverts, too, promoting the shows on the Nixon-Nirdlinger circuit, had lost all form of expression and creativity, especially when one considers the superb cartoon drawings the Karno appearances had sparked on previous circuits. At left is a typical example.

Before coming back to the States, the plan had been for the FKC to play two new sketches: *The Hydro*, and *The Village Sports*. The latter had similarities to *A Night in a London Club*, in that the premise was a sport's presentation evening in a village hall. But at least it would have given the company something new and challenging to perform. As for *The Hydro*, which was all about guests "taking the waters" at a health spa, maybe Chaplin could salvage some of that for a later film — say: *The Cure*.

Even the excitement of working and socialising with new acts had been denied them as, following a week off, it was back to the Sullivan-Considine circuit, where all the acts in their show were now touring as one complete package. Morale was at an all-time low. It was inevitable that, shortly, someone was about to make a break for it and, when they did, "The House That Karno Built" would come a-tumbling down.

CHAPTER 13

ONE FLEW WEST

Following a week-out, after finishing the Nixon-Nirdlinger Circuit, the next tour was to be twenty-two weeks on the Sullivan-Considine Circuit, with *A Night in a London Club* as the main sketch.

Archie removing his jacket in readiness for a punch-up with Mr. Meek.
[From the earlier show in Washington DC — June 16-21, 1913 (*Washington Post*)]

The tour started in Detroit (unconfirmed), after which came Chicago.

CHICAGO, Halstead Empress — (w/c Sunday July 6, 1913)

The Karno Company is playing a burlesque-pantomime called *A Night in a London Club*. Full of slap-stick humor, it is diverting, and Sunday afternoon the act had the house in an uproar of laughter. Charles Chaplin tumbles about in a surprising style and is the principal funmaker, although several others perform lively stunts and bring out numerous laughs. The character make-up of the people is excellent, and there are several moments in the sketch where laughter is at a high point.

(*Variety* – July 11, 1913)

The venue for Week 3 wasn't traced, but is thought to be Milwaukee. Then came a week in each of the "Twin Cities" of Minneapolis and St. Paul, Minnesota.

One Flew West

Sussman Studio, Minneapolis
week of November 10-16, 1912

Sincerely Yours
Stan Jefferson
1913.

BELOW:
Unknown snapshot, with similarities to one in the last chapter.
Far left: Edgar Hurley. Third from left: Stan Jefferson.
Kneeling: Amy Minister, and Ethel Hurley.
Three of the ladies are holding puppies.

Next, the company paid their third visit to Winnipeg:

WINNIPEG, Empress
(w/c Monday August 4, 1913)
"A Night in a London Club"

Karno's English Comedy Company, headed by Charles Chaplin, is the headline attraction at the Empress this week and well deserves the reputation as a merriment producer. Charles Chaplin, known as the only comedian who can act the part of a drunk realistically, without at any time approaching the vulgar, is the leading spirit of the sketch, and keeps the audience in an uproar from the rise of the curtain. Mr. Chaplin is remarkably supported, especially by Edgar Hurley and Amy Forest. The act itself is a farce of the extreme order, but it is so well carried out that the idea proves a fun maker - so "nuff said."

(*Winnipeg Telegram* – August 5, 1913)

The vast majority of reviews credit only Chaplin by name, but the above gives a very rare mention of two of the other featured players. Although the reviewer excuses himself from divulging more about the act itself, a couple of days earlier he had written a preview, using the advance publicity notes, which gives an insight into the premise of the sketch:

Charles Chaplin, who always portrays the very funny role of the inebriated gentleman of the productions, has a personal following that is always effusive and warm in its greeting, and in this elaborate and best of the Karno successes he is better—if such a thing is possible—than in any other of the comedies.

The scene depicts "ladies night" at the Bumblers' Angling Society, with "Archibald" (Charles Chaplin) in a hopelessly maudlin condition, while the other members have their "company manners," and are trying their unsuccessful best to squelch the pugnacious Archie. The antics and dialogue of the amateur entertainers to secure the attention of their fellow members while they add their songs and recitations to the enjoyment of "ladies night" are screamingly funny.

(*Winnipeg Telegram* – August 2, 1913)

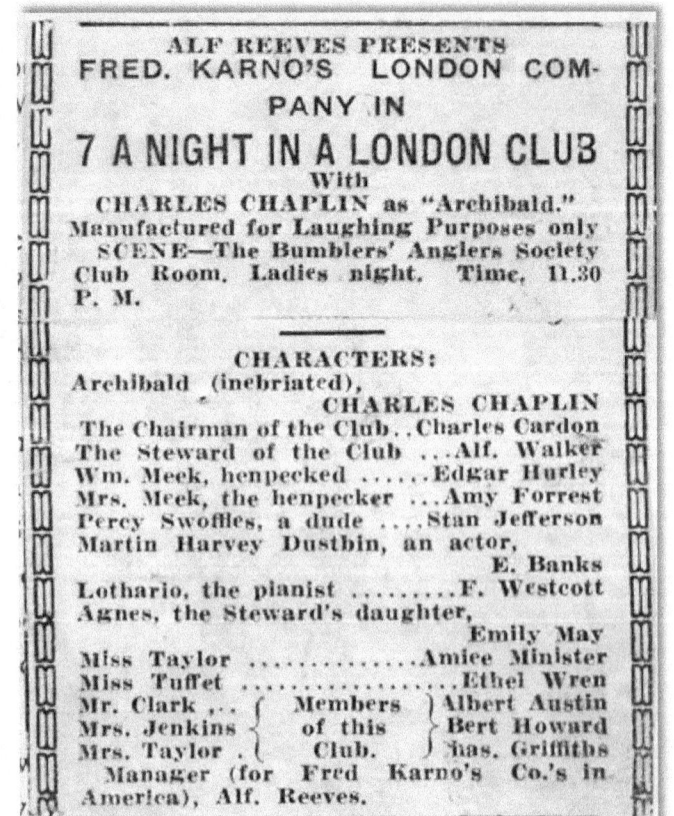

On the last night of the week in Winnipeg, Chaplin met and befriended one of four brothers from a touring sketch titled: *Mrs. Green's Reception Room*. Maybe you've heard of him – Groucho Marx.

In his memoirs, Groucho was relaxed enough to divulge:

> I was on the Pantages Circuit, the last act on the bill, doing four shows a day, rain or shine. There was a three-hour layover in Winnipeg before jumping to the Coast. As a rule, I made a bee-line for the pool room. It was generally warmer! This particular night I decided on the spur of the moment to take in a show.
>
> Well, sir, at this show, the audience was roaring with laughter. I looked at the stage and saw Chaplin for the first time. I had never heard people laugh like that. I began to laugh, too. His act was called *A Night at the Club.* It was supposed to be an English social club. Chaplin sat at a small table and ate soda crackers one after another. A woman up front was singing all the while, but nobody heard a note, I'm sure. They were intent on Chaplin's every move. A fine stream of cracker dust was slowly coming out of his mouth. He kept that up for exactly fifteen minutes.
>
> At the table was a large basket of oranges. Finally, he started to pick up the oranges, one by one, and throw them at the woman. One of the oranges knocked the pianist off his chair. People became hysterical. There never was such continuous laughter. I thought he was the greatest fellow I had ever seen on the stage.

Cartoon from Whimsical Walker's scrapbook, showing Chaplin spitting cracker crumbs at Charlie Griffiths.

(*Photoplay Magazine* – 1936)

Obviously, Chaplin didn't spit out crackers for fifteen minutes, otherwise he would have needed a mouth the size of a hippo. But this extract will show us what Groucho got right:

```
                              etc.
Mr. Basil Keene gets disgusted with interruptions and walks off.
Chairman calls for order and then on Percy Swoofles for the next
song.
Percy obliges with song and dance and finishes with being bombarded
with prop oranges from the members, finally he falls off rostrum
and Steward helps him to his feet.
Mr. Binks goes to him and presents him with a red ribbon, kisses
him on the forehead then pushes him and he finally lands knocking
over Taylor and Clark.
Chairman again regains order, then announces item - calling on
the Steward's daughter little Aggie for a recitation "The Colliers
dying Child".
Steward escorts Aggie to the rostrum.
Aggie "The Cottage was a thatched one" etc., the guests get very
sad and one or two start to shed a tear.
Mr. Binks starts eating crackers and blows them over Taylor and
Clark.
Steward helps Aggie off rostrum.  Mr. Meek overwhelmed goes
over to Aggie and gives her some money.
```

[Copy of original script — courtesy of the late- Olive Karno]

Groucho continues:

> I was so impressed by Chaplin that I sought him out after the show and we became friends. The two circuits that we were on made the same towns, and when we were on stage at the same times we would visit each other between shows.

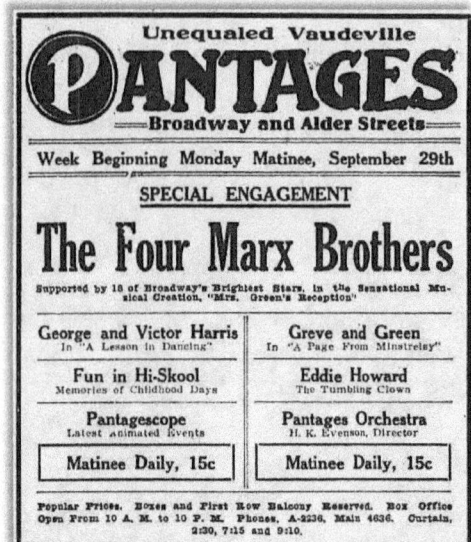

The Marx Brothers weren't yet on the Pantages circuit, but were on their way through to Edmonton, Alberta, Canada, where their tour was to commence on August 11. So what Groucho means when he says: "*There was a three-hour layover in Winnipeg before jumping to the Coast*," is that they had to wait for the connecting train. [Yes, I know Edmonton isn't on the Coast. Blame Groucho!]

However, his claim that: "…when we were on stage at the same times we would visit each other between shows …" doesn't seem to hold water, as I could find no incidences of the Marx Brothers playing the same week, in the same town, as the Karno Company. However, there are some dates when I couldn't trace the Marxes. Plus, they may have met if one company left town late, and the other arrived early. See the following date-sheet for both acts!

It's interesting to note that Groucho was happy to speak of this, and later contact with Chaplin, whilst Chaplin never wrote a single word about meeting Groucho. But, as has been noted many times, Chaplin was wont to omit from his records anyone who went on to be famous.

Date	State/Province	Town, Venue	Show
Aug 04-09	Manitoba	WINNIPEG, Empress (s-c)	*A Night in a London Club*
Aug 11-13	Montana	MILES CITY, Liberty (s-c)	*A Night in a London Club*
Aug 11	Alberta	EDMONTON, Pantages	MARX BROTHERS
Aug 14-15	Montana	BILLINGS, Babcock	*A Night in a London Club*
Aug 16-22	Montana	BUTTE, Empress (s-c)	*A Night in a London Club*
Aug 18	Alberta	CALGARY	MARX BROTHERS
Aug 24-30	Washington	SPOKANE, Orpheum	*A Night in a London Club*
Sep 01	Washington	SEATTLE, Empress (s-c)	*A Night in a London Club*
Sep 01	Washington	SPOKANE, Panatages	MARX BROTHERS
Sep 08	British Columbia	VANCOUVER, Orpheum	*A Night in a London Club*
Sep 15-20	Washington	TACOMA, Empress (s-c)	*A Night in a London Club*
Sep 15-20	British Columbia	VANCOUVER, Pantages	MARX BROTHERS
Sep 22-27	Oregon	PORTLAND, Empress (s-c)	*A Night in a London Club*
Sep 29-Oct 03	Oregon	PORTLAND, Pantages	MARX BROTHERS
Oct 04		no trace	
Oct 05-11	California	SAN FRANCISCO, Empress	*A Night in a London Club*
Oct 12	California	SACRAMENTO, Empress (s-c)	*A Night in a London Club*
Oct 20-25	California	LOS ANGELES, Empress (s-c)	*A Night in a London Club*
Oct 20-25	California	OAKLAND, Pantages	MARX BROTHERS
Oct 26	California	SAN DIEGO, Empress (s-c)	*A Night in a London Club*
Oct 26-Nov 01	California	LOS ANGELES, Pantages	MARX BROTHERS
Nov 04		no trace	
Nov 03-08	California	SAN DIEGO, Savoy	MARX BROTHERS

One Flew West

Nov 05-11	Utah	SALT LAKE CITY, Empress	*A Night in a London Club*
Nov 12	Utah	SALT LAKE CITY, Pantages	MARX BROTHERS
Nov 16-22	Colorado	DENVER, Empress (s-c)	*A Night in a London Club*
Nov 17-22	Utah	OGDEN	MARX BROTHERS
Nov 23-29	Missouri	KANSAS CITY, Empress (s-c)	*A Night in a London Club*

-----0-----

The next leg of the tour took the FKC through Montana, with stopovers in Miles City and Butte; then on through Washington State, to play Spokane and Seattle; before arriving in Vancouver:

VANCOUVER B.C., Orpheum — (w/c September 8, 1913)

The Fred Karno Company, with Charles Chaplin featured, are back once more in the city in *A Night In A London Club*, and were heartily welcomed by the many friends at the Orpheum yesterday. Chaplin's conception of the "inebriate" could not be improved upon, and he has made the part his own. While he is the star of the company, the rest of the members all do their part to amuse and they surely do make the audience laugh.

(*Daily News Advertiser* — September 9, 1913)

Groucho Marx, back in Winnipeg, may have found the "cracker spitting" hilarious, but the reviewer for the show in Tacoma could not have had a more opposing view:

TACOMA, Empress — (w/c September 15, 1913)

Save for the idea of comedy which consists of spitting water or chewed crackers into another's face, the *Night in an English Club* is still the funny slap-stick farce as on its former visit. It seems odd that this revolting feature of a successful act cannot be eliminated. Charles Chaplin is inimitable in his characterization of the drunk and the farce is reaping its usual harvest of laughs.

(*Daily Ledger* – September 16, 1913)

However, the following week the theatre critic found all the business to be "hilariously funny."

PORTLAND, Empress

(w/c September 22, 1913)

Archibald, Mr. Meek, the henpecked, Mrs. Meek, his better-half; the Chairman; Steward; a long-haired musician; and a would-be actor; and several other comical characters are to be seen in *A Night in a London Club,* which is presented this week at the Empress by a troupe of clever English character actors. The playlet is a satire on the organizations that are made up of supposed-to-be Bohemians and think-they-can-sing musicians.

There are eighteen in the company and stellar place is filled by Charles Chaplin who is noted for his comic portrayal of Archibald, the "souse." The latest act of *A Night in a London Club* is crowded with hilariously funny situations and the comedians are kept on the jump throughout the half-hour they hold the stage.

Percy Swoffles (Stan Jefferson) delivering a song to the members, and a swift kick to the pianist – Mr. Lothario (Fred Karno Jnr.) [Stan Laurel Scrapbook]
Percy is singing: "Yama! Yama! Yama! Man. Oh! Pop, while the pianist retorts:
"I say old chap! What the matter."

(*Morning Oregonian* – September 23, 1913)

It was while in Portland that Chaplin's contract to join the Keystone Company arrived, which he duly signed and returned. Now that Chaplin knew his time with the Karno Company was limited, the remaining weeks would have been agony. He would have just wanted to quit and start a new challenge.

Chaplin's imminent departure almost certainly had a negative effect on the rest of the cast, and maybe it began to show.

SAN FRANCISCO, Empress

(w/c Sunday October 5, 1913)

Fred Karno's Company with Charlie Chaplin, had the closing spot, but the offering only proved ordinarily entertaining to the Empress regulars.

(*Variety* – October 10, 1913)

This disappointing review was followed, in Sacramento, by one even more damaging:

SACRAMENTO, Empress — (w/c Sunday October 12, 1913)

Karno's Comedians comprised fifteen people, a number of whom could be dispensed with so far as the humor of the act. Their funmaking was of the slapstick variety, laughable in its ridiculousness but lacking in high-class comedy. None of the dialogue was distinguishable in the rough-house methods used to snatch the giggles from the audience and possibly it was just as well. The best part of the act was the way in which Charles Chaplin impersonated a stolid Englishman inebriated.

(*Sacramento Bee* – October 13, 1913)

These reviews would have had Charlie desperately worried. The troupe were about to revisit Los Angeles, where Chaplin was to meet Sennett, and he certainly did not want bad reviews preceding him. More importantly, when they got there, he wouldn't want a bad reception from any of the Los Angeles' audiences, especially on the night Sennett would be in the house. So! how *was he* received?

LOS ANGELES, Empress (w/c October 20, 1913)

> Charlie Chaplin is back with his amusing characterisation of a "souse." This time he appears in *A Night in a London Club*, a social affair where everybody has a good time and does exactly what he likes. Chaplin does his usual stunts at tumbling and knocking everybody down, he himself remaining preternaturally solemn all the time. There are no less than fifteen people in the cast, bright men and women, who know how to keep the ball of fun rolling.

(*Los Angeles Times* – October 21, 1913)

A second review ran:

> Mr. Chaplin is known from coast to coast as the original "souse." The word is not pretty, but neither is Mr. Chaplin. As the original dyed in the wool, dead in the face drunkard, Mr. Chaplin is immense. At this point the house slipped and stripped its gears, and went stark staring crazy with joy. Mr. Chaplin slammed and was slammed about the stage in a manner most miraculous. He inflicted falls upon others, but took a number himself. Everyone on the stage did weird topplings. The piano player stood on his ear and spun about—the woman—oh well, what's the use? See it yourself, but don't tear up the benches.

(*Los Angeles Herald* – October 22, 1913)

Chaplin adds a personal insight, from which one can feel his obvious relief at the turnaround in audience reaction from the ones in San Francisco and Sacramento:

> When we played the Empress in Los Angeles, we were a howling success, thank God. It was a comedy called *A Night at the Club*. I played a decrepit old drunk and I looked at least fifty years old. Mr. Sennett came round after the performance and congratulated me. But I wondered how sympathetic he would be in our future relationship. All through the interview I was extremely nervous and was not sure whether he was pleased with me or not.

(Chaplin's 1964 Autobiography)

There was one particular item on the bill which Sennett would undoubtedly have asked Chaplin his opinion on, namely:

> Exclusive of the new acts will be the Keystone comedies in which the popular comedian Ford Sterling figures as the star.
>
> (*Los Angeles Times* – October 21, 1913)

And there is no doubt that members of the Karno Company did watch the films they shared the bill with, as Stan Laurel testifies in a letter to a fan, dated June 2, 1958:

> Most of my picture viewing was done in my Vaudeville days when they used to run films on the same show, so to fill time between shows I'd go out front to watch them – I guess I got pretty fed up with them.

And Chaplin's confirmation, which came out at the first meeting with Kessel and Baumann.

> "Had I seen a Keystone Comedy?" Asked Mr Kessel. Of course I had seen several, I did not tell him that I thought they were a crude mélange of rough and tumble. However, a pretty dark-eyed girl named Mabel Normand, who was quite charming, weaved in and out of them and justified their existence. I was not terribly enthusiastic about the Keystone type of comedy, but I realised their publicity value.
>
> (Chaplin's 1964 Autobiography)

Obviously Chaplin did not reveal his thoughts to Sennett, but there is a very real probability that Sennett would have detected a coldness within Chaplin, hence his showing no outward liking for Chaplin, the man. Chaplin:

> He [Sennett] asked me casually when I would join them. I told him that I could start the first week in September, which would be the termination of my contract with the Karno Company.

[AJM. For a much more protracted account of just when Chaplin's contract with Karno actually began, and terminated, refer to my book: "CHAPLIN – Stage by Stage."]

So just who was Sennett, and what was his association with Kessel and Baumann? Already among industry's most active film producers by 1912, Kessel and Baumann were persuaded by Sennett to form another company, this one to specialise in comedies. Based on the reputation he had earned as a comic actor and director at Biograph, Sennett was given a one-third interest in the new company – Keystone. Sennett had then defected from Biograph with several key performers, including Mabel Normand, Ford Sterling and Henry "Pathé" Lehrman, and moved to a studio in Los Angeles, where he continued to build his roster of comedy performers. By the time Sennett instructed Kessel and Baumann to find Chaplin, Keystone had developed into Hollywood's pre-eminent fun factory of slapstick comedy.

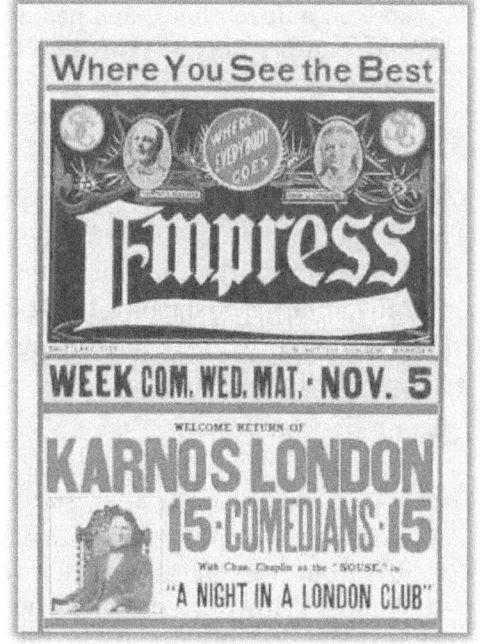

Original poster
Empress, Salt Lake City
w/c Wednesday November 5, 1913

But, for Chaplin, there was still the matter of more vaudeville dates to be fulfilled. From Los Angeles the company headed south, and stopped just short of the Mexico border, in San Diego, where, following the good reviews in Los Angeles, Chaplin would seem to have had an adrenalin boost.

SAN DIEGO, Empress (w/c October 27, 1913)

> Fred Karno's London comedians, in a sketch showing London music hall life, are as funny as ever. They have appeared in San Diego many times, but "bigger, brighter and better than ever" describes them. Charles Chaplin as "Archibald" seems to improve with every appearance.
>
> (*San Diego Union* — October 28, 1913)

Time was now going more and more slowly for Charlie. He had to endure another week in Salt Lake City, followed by two in Colorado, before the troupe finally reached Kansas City — where the tour was to end.

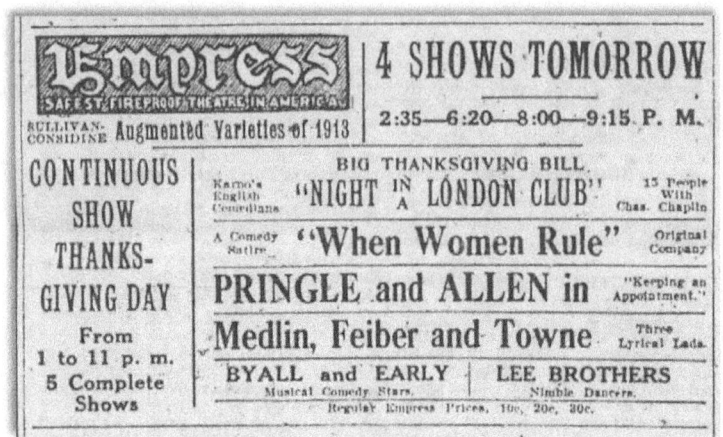

KANSAS CITY, Empress
(w/c November 23, 1913)

The Empress had its top-liner *A Night in a London Club*, with Karno's English company presenting the act. The usual big crowds were in attendance.

(*New York Dramatic Mirror* – December 3, 1913)

And that was the end of that. Despite having captured numerous headlines, having had euphoric reviews written about him, and having had countless numbers of cartoons of his stage characters printed in newspapers, Chaplin left the stage with only a whimper. The following is the only newspaper article found which mentioned the subject:

> Charlie Chaplin, who numbers his friends by the thousands, is going to desert the stage to become a movie actor and play the chief comedy roles with the Keystone Company. As a film actor Charlie should surely make good for, during the five years he has been with the Karno Company, and on all his visits to this city, he has not spoken a dozen lines, and has depended on facial expression and pan-drama, to gain him the laughs. We shall all be anxiously awaiting the Keystone films in which he appears, and it goes without saying they will be just as funny as he has been in his Karno offerings.
>
> (Chaplin's scrapbook – cutting not identified)

The only other two known accounts of his departure were given by Chaplin himself, and Stan Laurel, and these didn't exactly conform to the back-slapping, bear-hugging, handshaking, tear-jerking reactions we may have imagined from a troupe that had been together for nigh on four years.

Chaplin first:

> A member of our troupe, Arthur Dando[e], who for some reason disliked me, thought he would play a joke and conveyed whispered innuendos that I was to receive a small gift from the company. I must confess I was touched by the thought. However, nothing happened. When everyone had left the dressing-room, Fred Karno Junior confessed that Dando had arranged to make a speech and present me with the gift, but after I had bought drinks for everyone he had not had the courage to go through with it and had left the so-called 'present' behind the dressing-table mirror. It was an empty tobacco-box, wrapped in tin-foil, containing small ends of old pieces of greasepaint.

Chaplin had totally misunderstood the significance of the pieces of greasepaint. If only he'd asked his roommate, Stan Jefferson, he would have received an honest, but hurtful, answer. Instead it was some fifty years later before Stan revealed the secret:

There couldn't always have been bad feeling between Chaplin and Dandoe, as here they are enjoying some quiet timeout together. (Thought to be in San Francisco).

Arthur didn't like Charlie because he considered him haughty and cold. So in Kansas, on our last night with Charlie, he announced that he was going to present a special goodbye present. He told me what it was – about five pieces of old brown Leichner grease paint, looking just like turds, all of this wrapped up in a very fancy box. "Some shit, for a shit" is the way Arthur put it. This was Arthur's idea of a joke. I tried to argue him out of it but all Arthur said was, "It'll serve the superior ba****d right."

The so-called presentation never took place, however, and later Arthur told me why. First of all, Charlie stood the entire company drinks after the show. That fazed Arthur a bit but the thing that really shamed him into not going through with the so-called gag was this: just after his final curtain with us, Charlie hurried off to a deserted spot backstage. Curious, Arthur followed, and he saw haughty, cold, unsentimental Charlie crying.

(Charlie Chaplin, by John McCabe)

But let us not leave on a negative note. Chaplin's contribution and impact on his years with the Fred Karno Company should not be soured by one man's opinion of this comedy genius; a man who had almost single-handedly raised the standard of the Karno sketches to previously unreached heights, and saved his fellow comedians from being sent home on more than one occasion. So here to celebrate his glorious career with the Karno Company, is a glorious picture of them all, in full comedy mode, on stage.

So then came the parting of the waves. Not so very long ago, whenever Fred Karno had been asked, "Who's your star name?" he would retort: "My name's up there, and that's enough." But circumstances had changed. The student had become bigger than the master.

CHAPTER 14

THE LULL BEFORE THE LULL

Chaplin said of his departing:

> I had qualms about leaving the troupe in Kansas City. The company was returning to England, and I to Los Angeles, where I would be on my own, and the feeling was not too reassuring.

Chaplin is incorrect when he states that the company were returning to England, for they still had a twelve-week contract to complete on the Nixon-Nirdlinger circuit. The problem was — the terms were for Chaplin to be in the lead role.

Of Chaplin's decision to leave, Laurel offered:

> Then came the day when Charlie listened to the lure of the movies. We all prophesied, blindly, that he was making a great mistake, that he should remain true to the stage. But he passed off his departure with his usual clowning, and made a grand gesture of farewell. Still there was a trembling in his handclasp. After all, we had been trouping together for more than seven years.*[1] We all wished him well from the bottom of our hearts, but we secretly congratulated ourselves on possessing a superior wisdom.
>
> (*Film Weekly* – September 1929)

Chaplin's thoughts were:

> A year at that racket and I could return to vaudeville an international star.
>
> (Chaplin's 1964 Autobiography)

But after three years he was to spend in "that racket" Chaplin's views would change. He told the actor Fred Goodwin, whom he was to work with at the Essanay Studios:

> Back to the stage! I'll never go back to the stage again as long as I live. No. Unless my money leaves me, not ten thousand dollars would tempt me back behind the footlights again.
>
> (1915 *Pearson's Weekly* – Fred Goodwin article)

So how would Charlie fare now he was going into films? Well, first and foremost he would need a screen persona. Let us have a recap of his career to date:

At his first-ever stage appearance he had reprised his mother's singing act. In 'The Eight Lancashire Lads' he had synchronised with the other seven. In *Sherlock Holmes* he had portrayed the well-established character of 'Billy,' in the way he was coached. In *Casey's Circus* he had impersonated Dr. Walford Bodie and Bransby Williams. In the Karno Company he had copied Syd Chaplin's original comic creations – including "the drunk" in "*Music Hall*," *Skating* and *The Wow-Wows*; and not forgetting, of course, taking over Stan Jefferson's character improvisation in *Jimmy the Fearless*. Not once, in all that time had he created a single, original character. So why change the habit of a lifetime time now that he was going into film? All he need do was mimic the people he had worked, and others he had observed in passing, both on stage and in real life; but, first and foremost, reprise the role he had been playing on stage which was, after all, the character which had got him into films.

For the premise of his films he could call upon the numerous Karno sketches he had played in, plus all the other sketches he had observed during his years in variety and vaudeville. It could not have been easier. Mind you, it did help that he was a brilliant comedian and that, from hereon in, he would discard the 'crutches' he had borrowed from other performers, and go forward with his own comic creations.

---

*[1] Stan is known to have quoted this figure of 'seven years' in other instances. Why it stuck in his head is hard to fathom. He had actually spent less than FOUR years with the Karno Company. Chaplin became a Karno comedian in 1908, so not even he had been with the company for seven years.

The Lull Before The Lull

Chaplin's astronomical rise of fame and fortune in the film-world needs no recounting here. No! We shall stick with our subject — Arthur Stanley Jefferson. How long would it be before *he* was given the call to report to Hollywood, and then go on to enjoy a career parallel, and equal, to Charlie's?

With their star player gone, the Karno Company decided to struggle on, but it was going to be a bigger struggle than they could ever have imagined. The whole company had every reason, and every confidence, to believe that Stan Jefferson was going to step into the vacated principal role, and that the tour could carry on as if nothing had happened. After all, Karno had always trained the members of his companies so that, should one or more of the cast leave, there were always others who could step right into the vacant role(s). More than once Charlie Chaplin had learned a role from Syd Chaplin and then replaced him, in that role. So now it was the turn of Master Stanley Jefferson to repeat the process — and who better? Although Stan is not on record as ever having had the chance to showcase his interpretation of 'the drunk' to audiences, all the cast members surely knew he was more than capable of filling the part. Sorry to report, however, that the bookers for the Nixon-Nirdlinger circuit, for whom the Karno Company next had the aforementioned twelve-week contract to fulfil, didn't agree.

Alf Reeves tried to reassure the bookers that Stan Jefferson was every bit as good as Chaplin, but they wouldn't consider this option. Stan himself related:

> As I was the understudy, Charlie had taken a lot of trouble to rehearse me in his various parts, and I fondly imagined that I should take his place. But I was doomed to disappointment. Charlie had made quite a name for himself by this time, and the managers refused to accept a substitute. Our bookings dwindled, then petered out altogether.
>
> (*Tit-Bits* – November 21, 1936)

Adding, in another interview:

> It ended up, however, with their agreeing to accept the contract if Karno would bring over from England the principal comedian from the London Karno Company named Dan Raynor.

How misguided can one be? Stan had understudied Chaplin for almost three years, whereas Dan Raynor had never even set eyes on Chaplin. The Nixon-Nirdlinger people insisted that, if they could not have Chaplin, they wanted the nearest damn thing. But then, in their naivety, they had actually turned down the nearest damn thing, which was – STANLEY JEFFERSON. Alf Reeves even made the offer for them to let Stan play the part for one week and, if he wasn't successful, they would agree to the rest of the contract being cancelled. But, mystifyingly, the agency stuck to going with Dan Raynor. So, with Jefferson being blindly ignored, Raynor was duly sent for.

Stan continued:

> We laid off three weeks waiting for him. He came, we opened, but the show was a terrible flop and, after we played a couple of weeks, the contract was cancelled and the troupe disbanded. Those who wanted to return to England were given tickets, while those who didn't want to go could stay.
>
> (*The Comedy World of Stan Laurel* – John McCabe)

Stan's usual impeccable memory has galloped way-off course here. Let us rein him back and take it a little more slowly. Following is the first set of confirmed sightings of the Karno Company playing *A Night in an English Music Hall*:

[Dec 19			Dan Raynor arrives at New York, on the *SS Lusitania*.]	
Dec 22	Pennsylvania	PHILADELPHIA, Grand	*Music Hall*	[Dan Raynor debut]
Dec 29	Pennsylvania	PHILADELPHIA, Colonial	*Music Hall*	[week 1 of 2]
1914				
Jan 05	Pennsylvania	PHILADELPHIA, Colonial	*London Club*	[week 2 of 2]
Jan 12-17	Pennsylvania	PHILADELPHIA, Keystone		
Jan 19-24	Pennsylvania	PHILADELPHIA, Broadway		
Jan 26-31	Pennsylvania	PHILADELPHIA, Alleghenny		
Feb 02-07	Pennsylvania	PHILADELPHIA, Nixon		

1914 (continued)

Feb 09	New York	NEW YORK, Hammerstein's	*Music Hall*	
Feb 16		no trace		
Feb 23	New Jersey	TRENTON,		[unconfirmed]
Mar 02	Massachusetts	BOSTON, Keith's	*Music Hall*	

In studying this date-sheet, one can immediately see that the Karno Company not only played the twelve-week contract with Nixon-Nirdlinger, but actually went beyond that (a second list will follow) — totalling twenty-one weeks in all. So Stan's claim that the show was a flop, and the troupe disbanded after a few weeks, is totally incorrect.

The reason the Karno Company clung on so valiantly, is because Chaplin's 3-year contract was to run from March 6, 1911 to March 5, 1914, and bookings had been taken that far ahead to encompass those three years. Although Chaplin had seen out the tour up till the end of the Sullivan-Considine contract, he had in actuality terminated his contract some fifteen weeks early, and now the remaining company members were having to fulfil the dates, without him. So how did the FKC fare without Monsieur Chaplin? Well, here are contemporary reviews – as opposed to hearsay and conjecture:

Pennsylvania, PHILADELPHIA, Broadway

w/c January 19, 1914

At the Broadway this week the headline act will be the Karno Komedy Kompany in "A Night in an English Music Hall," in which Alf Reeves and 14 others will appear. This act is probably the most popular one now playing in popular priced vaudeville and has been the distinct hit of the bill wherever it has been shown.

(*Philadelphia Record* — January 18, 1914)

Massachusetts, BOSTON, Keith's

In less subtle but more uproarious style was the work of the original Karno Company of English comedians in "A Night in an English Music Hall." This is by no mean new to Boston, having being presented first at the Orpheum some half a dozen or more years ago. It contains those risible-exciting characteristics of which the average vaudeville audience never tires, and it was received last night with as much enthusiasm as ever.

(March 2, 1914)

Massachusetts, BOSTON, B.F. Keith's

The other comedy features of the week are Alf Reeves' spectacular farce, "A Night in an English Music Hall," with the original Karno Comedy company of 14 singers, dancers, and fun makers.

(*Boston Sunday Post* — March 1, 1914)

So, no mention that Chaplin had left the company — even to the point of claiming it was the "original" company. Even more encouraging was that they seemed to be doing well without Chaplin. So how was Chaplin doing without them?

"Between the Showers," featuring Chaplin, the inimitable comedian who was here recently with Karno's comedians in "A Night in an English Music Hall." No one should miss this side-splitter, for Chaplin is today considered one of the cleverest silent comedians in England.

(*Winnipeg Tribune* — March 7, 1914)

A second film review, just eight days later, further told us:

Charles Chaplin, the wonderful English pantomimist, who is well-known in this country for his wonderful work in "Fred Karno's Night in an English Music Hall," has up to the present time appeared in four Keystone comedies, and by the way he has been received by both exhibitors and public, he bids fair to be the greatest and most popular comedian in comedies today.

(March 15, 1914)

Top marks to the last reviewer who, with Chaplin's film career being only four pictures in, made such an accurate prediction.

The Lull Before The Lull

THE TEXT AT LEFT (below the 'Karno Comedy Company') READS: It has moments of vaudeville, musical comedy, burlesque, farce, satire, acrobatics, extravaganza and pantomime—"A STAGE UPON A STAGE" offers unusual opportunities in a thirty minute act that is built for comedy purposes only—and its mission is solely to entertain and that this mission has been fulfilled is shown by the long engagements the company enjoyed in the big New York houses—It's a whirlwind of hilarity. One of the biggest acts ever brought to a Canton vaudeville theatre.

Why it was felt necessary to compile such a long advertising spiel is puzzling. It seems almost as if they were desperately trying to give themselves credibility, when just having the name "Fred Karno" appended to the sketch title was more than enough to provide that. Maybe since Chaplin's departure they felt they were short-changing the audiences, and so needed to convince the public that the act was still a good one. It could be they were also trying to convince themselves.

But there had been a definite change in dynamics. Chaplin's rise in the film world seemed to be inversely proportional to the decline of the Karno stage company. It was as if he were sucking the air out of their balloon, and using it to inflate his own. Thus, one was slowly rising, and the other was slowly sinking.

All the company members would be aware of Chaplin progress in the film world. The two advertising blocks, above and at right, are both from the *Canton Repository* newspaper, April 5, 1914, showing that, while the FKC was playing at week at the Lyceum Theatre, *Kid Auto Races At Venice* (Chaplin's second film, and first-ever as 'The Tramp'), was running over at the Orpheum.

Is there anyone who doubts that Messrs. Reeves, Jefferson and company would have all gone to watch it?

As for their own show:

Ohio, CANTON, Lyceum — w/c April 6, 1914

> The English music hall act, a variation on the old country varieties, gives opportunity to Dan Rayner for a [indecipherable] portrayal of an inebriated [indecipherable]. Others in the cast include Edgar Hurley, Charles Griffith, Amy Minister and Ted Banks, all are show-stopping parts. A burlesque boxing match at the close causes gales of laughter.

[Note that the review says, "boxing match," and NOT "wrestling bout."]

LAUREL – Stage by Stage

From "The Drunk" to "The Tramp"

KID AUTO RACES AT VENICE

The business Charlie does, of repeatedly walking in front of the camera, was inspired by an event which happened while the Karno Company where appearing in Jersey (Channel Islands), during the summer of 1912. (See my book: "CHAPLIN – Stage by Stage" for a full account.)

-----0-----

The booking at the Orpheum, Montreal, Canada (see below!) marked the fulfilment of the company's contract (March 14). Montreal had been where the Karno Company had first set foot in Canada, back in September 1910. It was a coincidence, but maybe they should have taken it as an omen, and quit there and then. But, still unwilling to call it a day, they began taking scratch bookings. It didn't last.

-----0-----

1914 (continued)

Mar 09-14	Quebec (Canada)	MONTREAL, Orpheum	*Music Hall*	
Mar 16		no trace		
Mar 23	New York	Mount VERNON	*Music Hall*	[unconfirmed]
Mar 30		no trace		
Apr 06	Ohio	CANTON, Lyceum	*Music Hall*	
Apr 13		no trace		
Apr 20	New York	NEW YORK, American Roof	*Music Hall*	
Apr 27		no trace		
May 04-09	New York	BUFFALO, Shea's	*Music Hall*	[date may vary]
May 04	Ontario (Canada)	TORONTO, Shea's Hippodrome		

The Karno Company officially disbands here.

o-o-0-o-o

May 14, 1914   Karno Company sail for England, aboard the *Adriatic*.

-----0-----

So, despite Stan's claims, the Karno Company did not fold, and was *not* a flop. The members had seen out the remainder of the three-year contract, and had done so while still receiving decent reviews, right up to the very end — despite losing Mr. Chaplin.

It must have been a very sad parting for all troupe members. Around half of them had been together, seven days a week, since the beginning of the 1910 tour — some even during the earlier British Music Hall tours. Even most of the current bunch had been together around nineteen months, so there would have been a lot of bonding during those times, and much sadness now it had all ended and they were about to go their separate ways.

So what now? Well, those who wanted to return to Blighty were given return passage aboard the *Adriatic*, which sailed from New York Harbor on May 14, 1914.

Seeing no advantage in returning to England, Stan decided to stay on and make a go of it. This time, he hadn't chosen to leave, but he was still in the same predicament he had been in 1911 when he first left the Karno Company: i.e. no act, no bookings, and no management. And, if he did go back to England, instead of being engaged to tramp around the British music halls, he might well find his first engagement was tramping around the trenches, in France – where audiences were *really* hostile.

It isn't fair for me to say that Stan's reason for remaining in America was to avoid enlistment. In fact, he did later apply to join up, but was turned down on medical grounds. At this moment in time, though, he still wanted to continue his career in comedy. Like a footballer who has been dropped after spending several years with the best team in the top league, it didn't mean he had to quit the game. He still had lots to offer, and could still remain in the top league, with another team.

The young Jefferson's chances of forming a sketch company – which was his true forte, as opposed to becoming a solo comedian – were improved when other members of the Karno Company also chose to remain in America. So those of you who have read other accounts will know what happened next: Stan formed "The Three Comiques," then changed the name to "The Keystone Trio;" which he left, and formed "The Stan Jefferson Trio;" before meeting Mae Dahlberg in 1917, whom he toured with until 1922 as 'Stan & Mae Laurel.' Right? WRONG. That is a list of only half of the number of acts Stan was in. Plus, there are many more surprises along the way. For starters, try this one — a disclosure Stan made in the February 17, 1933 issue of *Film Weekly*:

> After Charlie had the left the Karno Company, and the members had disbanded, I hitch-hiked across the United States to claim a job in a small stock company playing British Columbia, where Boris Karloff was the leading man. He played a clergyman then—not a 'Frankenstein.'

By-passing the fact that Karloff's role was that of 'the monster' and not Frankenstein (who is the scientist), I did some in-depth investigation into this story of this hitherto overlooked tit-bit, but nowhere could I make the piece fit the puzzle in its correct chronological place. I even tried fitting the piece into the 1911 episode, when Stan first left the Karno Company, but nowhere could I place Stan and Karloff in the same place at the same time. Even two fellow researchers — one who specialises in Karloff's days in rep' in Vancouver, and the other who wrote a biography on Karloff — could not make the connection. So, the details of the whole episode will have to remain a mystery.

Karloff has signed this, and dated it 1914.

However, there are still many other previously unknown meetings, and partnerships, for which the answers *will* be supplied. Read on!

CHAPTER 15

WHERE DID HE WENT?

Other known members of the disbanded Karno Company staying on in America were Ted Banks, Billy Crackles, Edgar Hurley, and Ethel Hurley. Stan chose to form a trio with the Hurleys. Knowing well in advance that the Karno tour was about to end, Stan and the Hurleys would have been rehearsing their act weeks before, so that, when the break-off happened, they were ready to hit the ground running. Stan cited Chicago as where they made their debut. Confirmation has not been found but, as their last appearance with the Karno Company was on Saturday May 9, 1914, then the process of elimination puts it during week commencing Monday May 11 – although that isn't to say they did a full week there. This photo backs up the trio's presence in Chicago, as the original bears the photographer's studio logo "Celebrity, Chicago," but it is most likely from a later visit (not found).

Flossie – the Maid (Ethel Hurley); Tom – the Burglar (Stan Jefferson); Simple – his Accomplice (Edgar Hurley)

Just why they chose Chicago is hard to figure when, from Buffalo, New York [or Toronto, Ontario], where they parted from the FKC, they could have so easily made for New York, or Philadelphia, where bookings had been plentiful during the Karno tours. True, Chicago did have a decent number of vaudeville theatres at which to tout for bookings, but even the Karno Company, with all its fame and track record, had played there only once since November 1912 — so what hopes did an unknown bunch of wannabees hold?

My first thought would have been for "The Trio" to travel to New York with the Karno members who were going home, and then make appointments to negotiate work with the agents who had booked the Karno tours. Surely Alf Reeves could have introduced them to the agents who could give them the theatre work they so desperately needed. Failing that, they could always wear out a bit of shoe-leather, visiting all the New York theatres they had played whilst in the Karno Company, and maybe start with the line: "*Remember us? We have our own sketch show now. Any chance of a booking?*" But even this 'long shortcut' wasn't adopted. So, as was a regular trait with Jefferson Jnr., he did things the hard way, and started taking 'scratch' bookings — i.e. starting from scratch, and trying to build up a full book of engagements from nothing. The downside of this is that anyone doing so would not get booked into a chain of theatres controlled by one agency. As well as losing out on the security of advance multiple bookings, they would also lose out on playing venues which had been planned in a feasible geographical order. This left 'The Trio' having to take single bookings, and having to travel ridiculously long distances, in a zig-zag, criss-crossing fashion, to fulfil them.

So, Stan and the Hurleys set out to make a living in vaudeville, armed with only their talent. In the first eight months they must have scratched out a living well-off the main theatre circuit, and played what was referred to as 'the smalls,' as Big Foot has had more reported sightings than they have.

You may have noted that I have, as yet, omitted the name of Stan's trio. After you have studied the following date-sheet and reviews, you will understand why.

-----0-----

STAN JEFFERSON SOLO TOURS

1914 (continued)

Date	State	City, Theatre	Act	Billing
May 09		last appearance with the Karno Company		
May 11	Illinois	CHICAGO		[unconfirmed]
May 18-20		no trace		
May 21-23	Manitoba	WINNIPEG, Columbia		Three English Comiques
May 25	Manitoba	BRANDON, Sherman		Three English Comiques
Jun 01				
Jun 08				
Jun 15-20	Missouri	KANSAS CITY, Hippodrome	Breaking In	Stan Jefferson and Company
Jun 22				
Jun 29				
Jul 02-04	South Dakota	SIOUX FALLS, Majestic		Stan Jefferson and Company
Jul 06				
Jul 13				
Jul 19-22	Iowa	DES MOINES, Empress	The Nutty Burglars	Three English Comiques
Jul 23				
Jul 27				
Aug 03				
Aug 10				
Aug 17				
Aug 24	Missouri	ST. LOUIS, Hippodrome	The Burglars	Jefferson Hurley Wren
Aug 31				
Sep 07				
Sep 14				
Sep 21				
Sep 28				

-----0-----

Note that 'The Three Comiques' were also billed as: "The Three English Comiques" – "Stan Jefferson and Company" – "Stan Jefferson Troupe" – "Stan-Jefferson Trio – "Stan Jefferson, assisted by Edgar Hurley and Ethel Wren" – "Jefferson, Hurley & Wren" – and "Stan Jefferson, Edgar Hurley and Ethel Wren."

RIGHT: Review from: Sioux Fall Argus Leader July 3, 1914

Majestic.

Acrobatics, comedy and music make up the bill at the Majestic for the remainder of the week. The headline attraction is the Stan Jefferson company, billed as novelty knockabout acrobats, in an act combining the usual comedy with soft shoe dancing. The two gentlemen of the company appear in the role of burglars and their entire act is a sort of burlesque on housebreaking. In the course of their "job" they bring in comic talk and antics and do a turn at dancing. The scene is laid just outside a house, the window of which is their object of attack.

[AJM: Just to say that Ethel, being billed as "Wren," might well have been using the surname "Hurley" in real life as a name of convenience, in order to be allowed to book into accommodation with Edgar. For unmarried couples to co-habit was not only considered unethical, but was actually unlawful. These laws, aimed to prevent unmarried couples from registering in hotels and other places of accommodation, were in force in the USA right up to the 1960s. In fact, as of June 2016, cohabitation of unmarried couples remains illegal in three states – Mississippi, Michigan, and North Carolina.]

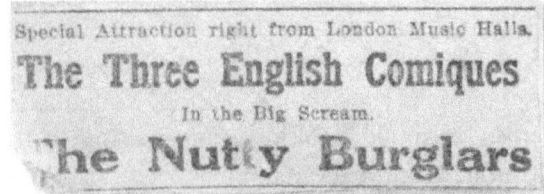

Manitoba, WINNIPEG, Columbia

(Preview) The new show which opens at the Columbia today [May 21st] includes the Three English Comiques, acrobatic marvels.

---o---

(Review 1) Laughter is the sole essence of the offering of the Three English Comiques at the Columbia's new show, which opened the last half of the week yesterday. This trio are from the famous Karno's London Comedians—so they need no further recommendation. There are three other first-class vaudeville acts, as well as first-run motion pictures and the Keystone.

(*Winnipeg Tribune* — May 22, 1914)

---o---

(Review 2) The class of acts being secured by the Columbia theatre is indicated by today's headliner—the Three English Comiques, a trio of the most talented members of Karno's famous London Comedians, who have toured America several times, gaining in popularity on each tour.

(*Winnipeg Tribune* — May 23, 1914)

-----o-----

Missouri, KANSAS CITY, Hippodrome

(Preview) Stan Jefferson Troupe, novelty English knockabout singers and dancers.

(*Kansas City Star* — June 13, 1914)

(Review) Stan Jefferson and Company, the Montgomery & Stone of London, are two of the funniest English comedians on the stage. They have a good act and can slide their feet around for the goods.

-----o-----

Iowa, DES MOINES, Empress

(Preview) The three English Comiques in a burlesque absurdity, billed as "the nutty burglars."

(*Des Moines Register* — July 19, 1914)

-----o-----

Missouri, ST. LOUIS, Hippodrome

Jefferson, Hurley and Wren are excellent fun makers.

(*Variety* — August 24, 1914)

---o---

Jefferson, Hurley and Wren, in the comedy sketch, The Burglars. The English trio produce some clever comedy. It was a hard spot for a foreign act. It pleased. Full stage, fifteen minutes, one call.

(St. Louis — August 24, 1914)

TALBOT'S HIPPODROME – Kansas City, Missouri

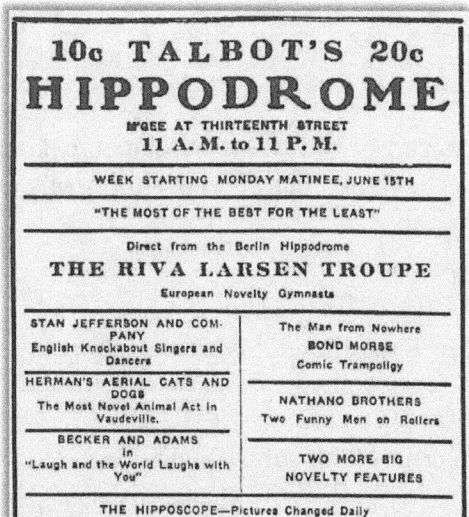

By "DOC BIRD" FINCH.

In accord with the retail merchants, Frank Talbot on "Dollar Day" has grouped a bunch of cracker-jack acts and is really giving a dollar show for a dime. Stan Jefferson and Company, the Montgomery & Stone of London, are two of the funniest English comedians on the stage. They have a good act and can slide their feet around for the goods.

-----0-----

STAN. JEFFERSON & CO.
(LATE - FRED - KARNO'S - KOMEDY - KO.)
PRESENT AN ORIGINAL BURLESQUE ABSURDITY ENTITLED
"BREAKING IN"
ASSISTED BY
EDGAR HURLEY & ETHEL WREN
SPECIAL SCENERY AND PROPERTIES
FIFTEEN MINUTES NOVELTY FUNSTORM

A well balanced bill of novelties holds the boards at the Hippodrome this week. The headline attraction is an aggregation of slapstick artists, Stan. Jefferson, Edgar Hurley and Ethel Wren of the late Fred Karno's comedians. Their absurdity, "Breaking In," affords opportunities for a good deal of rough fun, comic boxing and soft shoe dancing. It is an English company and good in its line.

HIPPODROME IS SHOWING CLEVER BILL THIS WEEK

An English company headlines a well balanced bill at the Hippodrome this week. Jefferson Hurley and Wren of the late Karo's comedians, in their comedy skit, "Breaking In," stage a continual round of good entertainment. They pull a lot of good comedy, do some comic boxing and are artists with soft shoe dancing. Trapeze and bal-

-----0-----

Unidentified clippings from the Stan Laurel Scrapbook:

this week is one of originalities. The first on the list in this order perhaps are the Three English Comiques. These three burlesque artists were formerly members of the Fred Karno "Night in a London musical hall" company, which disbanded in America a month ago after three seasons. Three of the members devised this little sketch, "The Nutty Burglars." They have been a success, and a career in big-time vaudeville is assuredly before them. Second on the bill is M

It is a treat to see three English comedians of the type of the Three English Comiques, who are the headline act at the Sherman this week. The three members of this little company were formerly members of Fred Karno's English London company, who have presented "A Night in a London Music Hall," which has been presented to vaudeville audiences all over the world. The sketch to know as "The Nutty Burglars," which is a burlesque on two members of that profession who are engaged in a house breaking expedition.

singing comedienne and the big laugh provoking act, Stan Jefferson and company, the "three English Comiques," in a singing and dancing knockout acrobatic act that will sure 'nough drive the "blues" and "dull care" to the "four winds." The pictures con-

three English comiques, late of Fred Karno's English companies, present a new and novel offering entitled "The Nutty Burglars," this act is full of laughs from start to finish, and was repeatedly encored. The pictures

As for the sketch, it was billed under four different titles: *The Nutty Burglars*, *The Natty Burglars*, simply *The Burglars*, and *Breaking In*. When I first saw the latter sketch billed as "*Breaking In*" I thought the title must have had originated from a

> No. 1—Jefferson, Hurley and Wren, in the comedy sketch, The Burglars. The English trio produce some clever comedy. It was a hard spot for a foreign act. It pleased. Full stage, fifteen minutes, one call.

lazy reviewer, who had read the press-notes, seen that the sketch was about some burglars breaking in, and then used the phrase in his newspaper preview and review. Imagine, therefore, my surprise when I found this, in Laurel's scrapbook:

> Missouri, KANSAS CITY, Hippodrome
> HIPPODROME IS SHOWING CLEVER BILL THIS WEEK
>
> An English company headlines a well-balanced bill at the Hippodrome this week. Jefferson Hurley and Wren of the late Karno's comedians, in their stage comedy skit, "Breaking In," stage a continual round of good entertainment.
>
> They pull a lot of comedy, do some comic boxing and are artists with soft shoe dancing.
>
> (Laurel scrapbook)

A second review ran:

> A well-balanced bill of novelties holds the boards at the Hippodrome this week. The headline attraction is an aggregation of slapstick artists, Stan Jefferson, Edgar Hurley and Ethel Wren of the late Karno's comedians. Their absurdity, "Breaking In," affords opportunities for a good deal of rough fun, comic boxing and soft shoe dancing. It is an English company and good in its line.

Along with the various names of both the act and the sketch, we also get varying descriptions of the actual business the three of them performed on stage. These include:

> acrobatic marvels – novelty English knockabout singers and dancers – a lot of comedy – do some comic boxing and are artists with soft shoe dancing – a good deal of rough fun, comic boxing and soft shoe dancing – a good act and can slide their feet around for the goods – a farce in which a number of clever performers show their art in a masterly manner – their grotesque eccentricities are fast and furious – a singing and dancing knockabout acrobatic act – comedy knockabout acrobats.

So we have all those descriptions, and yet we still don't fully know what the Trio did in their act. The comic boxing may well have been a reprise of the ending of *A Night in an English Music Hall*, wherein the 'drunk' fights the "The Terrible Turkey." Both Chaplin and Laurel went on to do comic boxing scenes in one of their films, which makes me suspect even more strongly that its origins are from the "Music Hall" sketch. It may also indicate that the wrestling match had been part-wrestling-part boxing, and that, over time the wrestling had been faded out, and the boxing aspect expanded.

Stan must have to come to realise that, unless they stuck to keeping just one name for the act, they would never become known. As for the on-stage business in the act itself, that too would need some attention. You can't go on stage and perform a succession of skills without structure. Nor, for instance, can a comedian just repeatedly fall over for no reason. There has to be an object or situation which makes him fall – hence the popularity of introducing a banana skin into the mix. Likewise, you can't just burst into song; nor have people walking on and off stage without a reason. What was needed was more "act" and less "action," and so this is when *The Nutty Burglars* was brought in.

Now, with a story and plotline they had a vehicle into which they could splice their own individual *and* joint stage talents. The sketch would also help to define each of them in their character roles. For an act to become successful audience members must recognise the character(s) and his/their mannerisms, and take the memory with them when they leave the theatre. Chaplin's 'drunk' is the perfect example. And if you feel that structuring the act would subdue the energy and freneticism, then just familiarise yourself with the Marx Brothers' stage sketches — *Fun in Hi Skool*, and *Mr. Green's Reception* — which are the definition of "mayhem." They also served to define the characters we came to recognise in the Marx Brothers' films.

So, let us have an objective look at *The Nutty Burglars* sketch.

"THE NUTTY BURGLARS"

Cast of characters

Tom, A Burglar

Simple, His Accomplice

Flossie, A Maid.

SCENE: Interior. Drawing-room or library.

(Curtain up slowly, girl discovered on settee reading. Clock strikes two. Girl turns lamp out and then exits)
(Black out and Tom enters) (Business)

(Tom Whistles, noise off)

Tom; Why don't you lift your big feet up?

(Enter Simple and both walk down stage for song)

Tom; Don't forget what I told you.

Simple: What's that?

Tom: If anybody catches us, tell them that we're the ice-men.

Simple. I see, ask them if they want any ice.

Tom: That's the idea. Now, here you are; sort these tools out.

Simple. Alright Horace.

Tom: No, don't call me Horace.

(Simple goes down by settee and drops tools out of bag)

Tom: Sh, sh, sh, sh.

Simple. (Business of running around like engine)

Tom: What are you doing?

Simple. I thought we were playing trains.

Tom. Ugh, come on, give me the hammer.

Simple: (Throws hammer over to safe)

Tom: Don't throw it, chuck it!

(Bus. of hammering loud. Simple sits on settee, looks round then gets up and treads on tray; falls.)

So, with their act still in a formative state, The Three Comiques continued to try to find work, but seemed to have as much luck as I did, in trying to find *them*:

1914 (continued)

Oct 05			
Oct 12			
Oct 19			
Oct 26			
Nov 02	Michigan	DETROIT, Palace	Three English Comiques
Nov 09			
Nov 16			
Nov 23			
Nov 30			
Dec 07			
Dec 14			
Dec 21			

-----0-----

I did say that the "Comiques" were armed only with their talent, while a more general term states that "Talent will out" – which I would translate as: "If you have talent, it will be discovered sooner or later." Happily, for Stan and the Hurleys, it was to be "sooner." 'Kalma the Great' – a magician they shared the bill with at one venue (believed to be in Cleveland) – thought the Trio deserved representation, and made an introduction for them to his management company, Claude W. Bostock.

Bostock operated from Room 305, Putnam Building, Times Square, New York, under the title: "Manager of Vaudeville Acts" — assisted by his brother Gordon, who was listed as "Representative." Stan did not know it at the time, but the Bostocks were to be as important to him during his vaudeville days, as Hal Roach was to be in his later film years. Management/representation was exactly what Stan needed. Now he wouldn't have to endlessly tout for work at individual theatres, or through individual booking agencies, as it was Bostock's job as his manager to do everything to keep him in work. Bostock was also able to negotiate the best work, in the best theatres, at the best fees — whereas, left to his own devices, Stan would have been forced to accept terrible jobs, in terrible venues, at terrible prices. The see-saw could not have tipped more markedly in his favour.

One of the first things the Bostocks did was to revamp the act. They would have known instinctively that the act was all over the place, and so needed to be brought into focus. The Bostocks also felt that the act would attract more interest, and be more memorable, by piggy-backing off the name of the most popular brand of film comedies then in circulation – the Keystone Comedies – which were shown not only in cinemas, but also shared the bill with live acts. Stan was well aware of the Keystone Comedies, and might possibly have been influenced by this one:

> Keystone had a near tragedy, in the making of the three-reel special, "Baffles, the Gentleman Burglar." The Keystone police force were pursuing Baffles over the roofs of ten and twelve story buildings. One of the cops, just as he was about to shoot, slipped on the edge of the roof, and for a moment it appeared as though he were going over.
>
> (January 6, 1914)

But now, Stan & Co.'s act was to take more than the seed of an idea from Keystone, by riding on the enormous wave of excitement being generated by the stratospheric rise to fame of their newest comedian — Chaplin. To reinforce their previous association with Charlie, and to make it clear to audiences that the Keystone Trio could perform the Keystone brand of comedy equally well, Bostock had Stan mimic the Chaplin film character; Hurley was to mimic one of Chaplin's more-regular co-stars, Chester Conklin; while Ethel was moulded into the Mabel Normand style of character.

In this comment made during an interview for a 1940 *Picture Show* article, Stan was revealed to have been blissfully unaware of the lack of ethics in this out-and-out steal of the characters from the Chaplin films:

Where Did He Went?

> If imitation be the sincerest form of flattery then I surely proved to Charlie the depth of my admiration in my vaudeville take-offs of his clowning pantomime. Since I had played with him for so long a time, and since, as his understudy, I had learned to copy every trick of his movements and speech, I found it easy. Charlie admitted that I made a pretty good job of it.

With the inconsistences of both the on-stage business and the name of the act ironed out, Bostock now needed to be one hundred per cent confident that Messrs. Jefferson and Hurley, and Ms. Wren, could consistently score at each and every venue he put them into. The big prize, if the act was deemed good enough, was an immediate forty-weeks' work, mainly in New York, with the odd out-of-town visits to the surrounding states of Pennsylvania, Ohio, Massachusetts, and New Jersey. If the trio failed to score heavily at their first few shows, the potential forty weeks of work would not even get into double figures, and they might well find themselves back to having to find their own bookings.

The first known engagement of The Keystone Trio was in Jersey City – away from the fierce glare of the New York critics. Next test was in Harlem which, although it is a suburb of New York City, was a well-known 'try-out' venue. By a strange coincidence, Harlem had been where the Karno Company too had played the second week of their debut tour – back in 1910. Then, Stan had played the Alhambra, whereas this time around he was going into the Opera House. This was a crucial week, as the Trio *were* within range of the New York critics. So how would they fare? Well, based on this one review by a critic from one of the trade papers – not too well:

HARLEM OPERA HOUSE

Neither "In Old Tyrol" nor Hurley, Stan and Wren lived up to being "in the lights" out front. An English trio, Hurley, Stan and Wren, two men and a woman, offered mediocre fun in a "noisy burglar" comedy turn. One of the men works as a tough character, while the comedian is made up to resemble the picture comedian Charlie Chaplin. The latter did some good falls and tumbles, and was the life of a "well done" idea, which they finish with a burlesque boxing bit. The little woman goes on and off a few times, and stays a while for some comic "love" business on a couch with the comedian.

(January 28, 1915)

-----0-----

The Bostocks were big enough and experienced enough to know that the word of one critic, describing the reaction of one audience, on one night, was not a deal-breaker, and so the planned trial period continued. Meanwhile note the reference in the last two reviews, to Stan being made up to resemble Chaplin.

Next stage was a showcase, the kind to which managers traditionally invite agents, theatre managers, and other management companies to come and watch their acts, with a view to getting bookings for them. The Bostock's showcase was at the Colombia Theatre, New York – for which one of the critics from the trade paper *Variety* opined:

Sunday January 31, 1915 – Keystone Trio – Comedy Sketch – 14 Mins: – Full Stage
(Parlor)

Depending on a skit that Harry Weldon is doing in England, a Charlie Chaplin make-up and their own slapstick capabilities these two men and a woman have fixed up a desirable rough comedy sketch. It deals mostly with burglars. The main idea is the part obtained from Weldon. The funniest fellow wears the Chaplin make-up and is entitled to do so, for the three in this act were formerly members of a Fred Karno organization which toured America. Nothing is forgotten in the rough material and the three get all that could be gotten out of it. The act proved a big hit at the Columbia Sunday.

-----0-----

This is a review from a critic who is trying desperately to impress his readers by telling them an insider secret, which only someone as clever and influential as he could possibly have been privy to. In this case his "secret" is that the sketch is: "Depending on a skit that Harry Weldon is doing in England" — but what utter nonsense that claim is. All three performers had been touring the USA for the last twenty months, so how could their act possible be dependent upon an act being performed by a comedian over in England? Harry Weldon was an extremely well-known former Karno Comedian but, even when Stan was touring Britain with various Karno Companies, he never worked with the guy, as Weldon had left Karno's employ before he joined. Chaplin had done three tours with Weldon, in *The Football Match*, which, it will not surprise you, had nothing to do with burglars. The sketch Stan had devised for the Trio was almost certainly a version of *An Unwilling Burglar* – a sketch he and his father had written back in 1908, so he can hardly be charged with plagiarism. At least the critic did give credit where credit was due, in acknowledging that the act was a big hit. Stan Laurel himself was still full of pride over their performance some forty-plus years later, when (so John McCabe informs us) he exclaimed: "*If I have to say it myself, we were a bloody sensation.*"

McCabe goes on to say that the Showcase clinched for them a booking on the Orpheum circuit, which is incorrect. When acts got onto this circuit, they were indeed in the 'Big Time' – with a guaranteed thirty-weeks' work, or more. Although the Orpheum represented theatres in over twenty US states, plus theatres in the bordering Canadian States, their sole New York City theatre was the Palace; whereas the main crop of venues Hurley, Stan & Wren were to play were in New York and New Jersey – at the Proctor's and the B.F. Keith's theatres. Others venues were booked through smaller agencies, such as Sun.

So, with all those concerned with the business side having full confidence that they had a 'sensational act' on the hands, it was time for a major launch — well almost, but first, one more tweak needed to be made. For the first two shows under the Bostocks' management, the Trio had somehow kept their old billing of "Hurley, Stan and Wren," even after the agreement had been for them to go out as "The Keystone Trio" — a point of order Gordon Bostock had to raise with them for immediate future billings:

February 10th 1915

Keystone Trio
Colonial Theatre.
Akron, Ohio

Dear Friends:-

Replying to your wire received this morning [would] say, I have just wired you as follows: "CRATE BEING SHIPPED AKRON YOU WORK UNDER NAME KEYSTONE TRIO " You evidently didn't understand what I mean when I tell you [that] you are booked under another name. The thing is:- your contract is made out in another name so that the booking office [books will] not show the Keystone Trio working for $200.00.

Pleased to hear you did well in Youngstown. Keep up the good work. Enclosed please find card, from which you will see that you play Johnstown, Pa. first half next week, and Altoona , Pa. last half.

Regarding the forty weeks blanket contract you were offered would say, that this was offered to me [by] Loew people, but they cannot see paying you [mor xxxxt] . They are talking about $150.00 and $175.00 week [xxx0.00] top money for the S. & C. time. Forget it.

With best wishes to you all, I remain.

Most sincerely,

Gordon Bostock

o-0-o

CROWN STUDIO
BRIDGEPORT
Connecticut

Note the change from Stan's 'burglar' costume in the earlier publicity shot of 'Jefferson, Hurley & Wren' (first page of this chapter) to this one in 'The Keystone Trio.'

Everything was now in place — revamped sketch; new characters, new name, publicity lined up, and the actors having thoroughly tried out, tested, and polished the act in front of representative audiences. But Bostock was still, I feel, reticent about bringing them into New York. In his letter, where he says: "*Keep up the good work*," there seems to be an unwritten proviso something like: "*Keep up the good work, keep rehearsing and, if the reviews continue to be good, we'll bring you into New York real soon.*"

The good news though is that Bostock *was* about to give The Keystone Trio a decent publicity launch, but there would be another two months of breaking in the act in nearby states before being offered the Big Apple.

CHAPTER 16

TOO GOOD TO BE TRUE

For the launch of his new act, Bostock emblazoned "The Keystone Trio" in a banner headline in the New Brunswick newspapers, so that the name would register with, and be remembered by, the public. It would also serve to remind Jefferson, Hurley & Wren what their new name was. Stan was so thrilled with the banner headline, that he cut it out, and pasted it into his scrapbook.

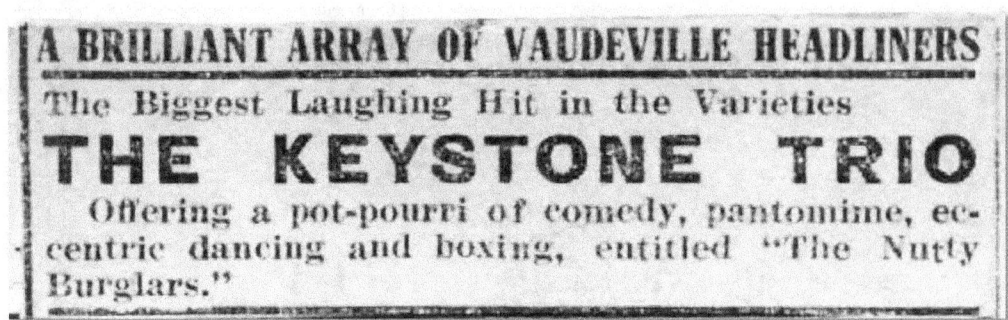

Question is now: "Would he want to keep the reviews?" But first, the preview:

GOOD VAUDEVILE BILL AT THE OPERA HOUSE

Vaudeville that will make the city forget the weather will be presented at the Opera House tonight, when a gladsome array of the most brilliant offerings of variety will give an entertainment unexcelled in New Brunswick's experience.

The outstanding stellar attraction will be The Keystone trio, the Biggest laughing hit in the vaudeville world, in a pot-pourri of comedy, pantomime, eccentric dancing and boxing, comical songs and more comical patter. Their act is entitled "The Nutty Burglar," and is built around a screamingly ludicrous plot.

(January 1, 1915)

-----0-----

Well that's a great preview, with some tremendous accreditations, such as: "most brilliant," "entertainment unexcelled," and "the Biggest laughing hit in the vaudeville world" — but then it ought to be, as previews were seldom custom-written by newspaper reviewers, but were simply the circulars of press and publicity notes which the management of the acts would send in beforehand, and from which the newspaper's theatre critic would then select which phrases to use.

Let us hope that the build-up Bostock had given the Keystones wasn't too big for them to follow. This review will tell us:

GOOD CROWDS SEE GOOD SHOW AT THE OPERA HOUSE

The Keystone Trio made a tremendous hit in their skit, "The Nutty Burglar," an English farcical comedy that is as funny a thing as ever came over the water. They say the English haven't a sense of humor. These capable people puncture that belief. They are comical in word and deed, with a lot of new "stuff" that is different and good. Songs, pantomime, excruciatingly funny boxing, eccentric dancing, and a ludicrous run of dialogue—on these they make their bid for popularity, and win out.

(January 2, 1915)

-----0-----

Good to know the KT were well-received, but wouldn't we all like to know who says: "the English haven't a sense of humor"? The Karno Company had been "killing 'em" in America for a decade, not to mention numerous other English acts who were "rolling them in the aisles."

So here is Stan's date-sheet under Bostock's management, so far:

Too Good to Be True

THE KEYSTONE TRIO in "The Nutty Burglars"

(aka: "The Nutty Burglar" and "The Noisy Burglar")

Dec 30	Pennsylvania	PHILADELPHIA, Cross Keys		['Keystone Comedy Four' – may not be Stan]
1915				
Jan 04		no trace		
Jan 11		no trace		
Jan 18		no trace		
Jan 25-27	New Jersey	JERSEY CITY, B.F. Keith's		Hurley, Stan & Wren
Jan 28	New York	HARLEM, Opera House	*Noisy Burglar*	Hurley, Stan & Wren
Jan 31	New York	NEW YORK CITY, Columbia		(one-night only Showcase)
Feb 01-03	New Jersey	NEW BRUNSWICK, Opera House		[the launch]

Following the successful launch, and good management skills from the Bostocks, multiple bookings on the East Coast were rapidly secured – the majority with the Proctor's, Poli's, and Keith's theatres. Now all that Messrs. Jefferson and Hurley and Ms. Wren needed to do was to make sure not to get them pulled out. Before we find out how they did, let us see exactly what they were *claiming* to do:

Pennsylvania, ALTOONA, Orpheum

(PREVIEW) The attraction uppermost among those that are to be shown will be The Keystone Trio, one of the cleverest funmaking organizations that recently has come to light. This trio, Hurley, Stan, & Wren by name, were formerly of the Karno Comedy company, the most famous laughing offering that ever the British sent to this country. They are travesty artists that have the art of burlesquing others down to a science and can easily give "cards and spades" to any of their competitors. In their present stunt they burlesque that famous film comedian, Charles Chaplin, the grotesque comique that brought the Keystone movies the public's highest regard. The number is claimed to be one of the funniest satires on filmdom that has ever been devised, therefore, if you want to be happy, you should make it your business to witness this one.

(*Altoona Tribune* – Thursday February 18, 1915)

Now let us see if they lived up to that claim:

Pennsylvania, ALTOONA, Orpheum

(REVIEW) The Keystone Trio comedians offer a bit of fast comedy quite unlike anything offered in this season. One of the trio depicts Charles Chaplin, the famous Essanay motion picture comedian, and his characterization of this peerless funmaker is excellent. He has mastered all the little jerks and motions that are peculiar to Chaplin and his walk reminds one so much of Chaplin in the pictures that one is never quite sure whether he is watching a motion picture or a comedy sketch.

(*Altoona Tribune* – Friday February 19, 1915)

-----0-----

This last review seems to be complimentary, but doesn't really answer the question: "Were they funny? Maybe this next one will tell us:

Pennsylvania, ALLENTOWN, Orpheum

The Keystone Trio are two men and a woman who do a real "nutty" act, and are true to their billing "Funnier than Keystone pictures." As the laugh provokers they make good every minute they are upon the stage.

(*Allentown Democrat* Tuesday February 23, 1915)

-----0-----

Pennsylvania, WILKES-BARRE, Poli's

The Keystone Trio, three real nuts in a nutty farce comedy entitled, "The Nutty Burglars," are positively the funniest ever, and furnish more laughs than any other trio ever before here.

(Wilkes Barre — March 9, 1915)

Now all we need to know is just how funny the Keystone pictures are.

LAUREL – Stage by Stage

It is ironic that, just two weeks before Stan, Hurley & Wren debuted as Chaplin, Conklin, and Mabel Normand, Charlie himself had left Keystone and signed for Essanay — meaning that The Keystone Trio were out of date before they had even started.

-----0-----

Feb 04-06	New Jersey	BAYONNE, Opera House
Feb 07	Ohio	YOUNGSTOWN,
Feb 11-13	Ohio	AKRON, Colonial
Feb 15-17	Pennsylvania	JOHNSTOWN,
Feb 18-20	Pennsylvania	ALTOONA, Orpheum
Feb 22-24	Pennsylvania	ALLENTOWN, Orpheum
Feb 25-27	Ohio	EAST LIVERPOOL, American
Mar 01-03	New Jersey	JERSEY CITY, Hudson
Mar 04-06	Pennsylvania	PITTSBURGH, Kenyon Street
Mar 08-10	Pennsylvania	WILKES-BARRE, Polis
Mar 11-13	Pennsylvania	WILLIAMSPORT, Family
Mar 15-17	Connecticut	BRIDGEPORT, Plaza

Crown Studio, Bridgeport.
Question is:
"Who is Stan turning his back on?"

-----0-----

Pennsylvania, WILLIAMSPORT, Family

Many of the city's most prominent citizens who have seen the show playing at the Family theatre this last half of the week have expressed their opinion that this is the best vaudeville show this season. Featured by a juvenile musical melange of six lively youngsters, a most refined diversion is offered. The Keystone Trio, in an acrobatic comedy sketch called the "Nutty Burglar," are a scream of laughs throughout.

(Williamsport — March 13, 1915)

-----0-----

Mar 18-20	Connecticut	NEW HAVEN, Bijou	
Mar 22-24	Connecticut	WATERBURY, Poli's	
Mar 25-27	Massachusetts	SPRINGFIELD, Poli's	
Mar 29-31	New York	NEW YORK CITY, 125th Street	
Apr 01-03	New York	NEW YORK CITY, Mount Vernon	
Apr 05-07	New York	AUBURN, Jefferson	Stanley, Hurley and Wren
Apr 08-10	New York	ITHICA, Star	

-----0-----

New York, ITHACA, Star Theatre

That Charles Chaplin is one of the most popular and evidently the funniest man of the movie screen is evidenced by his large number of imitators in vaudeville. "The Nutty Burglar" in The Keystone Trio, playing a three-day engagement at the Star Theatre, is one of the cleverest imitations ever seen in Ithaca, and his awkward antics are the source of much merriment and amusement to the audience.

(Ithica, New York — April 10, 1915)

Apr 12-13	New York	TROY, Proctor's New
Apr 15-17	New York	ALBANY, Proctor's Grand

-----0-----

New York, ALBANY, Proctor's Grand

It is one big laugh after another at Proctor's Grand. Charles Chaplin in one of his funniest roles in the photo-comedy, entitled "The Champion," keeps them in one big scream. Others on the bill are: The Keystone Trio, consisting of the well-known English stars, Messrs. Hurley and Jefferson, assisted by Miss Wren. They present a laugh absurdity, entitled "The Nutty Burglars." Mr. Jefferson impersonates Charlie Chaplin to the letter.

(Albany, New York — April 16, 1915)

Too Good to Be True

This bill shows you how good Stan had to be as a Chaplin impersonator, as he was having to perform 'live' whilst being compared to the real Chaplin on-screen, with all the film tricks, props, supporting company and scenery he had in his arsenal.

Good to note that, Messrs. Hurley and Jefferson, assisted by Miss Wren are now classed as "well-known" — especially when one considers they had barely appeared under that name. Do you think the reviewer was being kind?

 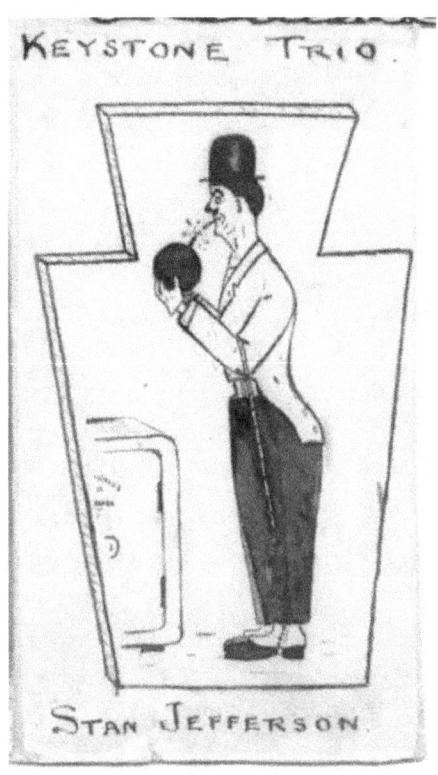

These two cartoons depict Stan in scenes from *The Nutty Burglars* sketch. The speech in the left-hand one reads: "ARE YER ASLEEP." While on the right we see Stan lighting a bomb with his cigarette, in preparation for blowing the safe. [Whether Stan himself drew these, and other similar cartoons found in his scrapbook, I am unable to establish.]

Thanks to a passage about the plot of *The Nutty Burglars*, in the book "Mr. Laurel & Mr. Hardy," I can now offer an edited synopsis of some of the business involved:

> The two burglars enter an apartment, with the intent of robbing it. While they are attempting to break into the safe, they are interrupted by a maid. They hastily come up with the story that they are icemen [i.e. delivering blocks of ice], an explanation which she falls for.
>
> One of the burglars flirts with her, while the other continues to try and crack the safe. Frustrated at the lack of impact from a hammer and chisel, he resorts to using a hand bomb. He lights the fuse but then, in a panic at what to do next, passes the bomb to the other burglar. This starts a pass-the-parcel-type game between all three occupants, but with the "parcel" being the bomb. Realising the bomb could explode any second, one of them throws it out of the window. There is the sound of an explosion, off-stage, immediately followed by the entrance of a cop, dressed in a shredded uniform, and with blackened face and sticking up hair.

-----0-----

New York, NEW YORK CITY, Fifth Avenue

The Keystone Trio of English comics have a likely [*sic*] skit composed of three characters, one essaying a Chaplin role. The material is bright and the speed of the vehicle kept the laughs running in rapid order. They were followed by the Essanay release showing Chaplin in "The Tramp."

(*Variety* — April 23, 1915)

LAUREL – Stage by Stage

An assortment of newspaper cuttings, from the Stan Laurel scrapbook, containing reviews for:

THE KEYSTONE TRIO in "The Nutty Burglars"

The Keystone Trio, consisting of the well known English stars, Messrs. Hurley and Jefferson, assisted by Miss Wren, and presenting a laugh absurdity entitled "The Nutty Burglars." Mr. Jefferson gives a clever impersonation of Charles Chaplin, the funniest man in the picture world today.

The Keystone Trio of English comics have a likely skit composed of three characterists, one essaying a Chaplin role. The material is bright and the speed of the vehicle kept the laughs running in rapid order. They were

CHARLES CHAPLIN'S DOUBLE IN "THE KEYSTONE TRIO" BIG HEADLINER AT UNION SQUARE TODAY.

As the headline attraction at the Union Square theatre the latter part of this week, the management has secured what is known as the greatest laughing act in all vaudeville It is the famous "Keystone" trio with Charlie Chaplin's double at the head of the funfest, which is entitled "The Nutty Burglars." This feature act keeps the laughs booming as this trio certainly do know how to handle the fun material. This act is for laughing purposes only, and the finish of their side-splitting farce is so novel and unexpected that the audience is left gasping. A great act, without an equal.

CHARLES CHAPLIN'S DOUBLE AT UNION SQUARE THEATRE THE TALK OF ALL PITTSFIELD.

Quality and quantity are both in evidence at the Union Square theatre the latter part of this week, and comedy holds full sway, for the show is one of the best laughing shows that ever appeared here before.

"The Keystone Trio" featuring George Holt, who is Charles Chaplin's double and who impersonates him to perfection, offered a 20 minute period of sure fire comedy and unrestrained laughter followed their every move. They set the mark for continuous laughter so high that it will take many many weeks for another act to equal their record. This act is entering upon an era of great vaudeville prosperity and after you see it, you will know the reason why this act is such a

excellent work. Another funny comedy sketch is the Keystone trio in a laughable farce, called "The Nutty Burglars." This is a riot of fun and, besides being a clever character sketch, introduces as one of the characters an impersonation of Charles Chaplin, the famous and popular moving picture comedian. Chaplin's double creates no end of fun in this offering and apparently has all the pleasing little mannerisms possessed by the real Chaplin. Pauline Saxton.

Say, Charlie Chaplin is at the Academy of Music; that is, his double is there and answers for the original from the ground up. Charlie is not billed as the headliner on the week-end program, but he's a big noise in one of the big acts and furnishes fun by the barrel.

Ralph Dunbar's Royal Dragoons top this excellent vaudeville bill. Eight men, all clever musicians, make up this organization, which is one of the best of the kind that has ever appeared here. Besides their concert work with brass instruments and a drum, and by the way, that fellow that taps the sheepskin is a "drummer" for fair, the Royal Dragoons have good voices and render many very pleasing songs. The audience was not slow to show its appreciation of the calibre of this act.

It is in the skit presented by the Keystone Trio that Charlie Chaplin's imitator appears, and while this unit of the trio is "doing stunts" he has the audience in an uproar. A very attractive girl is a member of the organization, and she does her share toward making the act a very pleasing one. She is also one of the only two female performers on the entire bill.

Another Charlie Chaplin entertainer—the pick of the lot, and a man who is accredited by the renowned Chaplin himself as having best mastered an imitation of the quaint film comedian—will be presented to Forsyth audiences this week in the Keystone Trio, a team of funmakers who worked in Keystone comedies and who present in real life the odd antics of the comedians in reel life.

One wouldn't expect much from "The Nutty Burglars," but one of them does a Charley Chaplin which is a scream in several spots. Ethel Mc-

1915

Apr 19-21	New York	NEW YORK, 5th Avenue City
Apr 22-24	New York	SYRACUSE [see May 17-23]
Apr 26-28	New York	SCHENECTADY, Proctor's
Apr 29-May 01	New Jersey	ELIZABETH, Proctor's
May 03-05	New Jersey	PLAINFIELD, Proctor's
May 06-08	Massachusetts	PITTSFIELD, Union Square

CHARLES CHAPLIN'S DOUBLE AT UNION SQUARE THEATRE THE TALK OF ALL PITTSFIELD.

The Keystone Trio, featuring George Holt [*sic*], who is Charlie Chaplin's double, and who impersonates him to perfection, offered a 20 minute period of sure fire comedy and unrestrained laughter followed every move. They set the mark for continuous laughter so high that it will take many weeks for another act to equal their record. This act is entering upon an era of great vaudeville prosperity and after you see it, you will know the reason why this act is such a success.

(Pittsfield — May 7, 1915)

[AJM. Just to make it clear, it was *not* George Holt, but Stan Jefferson. Don't ask!]

May 10-12	New York	NEW YORK CITY, 58th Street
May 13-15	New York	NEW YORK CITY, 23rd Street
May 17-23	New York	SYRACUSE, Temple
May 24-26	New York	SCHENECTADY, Proctor's
May 27-29	New York	ALBANY, Proctor's [see Apr 15-27]
May 31-Jun 02	New York	RICHMOND, Lyric

Virginia, RICHMOND, Lyric

Low comedy at its very funniest is supplied by the Keystone Trio, or rather by one of them, who appears in a Charlie Chaplin make-up, and tumbles about the stage doing comedy falls, slides, stumbles and other stunts quite as ingenious and amusing as any that the favorite of the knockabout screen has ever accomplished.

(Richmond — June 1, 1915)

-----0-----

Virginia, NORFOLK, Academy of Music

Say, Charlie Chaplin is at the Academy of Music; that is, his double is there and answers for the original from the ground up. Charlie is not billed as the head-liner on the week-end program, but he's a big noise in one of the big acts and furnishes fun by the barrel.

It is in the skit presented by the Keystone Trio that Charlie Chaplin's imitator appears, and while this unit of the trio is "doing stunts" he has the audience in an uproar. A very attractive girl is a member of the organization, and she does her share toward making the act a very pleasing one. She is also one of the only two female performers on the entire bill.

(Norfolk — June 4, 1915)

Jun 03-05	Virginia	NORFOLK, Academy of Music
Jun 07-09	Virginia	ROANOKE, Roanoke Theatre
Jun 14-19	Georgia	ATLANTA, Forsyth
Jun 21-23	New Jersey	NEWARK, Proctor's

-----0-----

Georgia, ATLANTA, Forsyth

[PREVIEW] Admirers of the phenom of the films, Charlie Chaplin, will have an opportunity to see him portrayed in real life at the Forsyth, when the Keystone Trio, a team of film actor folk, appear upon the bill. The impersonator of the popular Chaplin has been pronounced by Chaplin, himself, to be his most perfect mimic, and the others of the trio portray to a degree of surprising perfection other notables of the Keystone galaxy.

(Atlanta — June 13, 1915)

Let's jump to August and September:

New York NEW YORK CITY, 81st Street

The Keystone Trio closed with their acrobatic skit in which the Chaplin impersonator stands out conspicuously.

(*Variety* — August 6, 1915)

-----0-----

Connecticut, NORWICH, Davis Theatre

The show is one of the best presented at this popular playhouse this season. The vaudeville attraction is the Keystone Trio, one of the funniest acts playing the circuit. They present a an oddity called The Nutty Burglar, and is a scream from start to finish. One of the trio makes up like the famous Charlie Chaplin, and his imitation of Charlie is wonderful. You couldn't tell him from the original. His antics and actions, including the funny Chaplin walk, are an exact counterpart of the world famous fun-maker.

(Norwich — September 17, 1915)

-----0-----

So, with reviews like the latter, The Keystone Trio's act could run for ever. But there was just one problem: the man playing Chaplin at the latter two venues — the one whom "You couldn't tell from the original" — happens to be Edgar Hurley. Stan Jefferson had left back in June, at Newark.

CHAPTER 17

A BIT OF A HURLY-BURLY

The signs that Edgar Hurley had been totally dissatisfied with his role in The Keystone Trio were there to be seen very early on. In their first-ever incarnation, immediately after leaving the Karno Company, Stan, Edgar and Ethel had gone out as "The Three English Comiques" — which meant that no one member was favoured in the billing. But then, within a few weeks, the name had been changed to "The Stan Jefferson Company." An obvious internal rebellion must have occurred, as the name was soon changed back to "The Three English Comiques." But "star trouble" led to the act becoming "Jefferson, Hurley & Wren," before again reverting to "The Three English Comiques." Most-telling is that, when The Three Comiques signed for the Bostock Agency, the first two shows saw them billed as "Hurley, Stan & Wren" — so not only had Stan lost his surname, but he had also been relegated to second in importance.

Temporary peace and order was restored when Bostock had them change their name to "The Keystone Trio." Maybe he had been shrewd enough to realise that listing the three individual names would only lead to conflict, no matter what the order. But, even with the Trio's name favouring no-one, there was still a battle for the hierarchy within the ranks' and, in this, one has to empathise with Hurley's situation. At every performance Hurley had to play the straight role of "the tough" to set up all the laughs for the Chaplin character, played by Stan. Further pain would have been heaped upon Hurley whenever he read the reviews, as all would say how funny the Chaplin impersonator was, while he got no mention whatsoever. And, if we re-examine the review from the Harlem Opera House, we will see what was almost certainly another problem:

HARLEM OPERA HOUSE

... The little woman goes on and off a few times, and stays a while for some comic "love" business on a couch with the comedian.

[*Variety* — February 6, 1915]

Hurley having to stand aside, while his wife and Stan behaved like a courting couple billing and cooing on a park bench, must have caused ill-feeling both on and off stage. Add it all up, and one can see why Hurley wished to reverse the roles.

THE KEYSTONE TRIO

The look of disdain and jealousy on Hurley's face would not have been hard to summon up, while watching this scene of Jefferson making out with his wife, each night.

John McCabe gave this account of how the discord came to a head:

> Annoyed by the personal success of Stan's Chaplin, Hurley demanded the right to play the part on occasion. He did it—once—in New York at Proctor's Fifth Avenue Theatre. That day the act, in the words of Stan Laurel, "died a dog's death." Most of the laughs that had always greeted the Laurel Chaplin were missing when Hurley tried his hand at this performance. At one point in the act Stan-as-Chaplin invariably received a large and extended laugh followed by great applause. Hurley worked hard to duplicate this laugh and, failing to get the strong reaction at this moment, walked down to the footlights and sarcastically started to lead his own applause A few seconds later, he took the audience into his confidence with the remark that Stan always wanted to be the funny man in the act, and what did they think about that?
>
> [Extract from *Mr. Laurel & Mr. Hardy*]

As it happened, the act didn't survive much past when Laurel took back the role, as the three members decided to split. You would think it would have been Hurley who was given the push, as not only was Stan the comedy-star, but also the writer of the sketch. Again, we turn to an account Laurel gave to McCabe to find clarification:

> Hurley quickly copyrighted the act, not telling me about it, claiming it as his material as a means to stop me from doing the act with another couple. He replaced me in the act with another fellow, Ted Banks. Then the theatre managers discovered I was not in the act, and it had become an inferior act anyway. They couldn't get further bookings and *The Keystone Trio* folded forever. It was then I produced a three-person act known as *The Stan Jefferson Trio*.
>
> [Extract from *The Comedy World of Stan Laurel*]

Laurel reiterated in a 1957 taped interview for the radio show *Turning Point* that, after he had left The Keystone Trio, "the act was short lived," and in a letter to a fan he reinforced this claim for a third time:

```
                                                    JUNE 9th.1960.

The news article you read about Edward Coppin was very interesting,
he adopted the name of Teddy Banks when he joined the Fred Karno Co.
we used to share rooms together when we came to this Country - we
were only making $20 a week, so could'nt afford single rooms -
whoever wrote that article was mistaken in regard to Banks forming
the "Keystone Trio", it was I who started the act with another Karno
boy & his wife, whose names were Edgar & Ethel Hurley. I later left
the act & Teddy Banks then joined the Hurley's, but after a few
weeks the act folded up entirely.
```

But we have heard a similar statement from Laurel before, in similar circumstances: When Chaplin left the Karno Company, Stan stated that they played on only a few more weeks before folding; but, as we have seen, that was somewhat inaccurate. So let us see just how quickly The "New" Keystone Trio "faded and died."

The facts are: the "New Keystones" had continuous bookings for the remainder of 1915, through the whole of 1916, and right up till the end of February 1917.

And as for Hurley being, in Stan's opinion, "Dreadful," here again we find contemporary reviews holding totally contradictory evidence:

New York, NEW YORK CITY, American Roof Theatre

> The Keystone Trio brought a successful finish to the first part with their comedy burglar skit. The knockabout comedy appeared just right for the roof crowd, and the fellow in the Chaplin make-up did many a funny move, good for laughs. They derive the best results possible from the nonsensical comedy.
>
> [*Variety* — October 4, 1915]

-----0-----

A Bit of a Hurly-Burly

Indiana, LOGANSPORT, Colonial

Is it his double, or Charles Chaplin himself at the Colonial theatre today? Heaps of fun is offered by the Keystone Trio, who present a burlesque variety sketch entitled "The Nutty Burglars." One of these impersonates the famous screen comedian, Charlie Chaplin, and he has studied the big artist through working with him, so well that he has conquered many of his amusing tricks, so much so that his make-up and mannerisms are the best that has ever been attempted, and he can easily be considered a carbon copy. Hurley, Banks and Wren are the names of this trio. Edgar Hurley sets the mark for continuous laughter so high that it will take many weeks for another act to equal their record. This act is entering upon an era of great vaudeville prosperity, and after you see it you will know the reason why it is such a success.

[Logansport — October 15, 1915]

-----0-----

Ohio, EAST LIVERPOOL, American

The Keystone Trio in their comedy sketch, "The Nutty Burglars," furnish a laugh every minute. The act is funny from curtain rise to curtain fall.

[*East Liverpool Evening Review* — February 24, 1917]

-----0-----

The first and second reviews, above, are from the shows done in the first months of the Hurleys taking over the "New" Keystone Trio, and prove that Edgar Hurley hardly hit the ground face-first. The third review is from the last-ever performance the Hurleys made as The Keystone Trio, and confirms that the act was still attracting excellent reviews — some seventeen months of continuous work later — making Stan's claims what I would euphemistically label "a little untrue."

Stan had an unusual streak of meanness in him which led to his dismissing people who didn't come up to his exacting standards, and then destroying any creditability they may have had as capable performers. Hurley was not the first to receive this dismissive treatment, and would not be the last.

The reason the Hurleys discontinued the act was not because of any failure of Edgar Hurley as a performer, but because of a rival company. The Keystone Trio had been trading on the good name of the films of the Keystone Comedies for over two years, even making claims that their stage comedy was funnier than the Keystone films. This must have really irked some of the Keystone comedians, in the same way that it would have irked former members of the Karno Company if some outsiders had traded on the name 'Karno,' and then put themselves around as being better than the original Karno Comedians.

The rival trio was made up of comedians who had supposedly played in the Keystone Comedy films, and who went out under the name "The Keystone Comedy Trio." They also did a burglar sketch, titled "The Would-be Burglars" which, coincidentally or not, was a title Stan used for the embryonic "Crazy Cracksman" sketch. I can only surmise that, with the new trio on the scene causing confusion with the bookers and public alike, the Hurleys didn't want to fight anymore, and left the stage — but that is only *my* theory.

So what of Mr. Jefferson? Well, he almost immediately formed another act, which he named 'The Stan Jefferson Trio' — figuring that, if he used his own name, no-one could steal the act — well, leastways, not the name. The two new partners he invited to join were man-and-wife team Baldwin and Alice Cooke. I say "man and wife," but there is reason to believe that Alice was most likely still Alice Hamilton, a name she was using in her stage billing when she met Stan. (These vaudeville folks, hey?)

Stan would now be hoping that Baldwin and Alice could better be moulded to his designs than were Edgar and Ethel, and with whom he could top the success of The Keystone Trio. But would it be the Cookes' loyalty which would be tested – or Stan Jefferson's?

CHAPTER 18

A PUZZLE WITHIN A PUZZLE

It was Alice Hamilton, in her interview with John McCabe, who placed Stan's last appearance with The Keystone Trio at Newark, New Jersey (June 23, 1915). I could find no trace of any appearances by Stan Jefferson, in any guise, during the first twelve-and-a-half weeks which followed the split; but then, on September 20, we find him relaunching himself in "The Stan Jefferson Trio."

After informing McCabe that she and 'Baldy' (Baldwin Cooke) first became friends with Stan during a week they shared the bill at a theatre in St. Thomas, Ontario, Canada, (not found) Alice Hamilton goes on to relate what happened in those interim weeks:

> [After] Stan split with the Hurleys, we all got together to do our own three-act. This was The Stan Jefferson Trio. I think we were the three happiest people in the world, doing that act. When Stan first thought of the idea, he said he hadn't a vacation since he was a boy, and wanted one. So he had the idea for us to rent a cottage at some beach where we could go swimming, and that's where he would write an act for us. We would rehearse every day, as well as having a good time, and we'd get that act ready for a fall showing. This was June 1916.
>
> We rented a darling cottage near the Atlantic Highlands, in New Jersey. Stan wrote an act which he called *The Crazy Cracksman*, and we rehearsed hard every day, and he had it ready for our fall showing which Claude Bostock, brother of Gordon, Stan's old agent, got for us.

The said "fall showing" was at the Opera House, New Brunswick, New Jersey — the same theatre where Claude Bostock had launched The Keystone Trio, back in February. As Stan had left 'Keystone' while in New Jersey, followed by his and the Cookes' stay in New Jersey, and then culminating in their debut there, we can safely say this section of the puzzle is accurate.

STAN JEFFERSON TRIO

"THE CRAZY CRACKSMAN"

[Stan Jefferson – Alice Hamilton– Baldwin Cooke]

New Brunswick — September 21, 1915

It is disappointing to report that only nine nights' of confirmed bookings were found over the next five weeks; after which; sightings of 'The Stan Jefferson Trio' disappear altogether. The only footprints I could find are the unidentified newspaper cuttings, shown on the following page:

A Puzzle Within A Puzzle

The Stan Jefferson Company
IN THEIR LATEST ABSURDITY
THE CRAZY CRACKSMAN
With Imitations of the Popular Idol,
CHARLIE CHAPLIN

JEFFERSON TRIO ROUTED

The Stan Jefferson Trio, now appearing in a comedy skit, called "The Crazy Cracksman," have been routed by Claude and Gordon Bostock.

A SCREAM FROM CURTAIN TO CURTAIN
STAN JEFFERSON & CO.
FUN-MAKERS—"THAT'S ALL"
"THE CRAZY CRACKMEN"

...scribable. ... laughing hit of the entire show will be Stan Jefferson & Company, fun makers, "that's all" and their act, entitled, "The Crazy Cracksman" is a scream from rise to fall of the curtain. Built for laughing purposes only, and you need only to see this act to prove this statement.

songs and up-to-date stories. Stan Jefferson and company presented a laughable comedy called "The Crazy Cracksman." They have a funny bit of comedy introducing a Charlie Chaplin character, and keep the audience in a state of mirth from start to finish. Holmes and Wells in a musi-

batic absurdities. Stan Jefferson Trio, offering their "Charlie Chaplin" impersonations, were veritable sensation and a riot of mirth. Then the two Italian

cians with much talent. Stan Jefferson & Co. have an act that was built for laughing purposes, although the song and dance number by the girl and one of the men is pretty. The comedy of this sketch, however, is its real bid for popular approval, and the act has been approved by the big time audiences. One of the company does a Charlie Chaplin that looks as good as the orignal. Bob Tip and com-

numbers. The Stan Jefferson Trio offer a comedy playlet, called "The Crazy Cracksman." Stan Jefferson, who portrays the role of "Silent Jim" the burglar, does the best Chaplin impersonations ever seen here. The sketch is different from the usual comedy farce and kept the house laugh-

Stan Jefferson Trio, in a laughable and ludicrous comedy offering "The Three Cracksmen," have an interesting and amusing slapstick sort of an attraction that includes a Charlie Chaplin character.

All of the above newspaper cuttings are to be found in the Stan Laurel Scrapbook. Every effort was made to trace the original newspapers, but they proved to be elusive, so where and when these shows took place will have to remain unknown, for now.

STAN JEFFERSON — in pose and costume for "The Crazy Cracksman"
(New York 1915)

Meanwhile, here are some reviews we *were* able to trace:

New York, NEW BRUNSWICK, Opera House — September 18, 1915

The Stan Jefferson Trio will offer the funny absurdity "The Crazy Cracksman," a comedy playlet full of laughs. Stan Jefferson was last seen here as comedian in The Keystone Trio. [February 1, 1915]

---0---

New York, NEW BRUNSWICK, Opera House — September 21, 1915

The Stan Jefferson Trio in "The Amateur Cracksman," received many laughs.

-----0-----

New York, ALBANY, Proctor's Grand — October 6, 1915

Stan Jefferson and Company presented a laughable comedy called "The Crazy Cracksman." They have a funny bit of comedy introducing a Charlie Chaplin character, and keep the audience in a state of mirth from start to finish.

(*Albany Evening Journal*, New York)

-----0-----

The appearances so far:

1915

Date	State	Venue	Play	Act
Jun 21-23 Jun	New Jersey	NEWARK, Proctor's		[Stan leaves The Keystone Trio here.]
[Jun 28 to Sep 19				no trace of any bookings during the whole 12 weeks]
Sep 20-21 Sep	New York	NEW BRUNSWICK, O.H.	*The Would-be Burglars*	Stan Jefferson Co.
Sep 22-25				
Sep 27-29	New York	TROY, Proctor's New	*Crazy Cracksman*	Stan Jefferson Trio
Oct 04-06	New York	ALBANY, Proctor's Grand	*Crazy Cracksman*	Stan Jefferson Co.
Oct 07				
Oct 11	New York	NEW YORK CITY, 125th Street		Stan Jefferson Trio
Oct 14				
Oct 21				
Oct 28				

-----0-----

The absence of Stan's name in listings in the trade, and local, papers doesn't necessarily mean he wasn't making appearances — after all, the unidentified cuttings had to have come from shows not on this, and following, lists.

Another reason The Stan Jefferson Trio disappeared from the listings may well be because Stan changed the name of the act. Clues of the newly-named acts are to be found in his scrapbook — in which are newspaper cuttings for "The Stan Stanley Trio" and "The Stanleys."

Return Engagement of
THE STAN STANLEY TRIO
presenting the only recognized

CHARLIE CHAPLIN OF VAUDEVILLE

in the funniest sketch ever staged.
See Charlie's only competitor in life... You will not know the difference.

IMITATES CHARLIE CHAPLIN.

Stan Stanley in Vaudeville Sketch at Star Plays Part of Noisy Burglar.

The Stan Stanley Trio will present a comedy sketch, with Stanley in what is termed in vaudeville circles as the cleverest imitator of Charlie Chaplin at the Park Theatre, Stapleton, next Tuesday and Wednesday. The title of the playlet is "The Great Jewel Mystery," in which Chaplin's impersonator plays the part of a very noisy burglar. This is a return engagement, requested because of the tremendous popularity of the sketch during its last appearance.

STAN STANLEY TRIO in "The Great Jewel Mystery"

The above advert and review would seem to be from the same venue — the Park Theatre, Stapleton — but no further similar entries could be found, making it a bigger mystery than "The Great Jewel."

-----0-----

And then we have this:

> **THE STANLEYS**
> "One of Vaudeville's Best"
> A CHARACTER ACT THAT IS A SURE WINNER

These raise a few questions: "Were these acts ones which Stan Jefferson was actually in?" If so, "Was the sketch one we already know about – such as *The Nutty Burglars*, and/or *The Crazy Cracksman*?" "Where do they fall in the chronology of Stan's vaudeville tours?" "Which towns and theatres are the reviews and adverts from?"

Many hours of searching did unearth some promising leads: Could this be *our* 'Stan Stanley Trio'?

> The Stan Stanley Trio promises something out of the beaten path. In the fifteen minutes they occupy the stage the three display a wide-range of versatility. The act is made up of comedy, music, sleight-of-hand and acrobatics. The whole is woven into a most amusing story.
>
> (*Richmond Times Daily* — July 25, 1915)

Or this one?

> The Stan Stanley Trio offers comedy music and novelty.
>
> (*Courier Journal Sun* — January 23, 1916)

-----0-----

Or this newspaper advert, at right, from the *York Daily* — March 4, 1916?

The answer is "NO!" All three refer to "STAN STANLEY – The Bouncing Fellow" — aka: "Stan Stanley 'and relations'" —— an act which starts with Stanley doing a magic act, but then getting a "plant' from the audience to come on stage, at which point the magician, his wife, and the plant (his actual brother) go into a comedy trampolining exhibition. Dates for this act are numerous, and cover a number of years.

Another 'Stan Stanley' working the vaudeville circuit turned out to be a billiards champion, who did trick shots; and yet a third 'Stan Stanley' — described as: "an English entertainer — was ruled out owing to his touring the West Coast, at the same time as our Stan is known to have been on the East Coast.

Despite my best efforts to find further corroborating evidence, none surfaced; and so these scrapbook cuttings will have to stand alone, for now, as evidence of Stan's name changes — although the possibility remains that maybe Stan kept them on a whim, because he liked the act. If only he had taken care to include the dates and places of all the newspaper cuttings, and in chronological order, my task would have been shortened by a whole year or more.

And the hair-tearing frustration continues when we try to fill in the gaps over the next few months on Stan's date-sheet. Coincidental with The Stan Jefferson Trio disappearing from show business listings, the name "The Universal Trio" appears. This time, though, we do have confirmation of the names of its members:

> The Universal Trio, Stan Jefferson, Baldwin Cooke and Alice Hamilton, furnished a lot of genuine fun in which one of the men did a "Charlie Chaplin" stunt that was the best seen on a local stage.

A Puzzle Within A Puzzle

Between November 1915 and March 1916, the "Universal Trio" alternates as "The Universal Four."

> **THREE QUALITY ACTS FROM NEW YORK CITY!**
> The "Universal Four" in "The Cracksman"

> **UNIVERSAL FOUR.**
> A Variety Offering Consisting of Singing, Dancing and Talking, Coming Direct from Poli's, Scranton.

> Underwood calls "Pop." Then followed the laughing number of the whole program and carded as The Universal Four. Three men and a woman, who have a clever song and dance turn and presently introduce one of their members as a phony burglar, who turns out to have a remarkable makeup of the much advertised excruciatingly funny Charlie Chaplin. He has all the wellknown mannerisms, the funny walk, the funny pants, the funny mustache and the little cane that is always getting in people's way

-----o-----

[Transcript of the review at right:] Then followed the laughing number of the whole program, and carded as The Universal Four. Three men and a woman, who have a clever song and dance turn and presently introduce one of their members as a phony burglar, who turns out to have a remarkable makeup of the much advertised excruciatingly funny Charlie Chaplin. He has all the well-known mannerisms, the funny walk, the funny pants, the funny mustache and the little cane that is always getting in people's way.]

-----o-----

1915

Date	State	Venue	Billing
Oct 28	New York	BROOKLYN, Keeney's	Universal Trio
Nov 01			
Nov 08			
Nov 15			
Nov 22-24	New Jersey		
Nov 25-27	New Jersey	TRENTON, State Street	Universal Four
Nov 29			
Dec 05			
Dec 13			
Dec 20			
Dec 27			
Dec 30			

1916

Date	State	Venue	Billing
Jan 03			
Jan 10			
Jan 14	New York	ROME, Family	Universal Trio
Jan 17			
Jan 24			
Jan 31-Feb 02			

o-o-0-o-o

Alice Hamilton, in the McCabe interview, says of her time with Stan: "*Those happy days just seemed as if they would never end,*" but, just seventeen weeks after the debut of the Jefferson-Hamilton-Cooke partnership, they *did* end, when Jefferson dumped his partners, and jumped ship — AGAIN.

Alice told McCabe that Stan deserted: "*… because of the appearance on the scene of Mae Charlotte Dahlberg.*" After stating that Stan and Mae "*hit it off right away,*" Alice further revealed that a few weeks after meeting Mae, Stan told her and Baldy that he wanted to leave their three-act, but suggested as a replacement an old friend from the Karno Company – Billy Crackles.

We can now surmise that, when the Universal Trio had upped their number to "Four," it was because Billy Crackles had been brought in to learn the part, prior to Stan's departure.

After the subsitution of Crackles for Jefferson, sightings of The Universal Trio were infrequent, before disappearing not long thereafter. Alice Hamilton disclosed that Billy Crackles' close friendship with the bottle forced them back into their old double-act of 'Cooke and Hamilton.'

Advert naming Crackles–Cooke–Hamilton as 'The Universal Trio.' [Last sighting— Pennsylvania, April 6, 1916.]

So what of Mr. Jefferson, and his new partner? Every account to date of Stan's solo vaudeville years will tell you that he next formed a partnership with Mae Dahlberg, and toured with her as "Stan & Mae Laurel." Before we see if that is what actually happened, let us retrace our footsteps some ten months, to when Mae Dahlberg first entered the picture.

CHAPTER 19

MAE OR MAY NOT

We first pick up Mae Charlotte Dahlberg on July 26, 1915, beginning a three-night appearance at the 5th Avenue Theatre, New York City, in a song and dance duo called "The Hayden Sisters." This was immediately followed by three nights at the Halsey Theatre, in Brooklyn, N.Y.

The Hayden Sisters are featuring Shapiro-Bernstein Co. songs

Over the next few months, newspaper entries varyingly describe The Hayden Sisters as: "European Dancing Novelty" — "Those two dainty English Girls in their classy songs and dances" — and "Acrobatic Dancers." Nothing wrong there, except that the girls weren't sisters, and Mae wasn't a Hayden; nor was she English (but Australian) and so could hardly be described as "European." Apart from that, the rest seems to be accurate.

Just to re-iterate that we are showing interest in Mae Dahlberg because of the information Alice Hamilton revealed to John McCabe:

The Hayden act and Stan's act were on the same bill in a small Pennsylvania town in 1918 when Stan and Mae "Hit it off right away."

The year 1918 is so obviously wrong (it should read "1915"), and the first meeting being in Pennsylvania also causes a problem. To state the obvious: "For two people to meet, they have to be in the same place, at the same time," but no evidence of them even being in Pennsylvania at the same time, much less being on the same bill, was found – although that does not completely rule out the possibility.

THE HAYDEN SISTERS

1915

[Jun 21-23	New Jersey	NEWARK, Proctor's		Stan leaves The Keystone Trio here.]
Jun 28				
Jul 05				
Jul 12				
Jul 19				
Jul 26-28	New York	NEW YORK, 5th Avenue		Hayden Sisters
[Jul 29-31	New York	BROOKLYN, Halsey		Hayden Sisters
Aug 02				
Aug 09				
Aug 16				
Aug 23				
Aug 30 – Sep 1	New Jersey	JERSEY CITY, Keith's		Hayden Sisters
Sep 06				
Sep 13				
[Sep 20-21	New Jersey	NEW BRUNSWICK, O.H.		Stan Jefferson Co. (1st sighting)]

For Stan and Mae to have had regular contact *after* they first met, they would have had to have been circulating in the same areas for a length of time. It is possible they met somewhere in New Jersey, in August or September (when Stan and the Cookes were working-up their act); but the most-likely occasion was when both were playing in and around in New York City — as shown in the next section of the date-sheet. A quick look shows us that both the Stan Jefferson Trio *and* The Hayden Sisters were almost within touching distance during the last two weeks of September 1915. In fact, at the Proctor's Theatre in Troy, the SJT did the first half of the week, and the Haydens the second.

LAUREL – Stage by Stage

THE HAYDEN SISTERS

1915

Date	State	Venue	Show	Act
Sep 22	New York	SYRACUSE, Temple		Hayden Sisters
Sep 28	New York	CORTLAND, Temple		Hayden Sisters
[Sep 27-29	New York	TROY, Proctor's New	*Crazy Cracksman*	Stan Jefferson Trio]
Sep 30 - Oct 02	New York	TROY, Proctor's New		Hayden Sisters
[Oct 04-06	New York	ALBANY, Proctor's Grand	*Crazy Cracksman*	Stan Jefferson Co.]
Oct 11				
[Oct 11	New York	NEW YORK CITY, 125th St.	*Crazy Cracksman*	Stan Jefferson Trio]
Oct 14-16	New Jersey	BRIDGEWATER, Proctor's New		Hayden Sisters
Oct 18				
Oct 25				

Even if they never appeared on the same bill, this doesn't mean they never met. It was common practice for vaudeville acts to go and watch each other at neighbouring theatres, so Stan could have been attracted to Mae through seeing her on stage, and then maybe going backstage to pass on his compliments. There is also a distinct possibility that, at some time, both were staying in the same digs ("digs" being the term for temporary accommodation used by vaudeville acts). And a third option is that, after the show, they bumped into each other at one of the "drinking troughs" frequented by vaudeville acts, who went there to wind down after shows. Alice Hamilton spoke of one such venue:

> You could do a lot with $175 a week in those days [the amount the SJT got between them], and we did. We just spent it all (it seemed) when we got it, not giving a thought for the next day or the next week. When we were in Troy, New York, we used to go to this nice place, the Hofbrau, and spend it.

This particular Hofbrau House was located at Broadway and 30th Street; but there were others in Rochester, N.Y.; and Buffalo, New York. These clips indicate why the Hofbrau establishments were such a popular after-show gathering place, and give us an insight into the kind of after-show establishments the vaudeville acts frequented.

HOFBRAU—CABARET

The programme at Max Lubeiski's popular restaurant is sufficiently varied to please the tastes of all, embracing, as it does, grand opera, ballads, the latest sentimental songs, and now and then a bit of ragtime.

Between the singing numbers the orchestra plays the latest music, and it also furnishes music for those who care to dance. The dancing hours are from 10 o'clock until closing time. The entertainment begins at 6 o'clock and continues until 8:30 o'clock nightly.

After the theatre it begins at 10 o'clock and continues until 1 o'clock, except on Saturday nights when "taps" are sounded at midnight.

(*Buffalo New York Courier* — March 12, 1916)

This portrait of Mae matches the costume shot of Stan (inset) — which is confirmed as
having been taken in 1915 in New York (Note it is the same logo on both!).
So, it is plausible that Stan and Mae went to the studios together, which places their courtship
concurrent with when Stan re-formed "The Stan Jefferson Trio" with Baldwin and Alice Cooke.

o-o-o-0-o-o

(Mae Laurel portrait courtesy of Brian Clarry)

So, with their being in proximity and having late-night venues at which to effect a courtship, one can imagine how Stan and Mae's relationship was able to blossom. And not forgetting of course that, if Mae's shows finished first, she could pop round to the theatre where Stan was working – and vice versa. Then of course, there may well have been periods when one or both of them weren't working, and so could spend whole days together.

1915

Oct 28	New York	BROOKLYN, Keeney's	Universal Trio
Nov 01			
Nov 08			
Nov 15			
Nov 22-24			
Nov 25-27	New Jersey	TRENTON, State Street	Universal Four
Nov 30 (Tue)	Michigan	ESCABANA, St. Anne's Minstrel Show	Universal Trio
Dec 06			
Dec 13			
Dec 20			

[AJM: There were no engagements found for the Hayden Sisters in the above period. There were, however, other acts of similar name around, but these were gradually eliminated from having ties to The Hayden Sisters. Among them was "The Four Hayden Sisters" – "Hayden, Borden, and Hayden" (an act which was eventually revealed as being "Three Men and a Piano") – and Hayden & Hayden (who were simply what remained after Borden had left).]

With Stan 'on heat' and, I imagine, striving to be with Mae at every opportunity, it must have been a blow for him when, in December 1915, The Hayden Sisters brought in a third member, and made radical changes to the act:

> The feature act at the Family today is the Hayden Sisters and Ward in a variety act introducing singing, dancing, costume changes and a man monkey. This act consists of two pretty girls that can sing and dance. One of the ladies in the act does a very clever eccentric dance.
>
> (*Rome Daily Sentinel*, NY — December 23, 1915)

-----0-----

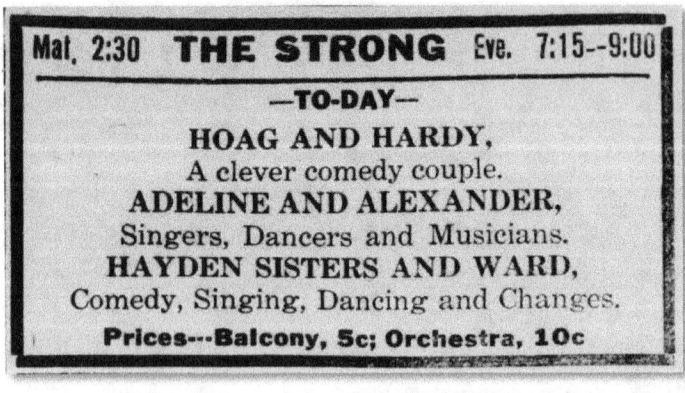

(*Burlington Free Press*, VT — December 28, 1915)

[Funny to see Mae dating Laurel, while working with a Hardy.]

1915

[Dec 20-21	New York	GLOVERSVILLE, Family	Hayden Sisters & Ward]
[Dec 22-23	New York	ROME, Family	Hayden Sisters & Ward]
[Dec 27-29	Vermont	BURLINGTON, Strong	Hayden Sisters & Ward]
[Dec 31 - Jan 01	New York	GLENS FALLS, Empire	Hayden Sisters & Ward]

1916

Jan 03			
[Jan 10	New York	FLATBUSH, Olympic	Hayden Sisters & Ward]

-----0-----

Glens Falls NY Post Star December 31, 1915)

The only way that bringing Mr. Ward into the partnership would *not* have caused conflict between Stan and Mae, would have been if Mr. Ward's eyes were only for Mae's stage-partner, Cossie. (Or, if Mr. Ward didn't have eyes for girls at all.) Ward's job may have been to create "monkey-business" on stage, but there was no way Stan would have allowed any off-stage. Or, or, or: What if Stan Jefferson were actually the mysterious "Mr. Ward"? There are no sightings of any act Stan was known to have worked in, during January and February 1916, which is when the Haydens were working as a three-act. This could have been a subterfuge, designed by Stan, to keep him close to Mae at all times. It certainly fits the known facts, and the immediate timeline after he had abandoned Cooke and Hamilton to go off with Mae. We will never know. But, just three weeks after their first appearance, 'The Hayden Sisters and Ward' totally disappeared. One would expect that the girls reverted to their former two-act, but the two of them were never sighted together again.*[1]

After The Hayden Sister's last-ever show on January 15, 1916, the date-sheets are much depleted: The only sighting in the last two weeks of January is one of "The Universal Trio." But then, in the first week of February, we see the re-emergence of 'The Stan Jefferson Trio' — a piece of the puzzle which we know for a certainty is in the right place, but which would seem to necessitate the displacement of some of the pieces around it.

UNIVERSAL TRIO — STAN JEFFERSON

1916

Jan 14	New York	ROME, Family	*Crazy Cracksman*	Universal Trio
Jan 17				
Jan 24				
Jan 31 - Feb 02				
Feb 03-05	New York	YONKERS, Orpheum	*Crazy Cracksman*	Stan Jefferson Co.

The Stan Jefferson Trio is known to be playing the sketch *The Crazy Cracksman*, but so too is The Universal Trio. In a complete surprise turn of events Stan had found two new, and formerly unknown, members to complete his Trio. A review of the show at the Orpheum Theatre, Yonkers, names the other two actors in the 'Stan Jefferson Co.' (*sic*) as Bessie Delberg, and Barry Preston (as 'Percy').

That Barry Preston was indeed one of the Stan Jefferson Trio is confirmed when, a week or so later, he places a "Looking for Engagements" advert in one of the trade papers in which he appends: "… *late of the Stan Jefferson Trio.*" So who are these two, and where did they come from? This question invites a piece of pure speculation on my behalf. Could Bessie *Delberg* actually be Mae *Dahlberg*? Her dance partner was named Cossie. Had Mae earlier adopted the name so that their first names were alliterative — "Cossie & Bessie"? It's a bit of a leap of faith, but would explain what happened to Mae when The Hayden Sisters split.

---

[1] Mae's former partner was later spotted with a new partner. MAJESTIC October 1, 1916 – Little Rock, Arkansas
"Hayden and Stewart, formerly the Hayden Sisters, comely young women, offer a dancing novelty containing fancy and eccentric dances."

If my speculative leap isn't correct, then what did happen to the mysterious "Bessie Delberg" following the departure of the equally mysterious Barry Preston? Well, for the next seven weeks, "nothing" seems to be the answer. But then, week commencing March 20, 1916, we find The Stan Jefferson Trio playing in Pittsburgh. This would have me believe that Mae was the female in the S.J Trio, and that, during the seven week gap, Stan had been training a new recruit. It may even have been the mysterious Mr. Ward, after he too had left The Hayden Sisters. And the above unidentified newspaper clipping does seem to confirm that Stan is touring with "Mrs. Jefferson" — although *we* know they never actually married. (The reason Stan was never to marry Mae, is that she already had a husband, back in Australia.) In later life Mae Dahlberg told John McCabe that when she first teamed with Stan: "*We travelled together as a double-act, sometimes called Stan and Mae Jefferson, or mostly Stan Jefferson, with me as assistant,*" so the above review does fit this time-frame.

Advert and review from the
Ada Meade Theatre
LEXINGTON, Kentucky
(The last know appearance of
The Stan Jefferson Trio – March 29, 1916)

For the second-half of the same week The Stan Jefferson Trio has had to make the considerable journey from Pittsburgh, Pennsylvania, to play the Ada Meade Theatre in Lexington, Kentucky — after which – "PUFF!" – The Stan Jefferson Trio disappears, never to be seen again.

1916 (continued)

Feb 07				
Feb 14				
Feb 21				
[Feb 25	New York	MALONE, Grand	Crackles, Cooke, Hamilton	Universal Trio]
Feb 28 – 29	Vermont	BURLINGTON, Strong		Universal Trio]
[Mar 02-04	Ohio	TOLEDO, Palace		Universal Four]
[Mar 05	Ohio??	COLUMBIA, Bell		Universal Trio]
[Mar 06	Michigan	DETROIT, Columbia		Universal Trio]
[Mar 13	New York	BUFFALO, Olympic		Universal Trio]
Mar 16-18	Indiana	MUNCIE, Star		Stan Jefferson Trio
[Mar 20-22	New York	NIAGARA FALLS, Cataract	Crackles Cooke Hamilton	Universal Trio
Mar 20-25	Pennsylvania	PITTSBURGH, Harris	*Crazy Cracksman*	Stan Jefferson Trio
Mar 27-29	Kentucky	LEXINGTON, Ada Meade	*Crazy Cracksman*	Stan Jefferson Trio
				[last known appearance]

-----0-----

No doubt you will be totally confused over the number of changes in Stan's stage acts; but bear in mind you are only *looking* at the picture. Imagine, if you had had to assemble it yourself. Before you read this book you had been led to believe that, after Stan left the Karno Company, he formed The Three English Comiques; which later became The Keystone Trio; after which he assembled The Stan Jefferson Trio; before going off with Mae Dahlberg to complete his vaudeville years as "Stan and Mae

Laurel." Having now read the book up to this point, you can see that the picture has rather changed somewhat, as follows:

> Jefferson leaves the Karno Company (three months later than first thought); runs away to Vancouver to join a stock company (not proven); forms "The Three English Comiques;" changes the name to "The Stan Jefferson Company;" reverts to "The Three English Comiques;" changes again, this time to "Jefferson, Hurley & Wren;" but then reverts to "The Three English Comiques." After yet another name change, this time to "Hurley Stan & Wren;" the act is revamped and becomes "The Keystone Trio." When the Keystones split, Stan forms a totally new act which he calls "The Stan Stanley Trio;" another name is possibly "The Stanleys" (not proven). He then recruits two new partners for "The Stan Jefferson Trio;" which is soon renamed "The Universal Trio;" quickly followed by "The Universal Four." He then reforms "The Stan Jefferson Trio" with two new partners; and then, after an interval of several weeks, relaunches "The Stan Jefferson Trio" with yet another revised line-up — which brings us bang up to date — March 30, 1916.

At this point in time we know that The Stan Jefferson Trio is no more, and that one pair of Stan's former stage colleagues are continuing with The Keystone Trio, and a second pair is touring with the Universal Trio. We also know that The Hayden Sisters have split, and that one of them has a new partner. So all you readers now know what happened next, which is that Mr. Jefferson and Miss Dahlberg struck out, together, as the comedy duo "Stan & Mae Laurel."

WRONG!

The act of "Stan & Mae Laurel" is not destined to hit the circuit until March 1917. What happened in those interim months has never before been recorded, and the events surrounding those 'lost' months will astound you.

CHAPTER 20

LIFE TO THE MAX

During the first week in January 1916, a San Antonio newspaper printed the following biography about a burlesque magic act called "Martini & Maximillian":

> Bob Martini, burlesquer of "black art" at the Majestic this week, began his career as a newspaper reporter in Philadelphia. Then he became press agent for Keller, the great magician. He graduated from that place into the ranks of vaudevillians after he had been— but thereon hangs this tale. As press agent for Keller, Martini learned nearly all of the simpler tricks of the master. It was quite profitable for him to give entertainments for churches and club benefits in spare moments ...
>
> ...The young Martini entered vaudeville. For a time he worked as a magician. But magicians better than he were so common he found it hard to procure engagements. Then he formed a partnership with Maximillian, with whom he still works. That was fourteen years ago. All these years, Martini and Maximillian have been burlesquing the latest feats of the world's greatest magicians. They show just how lots of seemingly difficult tricks are performed. And into their exposures, they inject some thoroughly wholesome comedy.

If this were a prelude to Martini and Maximillian celebrating their fifteen-year partnership, then it was ill-timed. Within three months the two of them had broken up, and Bob Martini carried on the act with a new partner. The world has no idea who that partner was, but we can now reveal it: The magician's new assistant was — STAN JEFFERSON.

This astounding revelation came to light only a few years ago, when my good friend, and fellow Laurel & Hardy researcher, Bernie Hogya, tipped me off. Bernie runs the Internet website "The Stan Laurel Correspondence Archive," which collects and catalogues letters written by Stan Laurel. One particular letter Bernie couldn't wait to share contained the following extract:

```
STAN LAUREL,
1111 FRANKLIN ST.
SANTA MONICA, CALIF.
U.S.A.

                                              May 20th.'57.
My Dear Charlie:-
          Appreciated very much your nice card,17th.inst.
     Not sure if I told you or not, I worked in a magic & illusion
act a few years ago with a Bob Martini,we were known as Martini &
Maxmillian,I was doing the comedy,after he had done his trick &
gotten big applause,I would by accident expose them - we played
Keith-Orpheum,around the East & later came West on the Pantages
time - those were the happy days!
     Well,all for now Charlie,it was nice to hear from you again &
once more,thanks for your kind thoughts & wishes.
          Bye,good luck & God Bless.
               Sincerely always:-
                              Stan Laurel.
                         Stan Laurel.
```

An entry in *Variety* in November 1918, does mention Stan having earlier partnered a magician; but, as the name of the act was not given, it was not possible to follow-up on.

> Stanley, son of Arthur Jefferson, a London manager, has been missing for some time. The last letter his family received was over a year ago and Mr. Jefferson has written to George Arliss asking help to locate the son. Jefferson, junior, was with the Keystone Trio ("The Nutty Burglars") at last reports and previously had been with a magician. Any information regarding the missing man should be sent to Mr. Arliss, care of Dixie Hines, 1400 Broadway. Jefferson may have enlisted with the British mission.

A second, similar review (circa November 1918) reads:
George Arliss Asks Aid in Finding Stanley Jefferson.

The search for a missing son by Arthur Jefferson, a theatrical man of London, brought a request from his friend, George Arliss, yesterday, that efforts be made to find him. The younger Jefferson's first name is Stanley. He is an actor. His father last heard from him when he was playing in Stamford, Ct., in 1916. He was later reported to be associated with Edgar Hurley in "The Keystone Trio," a vaudeville act. Mr. Jefferson states that while his son may be serving with the army in France, he believes that he may be in America instead: inasmuch as repeated requests for information from the military authorities have failed to show the young man's whereabouts. The elder Jefferson may be reached at 49 Colebrooke avenue, West Ealing, London. W. 13.

[AJM: George Arliss was an English actor, whom Arthur Jefferson had once managed. At the time of this letter of appeal, Arliss was making one of his many theatre appearances in the U.S. He later went on to star in many British and American films, and was the first British actor to win an 'Oscar' Academy Award.]

Here is a little information about the 'Maximillian' Stan was to replace. It dates from 1913.

MARTINI AND MAXIMILIAN AND ASSISTANT
Burlesque Magicians Who Show the Inner Workings of Some of the Tricks of the Great Magicians.

It is seldom that an act of such interesting calibre is presented as that of Martini and Maximilian. Martini is really a most clever illusionist, while his partner, Maximilian has not only the funniest make-up on the stage, but by his original silliness proves his artistic worth. Many of the tricks and illusions that are performed are from the repertories of the best-known magicians and illusionists that have ever appeared upon the stage, and the wholly unconscious manner in which they are disclosed by his idiotic helper are screamingly funny and at the same time gives the audience an insight into the methods of the average magician that is satisfying and unique.

Martini is a native of Philadelphia, and has made magic and illusion a life-long study. He is constantly inventing new tricks and frequently spends hundreds of dollars upon apparatus and equipment for the presentation of a new trick that is discarded after its first public appearance.

Had Maximilian chosen the profession of a clown instead of that of vaudeville performer, he would have become famous, as his pantomime is natural and unstudied. It is seldom that he gives two performances alike and his entire personality is such that it arouses laughter without conscious or labored effort. This is an excellent act that will fully demonstrate the ease and simplicity of seemingly wonderful and involved tricks of magic.

(Fort Wayne Journal — August 27, 1913)

How eerily prophetic the last paragraph would be, had it been written about Stan.

Upon learning the name of the magic act Stan had been in, I was able to begin tracing his theatre engagements, but this was still a task which could not be wholly fulfilled: During the months Stan was to tour with the magician, the duo's greatest trick was in disappearing from theatrical listings. Trade papers did cough up the odd bookings, but the rest had to be dredged up by the long, long task of trawling the local papers to find every venue where the magic act had played. If this weren't a big enough task in its own right, consider that, after searching on-line for "Martini & Maximillian," additional searches had to be repeated for each and every variant spelling, of which there are many: "Martin – Martine – Martino – Martina – Martinni; and then: Maxmllan – Maximllan – Maxmillian – Maximillian – Maxmilan – Maxmilian – Maximilan – Maximilian."

The spelling which occurs most frequently is "Maximillian," and here is why: When solo magician Bob Martini first teamed up with a partner, he chose Max Millian, a violin-playing clown, with the combined act billed simply as "Martini and Max Millian." When Mr. Millian left, however, Bob recruited a new partner and adjusted the name of the act to "Martini and Maximillian" so as not to infringe on the name of Max Millian. By employing this subtle change, and not "alerting the media," he wisely avoided the risk of losing future engagements.

MARTINI AND MAXIMILLIAN

At the Majestic

This cutting is in Stan's Scrapbook, so could this be him, behind that full-face clown's make-up? Thankfully, the answer is NO! This photo was in use long before Stan became Martini's comic foil.

You would have thought Laurel's scrapbook would be a goldmine of dates and venues; but, disappointingly, Stan had clipped all the newspaper cuttings to within one letter of their lives, thus omitting the precious information of the newspaper title, the date, the town/city, and the venue. So, although you may at first be disappointed that only just over a half of Martini and Maximillian's date-sheet has been reconstituted, please now adopt that well-known Irish saying and, "Be thankful for small Murphys!"

The downside of Stan's partnership was in not being credited under his own name. One solution would have been for a name-change such as: "Martini & Stan"; or "Martini & Jefferson;" but, as before, Bob Martini wanted to carry on trading off the name of "Martini & Maximillian," a name which was now even more well-known and respected, fourteen years on. That Martini had a new partner was never voluntarily released, and was certainly never promoted. In many of the previews and reviews, the act was billed as "original." The word "new" was sometimes used, but only to describe the tricks and props, and not the new man in the act.

From all this, one may conclude that Stan took the role because Bob Martini had guaranteed-bookings for several months to come, whereas he himself had failed to get regular bookings since quitting The Keystone Trio.

An additional reason may well have been because he was attracted to the role of Maximillian. It was exactly his kind of humour, the kind he had been party to throughout his years with the Karno Company — especially *A Night in an English Music Hall*, wherein performers are parodied; or as the Americans call it, "travested, or even "burlesqued." One of the acts in "Music Hall" was, as we know, a magician, doing what we English label "cod magic" — i.e. where an act behaves as if they are doing something really clever and skilful, but the audience knows that they are deliberately performing the discipline badly. And parody would be the type of humour which Stan Laurel was to favour, and enact so well, in his solo films.

When Stan was in The Keystone Trio, Edgar Hurley had mutinied after having to stand and watch each night as Stan got all the laughs. But here in this magic act, Stan's partner was happy for him to get ALL the laughs – and the bigger the better – especially as it covered over one of his shortcomings, as highlighted in this pre-Stan review:

> Martini and Maxmillian with their burlesque magic caused some merriment. The man in comedy make-up is the act. The straight does little that gets anything. He talks far too much, in a voice that does not impress. The other man knows how to handle the comedy.
>
> *(Variety — August 1, 1914)*

So now Stanley Jefferson was very happy with his lot: He had guaranteed work, and would be able to enjoy himself every night playing a character which suited every funny bone in his body, and for which he had free rein to improvise, improve, and build that comedy character — with thoughts in mind of how Chaplin had built up 'the drunk' in different Karno sketches.

But Stan did still have a major problem. What of Mae? What was she going to do now? Although she could tour with Stan, she would have to sit-out every show. Sitting out, when others were on stage getting the laughs, was not something Mae could suffer easily. Her urge to get into the action would later be perfectly demonstrated when she and Stan were to go in to filming.

In an earlier incarnation of Martini and Maximillian there had actually been a lady in the line-up — although uncredited. (See photo on page 165.)

MARTINI AND MAXMILLIAN

> After performing some marvellous tricks, which really is mystifying, it is usually exposed, apparently, by the comedy of the team. However, sometimes, just as the audience thinks it discovered how the thing was done, a new element of mystery will enter the game and the problem is further away from the solution than before.
>
> A woman, who is a silent member of the company, helps out the act greatly by sheer good looks.
>
> *(San Antonio Texas — June 12, 1911)*

-----0-----

Two days later, the same newspaper gave the lady a second mention, which brings the sum total of mentions of her I found, between 1904 and 1918, to TWO.

> For the briefest space, a pretty and shapely girl appears in one of the illusions and vastly ornaments the occasion.
>
> *(San Antonio Texas — June 14, 1911)*

-----0-----

However, it is extremely doubtful that Mae took even this, the smallest of roles, in the act. Nor was she found as a solo performer, or in any other act, touring concurrently with M&M. So with Stan Jefferson working under an assumed name, and Mae Laurel not working at all, the three of them hit the circuit.

It isn't going to be possible to confirm the exact date when Stan joined Martini. We will just have to go off the science of probability. The last-ever performance of The Stan Jefferson Trio was on Wednesday March 29, 1916 – in Lexington, Kentucky. The following day, Martini & Maximillian were in Richmond, West Virginia. As the two venues are in adjoining states, it *is* possible that Stan played both shows; although this would mean that he and Bob had met up weeks earlier, and done all the necessary rehearsing.

The more-likely scenario is that the two new partners teamed up shortly after the Richmond engagement. The ball-park area is highlighted by the briefest of mentions in the April 1st issue of *Variety*, which informs us: *"Martini & Maximillian have separated."*

A stand-out choice for when the 'new' Martini & Maximillian made their debut would be Monday April 17, 1916, in Atlanta, Georgia (which is a long-distance!!). This allows for the necessary rehearsal time, and then signals the start of a steady run of shows in New York, New Jersey, and Pennsylvania.

-----0-----

LAUREL – Stage by Stage

STAN JEFFERSON TRIO
"The Crazy Cracksman"

1916

| Mar 20-25 | Pennsylvania | PITTSBURGH, Harris | Stan Jefferson Trio | |
| Mar 27-29 | Kentucky | LEXINGTON, Ada Meade | Stan Jefferson Trio | [last-ever show] |

-----0-----

MARTINI & MAXIMILLIAN
[Bob Martini and Stan Jefferson]

1916

Mar 30-Apr 01	West Virginia	RICHMOND, Lyric	[Stan *could* have started here]
Apr 03	Pennsylvania	UNIONTOWN, Dixie	
Apr 10			
Apr 17	Georgia	ATLANTA, Forsyth	[most probable debut for Stan]
Apr 24			
Apr 27-29	New York	BROOKLYN, Prospect	
May 01-03			
May 04-06	New York	YONKERS, Orpheum	
May 08			
May 15-17			
May 18-20	New Jersey	TRENTON, Taylor's Opera House	
May 22	New Jersey	JERSEY CITY, Keith's	

FUNNY MAGICIANS HIT AT TAYLOR'S

What is considered a corking comedy show is the combination of five acts of vaudeville and four reels of high class motion pictures which are being offered at Taylor Opera House for the last three days. Three audiences received act and player with applause yesterday afternoon and evening, and the all-comedy feature of the bill proved popular.

Martini and Maxmillian, two of the best known members of the vaudeville stage, and for years identified with the real "big time," were finely received for their act of burlesque magic. The names of this couple are known from coast to coast as those of ideal exponents of high-class vaudeville. They have a new line of comedy magic and illusions, which Martini performs and which Maxmillian "unperforms," or rather ev-

Martini & Maximillian perform startling feats of legerdemain and then show how easily the tricks are done. Mr. Martini had them laughing for twenty two minutes last night.

Two more cuttings from Stan's Scrapbook, with reviews of Martini & Maximillian's shows at:
Taylor's Opera House, Trenton, NJ.
w/c May 18, 1916

> New Jersey, TRENTON, Taylor's Opera House
> Martini and Maxmillian, two of the best known members of the vaudeville stage, and for years identified with the real "big time," were finely received for their act of burlesque magic. The names of this couple are known from coast to coast as those ideal exponents of high-class vaudeville. They have a new line of comedy magic and illusions, which Martini performs and which Maxmillian "unperforms," or rather exposes.
> (Trenton, NJ — May 19, 1916)

As there are no known diary or biographical details of Stan's tours with Bob Martini, all we can do now is glean what information we can from contemporary newspaper sources. The following reviews and previews have been selected from the scores of those unearthed, as they offer genuine eye-witness accounts of the shows, as opposed to the ones which contain only oft-repeated extracts from the pre-publicity notes:

In the above set of newspaper clips, from the shows at Trenton, me suspects there is trickery going on with the wording. Twice the phrase: " … *two of the best known members of the vaudeville stage …*" is used; and then: "*They have a new line of comedy/burlesque magic and illusions ...*" but nowhere is it revealed that one of the duo is new — although we are told that Jersey is New!!

Stan Jefferson is by now definitely filling the role of Maximillian. How can I be so sure? Well, the clippings from Trenton are copies of the ones Stan Laurel cut and pasted into his scrapbook.

-----0-----

May 29	Pennsylvania	PITTSBURGH, Harris	
Jun 05	Pennsylvania	PITTSBURGH, Sheridan	
Jun 12-14	New York	BROOKLYN, Prospect	[re-booking – see April 27]
Jun 15-17			
Jun 19			
Jun 26	New York	NEW YORK CITY, Greely Square	
Jul 03-05	New York	BINGHAMTON, Stone	[Mon-Wed]
Jul 06-08	New York	ELMIRA, Majestic	[Thu-Sat]
Jul 10-15	New York	BUFFALO, Shea's }	[CLASH. When is this show?]
Jul 10-15	New York	LOCKPORT, Shea's }	
Jul 17-18	New York	GLOVERSVILLE, Family	
Jul 20	New York	SARATOGA SPRINGS, Broadway	

-----0-----

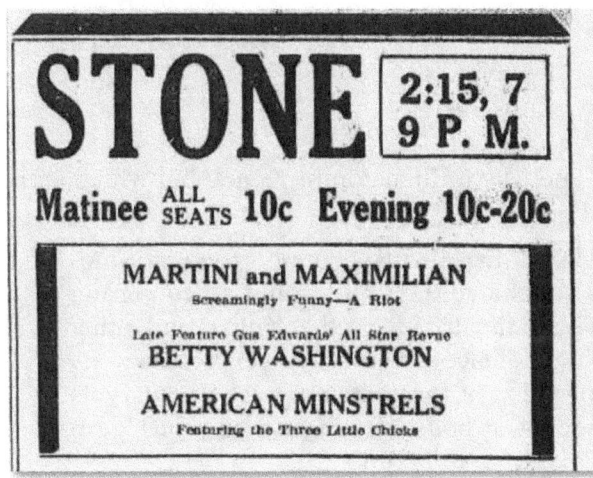

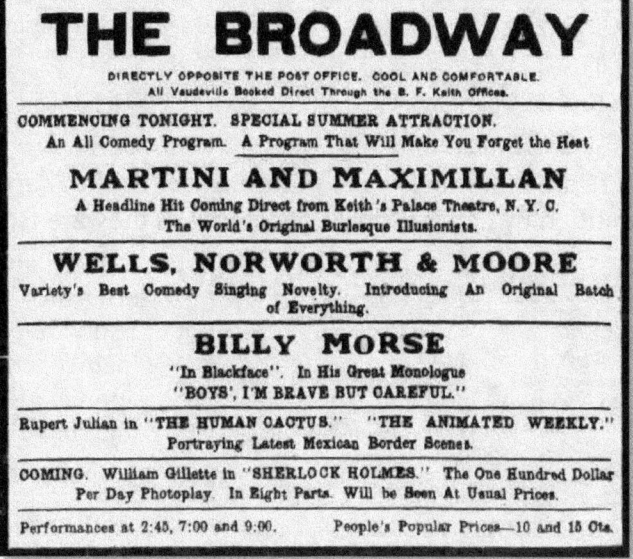

[Note the three different spellings of Martini's partner's name in these cuttings.]

Below, is all that Stan retained from the above advert.

-----0-----

Six weeks later, another reviewer tells us the act is "brand new," but, yet again, does not make the point that Martini has a new partner:

New York, ELMIRA, Majestic

Martini and Maximilian have a screamingly funny burlesque magic sensation. Everything in the act is brand new, from the scenery to the tricks and other features that combine to make an extraordinary performance.

(Elmira, NY — July 7, 1916)

-----0-----

MID-WEST

1916

Date	State/Country	Venue
Jul 24		
Jul 31		
Aug 07		
Aug 14		
Aug 21		
Aug 28		
Sep 04-06		
Sep 07-09	CANADA	OTTAWA, Dominion
Sep 11-16	CANADA	HAMILTON, Temple
Sep 18		
Sep 25		
Oct 02-04		
Oct 09		
Oct 16	Indiana	KOKOMO, Sipe's
Oct 22	Wisconsin	RACINE, Orpheum
Oct 23	Minnesota	MINNEAPOLIS, Palace
Oct 30-Nov 01	North Dakota	GRAND FORKS, Grand
Nov 03	Dakota	BISMARK, Auditorium
Nov 06		
Nov 12-14	Montana	ANACONDA, Empress

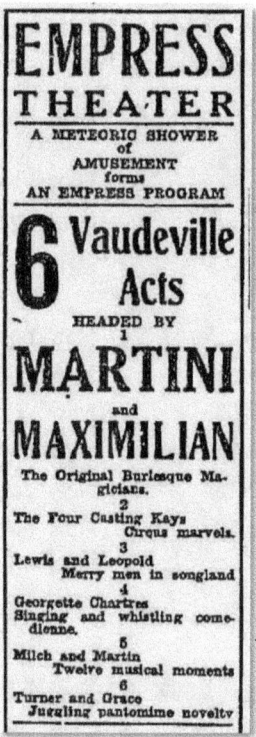

Anaconda Standard
November 13, 1916

-----0-----

Here are more reviews of performances of the Martini and Maxmillian conjuring act, but which aren't identified by date and location, seeing as they are from Laurel's scrapbook:

Martini and Maximilian had to come out several times after they had concluded their burlesques on conjuring, "Showing up" all the tricks of the Kellar and other magic. The audience certainly expressed its appreciation of the way these men expose the marvels that have made everybody sit up and at times gasp when feats of magic were in order.

[AJM: Keller was a highly-respected magician, considered one of the exponents of modern magic.]

-----0-----

The burlesque magic and illusions of Martini and Maximilian is another especially attractive number of the bill, which was thoroughly enjoyed by Monday's audiences. Some of their work was of the gilt-edged variety.

-----0-----

Martini and Maxmillian, burlesque magicians, have an uproarious and original offering, one perpetrating feats of magic and the other blunderingly exposing him. Their "illusion" is one long laugh, as is also their encore number.

A real bright act.

-----0-----

WEST and WEST COAST

1916

Nov 15			
Nov 20			
Nov 27	Washington	TACOMA, Regent	
Dec 04-06	Washington	SEATTLE, Palace Hippodrome	
Dec 07-09	Oregon	PORTLAND, Hippodrome	
Dec 10	Oregon	SALEM, Bligh	[Sun only]
Dec 11			

So far, none of the reviews has tipped us off as to what tricks Martini performed. One reviewer enticed the locals into wanting to go and see what the "remarkable ending" was, but then this idiot goes and completely gives it away, thus destroying any surprise the audiences would have enjoyed had they gone to the theatre un-informed.

> Martini and Maxmillian had the audience in one uproar of laughter, last evening, with their burlesque magic speciality. The nut comedian of this clever pair has some great fun, giving his very serious partner's tricks away. Funniest of all is the finish of the act when the comedian, while burlesquing one of his partner's tricks is buried under a bevy of newspapers falling from nowhere.

-----0-----

At least one other reviewer felt himself compelled to ruin the surprise ending:

Ohio, LIMA, Orpheum

> Martinni and Maxmillian have one of the cleverest acts that has closed a bill there in many weeks. In a special setting that gives a hint of real magic and real illusions, one fake after the other is exposed by the comedy member of the team. Usually such acts are somewhat annoying but Martinni and Maxmillian have put together some clever stuff. The act winds up with the dropping of about 1,000 newspapers from the flies, completely burying the comedy member of the team.
>
> *(Lima News — November 16, 1915)*

-----0-----

Here are a few rather more subtle hints at other tricks in the act, some of which have been gathered from write-ups pre-Stan, but which were almost certainly still in the act during his time as assistant:

> Martini and Maxmilian's act consists of the doing and undoing of wonderful tricks. They give a wonderful cage illusion and also manufacture snow. It's some act.
>
> (Lowell, MA — May 5, 1915

-----0-----

> The only trick, in a straight magical way, is the gold-fish bit which the straight does effectively.
>
> (*Variety* — August 1, 1914

-----0-----

> The act of Martini and Maxmillian is a happy mixture of comedy and magic. Some apparently difficult tricks are exposed by the magician's assistant in a most laughable manner, but the trick of catching gold fish on a hook and line, swinging over the heads of the audience, is mystifying all.
>
> (Hamilton, Ohio — November 19, 1915)

-----0-----

Virginia, RICHMOND, Lyric

> The bill closes with Martini and Maximillian in illusions and tricks. The pair jerk rabbits out of chafing dishes and then show how it is done, which always pleases the audience immensely.
>
> (Richmond — March 31, 1916)

[AJM: A chafing dish is a lidded pan with a source of heat beneath it, used for keeping food warm at the table.]

It is no coincidence that, when Stan joined Martini, the act was widely advertised as "new props and tricks." I have no doubt in my mind that Stan recycled one or more tricks from the act of Professor Bunco — the cod-magician in *Mumming Birds*. Why re-invent the wheel?

If you want an even better idea of Stan's character in the Martini & Maximillian act, just watch Laurel & Hardy doing a magic act in their cameo in the film *The Hollywood Revue of 1929*.

[Chaplin too had been taken by the cod-magician in *Mumming Birds* (*A Night in an English Music Hall*), and was all set to reprise the act in *The Circus*. For some reason, he dropped that idea (and substituted an over-elaborate one-trick-only apparatus, involving live animals); but the still, above right, shows the small magician's-table of tricks he originally meant to use This is an almost exact copy of the one in *Mumming Birds* — which Laurel too went on to copy. And both went for the 'stitched together card trick' in the publicity shot. Chaplin even went as far as to name his magician "Professor Bosco" – a thinly disguised alliteration of the Karno character "Professor Bunco."]

Now we have an idea of the business in the act, let us try and establish what Stan's character looked like? This next review may not be as helpful as it first appears, owing to a touch of ambiguity:

Montana, BUTTE, Empress

> Martini and Maximilian are very high class performers. The former is a magician and sleight of hand man, with few equals, while Maximilian is a comedian with great ability and a wonderful make-up.
>
> (*Anaconda Standard* — November 14, 1916)

In his earlier days as a Chaplin impersonator, Stan was referred to as being, "in Chaplin make-up." This wasn't referencing greasepaint on his face, but meant his overall appearance and dress — i.e., he was "made-up" to look like Chaplin. However, in the last review, the phrase could just as easily refer to facial make-up. Could it be that Stan actually applied clown make-up the same as, or similar to, his predecessor? This next review seems to hint that he did; but then, here again, there is ambiguity:

Oregon, PORTLAND, Hippodrome

> One could laugh until he cried watching Martini and Maximilian, comical tricksters, at the Hippodrome, the feature act in the show that opened today. The act is a perfect scream. One of the performers is a clever sleight of hand man; the other is a clown who exposes each trick performed by the other in a side-splitting way.
>
> (*Oregon Daily Journal* — December 7, 1916)

The ambiguity in the latter review comes from the usage of the word "clown." The most-common image of a clown is the circus performer who applies different coloured sticks of Leichner to enhance eyebrows, cheeks, and lips. But then we have the likes of Chaplin, Keaton, Lloyd, Semon, Langdon, and others, who are all described as "clowns" — none of whom wore the clown face. In their case, the word "clown" is used to describe a comedy acrobat who specialises in stunts, falls, slapstick, and general physical comedy.

Portrait of Stan's predecessor, in the role of Maximillian.
(I don't know about you, but I find the make-up more frightening than funny.)

So what kind of clown was Stan playing? Sorry to say that, in all the newspaper clips I unearthed, and among all those in Stan's scrapbook, there isn't a single picture showing Stan in clown make-up. Maybe he destroyed them, as he didn't want to be remembered in that guise, so we might never know what his stage character "Maximillian" looked like.

Going off the known dates, I would guestimate that Stan and Bob Martini did their last show together on February 7, at Sioux Falls, South Dakota. (But there is a twist, yet to come.)

Variety was again the only paper to publicly "out" that Martini had changed his stage partner, again, but was a little slow in volunteering the information:

RIALTO

Martini and Maxmillian with burlesque magic did well enough (the team has a new comic).

(March 1, 1917)

-----0-----

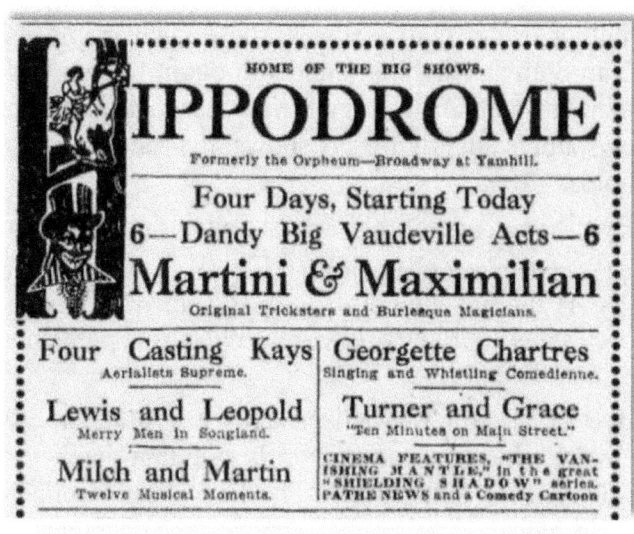

Portland Hippodrome — December 7-9, 1916

And so ends the chapter on Stan Jefferson's previously unknown tours with the magic act 'Martini & Maximillian' — leastways it would have been if I had not continued my research beyond the date the two separated, and — EUREKA! Just two months after the split, the picture, below left, was published in a newspaper in Des Moines, Iowa, advertising the appearance of the 'new' Martini & Maximillian:

Who could doubt that that high brow and elongated chin belong to a Jefferson?

Martini and Maximilian at Empress

I then found another newspaper advertisement, with picture (above, centre). Before you start debating whether or not that is Stan in these unclear images, please compare with the accompanying portraits (from Stan's scrapbook), and you ought to then feel as confident as I do that they are indeed Stan. My theory is that, in the same way Stan had had to accept pictures of his predecessor in some of the newspapers adverts for *his* shows; his successor too was misrepresented by these out-of-date publicity photos.

By the way, one of the earliest reviews of Stan's successor revealed:

> Martini and Maximilian offer a comedy magic act of a stereotypical yet pleasing nature. It is the old theme of the magician who wishes to startle the world by his feats and whose plans are rudely upset by a red-nosed gentleman.

(Lowell, MA — October 16, 1917)

If Bob Martini was indeed allowing his latest assistant to wear only a red-nose to mark him as a "clown," then one can feel fairly safe that that is the only make-up Stan wore. Jefferson Jnr. knew this role well. He had played "The Red Nose Comic" during the run of the 1912-1914 Karno Tours, so would have had no trouble reprising the character. In fact, it might be that Stan played the role so well, that Martini did not have his latest assistant revert to the full clown face make-up. An alternative view is that Stan worked in clown-face for the first few weeks after joining Martini, but then persuaded Bob he could be equally funny, if not even funnier, with just the red nose make-up.

And so, although we have not ended this chapter with a cliff-hanger, I do trust you will agree that, with these newly found images, we have finished on a high.

------0-----

Just one more "just one more" — Yes, Stan and Mae do come next.

CHAPTER 21

STANONIMTY

It is good practice to let readers get well into a chapter, before inserting any obstacles; but in this instance, I have to start with one before we can proceed:

After having spent countless hours trying to track down Stan's appearances with Martini & Maximillian, I thought I had identified the point where the two split. The list of continuous bookings for M&M takes us up to February 7, 1917, and then we get our first sightings of Stan & Mae Laurel. But then, just as I was happy with my conclusions, this newspaper article appeared; which puts Stan and Mae's debut some six or seven weeks earlier, to around December 18, 1916:

CHAPLIN'S OLD PARTNER
PLAYING IN CITY TODAY
Stan Laurel, Who Toured England
With Now Famous Star, Appearing at the
Temple

Probably as many people in America today know who Charlie Chaplin is as do who is president of the United States, and a whole lot more are familiar with his appearance and how he now earns his living. In fact, the American public probably knows more about Chaplin than any other one person.

The Temple theatre is announcing as a special attraction today and Christmas the comedy act of Stan and May Laurel, this same Stan Laurel having been the vaudeville partner of Chaplin during nearly all that time he toured the music halls and also coming to America with him. No other man in America knows as much of, nor was so interested in, the early struggles of Chaplin as was Stan Laurel. Stan and May Laurel have been appearing in Detroit all the past week and open on western "time" out of Chicago a week from today. It was only because they had one week between, that the Temple was able to book them as a special attraction.

Patriot Jackson
December 24, 1916

(*Patriot*, Jackson, Michigan — December 24, 1916)

-----0-----

The above preview, which is an advert (i.e. which had to be paid for by Stan or his agent) cites engagements during the week before and the week after this engagement. It adds that Stan & Mae are also about to begin a tour on the Western circuit. However, I found no other evidence to corroborate these claims, which leaves me wondering if they are factual. So I have edged my bets and printed the original date-sheet I compiled, whilst adding this new information for consideration. See next page!

Just why Stan split from Martini is open to speculation, but my theory reverts to the comments I made earlier that: "*Sitting out, while others were on stage were getting the laughs, was not something Mae could suffer easily.*" I can well imagine Mae chewing off Stan's ear, each and every day during his partnership with Bob Martini, wanting to get in on the act – literally. Whatever the case, Bob Martini walked off into the sunshine with his new partner, and Stan Laurel walked under a storm cloud with Mae. This was going to be a tempestuous relationship wherein it was not a matter of "when would the storm break," but "when would it stop?" However, let us concentrate on what happened on stage; which, after all, is the subject of this book — and not, "The Wifes and Strifes of STAN LAUREL."

Just as Stan had been rehearsing his new act with The Three English Comiques before jumping off the Karno wagon, here too Stan and Mae must have been writing, rehearsing, and polishing their new act before splitting from Martini.

STAN & MAE LAUREL
"Raffles the Dentist"

1916 (continued)

Dec 18	Michigan	DETROIT	Stan & Mae Laurel	[unconfirmed]
Dec 24-25	Michigan	JACKSON, Temple	Stan & Mae Laurel	[confirmed]
[Dec 25	California	SAN JOSE, Jose	Martini & Maximillian]	

1917

Jan 01	Illinois	CHICAGO	Stan & Mae Laurel	[unconfirmed]
[Jan 08	California	SAN DIEGO, Spreckels	Martini and Maximillian]	
[Jan 14-20	Texas	EL PASO, Crawford	Martini and Maximillian]	
[Jan 22-24	Kansas	TOPEKA, Auditorium	Martini and Maximillian]	
[Jan 25	Missouri	SPRINGFIELD, Electric	Martini and Maximillian]	
[Jan 29-31	Nebraska	LINCOLN, Lyric	Martini and Maximillian]	
[Feb 01-03	Nebraska	OMAHA, Empress	Martini and Maximillian]	
[Feb 05	South Dakota	SIOUX FALLS, Orpheum	Martini and Maximillian]	

[Logic says Stan left here – February 7.]

Feb 12	Illinois	CHICAGO, Academy	Stan & Mae Laurel	
[Feb 12	Minnesota	ROCHESTER, Metro	Martini and Maximillian]	
[Feb 18			*Variety* confirms Martini has a new partner]	
Feb 25-27	Montana	ANACONDA, Empress		

-----0-----

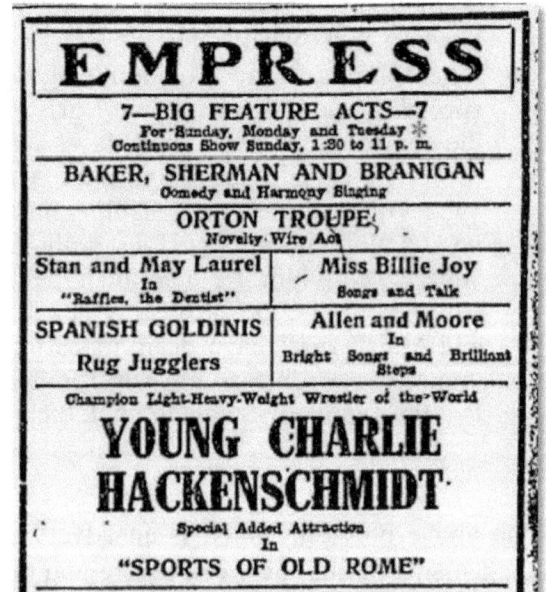

I am still not convinced that Stan had parted company with Martini at this juncture. Something went on between the end of December and beginning of January that we still don't know about. What we do know is that Stan has definitely left by February 24th, as on the 25th he begins a run of *confirmed* engagements as a double-act with Mae. Here is the first:

Montana, ANACONDA, Empress

Stan and May Laurel make up a team of high-class artists who will present a pleasing singing, dancing and talking act called "Raffles, the Dentist." Some bright, wholesome fun is promised.

(*Anaconda Standard* — February 25, 1917)

Stan Jefferson and Mae Dahlberg were about to launch themselves as "Stan & Mae Laurel" — that is, using a surname which belonged to neither of them. When questioned in later years as to why he chose the name "Laurel," Stan had no recollection. He did say that he changed from the name "Stan Jefferson" because it contained thirteen letters, which he considered to be a bad omen. But then "Stanley Laurel" contains thirteen letters, which hardly negates all the evil which falls on people with thirteen letters in their name. A more feasible reason for people in show business shortening their name is because of the print size in newspapers adverts and trade paper listings, and on posters. The more letters in the name, the smaller the font size has to be to accommodate them in the available space:

This explains why a shorter name is an advantage, but not the origin of the name itself. John McCabe believes that, during his interview with Mae Dahlberg (*ibid*), she gave the true origin — adding: "But on one matter," McCabe states, "she had total recall."

Stanonimty

I can remember just how Stan got the name Laurel. It was not long after we were teamed together, and we were traveling as a double act sometimes called Stan and Mae Jefferson, or mostly Stan Jefferson, with me as assistant.

[Before continuing I must point out that I never found a single billing for "Stan and Mae Jefferson," or just "Stan Jefferson" during that time period.]

In the McCabe interview, Mae goes on to tell how, in the dressing room of one theatre, she was thumbing through an old history book, left behind by a previous occupant, when she came upon an etching of an ancient Roman general. On his head was a laurel wreath, which prompted her to say aloud: "Laurel." She then repeated it aloud to Stan, this time adding his first name: "Stan Laurel." He too then voiced it aloud, and accepted the name change on the spot. *"That's how he got his name. It was that simple,"* related Mae to McCabe. So I guess we will have to accept it, as well.

As for Mae, she was now using the name of "Laurel" to surmount the problem that unmarried couples were not allowed to co-habit in professional accommodation — as outlined previously in the case of the Hurleys, and the Baldwins.

When it came to devising a new sketch to incorporate into the act, Stan once again stuck to the theme of a burglar caught entering a lady's apartment, and whose presence is accepted when he assumes the role of a legitimate professional. This time, he was mistaken for a dentist answering a call-out, hence the title *Raffles, the Dentist* — a close variant of both *The Nutty Burglars*, and *The Crazy Cracksman*. I could layout the premise in one complete hit, but I think you will have more fun gleaning the various bits of on-stage business as you read through the reviews which follow shortly. After all, what fun is there in being presented with a completed jig-saw puzzle?

Before letting Stan loose with this new act, consider the position he was now in: Any credibility he had gained as a comedy performer had almost totally evaporated. During the interlude with Martini & Maximillian, he had worked in total anonymity. Although he had earned glowing reviews as 'Maximillian' he wouldn't, or *couldn't*, let the show business world know that it was he, Stan Jefferson, who had been in that role. This negated the using of his body of work with the magic act as a promotional aid to generate work for his latest double-act. Even had he stuck with his own name, it would not have helped much, as any reputation he had gained in the Keystone Trio and the Stan Jefferson Trio, had now died, and trying to explain to agents and bookers about the many months out would not have helped his status. So, here in December 1916, almost three years after Stanley Jefferson had left the Fred Karno Company — we find Charlie Chaplin as the most famous and highly paid film comedian on the planet — and Stan Laurel starting out from scratch, as an unknown comic.

> Stan and May Laurel followed and achieved the seemingly impossible with an assortment of English low comedy songs, dances and pantomime bits. The male enters as a burglar and is mistaken for a doctor by the girl, who has just phoned for a dentist. After this the act devolves into a succession of comedy business by the man which was good for screams. He is a comic who reminds of the Karno school and has a fine knowledge of travesty values and an unusual amount of pantomimic talent. The big moment of the act was finished in one with the comic doing a "vamp" in a grotesque decolette gown, and the woman a "fool" trying to make him. This number weakens out at the finish, but could be built into a ladder that should vault this couple onto the big-time bills. He will make any gathering laugh, and the girl is a most capable partner.

In a move of desperation, Stan and/or his agent resorted to playing "the Chaplin card" as a way of giving Stan credibility, and so most of the earliest previews of Stan & Mae's act included reference to Stan's historical working relationship with Chaplin:

Washington, SEATTLE, Palace Hippodrome

Stan and May Laurel present a skit called "Raffles the Dentist," in which they have also singing and dancing, besides a lot of Charlie Chaplin comedy that is funny. Laurel was not long ago the understudy for Chaplin, and is expert at the latter's kind of acrobatics.

(*Seattle Daily Times* — March 19, 1917)

LAUREL – Stage by Stage

Oregon, PORTLAND, Hippodrome

"Raffles, the Dentist," a comedy skit, is presented by Stan and May Laurel. Stan is a brilliant burlesquer of types—and has further claim to attention as having appeared in vaudeville with Charlie Chaplin. The act he offers is replete with fun, and Miss Laurel adds to its effectiveness by appearing in smart toggery.

(Portland — March 23, 1917)

-----0-----

Oregon, PORTLAND, Hippodrome

Before Charlie Chaplain became world famous as a film celebrity, he was a vaudeville performer in a very clever variety skit known as "A Night in an English Concert Hall." Stan Laurel was Chaplin's head man for several seasons and after Charlie entered the movie business he started an act of his own and together with May Laurel has gained much fame on his own account in the vaudeville world. These two young persons are now touring over the Hippodrome circuit in "Raffles, the Dentist," a comedy skit including singing, talking and dancing. This little sketch gives Mr. Laurel ample opportunity to shine as a grotesque comedian of the type made famous by creating a riot at every performance at the Hippodrome theatre in Portland, and will be in Salem at the Bligh theatre in addition to two other headline acts from the same show, next Sunday matinee and evening.

(Salem — March 23, 1917)

[AJM: Stan had recently played these two Oregon theatres, in the Martini and Maximillian act, but that has been omitted from the reviews, in favour of the Chaplin reference.]

Oregon, SALEM, Bligh
Sunday March 26, 1917

Another bright vaudeville show was seen at the Bligh Theatre yesterday by crowds that filled the house to capacity on every performance including the matinee, which was packed, jammed in the doors.

Last but not least came the real riot act in the name of "Stan and May Laurel" playing "Raffles the Dentist." Mr. Laurel, the comedian in this set, for several years in connection with world famous film comedian Charlie Chaplin, they came to this from England, together in a comedy variety act "A Night in an English Music Hall."

Stan Laurel accompanied by May Laurel have gained considerable fame for themselves in the vaudeville world in their act. From his

Stan about to introduce Mae to "Painless Parker."

opening song "I'm a Burglar" the laughter began and continued all the while he was getting tangled up in the fly paper, extracting the lady's aching tooth, substituting a wallop on the head with a mallet for chloroform and calling it "Painless Parker," and a number of other funny capers including accidentally emptying the contents of a seltzer bottle in his lap, we believe that Mr. Laurel was the cause of a great many people going home with aching sides from laughter.

(Salem — March 26, 1917)

-----0-----

Through this period of wanting to catch some of Chaplin's reflected spotlight, Stan was starting to emerge as a comedy talent in his own right. Here are some of the more useful reviews which help us plot Stan and Mae's progress in developing the sketch:

> "Raffles, the Dentist," is a Chaplinesque comedy. It represents a burglar entering a hotel apartment, and being mistaken for a dentist. He makes the most of the situation, finds opportunity to make love to the lady occupant of the apartment, and indulges in a considerable deal of broad comedy.
>
> (Laurel scrapbook)

-----0-----

> "Raffles," Burglar-Dentist, Draws Down House with Act.
>
> Stan Laurel as "Raffles," the burglar-dentist, produces loads of humor. He is a grotesque comedian of the Charley Chaplin type and there are barrels of laughs every time he makes a turn. He is called upon the stage as a dentist, but everybody loses sight of this in the fun that he furnishes, capably assisted by May Laurel.
>
> (Laurel scrapbook)

-----0-----

The reviews for the current act continue:

> The star number on the bill is provided by Stan and Mae Laurel in "Raffles, the Dentist." Laurel is a capable comedian with a fondness for slapstick and burlesque methods. There is perhaps more than a suggestion of Charley Chaplin about his makeup and method, but he registers effectively. His partner is a pretty, well curved miss with red locks and bizarre frocks.
>
> (Laurel scrapbook)

So now we have an idea how Stan and Mae looked, on stage, let us get a bit more of an idea of the content of their performance.

> Stan and May Laurel presented "Raffles, the Dentist." The scene was laid in a hotel room, with the woman suffering from toothache. When a burglar appeared she thought he was a dentist, and he allowed her to think it. He was dressed and acted like one of those "perfect lady" type of men, and won a succession of laughs. Then, at the close of the act, May sang a song all about vampires and their methods. She appeared in a trailing black gown as the "vamp."
>
> (Laurel scrapbook)

-----0-----

> King Nebuchadnezzar, Egyptian potentate, perhaps used to laugh at seltzer bottle tricks. Endless funny things can be done with the business end of a fizz water bottle, but in "Raffles and the Dentist," a comedy skit by Stan and May Laurel at the Hip this half-week, a very simple little action by the pair, while seated at a table, discussing a bottle of spirits, brings down the house. It is something new.
>
> (Laurel scrapbook)

-----0-----

> Stan and Mae Laurel certainly brought down the house in a clever little comedy turn. If Stan didn't redden his nose it would be much more pleasant to look at him. He is downright funny in spite of it, but he gains nothing from it, and it is a handicap. His song, "I'm a Burglar," and his vamping are very clever.

Having stated that: "You couldn't be funny in those days unless you had a red nose," Laurel seems to be being told by the last reviewer that "those days" are over.

As for the song "I'm a Burglar," it may well owe its origins to the Karno musical sketch *His Majesty's Guests*, which was all about burglars. One review of HMG, from several years back, revealed:

> The knockabout business is smartly done, and the "Burglar's Chorus," as usual, is vociferously encored. The music is bright and tuneful.

-----0-----

LAUREL – Stage by Stage

1917 (continued)
Feb 28
Mar 05
Mar 11

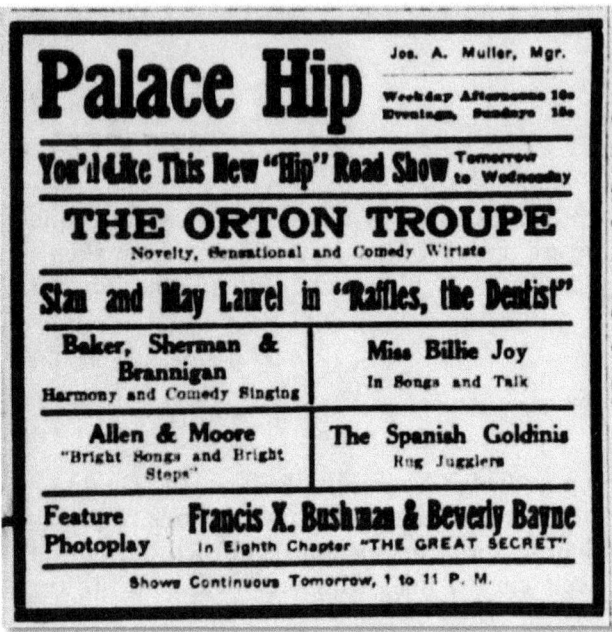

Seattle Daily Times
March 19, 1917

Mar 15-17	Washington	TACOMA, Regent	
Mar 18-21	Washington	SEATTLE, Palace Hippodrome	[formerly Majestic, then Empress]
Mar 22-24	Oregon	PORTLAND, Hippodrome	
Mar 25	Oregon	SALEM, Bligh	

Portland Oregonian — March 3, 1917

Sacramento Union — March 29, 1917

| Mar 26-28 | | ?? , Majestic |
| Mar 29-31 | California | SACRAMENTO, Empress |

-----0-----

California, SACRAMENTO, Empress

Stan and May Laurell have a comedy skit entitled "Raffles, the Dentist," replete with funny situations. Stan Laurell is a comedian of the type made famous by Chaplin.

(*Sacramento Union*, CA — March 28, 1917)

1917 (continued)

Apr 02			
Apr 04-07	California	OAKLAND, Hippodrome	
Apr 08-14	California	SAN FRANCISCO, Casino	[Sun-Sat]
Apr 16			
Apr 21-22	Nevada	RENO, T&H Hippodrome	[Sat-Sun]
Apr 23-26	California	SAN FRANCISCO, ??	
Apr 27-28	California	BAKERSFIELD, Hippodrome	
Apr 30			
May 03-06	California	SAN DIEGO, Spreckels Hippodrome	

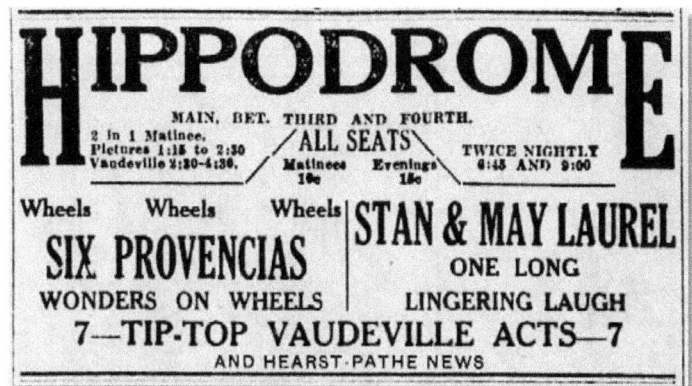

May 07	California	LOS ANGELES, Hippodrome
May 14		
May 21		
May 28		
Jun 04		
Jun 11		
Jun 18-24		

Cuttings from *San Diego Evening Tribune* (May 4, 1917) and *Los Angeles Herald* (May 8, 1917), both expressing their opinion that Stan Laurel ought to be in pictures. And how right they were.

-----0-----

Both Chicago and New Jersey seemed like popular places to break-in one's act before, hopefully, being offered a long run in New York. The biggest attraction of a long stay in New York, after the regular work and income it brought, was to be able to stay in the same apartment, and not have to pack up all of one's worldly goods every few days. However, that wasn't going to happen on the Laurels' current tour, as the agency they had signed with had them heading for the *West* Coast, and at a rate of speed that a rally-car driver would envy. Within just thirty-one days they traversed through Minnesota, and Montana, and hit the East Coast state of Washington. One week later they travelled south, into Oregon, and one week after that, they were in California. What was the rush? Chaplin had left for California three and a half years ago, and was more than well-established in the film world; so, by taking the slow route, Stan would hardly have been missing out on the action there. However, in this fable, the hare didn't take his time, but he did get there, and this time it was about to pay off. However …

Los Angeles, the film-capital of the world, was now about to be introduced to Stan Laurel, for the very first time.[*1] Here was the biggest chance of his career, so far, to impress the movie moguls by showcasing at one of the theatres they were known to monitor. Here they would see this new, fresh, funny comedy character, with his own unique style in comedy. So this newspaper preview announcing his forthcoming appearance, using a publicity blurb they had been sent, could not have been more ill-judged.

[*1] In the book *Laurel or Hardy*, author Rob Stone states that Laurel had played L.A. earlier in the year, under the guise of 'The Stan Stanley Trio' – but a quick check revealed this to be 'The Bouncing Fellow' with his trampoline act (*ibid*).

California, LOS ANGELES, Hippodrome

Other entertaining features of the bill will be Stan Laurel—regarded as the only legitimate imitator of Charlie Chaplin—and May Laurel, in "Raffles, the Dentist," one of the laughing hits of the season.

(Los Angeles, CA — May 6, 1917)

---O---

California, LOS ANGELES, Hippodrome

If any of the movie producers are looking for a successor for Charlie Chaplin there wouldn't be any harm in giving Stan and May Laurel in "Raffles, the Dentist," the once over.

(*Los Angeles Herald*, CA — May 8, 1917)

-----O-----

Stan has splashed out on a new stage costume, to impress the Hollywood set.
LEFT: Re-enacting part of the "eggs in the pocket" routine.
ABOVE: The matching head for the newspaper picture, at right. (This wouldn't be the last time Laurel would cut a lady out of his life).
RIGHT. Advert from *Los Angeles Times* — May 6, 1917.

But who the heck, in Hollywood, was looking for a Charlie Chaplin impersonator? Although Stan had been the first to realise the potential in the Chaplin character, he did say, in a later interview, that he had by then dropped the Chaplin impersonation, as so many others were now doing it. Just as today, where show business is saturated with Elvis Presley and Michael Jackson impersonators, to name but two, in 1917 there seemed to be a Chaplin impersonator on every bill. As well as comedians, there were singing acts, child acts, choirs, and even bands who had a member who would suddenly step out of the music line-up to give their own take. And let's not get started on Talent Shows, where so many amateurs believed that the gateway to stardom lay in spending two minutes walking across the stage with feet splayed, swinging a cane and wiggling a fake moustache.

Thankfully, our comedy subject did not regress to performing any of the above actions during his act, but delivered a polished composite of all he had learned during the ten years he had now spent in stage comedy — and this is what got him noticed. And the man who noticed him was the owner of the Los Angeles Hippodrome – Adolph Ramish. You can bet your bottom dollar, or, in Stan's case "your last cent," that film companies used theatre managers (and owners) as talent scouts, with the promise of a financial "thank you" if they came up with a good un'. Thus it was that film producer Isadore Bernstein was summoned to the Hippodrome to watch Stan Laurel perform. We will never know what so impressed Bernstein, but impressed he must have been as, just four weeks after Stan and Mae's week at the Hippodrome had ended, Bernstein let *Los Angeles Times* readers know of the plans for his latest comedy find.

Stanonimty

MORE COMEDY FLICKERS
ORPHEUM GETTING READY TO CELEBRATE BIRTHDAY

The film world has been quick to respond to the hysterical reaction from heavy drama to comedy which has taken place in public feeling since the outbreak of war. Nearly all the film concerns now have comedy companies at work. Latest among them to annex such organizations is the Bernstein Film Productions, which yesterday added two comedy companies to its forces. The first of these companies will be headed by Stan Jefferson, the output of the organization to be released by Isadore Bernstein under the name of Stanley Comedies.

Stan Jefferson is from the Fred Karno School of London, from which Charlie Chaplin graduated; indeed the two took the course of study at the same time, and are close friends. Jefferson was recently in vaudeville, where he was most successful.

(*Los Angeles Times* — June 15, 1917) [abridged]

-----0-----

[AJM: Give me a minute or two to stop laughing at the reviewer's literal translation of the "Karno Comedy School," and then I'll carry on writing.]

To have come into town under the introduction of "a Chaplin impersonator" and then, within a few stage performances, been offered his own film series – with his name on them – was a momentous leap for Laurel — or should that be "Jefferson"? But Stan had made momentous leaps before, all of which had ended with his landing at the bottom of the chasm he had tried to leap across. Could this leap be the one which brought instant fame and success? My advice would be, "if you've still got that bottom dollar, don't place it on this bet."

When he first landed in Los Angeles Stan had no idea that he would be making an extended stay there, so Bernstein would have had to get him out of the theatre bookings he was contracted for. As recompense for the lost bookings, Bernstein was about to pay Stan a $75 a week retainer. It was a little short of the $670,000 fee which Chaplin had been given to sign with Mutual, sixteen months earlier; but when you are absolutely skint, money to buy food and drink is an offer you can't refuse. But what was Mae going to live off, as $75 amounted to only half of their usual stage fee?

So, with Laurel *finally* about to enter into films, it is at this stage that I shall maintain strict discipline, and *NOT* even start to try to provide you with every bit of available information on Stan Laurel's solo films. To do so would be to double the content of this book, and dilute the theme. We shall just treat the films Laurel was about to make, pre-1922, as a pleasant interlude between his vaudeville engagements, and I shall leave you to read books which deal with the films themselves, to fill you in on the details. (I can heartily recommend "*LAUREL or HARDY — The Solo Films of Stan Laurel and Oliver "Babe" Hardy,*" by Rob Stone — which is my personal reference source for Laurel's solo films). However, I shall endeavour to add my own twopenneth of information on the films, consisting of trivia you may well not know about.

Stan's extended stayover in L.A. began on May 13, but it took till the end of June before cast and crew were able to start shooting. The film was titled *Nuts in May*, which is a play on the song title: "Here We Go Gathering Knots in May," although, ironically, most people wrongly refer to this song as "Here We Go Gathering *Nuts* in May." (As James Finlayson would have said: "You're all nuts.")

As for the finished film, *Nuts in May*, it seems to have disappeared without first appearing. Rob Stone (so called because he never leaves one unturned), has only ever found one mention of the premise, which was a snippet in a local paper making mention of a crew and cast involved in filming some action around a steam-roller, outside the Boyle Heights studio. Maybe the cans of film ended up under the steam-roller.

But not to worry — there was the rest of the series to shoot. But hang on a moment: we are talking about Stan the "Nothing Lasts Long With Me" man — and here, the jinx struck yet again. The series of "Stanley Comedies" didn't even get into the plural form as, for reasons best-known to Bernstein, he disbanded the comedy unit. The war-effected cinemagoers would have to continue watching "heavy dramas."

As for Laurel, he must have been housebroken. Seven years now he had been touring in vaudeville, playing two, three, and sometimes up to five shows daily; packing his bags every few days, and spending non-working days travelling — and all the time earning only just enough money to get him to the next town, and pay for food and digs. Being told he had his own film series must have made him believe that his vaudeville days were now over, and at last he could settle down in one location and live a fairly normal life. After that rise-and-fall of expectations, returning to vaudeville was going to be even harder to endure.

But then, as he viewed his future from the bottom of the chasm he had now hit, a rope ladder was tossed down, which just might allow him to get back to the level he was at before Bernstein withdrew the film offer. Sometime between August 6 and September 12, the film *Nuts in May* was previewed at the Hippodrome, Los Angeles. In attendance were Carl Laemmle and someone Stan knew very well — none other than his former roommate, but now the most famous film comedian in the world — Chaplin.

There are those who believe that Chaplin was there to watch Laurel on film, with a view to offering him work as part of his team. I don't. There is no way that Chaplin wanted someone of Laurel's comedy calibre in his company — i.e. a comedian capable of stealing every scene.

In analysing Chaplin's films, you will note that there is no second comedian. None of the parts were written for any of the supporting actors to get laughs, but only to act as stooges and foils for Chaplin's assaults of kicks, punches, and being the victims of food and/or water fights. When Chaplin is chased, the action focusses on only him and the chaser. Everyone else is a 'frozen' on-looker. No way could Laurel function in this kind of set-up. Methinks that Chaplin was there to see Laurel's entry-level into films, and to find out if his comedy crown was soon about to be dented.

If Chaplin had wanted to give his former companion a leg-up in the film industry, he could have done it in ways other than making him a support actor at his studios, AND he could have done YEARS earlier, but he chose to do — NOTHING.

-----0-----

Late Jun	California	LOS ANGELES	*Nuts in May*	filming
Early Jul	California	LOS ANGELES	*Nuts in May*	filming
Jul 09				
Jul 16				
Jul 23				
Jul 30				
Aug 06				
Aug 13		*Los Angeles Times*		
Aug 20		September 2, 1917		
Aug 27		[*Skidding Hearts* was the		
Sep 03		working title for Laurel's		
Sep 12		next film – *Phoney Photos*.]		

> A new company has been organized by Production Manager McRae for Director Frazee. The principal comedian is Stanley Laurel, who recently was one of the featured players at the New York Hippodrome. Rea Rogers, late of Vogue, and Neal Burns, of Christie comedy fame, will be the featured players, while supporting them will be Walter Belasco and Lydia Yeamins Titus.
> The picture is to be called "Skidding Hearts," and an automobile trip down a long stairway into a cafe is one of its thrilling scenes.

-----0-----

The only saving grace of the film *Nuts in May* is that it may well have been the preview showing at the Hippodrome which triggered an offer for Laurel to work under the Universal Pictures banner. Universal had two smaller companies under its wing — L-KO and Nestor Films, and it was with the latter two that Stan was now about to make films. The first of these was *Phoney Photos*, made for L-KO. In this, Stan joined up with the leading comedian Neal Burns, and support actress Rena Rodgers. If Stan were thinking he would soon be a famous film star, he was soon made to think again. *Phoney Photos* would only start its main first-run on the cinema circuit between June and August 1918 – some ten months after filming. So, here in October 1917 it was on to the next comedy short — *Hickory Hiram*.

Upon its release, one review (dated May 13, 1918) told us of the "Hickory Hiram" film:

Magazine advert, featuring a rare still from *Hickory Hiram*. Note that there is no mention of this being the start of a series. There isn't even a credit for the actor in the eponymous role — Stan Laurel.

"Hickory Hiram," Nestor Comedy, at Edisonia Today.

Trixie was a milkmaid, and Hiram was the hired man, but it seemed to Hiram that it was high time that he branched out and went into the city. Taking Trixie by the hand, he descended upon the metropolis with all of the confidence which a dollar and ninety-eight cents in the left trousers pocket naturally inspires. His adventures in the Metropolitan theatre, the Winter Garden restaurant, and the county jail, finally brought him to, and he discovered that he had been milking the cow all the time.

Both Laurel and Chaplin's introduction to the plot-device of falling asleep and dreaming of becoming the hero, was back in 1910, when they played in the Karno sketch *Jimmy the Fearless* — aptly subtitled *The Boy 'Ero*. Chaplin had already revised the device to similar effect in his films *The Bank*, and *Shoulder Arms*. [He would go on to employ dream sequences in both *The Kid*, and *Modern Times*, although with different premises.]

Dream-sequences would also later be utilised in outros for the Laurel & Hardy films *Oliver the Eighth*, and *The Laurel-Hardy Murder Case*, but, in both, the "dreams" have been switched to that of nightmares.

Although we know much about the production and content of *Hickory Hiram*, even though it is considered a lost film, it still causes head-scratching amongst film historians, as Laurel labelled it as the first in a series in which he starred in the eponymous role. But a simple analysis of the premise and characters in the two films which were to follow, reveal no such continuity of the 'Hickory Hiram' character. But then I unearthed a newspaper review, dated September 4, 1918, which advertised:

> At the Rex theatre tonight there will also be presented a side-splitting comedy featuring Hickory Hiram, entitled "Bread."

-----0-----

So! lots of speculation here: Has the film been mis-titled; did Laurel shoot a second 'Hickory Hiram' film; or did another actor take over the role? To all you film historians, you can have this snippet to play with – I have other puzzles to solve.

1917 (continued)

Sep 17-23				
late Sep	California	LOS ANGELES	*Phoney Photos*	[filming for L-KO]
early Oct	California	LOS ANGELES	*Phoney Photos*	
Oct 04-06				
Oct 08	California	LOS ANGELES		
Oct 15	California	LOS ANGELES	*Hickory Hiram*	[filming for Nestor]
Oct 15-20				
Oct 22			*Whose Zoo?*	[L-KO]
Oct 29 - Nov 01			*It's Great to Be Crazy*	[Nestor]

-----0-----

A few days after filming ended on *Hickory Hiram*, shooting began on *Whose Zoo?* — again through L-KO. Stan's character name in the credits is given as 'Stanley Laurel' (NOT 'Hickory Hiram') — playing second-comic to Rube Miller. His best scene, one review tells us, is a rooftop chase in which Laurel is pursued by a bear." *Whose Zoo?* was quickly followed by the shooting of *It's Great to be Crazy*, this one being with Nestor Comedies.

Laurel must now be in total bewilderment as to how one gets to progress in the film world. His first film (*Nuts in May*) appears to have never appeared at all; his third film (*Hickory Hiram*) was a series of ONE; and, of the five which were completed, it would be ten to sixteen months before they were released.

Only thing to do now is for Stan and Mae to go back on the vaudeville trail, and for us to follow them in the hope that it leads them back to the City of Angels.

CHAPTER 22

THE ROACH APPROACH

When filming of *It's Great to be Crazy* ended, circa November 1, 1917, Stan must have fully expected there would be a call to do more films; but, come the end of January 1918, no call had come in. Laurel's funds were now rapidly approaching zero. Bernstein's retainer of $75 per week had almost certainly been withdrawn after the making of *Nuts and May* and now, having received only paltry fees for the four films which followed, Stan had the choice of going back into vaudeville, or starving. He had already tried starving — during the time he returned to England between 1911 and 1912 — and did not want to suffer that again, so he and Mae revived the "*Raffles, the Dentist*" sketch and forced themselves back into a life they thought he had left behind some eight months earlier.

> For those who like the comedy style of Charlie Chaplin, the offering of Stan and May Laurel will come as a real treat. They present a medley of entertainment which includes a skit called "Raffles, the Dentist," singing, dancing and comedy. The antics of Mr. Laurel, who was formerly an understudy for Chaplin, are a scream for that type of acting. His song, "I'm a Burglar," is exceptionally funny, and Miss Laurel's dance and burlesques are good.

> Comedy of the typical "Hinglish" variety provoked the audience to mirth and laughter, when Stan and May Laurel began to unravel the burlesque threads of the comedy playlet, "Raffles, the Dentist." The antics of Mr. Laurel are humorous, and smack of the Charlie Chaplin variety. Miss Laurel sings and dances cleverly

> comedy. An unusual comedy act, a variety skit, called "Raffles, the Dentist," is presented by Stan and May Laurel. and includes about everything in the way of entertainment, singing, dancing and comical antics of the Charlie Chaplin kind that are very funny and very fast. Laurel was formerly an understudy for Chaplin, and has recently gained considerable fame with this type of comedy.

> "Raffles, the Dentist," is the title of a novel comedy playlet presented by Stan and May Laurel. A burlesque burglar with huge burglar tools, breaks into the flat of a young woman suffering with toothache and she mistakes him for a dentist. The situation develops a scream. Stan and May give extra measure of entertainment with songs and dances. The act is a hit.

STAN & MAE LAUREL — "Raffles, the Dentist"

1918

Date	State	Venue	
Feb 04-09	New Mexico	DEMING, Cody	
Feb 10-15	Texas	EL PASO, Texas Grand	
Feb 16			
Feb 18	Iowa	DES MOINES, Empress	
Feb 24-26	Montana	BUTTE, Empress	
Feb 27			
Mar 04			
Mar 11-13			
Mar 14-16	Washington	SEATTLE, Palace Hippodrome	
Mar 17	Oregon	PORTLAND, Hippodrome	
Mar 24-30	California	SAN FRANCISCO, Hippodrome	[Sun-Sat]
Mar 31-Apr 02	California	SAN FRANCISCO, Wigwam	[Sun-Tue]
Apr 03-05			
Apr 07-13	California	SAN JOSE, José	[Sun-Sat]
Apr 14-16	Nevada	RENO, Majestic	[Sun-Tue]

Portland Oregonian — March 18

> Stan and May Laurel presented "Raffles, the Dentist." The scene was laid in a hotel room, with the woman suffering from toothache. When a burglar appeared she thought he was a dentist and he allowed her to think it. He was dressed and acted like one of those "perfect lady" type of men, and won a succession of laughs. Then, at the close of the act, May sang a song all about vampires and their methods. She appeared in a trailing black gown as the "vamp."

-----0-----

LAUREL – Stage by Stage

Texas, EL PASO, Texas Grand — w/c February 10, 1918

Stan and May Laurel, in "Raffles the Dentist," also have a clever act which has lots of laughs. Miss Laurel is also a good dancer and a good looker.

(*El Paso Herald* — February 11, 1918)

-----0-----

Washington, SEATTLE, Palace Hippodrome — w/c March 14, 1918

"Raffles the Dentist," is the offering of Stan and May Laurel, which includes everything in vaudeville. Laurel is a comedian of Chaplin proclivities, and he does many clever falls.

(*Seattle Daily Times* — March 15, 1918)

-----0-----

Stan and Mae must have hoped they could get work in New York where, once they had made the 2,800 trip to get there, the amount of travel would be limited and therefore less exhausting. But St. Christopher wasn't looking after them and, in just forty-eight days, they made whistle-stop tours of *at least* six states — heading east as far as Iowa. The only good thing about this circular tour is that it brought them right back to California, where, when they hit Los Angeles, there was a ray of hope that some of the seeds Laurel had planted on the last visit would produce a yield. But better not to raise Stan's expectations. He had had enough disappointments to last a lifetime.

-----0-----

Apr 17-20	California	SACRAMENTO, Hippodrome	[Wed-Sat]
Apr 07-13	California	SAN JOSE, José	[Sun-Sat]
Apr 14-16	Nevada	RENO, Majestic	[Sun-Tue]
Apr 17-20	California	SACRAMENTO, Hippodrome	[Wed-Sat]

-----0-----

1st sighting of this publicity pose was in the *Sacramento Union* newspaper (April 17, 1918), although it seems to originate from the Kessler Photographic Studio, Chicago, which could date it as far back as February 1917, when Stan and Mae made their debut after Stan left Martini & Maximillian.

Note that Stan has completely discarded all make-up associated with Chaplin, and adopted a character very much like 'Percy Swoffles,' from Karno's *A Night in a London Club*, although there is no evidence that he appeared on stage like this, while with Mae.

The Roach Approach

I wonder if anyone ever turned up to see *Raffles, the Dentist* – expecting to see John Barrymore in it, as this is the film which was then doing the rounds:

> Thievery becomes a virtue in John Barrymore's characterization of "Raffles the Amateur Cracksman," The society crook has a thrilling career, in which he spans two continents. He seems to have none of the characteristics of a criminal, as he plies his trade for sheer love of adventure.

Apr 22		
Apr 29		
May 01-02	California	BAKERSFIELD, Hippodrome
May 03-04		
May 05-11	California	LOS ANGELES, Hippodrome [Sun-Sat]

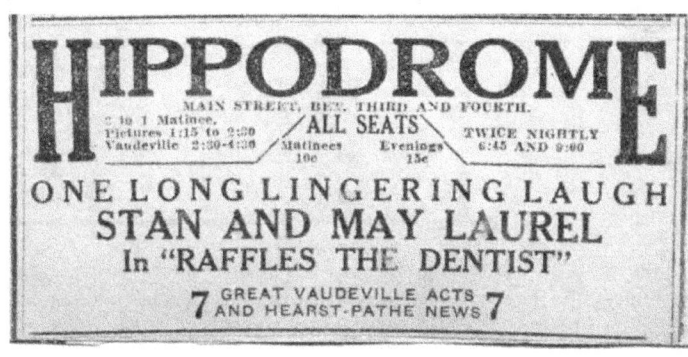

Week commencing May 5th Stan was back at the Hippodrome in Los Angeles, where the previous year he had been clocked by owner Aldolph Ramish. This time, however, Laurel was not approached by anyone with the well-used line: "Do you want to be in pictures?" and moved on to the next engagement. That's twice now that Laurel has left Los Angeles wondering just what the heck he has to do to get a film contract. He would have known that he could never hope to get a financial deal anything like Chaplin's, but he also knew he could be funnier than most any comedian in filmdom, and even give Chaplin a run for his money.

-----0-----

California, SAN DIEGO, Spreckels Hippodrome

Stan and Laurel have a number brimful of comedy. Stan Laurel as the dentist, who has disguised himself as a burglar, would make anyone laugh. His burglar's dance, his trick with the seltzer bottle, and his method of putting his patient to sleep drew howls of laughter.

(*San Diego Union* — May 14, 1918)

> There are several fine new features on the new Spreckels Hippodrome vaudeville bill which opened yesterday with three performances and among them it would be hard to determine on the headliner for the bill. Some thought that Scamp and Scamp, acrobatic comedians, should be awarded the plum and there were others equally determined that the biggest laugh on the bill was contributed by Stan and May Laurel in "Raffles, the Dentist." Both acts are immense.

The reviewer has made a couple of 'howlers' himself. Did you spot them?

But then, just when Stan thought he was going to be stuck on the not-so-merry-go-round called vaudeville, he received a telegram, recalling him to Los Angeles. The telegram, dated May 24, 1918, found Stan at the Portalo Theatre, Santa Barbara. Luckily it caught him just in time, as May 25th was his last date there, after which he would have moved on again.

May 13	California	SAN DIEGO, Spreckels Hippodrome
May 20-25	California	SANTA BARBABA, Portalo

-----0-----

So, on May 26th, Laurel caught the train back to L.A., and reported in at Bradbury Mansions, Court Street Hill, where a number of film companies leased space. The one he had been summoned to was Rolin Pictures – "Rolin" being an acronym formed from the initial letters of the surnames of Hal ROach and his financial partner Dan LINthicum. Roach was to become the most significant person in Stan's Laurel's life, but — slowly, slowly …

STANLEY LAUREL'S TEST FILM MADE IN QUICK TIME

Hal E. Roach in New York wired tht Rolin-Pathe studio a few days ago to make tests of Stanley Laurel and rush them East.

Laurel was in Santa Barbara filling a booking and by phone and wire another act was arranged to replace Mr. and Mrs. Laurel so that the vaudeville comedian could rush to Los Angeles. Old Sol was bashful that day, but finally the filming was done and in the Bloom Laboratory by 4 p. m. In 3 hours and 40 minutes positive and negative prints were made and 20 minutes later they patched the films into continuity form. A projection was made on the screen and by 8 that night the Santa Fe was carrying the test to the Director General in New York, where the Pathe officials examined 200 teet of the new find's work.

Following a quick viewing of the completed pilot in New York (see news clip, on previous page), the Pathe officials gave Roach the green-light to make five films with Laurel. Stan must have been thrilled. He was about to be paid for five consecutive weeks' work – a near-record. Mind you, he had lost the fees from his vaudeville bookings. Let us hope the sacrifice will prove more beneficial than his film-making exploits of a year ago – but I would still advise you to keep hold of that bottom dollar.

In May 1917 Hal E. Roach had signed a contract with film distributers Pathe, to produce five films starring well-known comedian Toto. But here, a year on, Toto had had cold feet, and quit. Maybe Toto went back to Kansas. This left Roach not only needing to produce five films, but to produce a comedian out of a top hat. So it was thanks to another talent scout having seen Laurel at the Los Angeles Hippodrome, that he had received this call. The man was one of Roach's directors, Alfred Goulding. Roach and Goulding's first job with Laurel was to shoot a test film, which was done (as we have learned from the news clipping) within a few short hours of his arrival in LA.

Advert April 6, 1918, proclaiming: "TOTO – The Funniest of all Comedians." I was hoping for a later one by Toto, proclaiming: "I have been replaced by Stan Laurel, the man who really *is* 'The Funniest of all Comedians.'

[May 26	California			test film – Rolin Studios]
Jun 03	California			
Jun 11-15	California	LOS ANGELES	*Do You Love Your Wife*	Rolin
Jun 18-22	California	LOS ANGELES	*Just Rambling Along*	Rolin
Jun 24-29	California	LOS ANGELES	*Hoot Mon!*	Rolin
Jul 01-05	California	LOS ANGELES	*No Place Like Jail*	Rolin
Jul 06-11	California	LOS ANGELES	*Hustling For Health*	Rolin
[Jul 12-13	California	LOS ANGELES		retakes]

-----0-----

On June 18th the *Los Angeles Herald* confirmed the Laurel-Rolin contract, by which time the above films were already in the can.

> Stanley Laurel, for years in the public limelight as a vaudeville star, has been signed by Hal E. Roach of the Rolin-Pathe studio for a series of one-reel comedies.

With the Pathe quota fulfilled, Roach had a lot to be grateful for, to Laurel. Roach had worked on all five films – actually credited as director – so had witnessed first-hand Laurel's comedy form, persona, and potential. So Stan was rightly awaiting the 5-year contract he so richly deserved, but all he got from Roach was a five-finger goodbye wave.

What in heaven's name was it about Laurel that everyone could see his potential, but no-one would invest in it? In the juvenile pantomime company run by Levy & Cardwell, the young Jefferson had done two long-running pantomimes, but had been given only minor roles, which barely got a mention. In the Karno Company, too, he had minor roles and little mention, and with no promotion during his four years-plus tenure. Then, after signing with a management company, the Bostocks had allowed him to be pushed out of the nest by Edgar Hurley, when it was he, Stan, who had written the sketch, and been the lead comic. And when Stan reinvented himself, in The Stan Jefferson Trio and other derivatives, the Bostocks failed to find him sufficient work, forcing him to abandon his new act completely, whereas the Hurleys continued in work, unabated. Upon Laurel's entry into films, Bernstein, Universal, L-KO, and Nestor Films had all let him go within a matter of weeks, and now Roach had followed suit by using Laurel to get him out of hole, then kicking him into one.

I hope this story has a happy ending, otherwise I'm not going to carry on writing it. It's just too heart-breaking.

The Roach Approach

HICKORY HIRAM

The good news is that, although Stan's little run of making films had ended, his first-ever films were now about to be released. *Hickory Hiram* hit the cinemas around mid-May, and continued its run until September. Stan must have thought this would launch his profile as not only a vaudeville performer, but also as a screen actor. Problem was, reading the publicity adverts was like playing a game of "Peek-a-Boo" with its routine of: "Now you see him — now you don't."

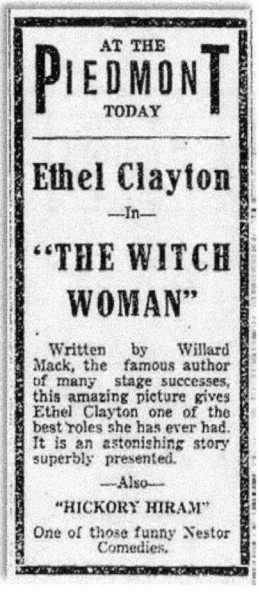

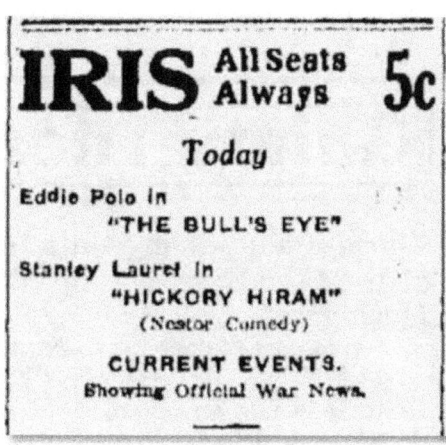

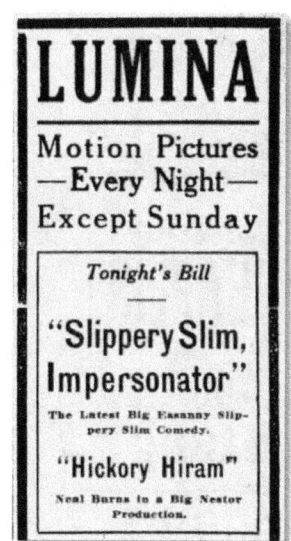

All clips dated between April and August 1918

This clip dated September 1918

"STANLEY COMEDIES" — FILM RELEASES

Below are various newspaper adverts for the releases of the five films Stan Laurel made between June and November 1917. Before you peruse them, let me just refer you back to the announcement in the *Los Angeles Times* — June 15, 1917.

> The first of these companies will be headed by Stan Jefferson, the output of the organization to be released by Isadore Bernstein under the name of Stanley Comedies.

Now imagine you are Stan Laurel and you have been waiting for over ten months for the Stanley Comedies to be released, and try to stop yourself from bursting out crying, followed by wanting to kill the film producers.

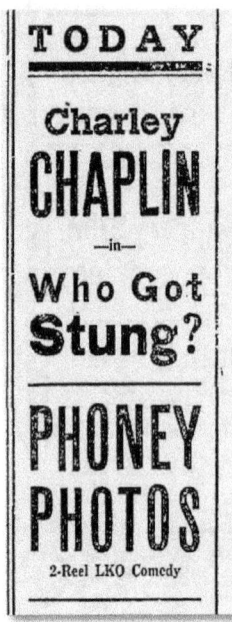

July 1918

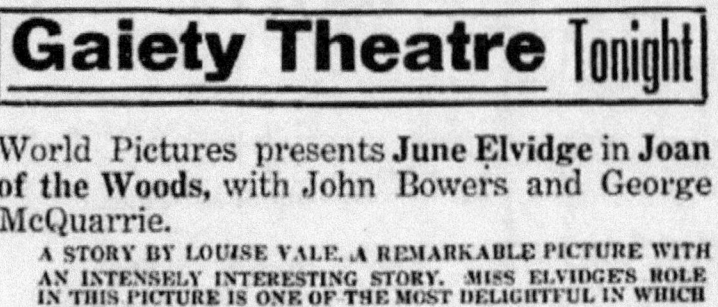

August 1918

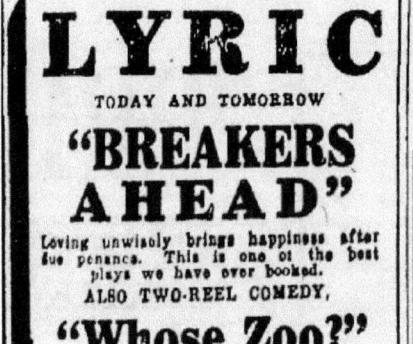

May 1918

January 1919

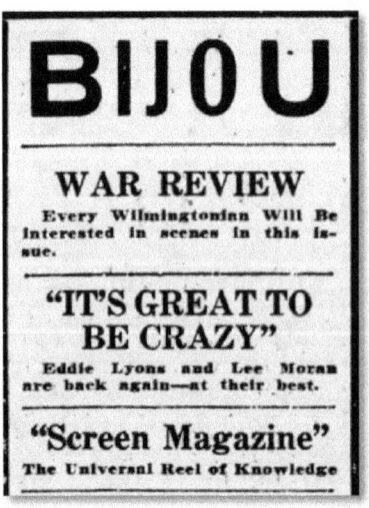

January 1919

The Roach Approach

I *am* happy to report that Stan did not have to wait long, or travel far, for his next spell in front of the cameras, as he bounced straight into the Vitagraph Studios, where he made three films as support to comedy star Larry Semon, but then bounced straight out again.

-----0-----

1918

late Jul	California	LOS ANGELES	*Huns and Hyphens*	Vitagraph/Semon
Jul 29 Jul	California			
early Aug	California	LOS ANGELES	*Bears and Badmen*	Vitagraph/Semon
Aug 12	California			
mid Aug	California	LOS ANGELES	*Frauds and Frenzies*	Vitagraph/Semon
Aug 26				
Sep 02				
Sep 09				
Sep 16				
Sep 23		All the California film studios are closed down, owing to the flu epidemic.		

-----0-----

It was the winter of 1918 and, just as Stan was making his mark in the Semon films, Los Angeles was stuck by a flu epidemic, and the studio had to close its doors until the epidemic could be controlled. But it wasn't just the one studio which had been effected by the flu epidemic — nor was it just the film industry which was hit:

> With the vaudeville circuits from Chicago to the Pacific Coast shut down, and their links in the East sadly weakened, the variety artist is in as bad a way as his fellow "legitimate," and probably worse. With few exceptions, he is own master dependent upon a booking agency, and booking agencies do not pay salaries at any time.
>
> With three and possibly four weeks of idleness confronting a large body of actors and other theatrical entertainers, it becomes a matter of public concern how those who are without funds are to exist during that period.
>
> (October 1, 1918 – abridged)

-----0-----

When the Vitagraph Studios re-opened, after a month of inactivity, Stan was already back in vaudeville. Larry Semon was not keen for Laurel to be recalled, as the latter had been getting too many laughs for Semon's liking. One story goes that, during a showing of the daily rushes of the Larry Semon film *Frauds and Frenzies*, actor Antonio Moreno, whilst killing himself laughing at Stan Laurel's on-screen actions, blurted out: *"This guy's funnier than Semon."* If that story is true, it does give a good reason why Laurel was not invited back to work with Semon. It also gives a good insight into why Chaplin never invited Laurel to work with him.

HUNS & HYPHENS
Semon seems to be thinking:
"Hmm! This guy's far too funny.
How do I get rid of him?"

LAUREL – Stage by Stage

STAN & MAE LAUREL — Raffles, the Dentist

1918 (continued)

Sep 29	Missouri	KANSAS CITY, Globe	[Sunday start]
Oct 04-05	Kansas	ATCHISON, Crystal	
Oct 06	Kansas	ATCHISON, Orpheum	
Oct 07-09	Kansas	TOPEKA, Novelty	[Mon-Wed]
Oct 10-12	Kansas	WITCHITA, Princess	
Oct 14			
Oct 21			
Oct 28			
Nov 04		Studios and theatres re-open after flu epidemic.	

-----0-----

Kansas, ATCHISON, Crystal

One of the cleverest acts sketches ever seen on the Crystal stage is one of the several high-class features of the week-end bill. It is "Raffles, the Dentist," by Stan and Mae Laurel. Stan Laurel is a knockout from the time he comes upon the stage and sings his little ditty, "I'm a Burglar." The act is crammed with real comedy, and keeps the audience in an uproar.

(*Atchison Daily Globe* — October 4, 1918)

Although the flu epidemic (highlighted October 1st) was still set to run for several more weeks, some states seemed to be unaffected, and had kept their theatres open. Thus it was that Stan & Mae were able to secure some much-wanted work in Missouri and Kansas. (See above Date-Sheet!) For other towns and cities, though, they would have to sit it out before their doors opened.

The lay-off did Stan a bit of good, as it gave him time to write and rehearse a new sketch, entitled *No Mother to Guide Her*, which "Stan & Mae Laurel" then performed on the circuit. It would be a fresh start in every sense.

[The title *No Mother to Guide Her* was taken from a popular stage play of the same name, which was playing at the Metropole Theatre, Glasgow, on the very week that Stan left for the U.S. in 1910. Although Stan borrowed the name, the premise bore no similarities whatsoever.]

-----0-----

STAN & MAE LAUREL
"No Mother to Guide Her"

Nov 04-06	Illinois	CHICAGO, Kedzie	*No Mother to Guide Her*	[debut]
Nov 07				
Nov 11				
Nov 14-16	Illinois	SPRINGFIELD, Majestic		
Nov 17-20	Indianapolis	FORT WAYNE, Palace		[Sun-Wed]
Nov 21	Michigan	BATTLE CREEK, Bijou		
Nov 24-27	Michigan	JACKSON, Orpheum		[Sun-Wed]
Nov 28-30	Michigan	LANSING, Bijou		[Thu-Sat]

-----0-----

Indiana, FORT WAYNE, Palace

[PREVIEW] The Palace is celebrating the lifting of the "flu ban" with a smashing program that includes a list of crack vaudeville attractions with Charlie Chaplin's newest million dollar film, "Shoulder Arms" as a special added attraction

One of the cleverest bits of fun that will be enjoyed this season is offered by Stan and Mae Laurel in their skit "No Mother to Guide Them," a hodge podge of foolishness in which Stan Laurel wins some new laurels. He is well known to fun lovers as one of the starred comedians of the Pathe company. He's funnier in the flesh that he is on screen, which is by way of saying something.

(*Fort Wayne Journal* — November 18, 1918)

Indiana, FORT WAYNE, Palace

"No Mother to Guide Them" [*sic*] is the title chosen by Stan and Mae Laurel, for their howling scream. Stan Laurel is no stranger to the lovers of light comedy as he has appeared in scores of Pathe comedy films and created twelve of the best of them including, "No Place Like Jail," "Do You Love Your Wife?", "Hoot Mon," etc.

He has brought to vaudeville all the droll mannerisms and excruciatingly funny antics and endeared him to the public on the screen. His support, Mae Laurel, is a prepossessing looking girl who serves as a splendid foil for his comedy efforts.

(Fort Wayne — November 17, 1918)

-----0-----

Michigan, JACKSON, Orpheum

Joyous Laughter in Abundance at the Orpheum

If there was ever an act at the Orpheum that caused any more laughter than Stan and May Laurel do, the first half of this week, it is at least a season or two ago, for from the time this clever English comedian makes his entrance, even before he has spoken a word, until his encore finish when he does a burlesque on Theda Barra, there is just one happy roar after another from the audience.

(*Jackson Citizen* — November 26, 1918)

HOOT MON!
Laurel displaying the legs that launched a thousand quips.

-----0-----

Michigan, LANSING, Bijou

[PREVIEW] Stan and Mae Laurel, a slim built young man with most prepossessing mannerisms and a beautiful young woman comprise this duo of entertainers who keep an audience screaming with laughter with their comedy antics and burlesque dramatics in their offering which they call "No Mother to Guide Them."

Stan Laurel is not by any means a new face in vaudeville though well known as a screen star, having been the leading comedian with the Pathe company. Prior to his appearance in the movies he was featured with Charlie Chaplin when that famous English pantomimist first came to America in Fred Karno's "Night in and English Music Hall." Mr. Laurel at that period was offered a position by the silent drama directors, but could not be induced to sign a contract at that time, preferring to remain in vaudeville. Later he accepted an offer made him by the Pathe people, appearing in 12 warring comedies of which "No Place Like Jail," "Just Rambling," "Do You Love Your Wife?", "Rest Cure," and "Hoot Mon," have been released.

Any patron of the movies will remember the droll comedy situations and excruciatingly funny antics of this popular comedian in his screen performances, but to see him in real life "carrying on" is a joy that very theatre-goer will appreciate. The present vehicle was concocted by Mr. Laurel during his experience as a screen star, and he advises it cannot be explained, but he vouches for its entertaining qualities, and he says it is for the lighter amusement, and seriously minded dramatic lovers would shun his offering.

(*Lansing State Journal* — November 28, 1918)

-----0-----

LAUREL – Stage by Stage

1918 (continued)

Dec 01-02	Michigan	FLINT, Palace	[dates may vary]
Dec 03-04	Michigan		
Dec 05-07	Michigan	SAGINAW, Strand	
Dec 08-11	Michigan	BAY CITY, Bijou	
Dec 12-14	Michigan	SAGINAW	[See 5-7 Dec]
Dec 15-18	Michigan	MUSKEGON, Regent	[Sun-Wed]
Dec 19-21	Indiana	SOUTH BEND, Orpheum	
Dec 23	Nebraska	LINCOLN, Orpheum	
Dec 24-25	Wisconsin	MADISON, Orpheum	
Dec 26-28	Illinois	ROCKFORD, Palace	
Dec 30-Jan 01	Illinois	CHICAGO, Wilson	

Bay City Times — December 7, 1918

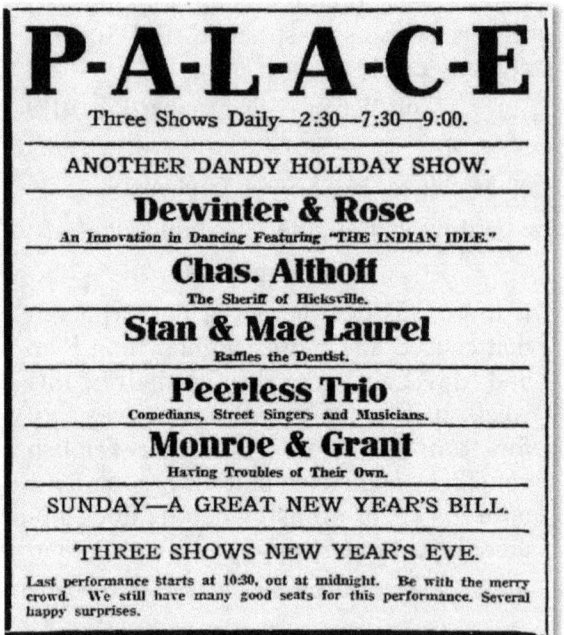

Rockford — December 26, 1918

-----0-----

Wisconsin, MADISON, Orpheum

Stan and Mae Laurel in "Raffles the Dentist," failed to reach town in time for the Monday night show, but promise a good laughing act at the following performances.

(Madison — December 24, 1918)

-----0-----

There is no record to say if Stan and Mae fulfilled the two shows on Christmas Eve and the three on Christmas Day. I am sure they would have preferred to spend their time on stage, rather than partying – along with the rest of the country.

Come Boxing Day, Stan and Mae had gotten over whatever obstacle it was, and were able to treat the good people of Rockford to their stage show:

Illinois, ROCKFORD, Palace

Stan and Mae Laurel in "No Mother to Guide Them," get away very well with a comedy skit. Stan is a former Pathe film comedian and he knows how to "register." He is built on the Charlie Chaplin order, but is original. He threw his audience into ecstasies of mirth at the first show last night.

(*Rockford Republic* — December 27, 1918)

---0---

Illinois, ROCKFORD, Palace

Stan and Mae Laurel have third spot with a song and dancing sketch, which scored yesterday. All the old farce expedients of your childhood days are used in this act, the seltzer bottle, the eggs in the pocket and the like, yet Laurel makes them productive of a good many laughs. There was never a harder-working pair on the local stage and they deserve well of their audiences.

(Rockford Register — December 27, 1918)

Interesting to note the reference to "the eggs in the pocket" routine. Maybe Stan could use that in a future film, as there had been no films for him to include it in, in 1918.

> Stan and May Laurel have a comedy offering they call "Raffles the Dentist." Stan and May were formerly with Charlie Chaplin and his company when they played the Empress circuit in "A Night in a London Music Hall." They have received several attractive offers from Chaplin to appear with him in pictures, but so far have refused to leave the vaudeville stage.

Laurel kept this cutting – possibly with the thought in mind:
"Oh yeh! What offers were them, then?"

Let us hope 1919 will find him working in films — at a studio which will keep him on for longer than the odd few weeks.

CHAPTER 23

BACK IN THE OLD ROUTINE

The good news is that the dip into the film world seemed to be paying off, as Stan and Mae were to be in continuous work for almost the entire year of 1919. The bad news is that NONE of it was *film* work. So if you feel that this book is getting repetitious, that is because Stan and Mae's lifestyle *was* repetitious: They would travel to a town or city, appear at a theatre for anything from one to six days; and then move on. That's the story – and I'm stuck with!

Having spent New Year's Day in Chicago, our intrepid travellers were reported to have hit St. Louis, Missouri the following day, but this could not be confirmed.

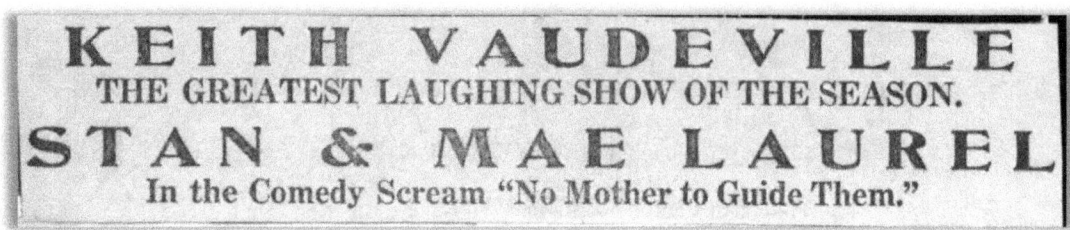

1919

Jan 02-04	Missouri	ST. LOUIS, Park	[unconfirmed]
Jan 06-08	Illinois	E. ST. LOUIS, Erber's	
Jan 09-10	Illinois	ALTON, Hippodrome	
Jan 13	Illinois		
Jan 16-18	Illinois	CHAMPAIGN, Orpheum	
Jan 19-22	Illinois	DECATUR, Empress	[Sun-Wed]
Jan 23	Illinois	PEORIA, Orpheum	
Jan 27-29	Indiana	EVANSVILLE, New Grand	
Jan 30-Feb 01	Indiana	TERRE HAUTE, Hippodrome	
Feb 03	Illinois	ST. LOUIS, Grand	
Feb 10			
Feb 17	Illinois	CHICAGO, Lincoln	
Feb 20-22	Illinois	MOLINE, Palace	[Rock Island]
Feb 23-26	Illinois	DES MOINES, Empress	[Sun-Wed]

-----0-----

Iowa, PEORIA, Orpheum

Stan Laurel, Pathe picture star and late partner of Charlie Chaplin in vaudeville, turns out to be the funniest man ever seen on a Peoria stage, and precipitates a huge riot of laughter on his very first appearance. Laurel's smile is alone worth the price of admission. Entering as a burglar and mistaken by a lady for with a toothache for a dentist, he proceeds to burgle the lady's mouth with a jimmy [sic]. And when he uses a huge mallet on her she immediately disappears and returns with hardly any clothes on and proceeds to do some of the highest kicking on record.

The act is screamingly funny and deserves the applause it gets.

(Peoria — January 24, 1919)

Doing high kicks when you've got hardly any clothes is either a very bad idea, or a gross exaggeration. I think, the latter.

Mae's dress was certainly very conservative when she and Stan went to have their portraits done at a photographic studio in Peoria, as can be seen on the next-but-one page.

NO MOTHER TO GUIDE THEM
Cartoon by Orald Cloakey — dated 1919 (from the Stan Laurel Scrapbook)

Depicted are the various scenes from the sketch and accompanying "vamp" routine, plus previously undisclosed key phrases from the dialogue.

Upon being crowned with a rolling-pin Stan declares: "The King shall hear of this." When entering the lady's apartment he introduces himself with: "Sh .. I'm a burglar." This prompts the reply from Mae: "Yer jist spoofin' me." [You're just spoofing me"], to which Stan reiterates: "Honest Miss … I'm a burglar" — which is his cue to go into the song "I'm a Burglar"

In the vamp sketch, where both San and Mae cross-dress, Mae triumphantly announces: "Ah! Ah! So I've found you at last." At one stage, Stan comes back with the line: "Oh! Fer 'eavings sake, you stop lur'n me on." [Oh" for heaven's sake, you stop luring me on.]

And in the incident where Stan accidently discharges some of the liquid from the seltzer bottle (or "soda" as we call it in Britain) it would seem he blames it on the puppy dog. [Whether they toured with an actual puppy, I couldn't say.]

Laurel signed and presented this portrait to one of the acts on a later show — Frankie Mason of the double-act "Mason & Austin – Frolics of Comedy and Song."

> *Mason and Austin have a budget of songs which strike a popular vein, and Mason's roly-poly figure and infectious smile help along on the comedy side of the act.*

Like a future partner of Stan Laurel, Frank Mason's large physique was promoted as an asset which defined his character and personality.

Laurel even made reference to Mason's larger-than-average size in the tongue-in-cheek inscription on the portrait.

It reads:

> *To Fatty Arbuckle from Geo. M. Cohan*
> *Good luck Frankie*
> *Yours as Ever*
> *Stan Laurel*
> *March 1919*

Most photos of Stan and Mae were taken in stage costume, some even on the stage set, and some as gag shots — which could then be used for publicity purposes in newspapers and in theatre displays. But these ones are more like classical Greek poses, which hardly depict a couple of vaudeville comedians.

Another feature is that both are tinted, with the dominant added colour being red – which is yet another rarity for photos from that era.

The inscription on Mae's portrait reads:

> *Lots of good wishes and things,*
> *Sincerely Yours, Mae Laurel.*

For some strange reason, Stan wrote and signed that, as well — only in *Mae's* name.

Colorgraph Peoria, Ill.

Back in the Old Routine

Illinois, MOLINE, Palace

When someone tells you that Stan and Mae Laurel, the late stars in Pathe comedies, are comical, believe 'em. They proved it last evening at the Palace theatre, Moline, when "gales of laughter," as O.D.K. would say, resulted from their antics in "No Mother to Guide Her." What was it all about? No one knows, not even Stan and Mae, but it went big and put everybody in a happy frame of mind—especially when the former did a Theda Bara "vamp." It would convulse a stone image.

(*Rock Island Argus* — February 21, 1919)

-----0-----

Illinois, DES MOINES, Empress

Stan Laurel is an English comedian who came to this country with Charlie Chaplin. They were featured together in "A Night in an English Music Hall," a vaudeville act.

Chaplin took up the movies, but Laurel stayed with vaudeville. Their work is similar, and critics claim Laurel is Chaplin's only rival. Assisted by May Laurel, he is headlining the bill in a dramatic burlesque, "No Mother to Guide Them."

(Des Moines — February 23, 1919)

-----0-----

That's a bit of a bold statement — "Laurel is Chaplin's only rival." Chaplin had been making films since 1914 — films which were shown around the world, and which had made Charlie a millionaire, and one of the most-famous people on the planet. Laurel was in vaudeville, being seen only by the number of locals who could fit into each theatre; was only just keeping his head above water; and was virtually unknown. If Laurel was Chaplin's nearest rival, then Chaplin had no rivals. But Laurel's day will come and, though he will never match Chaplin on a financial level, he will undoubtedly be his rival on the "Who is the funniest?" scale.

-----0-----

Feb 27-Mar 01	Iowa	CEDAR RAPIDS, Majestic	
Mar 02-05	Iowa	DUBUQUE, Majestic	[Sun-Wed]
Mar 06	Iowa	DAVENPORT, Columbia	
Mar 09	Iowa	WATERLOO, Majestic	[Sunday only]
Mar 10-12	Nebraska	LINCOLN, Liberty	
Mar 13-15	Iowa	DAVENPORT, Columbia	
Mar 17-19	Iowa	SIOUX CITY, Orpheum	
Mar 20-22	Nebraska	OMAHA, Empress	

-----0-----

Iowa, CEDAR RAPIDS, Majestic

Right out of the film studio, Stan and Mae Laurel come to town to chase out whatever gloom they may encounter. The Laurels are known all over the world through their engagement with the Pathe comedy films. In their ridiculous act "No Mother to Guide Them" patrons may be assured of an act as funny as the old favourites Williams and Wolfus of "Hark, Hark, Hark" fame. By all means see this act.

(Cedar Rapids — February 28, 1919)

Ah yes! We all remember with fondness the old favourites 'Williams and Wolfus' of "Hark, Hark, Hark" fame. Plus, Stan and Mae are now, like Jeannie Weenie, claimed to be "known all over the world" – but that pails into insignificance when compared to local favourites Williams and Wolfus.

-----0-----

Iowa, DUBUQUE, Majestic

MOVIE STAR AT MAJESTIC TODAY

Stan Laurel, a former screen star and leading comedian with the Pathe company for several years, is prepared to manufacture laughs at the Majestic for four days, starting this afternoon. He and his wife perform 18-karat comedy antics and burlesque dramatics in their offering, which they call "No Mother to Guide Them."

Laurel was featured in twelve comedy films released by the Pathe company. A number of these were exhibited in Dubuque movie theatres, but this will be the first opportunity Dubuquers will have to see him in real life "carrying on" his laughable stunts. His wife, Mae Laurel, is a nifty looker and a splendid entertainer.

(Dubuque — March 2, 1919)

STAN LAUREL ON DECK

Stan Laurel, the English comedian, who has signed for a series of one reel stories by the Rolin Company during his recent vacation, has, in "Rambling Along" probably the best of the lot, it is said. With a proper appreciation he has characterized it as "Hoover hilarity," which, though it has to do with food, is nevertheless entirely unstinted.

Laurel extracts many laughs as the waiter in a beanery. Business has been so dull the cash register is losing its voice, but he is just rambling along and has had nothing to eat for two days and four nights when he addressed a woman at a back door, saying: "I am wasting away. I would crawl through a piccolo for a ham sandwich."

She immediately gives him a job telling him that all he has to do is lure the folks into the Cafeteria. Then fun and trouble start simultaneously. Pathe releases this comedy the week of Dec. 8.

-----0-----

Iowa, DUBUQUE, Majestic

"He's one of the funniest fellows I ever seen." That seems to be the unanimous verdict of Dubuquers who have been entertained by Stan Laurel, former movie star, who is appearing with Mae Laurel in a burlesque skit at the Majestic called "No Mother to Guide Them."

Laurel is a stellar comedian. He was starred in numerous comedies released by the Pathe company. One of the comedies in which he featured, "Just Rambling," is to be exhibited at the Majestic the first four days of next week. Strange coincidence, isn't it? Majestic patrons see Laurel in person the first part of this week; next week they will see him in the movies.

(Dubque — March 4, 1919)

-----0-----

STAN LAUREL COMING BACK IN THE MOVIES

Although Stan Laurel closes his engagement at the Majestic tonight, Dubuquers will not have much of an opportunity to forget one of the best comedians that has ever hit the town. Laurel is coming back next Sunday, but this time he'll be in the movies. He will be seen in

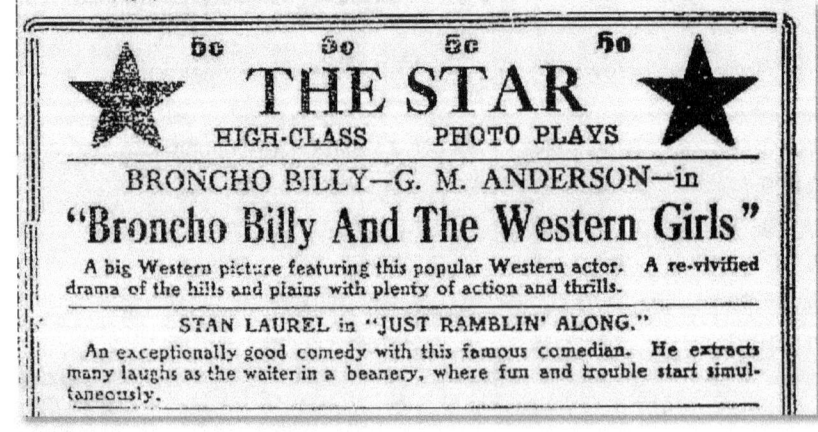

the Pathe comedy "Just Rambling." If Laurel is half as good in the movies as he is "in real life" on the stage, "Just Rambling" should be a picture worth seeing.

(Dubque — March 5, 1919)

-----0-----

Iowa, WATERLOO, Majestic

Stan and Mae Laurel went big in their sketch, "No Mother to Guide Them," until Mae sung, and then—

(*Waterloo Courier and Reporter* — March 9, 1919)

Ouch! It had all been going so well.

-----0-----

Mar 24			
Mar 31	Minnesota	ST. PAUL, New Palace	
Apr 03-05	Minnesota	MINNEAPOLIS, New Palace	[*Sussman* shoot]
Apr 06-08	Minnesota	DULUTH, New Grand	[Sun-Tue]

Minnesota, DULUTH, New Grand — April 6, 1919

This gag photo, shows not only Stan cross-dressing, but also Mae; who, is sporting two necessary manly identities – a bowler and a moustache (held on by an elastic strap). [I know it looks like a beard, but that is just shadow.] Both took on these guises in the second part of the stage act — after the *No Mother to Guide Her* sketch.

With the accompanying text to the above picture being solely centred on Stan (see below), the *Duluth News Tribune* did address the balance by posting this photo and mini write-up on Mae.

A slim built young man with most prepossessing mannerisms and a beautiful young woman comprise this duo of entertainers who keep an audience screaming with laughter with their comedy antics and burlesque dramatics in their offering which they call "No Mother to Guide Them."

Stan Laurel is not by any means a new face in vaudeville though well known as a screen star, having been the leading comedian with the Pathe company, prior to his appearance in the movies he was featured with Charlie Chaplin when that famous English pantomimist first came to America in Fred Karno's "Night in an English Music Hall." Mr. Laurel at the period was offered a positon by the silent drama directors but could not be induced to sign a contract at that time, preferring to remain in vaudeville.

Later he accepted an offer made him by the Pathe people appearing in 12 warring comedies of which "No Place Like Jail," "Just Rambling," "Do You Love Your Wife," Rest Cure, and "Hoot Mon" have been released. Any patron of the movies will remember the droll comedy situations and excruciatingly funny antics of this popular comedian in his screen performances, but to see him in real life "carrying on" is a joy that every theatregoer will appreciate. The present vehicle was concocted by Mr. Laurel during his appearance as a screen star, as he advises it cannot be explained, but he vouches for its entertaining qualities, as he says it is for the lighter amusement, and seriously minded dramatic lovers would shun his offering.

MISS MAE LAUREL
Miss Mae Laurel, one of the team of Stan and Laurel, will come to the New Grand tomorrow in a comedy novelty entitled "No Mother to Guide Them."

(*Duluth News Tribune* — April 6, 1919)

I wonder if Mr. Laurel also said: "The moving picture industry is still in its infancy"?

1919 (continued)

Apr 09-11	Wisconsin	SUPERIOR, New Palace	
Apr 14	Minnesota	MINNEAPOLIS, Palace	
Apr 17-19	Wisconsin	GREEN BAY, Orpheum	
Apr 21	Illinois	CHICAGO, Hippodrome	
[Apr 28-30	Illinois	CHICAGO, Academy]	
May 01-03	Illinois	CHICAGO, Empress	

-----0-----

In Chicago, the Laurels walked out of the Academy, theatre, refusing to perform there. It may have been named "The Academy" but it didn't win any awards. It was said that charges may be preferred against the Laurels by the W.M.V.A. via Joe Pilgrim, manager for the Kohl & Castle interest. However, bookings seem to have continued without a hiccough.

May 05-07	Indiana	KOKOMO, Sipe
May 08-11	Indiana	LAFAYETTE, Family
May 12-14		
May 15-17	Indiana	LOGANSPORT, Colonial

-----0-----

Waterloo, Iowa — March 9, 1919
Note 'Mason & Austin' on the bill (*ibid*).

Indiana, KOKOMO, Sipe

A familiar face to screen patrons is seen in a decidedly clever comedy sketch, "No Mother to Guide Them," offered by Stan and May Laurel, one of the Pathe luminaries frequently encountered in Kokomo in the "silent drama." There is nothing "silent" about the present offering. It is something more than a shout. It is a shriek from the entrance of unsophisticated burglar to the exit of the vanished "vamp." Nothing in this line has been more admirably acted since Kokomo was first introduced to vaudeville.

(Kokomo — May 6, 1919)

Indiana, LOGAN, Colonial

Stan & Mae Laurel had their audience screaming with laughter with a comedy skit which they term "No Mother to Guide Them." Stan is one of those really funny English comedians whose every word and movement is a laugh. In the first part of his vaudeville offering at the Colonial he takes the part of a bold burglar and is a vampire in the latter part of the act. The result is one scream of laughter after another. His partner ably assists in the comedy and contributes singing and dancing.

(Logan — May 16, 1919)

May 19-21	Missouri	ST. LOUIS, Rialto	
May 22-24	Missouri	ST. LOUIS, Skydome	
May 26-28			
May 29-31			
Jun 02	Michigan	OWOSSO, Strand	
Jun 09-11	ONTARIO	LONDON, Grand Opera House	Canada
Jun 12-14	ONTARIO	BRANTFORD, Brant	Canada
Jun 16-18	ONTARIO	PETERBOROUGH, Grand Opera House	Canada
Jun 19	ONTARIO		Canada
Jun 23	ONTARIO	KINGSTON, Grand Opera House	Canada
Jun 30	ONTARIO	TORONTO, Younge	Canada
Jul 07			
Jul 14			
Jul 21	Illinois	CHICAGO, Rialto	
Jul 26-27	Indiana	HAMMOND, Orpheum	
Jul 28			

Back in the Old Routine

Like Two Peas in a Pod-uh!

THEDA BARA — vastly popular actresses of the silent era, and one of cinema's earliest sex symbols. Her femme-fatale roles earned her the nickname "The Vamp."

[You will have to decide for yourself just who is who.]

Stan and Mae were now about to embark on a twenty-nine-week tour on the Pantages circuit, for which the following posters were made up, to display in the frames outside the theatres.

PANTAGES

1919 (continued)

Aug 03	Minnesota	MINNEAPOLIS, Pantages	[starts Sunday]
Aug 11	Manitoba	WINNIPEG, Pantages	Canada
Aug 18-20	Saskatchewan	REGINA, Pantages	Canada
Aug 21-23	Saskatchewan	SASKATOON, Pantages (Empire)	Canada
Aug 25	Alberta	EDMONTON, Pantages	Canada
Sep 01-06	Alberta	CALGARY, Pantages	Canada
Sep 09-10	Montana	GREAT FALLS, Grand Opera House	
Sep 11-12	Montana	HELENA, Marlowe	
Sep 13-16	Montana	ANACONDA, Pantages	
Sep 17-18	Montana	BUTTE, Broadway	
Sep 19-20	Montana	MISSOULA, Pantages	

-----0-----

Back in the Old Routine

Montana, GREAT FALLS, Grand Opera House

There have been few acts at the Grand that proved bigger fun screams than the one being presented in this bill by Stan and Mae Laurel under the title "No Mother to Guide Her." The finish of the act is one of the biggest hits that has played the house, and it literally stops the show.

(Great Falls — September 10, 1919)

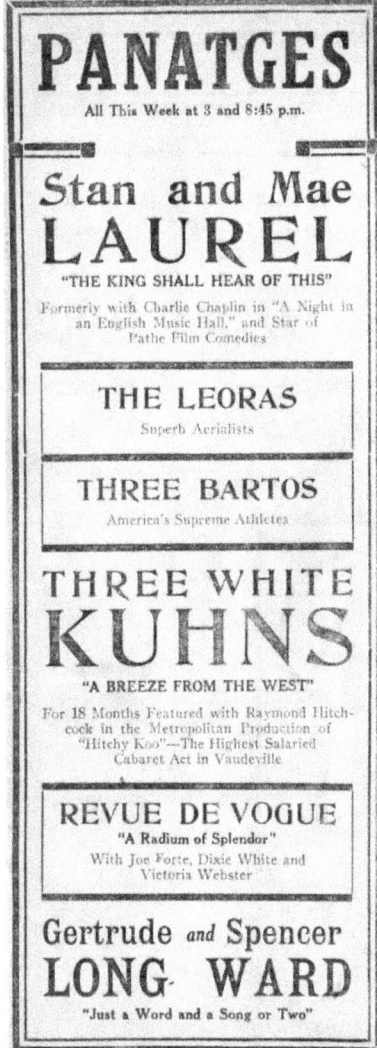

[Note the use of the phrase "THE KING SHALL HEAR OF THIS." in the bill matter, at left]

GOOD COMEDY AT THE PANTAGES

There is space for an argument as to whether Stan and Mae Laurel, in their up-to-the-minute skit, headline the bill or the Revue de Vogue — which consists of seven pretty girls and a man. This acts produces excellent music, delightful dancing and five changes of costumes with the singing of a number of popular songs and, on a whole, the act is of high quality.

"No Mother to Guide Her," is the billing of Stan and Mae Laurel's offering. Their act occupies no less than twenty valuable minutes of the show during which space of time this pair create screams of hysterical laughter among their audience, and at the close of the act they put across one of the breeziest turns ever witnessed on the Pantages stage. Last but not least, the comedy and wit of these two is absolutely clean.

The Pantages Circuit worked differently from others as, instead of changing the bill at each and every town, the same acts were kept as a package, and travelled and appeared on the same bill together, with few changes. Above left, Stan has managed to find a poster with "Stan & Mae" topping the bill. In the write-up above, opinion is divided as to who should top the bill, but this should not be taken to indicate that the top-of-the-bill was alternated as, in all the other adverts I found, it was the Revue de Vogue which retained that position.

1919 (continued)

Sep 22-27	Washington	SPOKANE, Pantages
Sep 29-Oct 04	Washington	SEATTLE, Pantages
Oct 06-11	British Columbia	VANCOUVER, Pantages
Oct 13	British Columbia	VICTORIA, Pantages
Oct 20-25	Washington	TACOMA, Pantages
Oct 27-Nov 01	Oregon	PORTLAND, Pantages
Nov 03		
Nov 07-08	California	SAN JOSE, Victory

-----0-----

California, SAN JOSE, Victory

Stan and Mae Laurel in a little skit which was unique and indescribably amusing. Mr. Laurel as a burglar and later as a "vamp" made the audience literally hold its sides with laughter.

(*San José Evening News* — November 8, 1919)

-----0-----

Nov 09-15	California	SAN FRANCISCO, Pantages	[Sun-Sat]
Nov 17-22	California	OAKLAND, Pantages	
Nov 23-29	California	LOS ANGELES, Pantages	[Sun-Sat]

Los Angeles Herald — November 24, 1919

-----0-----

California, SAN DIEGO, Savoy

"No Mother to Guide Her" is the title of the highly enjoyable sketch presented by Stan and Mae Laurel. Not the least enjoyable feature of the production is the clever stagecraft employed, which sets something of a new standard for vaudeville offerings.

(*San Diego Union* — December 4, 1919)

1919 (continued)

Dec 01	California	SAN DIEGO, Savoy	
Dec 08	California	LONG BEACH, Pantages	
Dec 15			
Dec 17-23	Utah	SALT LAKE CITY, Pantages	
Dec 24			
Dec 25-27	Utah	OGDEN, Pantages	[Mae is ill.]
Dec 29-Jan 03	Colorado	DENVER, Empress	

-----0-----

In San Diego, the Pantages' package show landed at the beginning of four days of festivities, to celebrate the opening of the "San Diego & Arizona Railway." This brought it home to me that one should not take it for granted that the whole of the railway system throughout the USA was completed, and that there must have been many occasions during Laurel's years of touring when alternative modes of transport would have been employed.

There was also great cause for celebration when the company hit Ogden, Utah, as they were there over the 3-days commencing with Christmas Day. However, the local papers had the sad news to announce that: "Stan and May Laurel did not appear because of the illness of Miss Laurel." Gosh! that is really sad. Poor Mae, having to miss work and stay at home over Christmas. That is THREE years in a row now in which the Laurels had not worked over Christmas, which makes this newspaper advert a bit of an empty greeting:

The Laurels were, however, back in time to complete the last engagement of the year:

Colorado, DENVER, Empress

Stan and Mae Laurel in "No Mother to Guide Her," present the funniest vaudeville satire that has ever appeared in Denver this season. Stan as a vampire is a scream, and his petite wife is equally clever. Stan has won distinction as a motion picture comedian, but he has never done anything in the movies as funny as his present act in vaudeville.

(*Denver Post* — December 30, 1919)

-----0-----

That's a great note to end the year on, but there is one drawback: Throughout 1919, Stan Laurel had gained consistent work in *Vaudeville*, by playing on his popularity as a *film star* — but hadn't made a single film in that year. That can't be right. Surely someone will give him a film contract in 1920. Have you got that bottom dollar ready to place a bet?

CHAPTER 24

A SPECIAL KIND OF NOTHING

The year 1920 started off well. Stan and Mae had been signed up by the Horwitz-Kraus Agency, on a twenty-week "pay or play" contract. This was a bit of a gamble for the agency, as they would have to pay the Laurels even if they found them no work. If the trial period went well, Horwitz-Kraus would then offer a second twenty-week option.

Even better news was that Stan and Mae had also been booked onto the Loew's Circuit, again for twenty weeks; so a possible sixty weeks of work to be had — if you count your chickens. Working for Loew's was different to working for an agency. Lowe's had a huge circuit of their own theatres which they exclusively booked acts into, whereas an agency can only *request* theatres to take their acts. This is an arrangement built on trust that the agency will consistently supply good acts, but on threat of those theatres turning to other agencies if they didn't. But, neither party should have any problems with the 'Stan & Mae Laurel' act, which was constantly being polished and even upgraded.

-----0-----

Colorado, COLORADO SPRINGS, Burns

The use of a carpenter's mallet as a sleep-producer by a burglar is a feature of one of the acts on the Pantages bill at the Burns theatre today. The act is entitled "No Mother to Guide Her," and Stan and Mae Laurel have worked up a humorous burlesque in which some slapstick comedy and some clever lines have been well mingled.

(Colorado Springs — January 6, 1920)

In the above cutting, Stan has cut out all reference to the rest of the show but, as I found the original newspaper entry, I can now reveal the bit which he most-wanted to lose:

> The headline attraction is the Revue de Vogue, an act of seven scenes and five changes of wardrobe.

Stan and Mae still had another eight weeks to run on the Pantages Circuit and, as such, were still touring in a package show. At the smaller theatres, which were unable to afford the full show, the act 'Revue de Vogue' was taken out, and found work elsewhere. Even so, Stan & Mae didn't take over the top-of-the-bill — as is illustrated in this advert for Muskogee.

-----0-----

1920

Jan 05-06	Colorado	COLORADO SPRINGS, Burns
Jan 07		
Jan 13-15	Oklahoma	MUSKOGEE, Broadway
Jan 16-17	Texas	WACO, Orpheum
Jan 19-24	Texas	SAN ANTONIO, Royal
Jan 26-31	Texas	WITCHITA FALLS, Wichita
Feb 02-07	Texas	DALLAS, Jefferson
Feb 09		
Feb 16		
Feb 19	Michigan	DETROIT, Majestic
Feb 23-25		

-----0-----

When the Pantages Circuit ended, at the end of February, the Laurel's went straight onto the Loew's Circuit, but then the tour was temporarily halted for the second week, as one or both of them had reported in as being unwell. Is it Christmas already?

LOEW'S CIRCUIT starts here

1920

Feb 26-28	New York	BROOKLYN, Fulton	
Mar 01-03	New York	NEW YORK CITY, National	}
Mar 03	New York	KYRA, Century Roof	} cancelled through illness
Mar 04-06	New York	NEW YORK CITY, Delancey St.	}

-----0-----

After taking the first week in March out, Stan and Mae got back into gear to fulfil the Loew's bookings, including ones which had been rescheduled:

Mar 08-14	Washington DC	WASHINGTON, Cosmos
Mar 15-20	Ohio	AKRON, Colonial
Mar 22		
Mar 25-26	ONTARIO	LONDON, Loew's
Mar 28-Apr 03	New York	ROCHESTER, Fays

Cosmos, Washington, DC – March 7

Fay's, Rochester, New York – March 28

As can be gleaned from the two adverts above, Stan & Mae where now appearing on a bill which changed at each and every theatre. Note too, that a feature film is now the main attraction. The times they are a changin'.

------0-----

District of Columbia, WASHINGTON, Cosmos

Stan Laurel is a veritable scream in "No Mother to Guide Her," a farce for which he furnishes all of the laughter, and a great deal of it at that.

(Washington DC — March 9, 1920)

-----0-----

1920

Apr 05-10	ONTARIO	TORONTO, Loew's	
Apr 12-17	ONTARIO	HAMILTON, Loew's	
Apr 19-21	New York	NEW YORK CITY, American Roof	
Apr 22-24	New York	NEW YORK CITY, Boulevard	
Apr 26-28	New York	NEW YORK CITY, National	[rescheduled from March 1]
Apr 29-May 01	New York	NEW YORK, Lincoln Square	
May 03-05	New York	NEW YORK CITY, DeKalb	
May 06-09			
May 10	New York	BROOKLYN, Metropolitan	
May 13-15	New York	NEW YORK CITY, Delancey St.	[rescheduled from March 4]

-----0-----

New York, NEW YORK CITY, American Roof

Stan and Mae Laurel pulled down the comedy honors of the evening. When they came down to "one" for their travesty comedy vamping, giving their low comedy proclivities full play, they had the house at the mercy. Stan doing a comedy dance and **Miss Laurel playing opposite in her hoke male get-up**, provides a sure-fire comedy finish for their act.

(New York City — April 21, 1920)

-----0-----

The last sentence, in this review from the American Roof Theatre, contains a most interesting line, as it is the only instance I have seen where Mae is revealed as dressing up as a male, to counter Stan's role in drag. And here, if proof were needed, is Mae in that very (dis)guise:

Yes that really is Mae on the right. We have seen her dressed like this before, (in the news clip from Duluth – April 6, 1919), but there was nothing then to suggest that this is how she dressed at some point in the stage act.

We do know that Stan and Mae's publicity photos, in costume, were taken during their week in Minneapolis (See next page!)

-----0-----

A Special Kind Of Nothing

NO MOTHER TO GUIDE HER

No this isn't 'Stan & Mae' — it's 'Stan & Stan'
In costume as both the 'vamp' and the 'burglar.'

[*Sussman* Studio — Minneapolis (w/c April 3, 1919)]

1920 (continued)

May 17-19	Massachusetts	BOSTON, Loew's Orpheum
May 20-22	Massachusetts	FALL RIVER, Empire
May 24		
May 27-29	Massachusetts	SPRINGFIELD, Broadway
May 31-Jun 02		
Jun 03-05	New York	NEW YORK, Greeley Square
Jun 07-09	New York	NEW YORK, Victoria
Jun 10-12	New York	NEW YORK, Lincoln Square
Jun 14-16	Pennsylvania	PHILADELPHIA, Nixon
Jun 21		
Jun 28		
Jul 05		
Jul 12		
[Jul 17	NY, Times Square — Teddy Jefferson arrives]	
Jul 19		
Jul 26	New York	NEW YORK, Orpheum

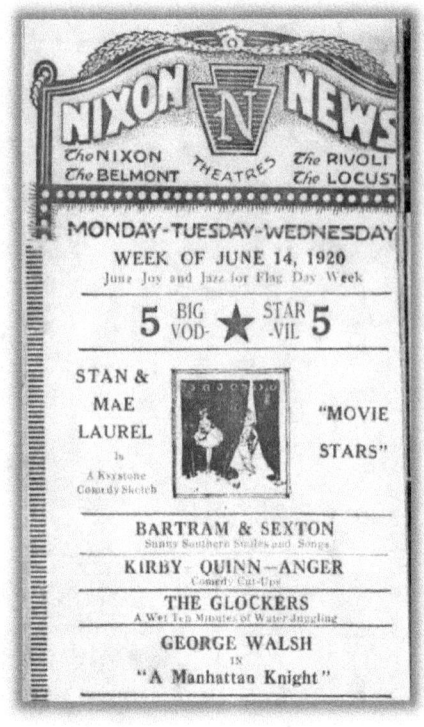

-----o-----

LOEW'S CIRCUIT ends here — July 31, 1920

-----o-----

When Stan & Mae were touring with *Raffles, the Dentist* it made me wonder if anyone went to the theatre expecting to see the film featuring 'Raffles,' which was doing the rounds concurrently. Now that Stan & Mae were playing *No Mother to Guide Her* there might well have been similar confusion, as not only was there a touring play titled *No Mother to Guide **Them***, but also a film titled: *No Mother to Guide **Him***. It certainly caused confusion in newspapers, as many adverts and reviews named Stan & Mae's sketch by one of the other titles. It also caused me much frustration, as far too many of the on-line searches to locate the Laurels' sketch, gave me either the play or the film. I surmise Stan chose the title to piggy-back on the publicity for the similarly-named productions, but just whether that was help or hindrance I cannot decide. It was certainly a hindrance to me.

Newspaper advert for the recently-released Ben Turpin film *No Mother to Guide Him*.
[By the time I had sifted out all the false leads which a search for the
Stan & Mae sketch brought up, I was as cross-eyed as Turpin.]

Two weeks before the Loew's tour ended, Stan had a special visitor, from England — his younger brother, Teddy Jefferson. The last time he had seen Teddy would have been in 1912, or earlier. We do know that Stan met up with his older brother, Gordon, in 1911 when Gordon was managing the Prince's Theatre in London, but have no records of any contact with Teddy.

I could find no theatre engagements for the Laurels during the first four weeks of August, but maybe Stan was happy to have the time off, and spend it as tour guide to his brother. However this was no tourist trip for Teddy — he was in America to stay, and would soon have to find a job, although it would not be on the stage. One job he is known to have had is that of Stan's driver; although what he drove, and the time period, is unknown. It could have been a few years later, when Stan becomes domiciled in Los Angeles.

Here in 1920, the train was almost certainly Laurel's mode of transport when vaudeville bookings resumed on the Poli's-Proctor's Circuit, although Stan may also still be using that car we know him to have driven, and Teddy taken over as chauffeur already.

-----0-----

1920 (continued)

Date	State	Venue
Aug 02		}
Aug 09		} no bookings found
Aug 16		}
Aug 23		}

POLI'S–PROCTOR'S starts here

Date	State	Venue
Aug 26-28	Connecticut	HARTFORD, Palace (Poli's)
Aug 30-Sep 01	Massachusetts	SPRINGFIELD, Palace (Poli's)
Sep 02-04	Connecticut	BRIDGEPORT, Poli's
Sep 06	Pennsylvania	WILKES-BARRE, Poli's
Sep 9-11	Pennsylvania	SCRANTON, Poli's

-----0-----

WILKES-BARRE

Stan and Mae Laurel are entertainers well known from former visits.

(*Wilkes-Barre Record* — September 6, 1920)

-----0-----

WILKES-BARRE

Stan and Mae Laurel generate heaps of joy through the travesty of a hodge podge of merriment and Mr. Stanley is a most capable comedian who gets falls and bumps in abundance.

(*Wilkes-Barre Record* — September 7, 1920)

-----0-----

GOOD PLAY PICTURED.

"39 East" With Constance Binney Feature of Poli Bill.

The strongest feature of the bill at the Palace for the first three days of the week is certainly the picture, Constance Binney in a dramatization of "39 East." Although many have seen the stage edition of Rachel Crothers' play they cannot fail to enjoy Constance Binney in the role of the simple country girl who is forced to enter the chorus in New York to help her family financially.
Davis and Pelle shared the honors in the show yesterday afternoon with those billed as headliners. The former are equilibrists and capable ones. Jed Dooley, billed as headliner does an act something like Will Rogers', something. He has a pleasant personality but couldn't seem to put over his act yesterday.
Kafea and Stanley open the bill, doing stunts on the slack wire, and they have a surprise at the end. They are followed by Williams and Pierce. The man of the team dances well and the woman takes delight in annoying helpless members of the audience, but it fell painfully flat. The audience liked Stan and Mae Laurel, who sort of burlesqued the skit they presented. The man is a low comedian, but quiet in his methods and he seemed to take. "Bringing up Father," a comedy and the Selznick News complete the bill.

SPRINGFIELD — August 30, 1920
Why Laurel kept this particular cutting is puzzling, as many others were far more flattering.

1920 (continued)

Date	State	Venue
Sep 13	New York	BROOKLYN, Chester
Sep 20	Pennsylvania	CHESTER, Edgemont
Sep 27-Oct 02	Pennsylvania	PHILADELPHIA, Keystone
Oct 04		
Oct 11		
Oct 14-16	New York	SYRACUSE, Temple
Oct 18-20	New York	SCHENECTADY, Proctor's
Oct 21-23	New York	TROY, Proctor's
Oct 25		
Oct 28-30	New York	POUGHKEEPSIE, Collingwood
Nov 01		
Nov 08-10	New York	ALBANY
Nov 11-13	New York	BINGHAMTON

-----0-----

New York, SCHENECTADY, Proctor's

Stan and Mae Laurel present an original comedy travesty. Both are clever impersonators, with good singing voices.

(*Schenectady Gazette*, NY — October 18, 1920)

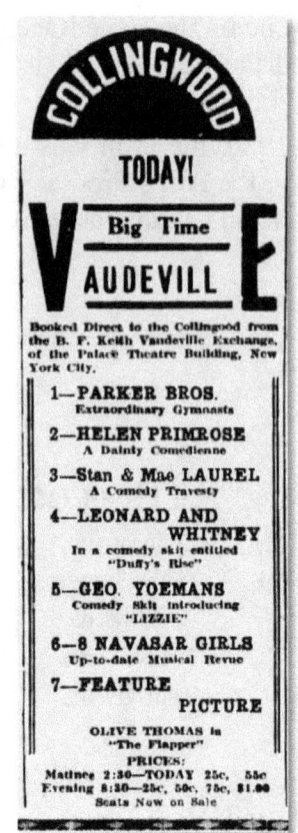

| Pennsylvania, SCRANTON September 9, 1920 | Pennsylvania, SCRANTON September 10, 1920 | New York, POUGHKEEPSIE October 28, 1920 |

Maybe you, too, have noticed that Stan & Mae have been sliding further and further down the bill, and receiving only scant reviews, as opposed to previous "show-stealing" ones. But worse was to come: After the twenty-week contract on the Poli's–Proctor's, in mid-November, it would appear that the option for the third twenty-week booking was either not offered to Stan and Mae, or simply not taken up by them; as, between November 15th and December 31st, no theatre bookings were traced.

-----0-----

It was during the latter period that mystery comments, about Laurel appearing in films again, began to be published in trade papers:

> Ted Laurel, the little English comedian, who played a character part in "Ham" Hamilton's comedy, April Fool, has accepted a comedy role with his brother, Stanley Laurel, English music hall comedian, who will shortly be featured in two-reel comedies.
>
> (Camera! — November 11, 1920)

[AJM: In the later stages of my writing this book, speculation was circulating that it was actually Stan Laurel who played a cameo role in the film *April Fool*; but, upon my viewing the said film, I immediately recognised the sailor in the ship scene as Teddy Jefferson, not Stan. Sometime later, I came across the above clipping, which confirmed my identification. And here are my initial comments, which show why Stan could not have been in that film:

April Fool was shot late-October to early-November, then released November 21, 1920; but, as Stan was only to end his vaudeville tour on November 13, in Binghamton, NY, the earliest he could have made Los Angeles was November 16, which rules out his being in the film *April Fool*. However, Teddy could have gone on ahead, to do a reconnaissance for Stan's pending arrival.]

-----0-----

Teddy's lantern-jaw makes him easy to distinguish in his film roles. Here it can be seen in all its prominence, in this still from the 1922 Stan Laurel film *Mixed Nuts*.

Further developments ensued:

SIGNS CONTRACT

Stanley Laurel, the popular English music hall comedian, who has just finished a tour of the Keith and Orpheum circuits in his own vaudeville headline act, has been placed under contract by the Special Pictures Corporation.

(*Los Angeles Herald* — December 6, 1920)

-----o-----

SPECIAL PICTURES

Stanley Laurel, after playing in an all-star Reggie Morris Comiclassic with Neely Edwards, Charlotte Merriam, and Dave Morris, he is to be given his own company and featured in his own releases.

(*circa* December 24, 1920)

-----o-----

"So what is the mystery," I hear you ask. Well, unless I've misinterpreted something, Stan Laurel had not just finished on the Keith and Orpheum circuit, but on the Poli's–Proctor's circuit. What I can say with certainty is that he was *not* the headline act, as claimed in the write-up. My comments on the previous page, about the act's slide down the bill, confirm this. The Keith and Orpheum networks of theatre chains would go on to become RKO pictures, so maybe they were just bigging-up Laurel to make it look as though they had nurtured an outstanding vaudeville act through their theatres, and raised him to the level where he was ready to be launched as a film comedy star.

And the biggest question arises from the statement: "*Stanley Laurel, after playing in an all-star Reggie Morris Comiclassic ...*" Are we to take it from this that Stan had actually just made a film via Special Pictures corporation? If so, it is not known to have been released. In fact, it is not known of — at all.

A third announcement tells us more about the aims of the company:

PLAN TO INCREASE 1921 PRODUCTION

An extensively increased production schedule for 1921 has been arranged for by the Special Pictures corporation, following the turning of their distribution over to the Federated Film Exchanges of America and the elimination of their own exchange system.

With the money that has formerly been used in maintaining their own distribution organization the Special pictures will be enabled to more than double production activities at their studios in Hollywood. According to Louis W. Thompson, president, the output of Comiclassics will be doubled. Instead of releasing one every two weeks, there will be one release a week. Such well-known stars as Ford Sterling, Neely Edwards, Charlotte Merriam, Stanley Laurel and Eddie Baker will be seen in the Comiclassics, of which Reggie Morris will continue as director general.

(*Los Angeles Herald* — December 27, 1920)

-----o-----

I could follow this through, at some length, and outline how G.M. Anderson was first involved, than removed from the company plans, but to do so would gain nothing. Suffice it to say Stan Laurel has been given a film contract, with his own company, and will be featured in a series of films bearing his name.

This is the fourth year running that the Laurels hadn't worked over Christmas, but what a present Stan had been given. He must have been so excited to be finally quitting vaudeville, and going into films — but we aren't. Hindsight is a wonderful thing!

CHAPTER 25

BREAKING NEWS

We have all seen those high-energy waves which come rushing in from the world's seas, and then crash onto the beach. They are known as "breakers," as they break twice — once when they rise up from the water, then a second time as they break onto land. Well those are the kind of breaks Stan Laurel was getting — a huge wave of high energy, which promises to carry you forward at great speed, but then hits the ground and dissipates within seconds.

This analogy can be applied to the offer, made by Special Pictures, to feature Stanley Laurel in his own series; as; after promising so much, it died almost instantaneously. And that would have been that, if it had not been for the arrival in Los Angeles of one G. M. Anderson.

Anderson had been in pictures since 1903, appearing in over three hundred films — the most-popular of which were the series of westerns in which he starred as 'Bronco Billy.' He was also founder of Essanay Studios, along with partner George Spoor ("S" and "A" — get it?). Essanay's biggest star name was Charlie Chaplin, who had made eleven films with them during 1915, after being lured away from Keystone. But then, in 1916, Anderson had sold his stake in the Essanay studios and retired from films.

Here in 1921, Anderson was planning a comeback as a film producer. One of his aims was to set up a comedy unit, and make a series of films with Stan Laurel as the star. First thing on the agenda was a pilot film, which Anderson could then use to showcase Laurel's talents to potential backers. The film, *The Lucky Dog*, was duly shot sometime during the last week in January, and the first week in February 1921.

It was now a waiting game for Laurel, to see if Anderson could get a distribution deal for the 'Stan Laurel Comedies' series. Little did anyone know then, but Laurel would, in the near future, make a series of films, totalling over one hundred, with one of the actors he had just appeared with — for the "heavy" in *The Lucky Dog* is none other than Oliver "Babe" Hardy. Hardy had spent the whole of 1919 and 1920 making films with Jimmy Aubrey, for Vitagraph. In March 1921 he would go on to team up with Larry Semon, with whom he would spend two and half years. Here, though, in January 1921, Babe was happy to tag along when Anderson asked Vitagraph director Jess Robbins to work with him on the Stan Laurel pilot.

Jess Robbins, along with Babe Hardy and Jack Lloyd, has been loaned by Vitagraph to G. M. Anderson, who will sponsor production of two-reel comedies which Jess Robbins will direct. Among others who have been engaged is Stanley Laurel.

* * *

Such was the briefness, though, of the on-screen time Laurel and Hardy spent together that no-one had had a chance to assess any chemical mix between the two, so evident in later years, and so both comedy actors went their separate ways – Hardy back into films, and Laurel back into vaudeville.

With nothing to be achieved, and no money to be earned, by lingering in Los Angeles, Stan and Mae high-tailed it over to San Diego, to catch up with the touring show they had been booked for on the Pantages circuit, having missed the first few bookings. Returning to vaudeville, a medium he had come to hate, must have been even more gut-wrenching than ever before for Stan. Back in 1917, when he had first made films, he had been led to believe that his vaudeville days were over, and that, in his own words: *"I didn't have to work seven days and seven nights a week, and could live like a human."* Going back into vaudeville, therefore, must have been comparable with a boxer who has to keep climbing back into the ring, despite having been knocked down so many times.

-----0-----

PANTAGES – ORPHEUM Circuit

1921

Jan 03	Oregon	PORTLAND, Pantages		[Stan and Mae NOT billed]
Jan 10				
Jan 15-21	California	BERKELEY, Pantages		[Stan and Mae NOT billed]
Jan 24				
Jan 31	California	LOS ANGELES	*The Lucky Dog*	filming
Feb 07	California	LOS ANGELES	*The Lucky Dog*	filming
Feb 10-13	California	SAN DIEGO, Hippodrome		Stan & Mae Laurel
Feb 14				
Feb 17-18	California	RIVERSIDE, Loring		

-----0-----

The Pantages Circuit was one that most run-of-the mill acts wanted to be on, mainly because of the amount of work it offered per annum. But that came at a price — and the price was a low price. Back in 1915, Stan had been getting at least a third-share of the $175 per week The Keystone Trio were on. And now here in 1921, with a track record of having spent six years in vaudeville as a solid act, plus having starred in his own film series, he was being marketed in no better light than an absolute beginner, with pay to suit — a guesstimated $100 per week, which barely covered inflation, much less a pay rise.

It must be the case that the advance publicity sheets, sent to theatres by the Pantages' office, contained very little to "sell" the act. Gone were mentions of Laurel's tie-ins with Chaplin (which perhaps wasn't a bad thing); but missing too were a description of the act, and adjectives and superlatives meant to excite readers into going to see the artistes (what we would call in today's computer language "keywords"). Without decent publicity sheets, from which to extract usable lines and phrases, reviewers employed by newspapers were left to do some "creative writing," which proved to be a step too far for a large percentage. The resultant previews and reviews were so badly written, containing little decipherable text relating to the actual act and/or its quality, that they have no place of merit here. I include these next two, only to give you an insight into just how poor they are. I would go as far as to say "gobbledegook":

-----0-----

California, SAN DIEGO, Spreckels Hippodrome

Stanley and Mae Laurel will demonstrate the position or activities of one who has "no mother to guide him."

(*San Diego Union* — February 10, 1921)

-----0-----

California, SAN DIEGO, Spreckels Hippodrome

Foolishment, impersonation, burlesque and whatnot comprise a pleasing act by Stanley and Mae Laurel which they call "No Mother to Guide Him," and mean nothing in particular. Some of the gowns in this turn are smart freaks that demand attention.

(*San Diego Evening Tribune* — February 12, 1921)

-----0-----

Finally, the Laurels received a preview worth quoting:

California, RIVERSIDE, Loring Theatre

Stanley and Mae Laurel, comedians and musicians supreme, have an act that never fails to "bring down the house" with applause.

(*Riverside Enterprise* — February 2, 1921)

However, this part of the same review would have had Stan gagging:

California, RIVERSIDE, Loring Theatre

The Loring theatre is offering today on its regular vaudeville program one of the highest salaried artists on the vaudeville stage, Jan Rubini.

(*Riverside Enterprise* — February 2, 1921)

Thirty-two years after touring with Rubini, the bitterness Laurel felt towards him had not diminished, as is more than evident in this letter to a confidante, Betty Healy (wife of Ted Healy — he of 'The Three Stooges' fame.).

June 4th.'53.

```
My Dear Betty [Healy]:-

I know Jan Rubini very well, was on the Pantages show with him a few
years ago when he was with his first wife Dianne, (A French Girl -
from Spokane!) before he joined our show, he had visited Charlie
Chaplin at the Studio & had some snapshots taken with him. He had
them enlarged & used them for Lobby display & was showing off to the
rest of the acts what a big shot he was, & everything was Charlie &
I etc. He didn't know I had come to this Country with Chaplin & was
his understudy & roomed with him for a couple of years, so one day I
put out in the Theatre Lobby, personal pictures that Charlie had
autographed to me & photos of Charlie & I on the Boat & in the show
etc. You should have seen Rubini's face! he went bloody mad! & to
make matters worse, after the first week, Pantages Headlined me
instead of Rubini for the rest of the trip. From then on he did
everything he possibly could to have me taken off the show. Dianne
even accused the Girl I was working with of stealing her pocket book
out of the dressing room. However it ended up, he was taken off the
show in L.A. here. I'll never forget that trip as long as I live.
What an impossible little Squirt he was, it would take too long to
tell you of the many other incidents with him. I would like to go
over to Malibu & teach him how to DROWN!.
```

Laurel had excellent recall, in general; but, when he gets into a fit of pique — as we have witnessed before with the likes of his working relationship with Edgar Hurley (*ibid*) — Stan abandons all accuracy, even truthfulness, and just goes for character assassination. Let us analyse this letter in its entirety:

On a minor point: in Stan's opening line he uses the phrase "*a few years ago,*" which is strange turn of phrase to describe THIRTY TWO years ago.

I can't begin to fathom what made Stan come up with the statement (in the letter): "... *to make matters worse, after the first week, Pantages Headlined me instead of Rubini for the rest of the trip...*" I have copies of nearly all of the adverts, bills, and reviews for the shows Jan Rubini and Stan & Mae did together, and *not once* were the Laurels the headline act. The falsehood of Laurel's statement is exposed to the fullest by the preview in the *Los Angeles Herald*, in which — out of the five acts mentioned — Stan & Mae Laurel aren't one of them.

Another strange turn of phrase in the letter is when Stan says: "... *the Girl I was working with ...*" Why not say something like: "My touring and stage partner ..." and then use the girl's name? It is as if he wanted to keep Mae's name and his relationship with her a secret — which is quite a surprising omission considering the passage of time.

And for Laurel to finish the letter with such bitter recrimination, when you would have thought that the passing of three decades would have made him look back and laugh at the one-upmanship he had gained over Rubini, is both a disappointing and excessive reaction.

Meanwhile, it is on with the 1921 tour — leastways, what we found of it:

-----o-----

Feb 19-20	California	SAN BERNADINO, Opera House
Feb 21		
Feb 25-26	California	BAKERSFIELD, Hippodrome
Feb 28		
Mar 03-05	California	RIVERSIDE, Orpheum
Mar 07		
Mar 10	California	SAN FRANCISCO
Mar 14		
Mar 21		
Mar 28		
Apr 04		
Apr 06-12	Utah	SALT LAKE CITY, Pantages

 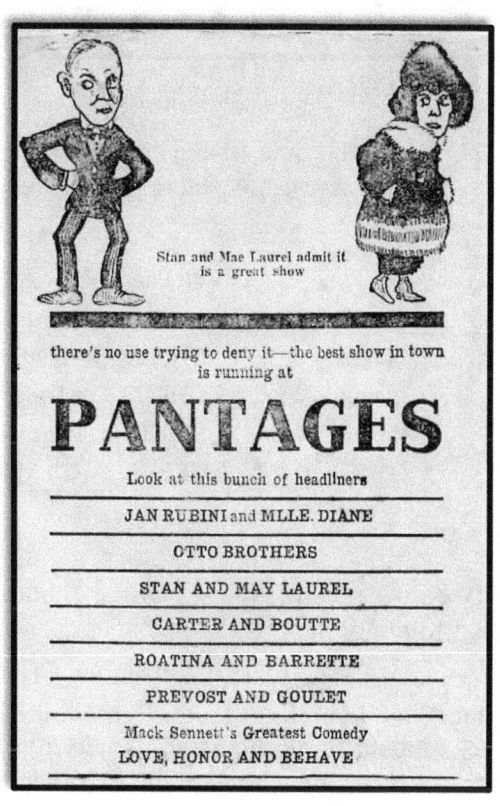

The feud continues: When Rubini had a cartoon featured in this advert from a Salt Lake City newspaper, Stan retaliated with a similar one.

Apr 14-16	Utah	OGDEN, Pantages	
Apr 18-23	Colorado	DENVER, Empress	
Apr 25-26	Colorado	COLORADO SPRINGS, Burns	
Apr 27			
May 02	Oklahoma	MUSKOGEE, Broadway	[1 night only]
May 04-07	Texas	WACO, Hippodrome	
May 08-14	Texas	SAN ANTONIO, Grand	
May 16			
May 22-28	Texas	DALLAS, Hippodrome	

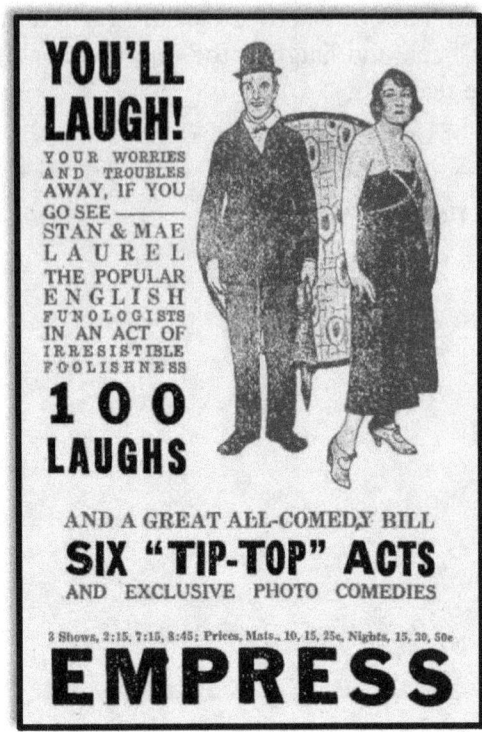

Denver — April 20, 1921   Waco — May 4, 1921

This time, Stan wins the battle of the pictorial feature, when he secures a real-life picture in *his* advert, as opposed to a cartoon in Rubini's.

May 30		
Jun 06		??, Pantages
Jun 13		
Jun 20	Illinois	CHICAGO, Chateau
Jun 21	Illinois	CHICAGO, Hippodrome
Jun 27-29	Illinois	DETROIT, Regent
Jun 30	Ohio	CLEVELAND, Miles
Jul 04		

-----0-----

This reviewer wasn't impressed with the Stan & Mae act but, ironically, gives one of the best descriptions I found of the on-stage business:

Illinois, CHICAGO, Chateau

Stan and Mae Laurel got laughs; entertained, but did not draw any encores. The plot of the act lacks much; some things are done without rhyme or reason; it even appears jumbled up at times. A girl comes home with a toothache. She phones for a dentist and exits. A burglar, bearing the earmarks of an amateur, comes in. Girl re-enters, thinks burglar is dentist. He has a tough job convincing her he is a burglar. After which he asks her to marry him. (Some speed.) Man exits and girl sings song. Man comes back dressed as a girl vamp; girl dressed as a man to be vamped. Talk foolishness, and then exit, after taking up too much time and offering nothing to brag about. The man acts comical, sometimes succeeds, and the girl carries a diva air about her.

(Chicago — June 22, 1921)

-----0-----

PANTAGES – ORPHEUM Circuit

Jul 10		??, Pantages
Jul 18-23	Manitoba	WINNIPEG, Pantages

-----0-----

Breaking News

Manitoba, WINNIPEG, Pantages

"No Mother to Guide Her," the burlesque travesty presented on this week's vaudeville bill at the Pantages theatre, serves to introduce Stan Laurel in his impersonation of a female impersonator. His depiction of the wiles of the average vampire keeps the audience in one continual peal of laughter. This chap, Stan Laurel, who appears in the act with his fair partner, Mae Laurel, has been at the Pantages on former occasions, and his unique sense of humor has made him a favorite on every bill upon which he has appeared.

But even though Stan got this glowing review, the next part took off the gloss:

The headline feature of the week is supplied by Jan Rubini, the wonderful Swedish violinist, and Mdlle. Diane, the French songbird. Rubini's own arrangement of an Irish melody is one of the most appealing bits of music heard here in a long time, while he simply captivates one and all with his closing number, "Oh, Promise Me," played in subdued tones that hold the attention of the house so that the proverbial pin dropping would sound like a crash.

(Winnipeg — July 21, 1921)

-----0-----

Still in Winnipeg, a new act to the show was 'Burns and Lorraine,' who are worthy of a mention here:

Manitoba, WINNIPEG, Pantages

Burns and Lorraine call themselves "The Broadway Thieves" because they have "purloined" the latest song and dance hits of "The Great White Way." But they return credit to the original performers by their clever impersonations.

(*Winnipeg Tribune* — July 16, 1921)

Just what impersonations they did was revealed in this review from San Francisco:

Burns and Lorraine, a nifty appearing male team, consisting of dancer and singer, featuring impressions of stars, were next to closing. The Cantor and Jolson and George White and Cohan imitations won them deserved recognition.

Stan and Mae Laurel took the comedy hit. They had them laughing throughout, and Stan's burlesque woman got howls.

(*Variety* — September 21, 1921)

A later review tells us:

Nat Burns and Will Lorraine demonstrate their cleverness as dancers in a most acceptable manner, and also prove that they are comedians of ability.

(*San Diego Union* — October 11, 1921)

It is good know that Nat Burns was considered to be a vaudeville "comedian of ability," as he certainly went on to be a comedian of some considerable ability. For those of you who don't already know, Nat Burns later changed his name to George Burns, and went on working as a comedian right up until his 100th Birthday. As well as continuing to perform stand-up, he had his own long-running radio *and* TV series, with wife and partner Gracie Allen, whom he was to meet on the vaudeville circuit in 1922. He also starred in many films, the most-notable being *The Sunshine Boys* — playing an old vaudeville comedian, trying to make a comeback.

At a Masquers Club meeting in Hollywood, in 1975, during a snatched interview with film historian Jordan R. Young, George Burns revealed his overriding memory of sharing the bill with Stan and Mae:

The Laurels seemed to be fighting day and night and, with the thin-walled dressing-rooms on the Pantages circuit, they could easily be heard all over the theatre.

When the dressing-room door would open, they would both be smiling at each other as if nothing were going on, but the minute the door was closed, the battle would begin again. She had the voice, he had the talent.

The quarrelling in San and Mae's lives was constant, and would continue throughout their future film career together, where it was about to have serious consequences. But first …

1921 (continued)

Jul 25	Alberta	EDMONTON, Pantages
Jul 26-27	Montana	GREAT FALLS, Grand
Jul 28-29	Montana	HELENA, Marlowe
Aug 01-05		
Aug 06-09	Montana	ANACONDA, Pantages
Aug 10	Montana	BUTTE, Pantages
Aug 11	Montana	MISSOULA, Pantages
Aug 15-20	Washington	SEATTLE, Pantages
Aug 22-28	British Columbia	VANCOUVER, Pantages
Aug 29	Washington	TACOMA, Pantages
Sep 05-10	Oregon	PORTLAND, Pantages
Sep 12		

Seattle — August 15-20

-----0-----

The touring show was now about to enter California, the highlight of which should be Los Angeles.

Sep 16-17	California	SAN JOSE, Victory
Sep 18-24	California	SAN FRANCISCO, Pantages
Sep 25	California	OAKLAND, Pantages

-----0-----

But before we hit L.A. let us have another look at part of what Laurel said in the letter in which he maligned Rubini: When Laurel says: *"... he [Rubini] was taken off the show in L.A. ..."* this is again a bit of wishful thinking. Jan Rubini had planned well-ahead to leave the show in Los Angeles, and with willing agreement from Pantages — as this article published nine months earlier will confirm:

> For quite a few years the many advantages of Los Angeles have appealed to the virtuoso Jan Rubini. He conceived the ambition to head and direct a symphony orchestra in this city. After a conference with Alexander Pantages, Rubini cancelled his long series of vaudeville engagements, and set himself the task of organizing an orchestra that would meet with the approval and approbation of the city's most exacting musical lover. Tomorrow Los Angeles will have the opportunity to witness the results of his musicianship.
>
> (*Los Angeles Herald* — February 2, 1921)

-----0-----

Six weeks on and Rubini's ambition is gradually becoming a realisation:

Jan Rubini

> *Tomorrow will mark the fourth Sunday morning concert at the new Panatages, and the scheduled program is considered a happy augury for the continued success of Jan Rubini's Symphony orchestra. ...*
>
> *... A steadily increasing attendance proves that the young virtuoso has won a warm place in the hearts of music-loving Angelenos.*
>
> (*Los Angeles Herald* — March 19, 1921)

So Rubini had been touring with the weekly vaudeville package show, but then playing Sunday concerts with his orchestra at the Pantages theatre, Los Angeles. Now, in October, the whole show was here:

Breaking News

California, LOS ANGELES, New Pantages

> After the film ... Jan Rubini, always welcome, plays for us once again on his wonderful violin. Signor Jan has two charming assistants, Mlle. Diane, who sings cute songs in a chic way, and Miss Voelker, the talented violinist's able accompanist [on piano]. Their number is a great musical treat.
>
> Joe Whitehead delivers the jokes that produce the laughs—his goods are perennially fresh, despite their age. The burlesque of Stan and Mae Laurel "No Mother to Guide Her," though occasionally a little rough, is very funny. It hits hard, and it makes a hit. Nat Burns and Bill Lorraine, "Broadway Thieves," sing and dance to the accompaniment of applause. In "White, Black and Useless" we have three humans and a mule, all in a grand mix-up of kicks and falls—lots of hilarious fun. Maud and Frank Cromwell, who come from the Barnum and Bailey, do the trapeze in a breezy style. Which ends a very good show.
>
> (*Los Angeles Herald* — October 6, 1921)

So did Stan & Mae top the bill? No! And was Rubini taken off the show? Well, yes and NO. Here is a contemporary account of his "enforced" departure:

> Jan Rubini, the violinist, appearing at Pantages this week, slept for the first time last Monday night in the $25,000 home which he purchased at Ninth street and Third avenue last winter, just two days before leaving for the tour of the Pantages circuit, just concluding. Rubini plans to settle down and enjoy life for a time, growing roses and perhaps training a few budding geniuses in the intricacies of violin virtuosity.
>
> (*Los Angeles Herald* — October 7, 1921)

So, after the last show in Los Angeles, Jan Rubini retired to his $25,000 dream home, while Laurel returned to his $100-a-week nightmare ordeal on the vaudeville circuit.

Oct 03	California	LOS ANGELES, Pantages	
Oct 10-16	California	CORONADO, Savoy	
Oct 17	California	LONG BEACH, Hoyt	
Oct 24	Utah	SALT LAKE, Pantages	
Oct 31	Utah	OGDEN, Pantages	
Nov 07	Colorado	DENVER, Empress	
[Nov 11	California	PETALUMA, Hill Opera House	date may vary]
Nov 14			
Nov 21	Missouri	KANSAS CITY, Pantages	
Nov 28	Missouri	ST. LOUIS, Pantages	
Dec 05	Tennessee	MEMPHIS, Pantages	

As can be gathered from this poster (used for display outside each theatre), Stan and Mae had been booked to tour on the Pantages Circuit for the 1921-1922 Season. But from December 12, 1921 onwards, no further stage appearances were found. This was more than avoiding having to work over Christmas.

And this was what had triggered the departure:

"Broncho" Billy, Screen's First Star, at It Again

G. M. (Bronco Billy) Anderson is back in San Francisco preparing to re-enter the moving picture production field, and already has started a comedy company at work. This unit will be headed by Stan Laurel, and the first picture is to be called "The Nut."

The company will locate in the Montague studio here temporarily.

Anderson says he intends to make a series of two-reel comedies, a series of westerns and a number of five-reel features.

G. M. ANDERSON

Finally, after eleven years in Vaudeville, Stan Jefferson Laurel was about to go into films. For him, this was — THE LAST STAGE.

CHAPTER 26

I WANNA BE IN PICTURES

"Bronco Billy" Anderson had managed to contact Laurel by phone, while he was still on tour, and invited him to return to L.A. On the strength of his having sold *The Lucky Dog*, Anderson took a chancy gamble by beginning to shoot the series of films he had proposed to do one year earlier, with Stan as the star:

> A new English comedian is shortly to be introduced on the screen by the Amalgamated Producing Company of Los Angeles, according to the announcement made by G. M. Anderson, the head of the new organization producing on the West coast. The comedian is Stan Laurel, known for his work in numerous American vaudeville engagements.
>
> *"In Stan Laurel I believe I have found a comedian who will prove as popular as Chaplin,"* Anderson said in speaking of his new comedian. *"He is not an imitator of Chaplin, but is a graduate of the same school of experience. In fact, Laurel came to America with the same company of players as Chaplin."* For five months G. M. Anderson has been giving his personal attention to the production of comedies starring Laurel. Three are now completed.
>
> (*The Era* — July 22, 1922)

In all, seven were filmed throughout 1922, as follows: *The Weekend Party* and *The Handy Man* (shot back-to-back – January 1922); *The Egg* (April); *The Pest* (August); *Mixed Nuts* (August); *Mud and Sand* (September); and *When Knights Were Cold* (December).

Stan in one of his favourite-ever gag-sequences — the basket-horse from *When Knights Were Cold*.

Come the completed Anderson-Laurel 12-month contract, there was a clause for an extension, in which more films would be made. Disappointingly, the distribution company, Metro (in conjunction with Anderson's 'Amalgamated Pictures') did not take up the option; and so Anderson and Laurel were forced to part company. Metro Pictures did, though, release six of the 'Stan Laurel Comedies,' at one-monthly intervals up till March 1923.

LAUREL – Stage by Stage
KEEP IT IN THE FAMILY – ALBUM

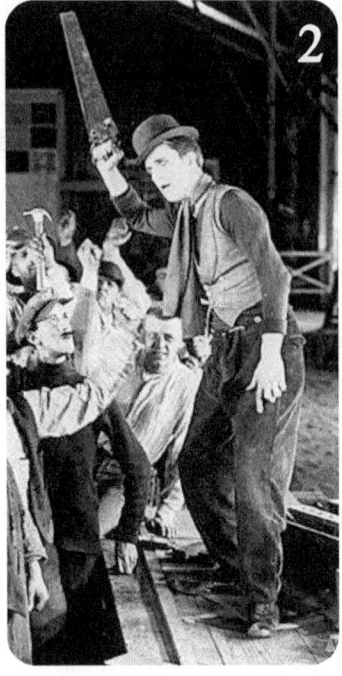

1) Cast and production team of *The Pest* – second from left Teddy Jefferson – third: G. M. Anderson. Front row right: Stan and Mae. 2) A scene from *The Egg*. Teddy is the man with cap and moustache. 3) Teddy's second role, as the butler, in *The Egg* [a role he also played in *The Lucky Dog* (in the same costume)].
4) Teddy as a guard in another Stan Laurel Comedy.

BELOW: Teddy and Stan in *Mixed Nuts*

Hal Roach Signs Stan Laurel

Moving Picture World, March 31, 1923

Hal Roach has signed Stan Laurel on a five year contract to star in one-reel comedies for Pathe release. This was the action taken by the producer, according to advices just received by Pathe, on seeing Laurel's first two pictures.

As recently announced from the Pathe offices, Stan Laurel is to alternate with Paul Parrott as star in weekly one-reel comedy releases under the production specifications which add considerably to the average cost of these short comedies in the past.

At the Hal Roach Studios a General Committee discusses every picture before it starts, watches it during the course of production, and assists in making eliminations and retakes where desirable.

TWO PATHE COMEDY STARS
Stan Laurel, on left, who has been signed by Hal Roach for five years to alternate with Paul Parrott, on right, as stars of single reel comedies for weekly release through Pathe.

Hal Roach, having seen one or more of the Anderson-Laurel comedies, had been impressed enough to recall Stan for a trial period to his studio. Roach, it may be remembered, had been half of the Rolin Film Company, with whom Stan had made five films back in the summer of 1918. Roach was now sole-owner of the Hal Roach Studios, which had a permanent new base in Culver City. The contract signed late January 1923 was for twelve weeks, with a one- or two-year extension.

The full list of the twenty-five titles, in order, is: *Under Two Jags, The Noon Whistle, White Wings, Pick and Shovel, Kill or Cure, Collars and Cuffs, Gas and Air, Oranges and Lemons, Short Orders, Save the Ship, A Man About Town, Roughest Africa, Scorching Sands, The Whole Truth, Frozen Hearts, The Soilers, Mother's Joy, Near Dublin, Smithy, Zeb vs. Paprika, Postage Due, Brothers Under the Chin, Wide Open Spaces,* and *Rupert of Hee Haw*, with the last one being *Short Kilts*.

Stan Laurel Comedies

Two Parts

With the release of the first Hal Roach Comedy in which he was featured, Stan Laurel was a star.

Succeeding Hal Roach Comedies definitely established him as a real personality, a natural comedian, a certain favorite-to-be.

Pathe hailed Laurel as a "comer." He has now arrived. He is to be presented in two-reel comedies made the way Hal Roach makes them.

Pathe prophesied that he would be popular. Pathe now prophesies that the season of 1923-1924 will bring him pretty close to the very top.

WATCH STAN LAUREL!

13—Sold in Series of Six

Hal Roach *presents*

One reviewer gave this very astute observation about the Stan Laurel Comedies:

> Two uproarious satires by Stan Laurel are high laughing marks in the new few-reel comedies on view this week.
>
> I must think up some really suitable way to apologize to Stan Laurel for not noticing his existence before. He's probably the only comic in the movies who doesn't use any patented makeup or wardrobe.
>
> Believe it or not, but Stan Laurel is making people laugh without benefit of busy eyebrows, walrus mustache, baggy pants, cane, monocle, or horn-rimmed glasses. He is not funny on

account of any peculiar shape, color, size of previous condition of servitude. He doesn't jump off the Santa Monica Palisades or dodge traffic at Hollywood and Cahuenga. He doesn't get shot in the pants oftener than every third picture, and I haven't seen him take a prat fall yet. I don't see how it can be accounted for. He's just funny.

You can see him in "Roughest Africa" at Clune's this week or in "Frozen Hearts" at the Rialto. And they're both cartilage-stretching satires well worth the chortling.

UNDER TWO JAGS (1923)

The first film Laurel made with Roach was a parody of *Under Two Flags*. The above still however, looks like a parody of Stan & Mae's 1918 publicity photo (except that they've swapped positions).

Happy with the nine films they had in the can during the provisional twelve weeks, the two parties agreed to the 1-year extension, during which an additional sixteen films were shot, ending almost exactly one year to-the day later (January 1924).

It is believed that Roach didn't take up the second-year option on Laurel's contract, because of Mae Laurel. He wasn't enamoured with her looks, didn't like her on-screen antics, and was totally infuriated by her private life, and the way it affected Stan and his film work. As Stan wouldn't agree to Mae being left out of the films, Roach felt he had no option but to keep Stan out of the frame as well – literally.

Luckily for Laurel, a friend of his persuaded independent film producer Joe Rock to take him on. Rock, however, had heard of the trouble Mae could make, and made it quite clear from the outset that her face wasn't about to be seen on film, nor even on set. However, things came to a head when Mae was allowed to accompany Stan on location during filming of the *Snow Hawk*. A few days in, she caused a major incident by implying that Joe Rock had made a pass at her. After convincing Laurel that he had been nowhere near her, Rock finally persuaded Laurel to send Mae packing, and even paid for her boat fare back to Australia.

Promotional photo for the 'Stan Laurel Comedies' made by Joe Rock films.

With Stan now able to concentrate fully on film-making, Joe Rock was able to finish the rest of the series of twelve films: *Detained, Mandarin Mix-Up, Monsieur Don't Care, West of Hot Dog, Somewhere in Wrong, Twins, Pie-Eyed, The Snow Hawk, Navy Blue Days, The Sleuth, Dr. Pyckle and Mr. Pride*, and *Half a Man* — making Stan Laurel the first-ever star of "Rock and Rolin." (Boom, Boom!)

MANDARIN MIX-UP
Laurel resting between takes, while director Percy Pembroke
discusses the scene with producer Joe Rock (right) 1924

When Laurel's one-year contract with Joe Rock expired, Hal Roach seized the day and invited him back to the Hal Roach studios — but there would be a catch: The twelve films Laurel made with Rock were pretty good quality, even though Rock had made them in an average of ten days, but thereby lay the problem: Rock was making out that the films were taking a whole month to shoot, and was charging the distributors accordingly. Consequently, when the films came in five months ahead of schedule, Rock had to keep up the pretence that some of the films were yet to be produced. This meant he wasn't able to start shooting any further films with Laurel, until that time was up.

The problem now was that, during the wait, Stan would have no income, and could not appear on film for another studio for fear of blowing Rock's ruse.

However, the move to the Hal Roach Studios was about to have life-changing outcomes. Laurel was now in the right mixing-bowl, working with all the best ingredients. There was just one more ingredient yet to add, to get that something really special.

-----0-----

With Laurel unable to work in front of the camera, Warren Doane, General Manager at the Roach Lot, positioned him as a writer and gag-man — a role which Stan was happy to accept, as he had never rated himself as a film comedian in any case. Of this sudden change in direction Laurel was to say in a 1957 taped interview:

> I wasn't too successful as a [film] comic. They told me my eyes were too blue to photograph. There was a kind excuse. I didn't feel I was so hot myself, so I was very happy to get into some other end of the business.

Laurel commenced work on the Roach Lot in May 1925; and a short time later, after he had shown interest in everything about film-making, was rewarded by supervisor F. Richard Jones offering to train him as a director. By 1926, he had co-directed a handful of films, including three with Oliver Hardy – who was now also working on "the Lot." When one day Hardy was unable to turn up for filming, having badly scalded his arm, Laurel was reluctantly coaxed back in front of the cameras to fill the vacant role. Roach liked Stan's contribution in the film *Get 'Em Young*, and gave him the go-ahead to write himself a part in the next picture. Hardy had by then recovered sufficiently to return, whereupon the two of them inadvertently appeared in the same film – *45 Minutes From Hollywood*. For Stan Laurel and Oliver Hardy, the wheels of fortune had been set in motion. It was now only a matter of time! Further films ensued in which the two of them appeared, until – by a process of almost "natural selection" – the potential of playing them against one another was spotted, and exploited.

And Here They Are — The Big Three

HRS is the initials of the Hal Roach Studios, but it also stands for:
HARDY, ROACH, and STAN
Three people who were in the right place, at the right time.
They knew they were good together, but none of them ever thought
they would go on to conquer the film world.

-----0----

Twelve months, and just as many films later, Laurel and Hardy made *Hats Off* (August 1927). In this film are the two characters, so consistent throughout the next thirteen years in the Roach films. Gone are the false moustaches, wigs, and costumes from their differing characters in previous films, and in their place is seen what was to become their regular clothing: Laurel's ill-fitting suit, spotted bow-tie, wing-collar shirt, and flat-heeled shoes; and Hardy's dark trousers, jacket, and the inseparable tie. The two of them have also permanently adopted their most famous of trade-marks – the hats.

[AJM: "Twin bowlers" is a misnomer used to describe the headgear worn by Laurel & Hardy. Hardy wore an English-type "Bowler," whereas Stan wore an Irish "Derby" – which is rounder, taller, and has a flat rim. See next photo!]

It is absolutely amazing when one realises that — though Laurel had been influenced by so many stage comedians, especially Chaplin; and Hardy had played the heavy/foil/villain to screen comedians like Jimmy Aubrey, Billy West, and Larry Semon — both had, within the incredibly short space of time since coming together, magically created two totally original, and fully-formed characters.

Because the comedy of the screen Laurel & Hardy was based on these two characters, and the situations in which they found themselves, audiences could easily relate to them. Their popularity grew rapidly and, even with the advent of talking pictures, their style of comedy was not hindered – but advanced.

Is it any wonder that, more than seventy years after making their last Hollywood film, they are still loved and lauded throughout the world? Both men had played the stage, but you might say they had taken it that one stage further.

THE END

CHAPTER 27

REMEMBER ME?

Many of the acts who Stan met on the British, American, and Canadian stage went on to become famous stars of stage and screen. This wouldn't have bothered Stan — known or unknown, star or support act, rich or destitute, working or retired — he would welcome them all when he met up with them in later years.

Many stars would not admit to their roots, and would pull away from people from their past who brought up the subject, but not Stan Laurel. He would spend time with whomsoever took the time and trouble to go and meet him. Here are just some of the people who he got to reminisce with:

VAUDEVILLE DAYS

Let's start where we finished off:

MAE DAHLBERG

LEFT: Mae on the set of the Roach-Laurel film *Near Dublin* (filmed September 1923). Early in 1925 she was supposedly shipped off to Australia, never to be seen again. However, in November 1936 she turned up in Los Angeles, claiming alimony off Stan, backed up by cuttings in her scrapbook to prove they had lived as common-law man and wife. Well we won't go into that. It was such a shame that, having partnered Laurel through those hard times in vaudeville (which directly resulted in his being spotted as a potential film star), their parting should have seemingly been so heartless. Mae did know in her heart, though, that had she hung around she would have only ruined Stan's chances of progressing in films.

GEORGE BURNS

When Stan first met George Burns, in 1921, he was touring with Bill Lorraine. But then in 1922 Burns met and later married Gracie Allen, and together the two went on to become huge Radio and TV stars.

Laurel met up with George at Eddie Cantor's birthday party (January 1952), along with a host of other comedy stars, including Jimmy Durante, Joe E. Brown, Oliver Hardy, Norris Goff, and Charles Corell (pictured right).

DIANE RUBINI

Of the people Stan Laurel did not want to meet again, Swedish violinist Jan Rubini was high on the list. However, that didn't hold for Rubini's former-wife, the charming French singer Mdlle. Diane Rubini, who visited Stan at the Hal Roach Studios.

When Diane and Stan shared the bill on their 1921 vaudeville tour, she was the wife and stage partner of Jan Rubini. However, when the two were reunited on the Roach Lot, during filming of *Below Zero* (February 1930), Diane was a divorcee.

CHARLES ALTHOFF

Althoff busking with Stan and Viola Richard on the set of *Why Girls Love Sailors* (1927). [Amazing to see that Althoff has the same stance in all three stills.]

The Sheriff of Hicksville Publicity photo from 1918, when Althoff and Stan did shows together. [Chapter 22]

A second reunion on the set of *Below Zero* (1930), with Charles looking more 'slick' than 'hick.'

BALDWIN COOKE

Stan had worked with Baldwin (and Alice) Cooke in two stage acts, playing *The Crazy Cracksman* (Chapter 18). But then in 1927 Baldy began working as an extra at the Roach studios. Although he was mainly in the background on thirty-one L&H films, his moment does come in this scene as the irate neighbour in *Perfect Day* (1929).

He and Alice were also close friends of Laurel in his private life. I guess Stan was making up for the way he had dumped the Cookes to run away with Mae.

KARNO COMEDIANS

TED BANKS

This is an extract from a letter written by Stan – June 9, 1960.

```
The news article you read about Edward Coppin was very
interesting,he adopted the name of Teddy Banks when he joined
the Fred Karno Co. we used to share rooms together when we came
to this Country - we were only making $20 a week,so could'nt
afford single rooms - whoever wrote that article was mistaken
in regard to Banks forming the "Keystone Trio",it was I who
started the act with another Karno boy & his wife,whose names
were Edgar & Ethel Hurley. I later left the act & Teddy Banks
then joined the Hurley's,but after a few weeks the act folded
up entirely.Banks then joined another act called "A Night in the
Park". I met him a few years later when he was with 'Blackstone'
in Los Angeles.
```

Stan and Babe giving attention to Ted, during a break on the set of *Oliver the Eighth* (1934). He was then tour manager with magician Harry Blackstone.

[Ted Banks is pictured with the Karno Hockey Team in Chapter 5.]

FRED KARNO Jnr.

Freddie, Stan, and George Rowe enjoying a beer-break during filming of *Near Dublin* – 1923

Freddie was one of the Karno Company who returned to England in March 1914, and one of the few who subsequently joined the army, to partake in World War 1. But then, in the summer of 1923, he was to be found living in Los Angeles, with a wife and two children. He also had two surprising lodgers during his tenure — namely Stan and Mae Laurel. The reciprocal arrangement was that Stan got Freddie work as an extra on the Roach Lot, in which capacity he made glimpsing appearances in *Near Dublin*, *Smithy*, *Zeb vs. Paprika*, *Postage Due*, *Brothers Under the Chin*, and *Wide Open Spaces*.

After twelve months in L.A., Freddie upped sticks, and moved to Canada (probably because he had only a temporary visa), where he attempted a revival of *A Night in an English Music Hall*. Further details are sketchy, except to say his stay in Canada was a short one, and that he returned to England where, sometime later, he re-married and ran a guest house in Kent. He was also still doing infrequent tours with *Mumming Birds*. Stan was known to be still exchanging letters with him as late as 1959.

FRANK O'NEIL

Although Fred Karno was the figurehead, Frank O'Neil was the manager of the various Karno Companies which Stan toured with in the UK in 1909-10. It would therefore have been O'Neil who coached the young Jefferson, rehearsed him, and selected him for the various roles.

[See Chapter 5)

Stan was thrilled when Frank O'Neil paid him a visit at the Savoy Hotel, London, during Laurel and Hardy's 1932 British tour. Babe thought he had come to check his passport.

(At right is comedian Bobby Howes).

This almost looks like a dress-rehearsal for the photo at left, with Frank O'Neil again seated, and Bert Williams, Charlie Chaplin, and Freddie Karno standing in for the other players. (1910)

(With thanks to Paul Duncan)

FRED KARNO

I am pretty certain Laurel's meeting with Karno in 1927 (see letter below) led to Fred being invited to the Roach Studios as a comedy writer. Things didn't work out, and he soon went back to England, but no doubt he would have enjoyed being reunited with his star pupil.

```
Yes, I had a long chat with Stan and thought he looked
very fit, he seems to have got on very well, and I
was pleased to hear of his success.   I would very
much like to come over, and will certainly do so at
the first opportunity.   Things are very quiet over
here in our business, and it does not look as if
there is going to be any improvement.
            Best love to the boys and good wishes
to you,                    Sincerely,
```

Karno (on overturned dustbin), trying to think up funny business for the Laurel & Hardy film *Night Owls* (filmed November 1929).
James Parrott (right) awaits the killer gag.

TEDDY DESMOND

Another comedy partner from the past, whom Stan was delighted to see, was Teddy Desmond. Back in 1911 he had worked under the name of Ted Leo, and was the other half of the re-formed 'Barto Bros.' Teddy had previously met Stan during the 1932 tour, when he was leader and trumpet player of the "Savannas Orchestra," in residence at the Dennistoun Palais, in Glasgow.

This second meeting was at Southend, Essex in 1952, where Teddy was now manager of an amusement arcade.

No doubt the ill-fated tour of the 'Continent' was their main topic of conversation (see Chapter 10).

CARY GRANT, CHICO MARX, GROUCHO MARX

Stan didn't appear on the bill with Cary Grant, but did see him on stage at the Hippodrome, New York, when Cary was in a stilt-walking troupe.

As for Groucho and Chico, they first met backstage in Vancouver (see Chapter 13).

Groucho on piano, *sans* moustache.

To find out where these reunions took place, you will need to treat yourself to a copy of my "US Tours" book.

LEVY & CARDWELL'S JUVENILE PANTOMIME COMPANY

JACKIE GRAHAM
Stan reminiscing with Jackie Graham, backstage at the Glasgow Empire – March 1954 (see Chapter 3).

BENNY BARRON
Stan with the other half, at the Sunderland Empire – March 1952

JOHN ARMSTRONG
John as he looked when Stan met up with him in North Shields, in 1932. And right, how he looked back in 1907 when he played the 'Queen' in *The Sleeping Beauty*.

WEE GEORGIE WOOD

Wee Georgie remained short in stature throughout his life, and so continued in show business playing the role of a boy.

Georgie seeing off Stan and Babe at Los Angeles Railway Station, at the beginning of the 1952 British Tour. (See Chapter 3.)

Remember Me?

BEATRICE OLGA JEFFERSON (also Woods, and then Healey)

Olga as she would have looked while Stan was touring America in the mid-1910s.

In March 1947 Stan and Babe dropped in at the *Plough Inn*, Barkston, where Olga and husband Bill Healey were the landlords.

Olga and Bill are now landlords at the *Bull Inn*, Bottesford, where Stan and Babe were treated to lunch on Easter Sunday, in 1952. They also had Christmas dinner there, in 1953.

ARTHUR JEFFERSON Snr.

Stan was reunited with his father in 1927, when he paid a short visit to England. He returned in 1932 with comedy partner Hardy.
On board the *Aquitania*, Southampton (July 1932)

In 1935 it was Arthur who made the trans-Atlantic trip (with his second wife, Venetia) and enjoyed his son's hospitality for several months in Los Angeles.
Catalina Island (August 1935)

In 1947 "A.J", now eighty-four, was living with his daughter Olga (top right) when Stan and Babe dropped in at the *Plough Inn*.

Top Left: Ida Laurel.
Barkston, Lincs. (March 11, 1947)

ARTHUR JEFFERSON Snr. and Jnr.

So now we are back where we started — with Arthur Jefferson

Father of a Comic Genius

DATE-SHEETS

Stan Laurel's stage appearances in the United Kingdom, U.S.A., and Canada

On the following pages are date-sheets containing every known stage appearance which Stan Jefferson/Laurel made between 1907 and 1921; before entering films and then meeting with his legendary partner – Oliver Hardy.

In the United Kingdom the standard "week" for theatre engagements is six days, Monday to Saturday. Any exceptions have been notated as such. But, *no performances* were ever played on a Sunday. God would have struck the theatre with a bolt of lightning if they had ever dared.

How to read the tables.

UNITED KINGDOM:

Column 1 is the DATE — termed as "week commencing" (often abbreviated to w/c) which starts on a Monday – unless otherwise stated. Column 2 is the COUNTY. Column 3 is the TOWN or CITY where the theatre was located. Column 4 is the name of the THEATRE. Column 5 is the name of the PRODUCTION. Column 6 is for the NAME of ACT, and/or author's COMMENTS, and/or additional INFORMATION.

-----0-----

U.S.A. and CANADA

Column 1 is the DATE. Column 2 is the STATE. Column 3 is the TOWN or CITY where the theatre was located. Column 4 is the name of the THEATRE. Column 5 is the name of the PRODUCTION. Column 6 is for the NAME of ACT, and/or author's COMMENTS, and/or additional INFORMATION.

-----0-----

To repeat what I wrote in the Preface:

> In America and Canada there were numerous permutations of the working-week: Monday to Saturday did sometimes happen; but the following were more common — Monday to Wednesday, or Sunday to Wednesday; Thursday to Saturday, or Thursday to Sunday; but then comes Sunday only; or the pairing of any two consecutive days, and then, of course, single days. This makes it almost impossible to compile totally accurate date-sheets.
>
> Any corrections of wrong dates and/or information, and/or additional dates will be gratefully received, and the date-sheets duly amended in any future publications.

-----0-----

It has taken many years to find and collate these dates, so now that they are in print does not give anyone the right to reproduce them for their own projects. So, please note that:

THESE TABLES ARE COPYRIGHTED

THE PUBLISHERS WILL NOT HESITATE TO TAKE LEGAL ACTION AGAINST ANYONE WHO REPRODUCES THEM BY WAY OF PRINTED MATTER, WEB-SITES, INTERNET, ELECTRONIC DATA or IMAGES, PRESENTATIONS, DISPLAYS, OR ANY OTHER FORM, WITHOUT PRIOR CONSENT.

"A.J" Marriot

for Marriot Publishing

Stan Jefferson — Date-Sheets

THE SLEEPING BEAUTY
Levy & Cardwell Company

1907

August 12	Lancashire	BACUP, New Court
August 19	Lancashire	CHORLEY, Grand
August 26		no trace
September 02	Lancashire	LANCASTER, Athenaeum
September 09	Scotland	LEITH, New Gaiety
September 16	Scotland	LEITH, New Gaiety
September 23	Durham	SOUTH SHIELDS, Royal
September 30	Durham	SUNDERLAND, King's
October 07	Scotland	GREENOCK, Alexandra
October 14	Scotland	MOTHERWELL, New Century
October 21	Yorkshire	CASTLEFORD, Royal
October 28	Wiltshire	SWINDON, Queen's
November 04	Cheshire	CREWE, Lyceum
November 11	Staffordshire	LONGTON, Queen's
November 18	Lancashire	DARWEN, Royal
November 25	Lancashire	TYLDESLEY, Royal
December 02	Lancashire	RAWTENSTALL, Grand
December 09	Yorkshire	MEXBOROUGH, Prince of Wales
December 16	Lancashire	WIDNES, Alexandra
December 23	Cheshire	STOCKPORT, Royal
December 30	Cheshire	STOCKPORT, Royal

1908

January 06	Manchester	SALFORD, Regent
January 13	Manchester	SALFORD, Regent
January 20	Lancashire	ASHTON-under-LYNE, Royal
January 27	Lancashire	ASHTON-under-LYNE, Royal
February 03	Lancashire	OLDHAM, Colleseum
February 10	Staffordshire	STAFFORD, Lyceum
February 17	Staffordshire	DUDLEY, Royal Opera House
February 24	Wallasey	SEACOMBE, Irving
March 02	Durham	JARROW, New Royal
March 09	Durham	SEAHAM HARBOUR, New Royal
March 16	Northumberland	BLYTH, New Royal
March 23	Cumberland	CARLISLE, His Majesty's
March 30	Durham	NORTH SHIELDS, Royal
April 06	Durham	CONSETT, New Royal
April 13	Durham	WEST STANLEY, Royal
April 20	Durham	HARTLEPOOL WEST, Grand and Opera House
[April 25		*The Sleeping Beauty* ends here.]

-----0-----

Stan Jefferson appeared in all the above.

THE GENTLEMAN JOCKEY
Edward Marris Company

1908

April 27	Oxfordshire	OXFORD, East	
May 04			
May 11			
May 18	Ireland	DUBLIN, Theatre Royal	
May 25	Oxfordshire	OXFORD, East	
June 01	Cheshire	CREWE, Lyceum	
June 08	Manchester	BROUGHTON, Victoria	
June 15	Scotland	EDINBURGH, Royal Lyceum	
June 22	Northumberland	NEWCASTLE, Tyne and Opera House	[Stan joins here.]
June 29	Scotland	GLASGOW, King's	
July 06	Yorkshire	YORK, Royal	
July 13	Hampshire	SOUTHAMPTON, Grand	
July 20	Dorset	BOURNEMOUTH, Royal	
[July 25		Stan leaves *The Gentleman Jockey* at the end of its run.]	

-----o-----

AJM: The first time Stan is named in a review is June 29, 1908, at the King's Theatre, Glasgow, when the reviewer writes: "*Stan Jefferson is very humorous.*" But, in a 1936 article in *Tit-Bits* (*ibid*) Stan cites his debut as being at the Tyne Theatre and Opera House, Newcastle – so his joining there has to be taken as correct. BUT, he must have rehearsed the week before, at Edinburgh.

o-o-o-o-o

HOME FROM THE HONEYMOON
Arthur Jefferson's Company

1908

July 06	Wales	SWANSEA, Empire	
July 13	Wales	NEWPORT, Empire	
July 20	Leicestershire	LEICESTER, Palace	
July 27	Worcestershire	BIRMINGHAM, Empire	[Stan is believed to have joined here.]
August 03	Northumberland	NEWCASTLE, Empire	
August 10	Durham	SUNDERLAND, Empire	
August 17	Scotland	DUNDEE, Palace	
August 24	Scotland	EDINBURGH, Empire	
August 31	Scotland	GLASGOW, Empire	
September 07	Scotland	GREENOCK, Alexandra	
September 14	Scotland	PAISLEY, Hippodrome	
September 21	Liverpool	LIVERPOOL, Empire	
September 28	Manchester	MANCHESTER, Hippodrome	
October 05	Yorkshire	BRADFORD, Empire	
October 12	Yorkshire	LEEDS, Empire Palace	
October 19	Yorkshire	HULL, Palace	
October 26		vacant	
November 02	Yorkshire	SHEFFIELD, Empire	
November 09	Nottinghamshire	NOTTINGHAM, Empire	
[November 14		Stan leaves *Home From The Honeymoon* at the end of its run.]	

Stan Jefferson — Date-Sheets

THE HOUSE THAT JACK BUILT
Levy & Cardwell Juvenile Pantomime Company

1908

November 23	Staffordshire	STAFFORD, Lyceum	[Stan starts here.]
November 30	Cheshire	HYDE, Royal	
December 07	Lancashire	TYLDESLEY, Royal	
December 14	Yorkshire	CASTLEFORD, Royal	
December 25	Worcestershire	DUDLEY, Royal Opera House	
December 28	Worcestershire	DUDLEY, Royal Opera House	

1909

January 04	Worcestershire	DUDLEY, Royal Opera House	
January 11	Wiltshire	SWINDON, Empire	
January 18	Lancashire	DARWEN, Royal	
January 25	Manchester	SALFORD, Regent	
February 01	Durham	BLYTH, New Royal	
February 08	Durham	CONSETT, New Royal	
February 15	Durham	JARROW, New Royal	
February 22	Durham	SEAHAM HARBOUR, Royal	
March 01	Northumberland	NEWCASTLE, Palace	
March 08	Scotland	DUNFERMLINE, Opera House	
March 15	Scotland	KILMARNOCK, King's	
March 22	Scotland	KIRKCALDY, King's	
March 29	Scotland	DUMFRIES, Royal	
April 05	Durham	WEST STANLEY, Royal	[tour ends here – Saturday 10th.]

o-o-0-o-o

ALONE IN THE WORLD
Percy Williams' Company

1909 (continued)

[Apr 12–Aug 01		Stan is disengaged.]	
Aug 02	Wales	PONTPRIDD, Royal Clarence	
Aug 09	Manchester	MANCHESTER, Metropole	
Aug 16	Yorkshire	WAKEFIELD, Opera House	
Aug 23	Manchester	QUEEN'S PARK, Hippodrome	[pulled out]
Aug 23	Yorkshire	BRADFORD, Prince's	
Aug 30	Yorkshire	LEEDS, Royal	
Sep 06	Manchester	SALFORD, Hippodrome	[pulled out]
Sep 06	East Riding	HULL, Alexandra	
Sep 13	Yorkshire	TODMORDEN, Hippodrome	
Sep 20	Manchester	LONGSIGHT, King's	[pulled out]
Sep 20	Lancashire	HORWICH, Prince's	
Sep 27	Worcestershire	KIDDERMINSTER, Opera House	[pulled out]
Sep 27		vacant date	
Oct 04	Northumberland	ASHINGTON, Miners'	[tour ends prematurely — Oct 11]
	NEWCASTLE, Empire Palace; SCARBOROUGH, Royal; WEST STANLEY, Royal		[all cancelled]

-----0-----

DICK WHITTINGTON
Christmas Pantomime

[Nov 29	Tyne & Wear	SUNDERLAND, King's	Stanley Jefferson	withdrew]

o-o-0-o-o

FRED KARNO COMPANY
British Tours 1909 — 1910

1909 (continued)

Date	Region	Venue	Show	Notes
November 29	Scotland	GLASGOW, Grand	*Mother Goose*	[Stan's interview with Karno]

[Pantomime is in rehearsal. Opens on Wednesday December 8, 1909]

Date	Region	Venue	Show	Notes
December 06	Manchester	HULME, Hippodrome	*Mumming Birds*	[Stan Jefferson's DEBUT]
December 13	Lancashire	WARRINGTON, Palace	*The Casuals*	
December 13	Lancashire	WARRINGTON, Palace	*Mumming Birds*	
[December 20	Manchester	MANCHESTER, Palace	*Skating*	Syd Chaplin]
December 20	Manchester	SALFORD, Royal Hippodrome	*Mumming Birds*	
[December 27	Manchester	MANCHESTER, Palace	*Skating*	Syd Chaplin]
December 27	Scotland	DUNDEE, King's	*Early Birds*	
December 27	Scotland	DUNDEE, King's	*Mumming Birds*	

1910

Date	Region	Venue	Show	Notes
January 03	Yorkshire	WAKEFIELD, Empire	*Mumming Birds*	Syd Chaplin
January 03	Yorkshire	WAKEFIELD, Empire	*Skating*	Syd Chaplin
January 10	Liverpool	LIVERPOOL, New Pavilion	*Mumming Birds*	Syd and Charlie Chaplin

[Stan meets Charlie here, for the first time.]

Date	Region	Venue	Show	Notes
January 17	Lancashire	ROCHDALE, Hippodrome	*Early Birds*	
January 17	Lancashire	ROCHDALE, Hippodrome	*Skating*	Stan Jefferson AND Charlie Chaplin
January 24	Lancashire	BURY, Royal and Palace	*Early Birds*	
January 24	Lancashire	BURY, Royal and Palace	*Skating*	

[Hockey team – 1st match: M. Schofield; Gertie Jackson. Ernie Stone, Ted Banks, James Barrasford.]

Date	Region	Venue	Show	Notes
January 31	Lancashire	WIGAN, Grand Hippodrome	*The Casuals*	
January 31	Lancashire	WIGAN, Grand Hippodrome	*Skating*	Charles Chaplin, Johnny Doyle
January 31	Manchester	HULME, Hippodrome	*Skating*	
February 07	Scotland	GLASGOW, Pavilion	*Skating*	
February 14	Yorkshire	LEEDS, Hippodrome	*Skating*	Charles Chaplin, Johnny Doyle
February 21	Warwickshire	BIRMINGHAM, Hippodrome	*Skating*	Charles Chaplin, Johnny Doyle

[Saturday – City Rink Hockey]

Date	Region	Venue	Show	Notes
February 28	Yorkshire	SHEFFIELD, Hippodrome	*Skating*	(Charles Chaplin in good form.)

[Cast had great fun every day at the American Rink.]

Date	Region	Venue	Show	Notes
March 07	Liverpool	LIVERPOOL, Royal Hippodrome	*Skating*	Syd Chaplin, Charles Chaplin
March 14	Northumberland	NEWCASTLE, Pavilion	*Skating*	Syd and Charles Chaplin
March 21	Lancashire	ECCLES, Crown	*Skating*	Syd Chaplin, Charles Chaplin
March 28	Manchester	LONGSIGHT, King's	*Skating*	

[Hockey Team at Levenshulme: Charles Chaplin, Ernie Stone, James Beresford, F. Jordan, Ted Banks]

Date	Region	Venue	Show	Notes
April 04	London	HACKNEY, Empire	*Skating*	
Apr 09		Charlie and Stan end their run in *Skating*		

-----0-----

Date	Region	Venue	Show	Notes
April 11	London		*Jimmy the Fearless*	rehearsals

[Saturday 16th – Charlie's 21st Birthday]

Date	Region	Venue	Show	Notes
April 18	London	EALING, Hippodrome	*Jimmy the Fearless*	Stan as 'Jimmy'
April 18	London	WILLESDEN, Hippodrome	*Jimmy the Fearless*	Stan as 'Jimmy'
April 25	London	STRATFORD, Empire	*Jimmy the Fearless*	[Chaplin replaces Stan.]
May 02	London	HOLLOWAY, Empire	*Jimmy the Fearless*	
May 09	Yorkshire	SHEFFIELD, Empire Palace	*Jimmy the Fearless*	
May 16	Durham	SOUTH SHIELDS, Empire Palace	*Jimmy the Fearless*	
May 23	Northumberland	NEWCASTLE, Empire Palace	*Jimmy the Fearless*	

Stan Jefferson — Date-Sheets

1910 (continued)

May 30	Scotland	GLASGOW, Coliseum	*Mumming Birds*
June 06	Scotland	GLASGOW, Coliseum	*Jimmy the Fearless*
June 13	Staffordshire	WALSALL, Her Majesty's	*Jimmy the Fearless*

[Thursday June 16th – Stan's 20th Birthday]

June 20	Leicestershire	LEICESTER, Palace	*Jimmy the Fearless*
June 27	Wales	CARDIFF, Empire	*Jimmy the Fearless*
July 04	Wales	NEWPORT, Empire	*Jimmy the Fearless*
July 11	Wales	SWANSEA, Empire	*Jimmy the Fearless*
July 18	Yorkshire	LEEDS, Empire Palace	*Jimmy the Fearless*
July 25	Warwickshire	BIRMINGHAM, Empire Palace	*Jimmy the Fearless*
August 01	Yorkshire	HULL, Palace	*Jimmy the Fearless*

[Hockey match at Newington. Charles Chaplin, Stan Jefferson]

August 08	Liverpool	LIVERPOOL, Empire	*Jimmy the Fearless*

[Company pulled out. Could have been rehearsing *The Wow-Wows* – with Syd]

August 15	Manchester	ARDWICK, Empire	*Jimmy the Fearless*
August 22	Nottingham	NOTTINGHAM, Empire	*Jimmy the Fearless*
August 29	Yorkshire	BRADFORD, Empire	*Jimmy the Fearless*
September 05	London	WOOLWICH, Hippodrome	*The Wow-Wows*
September 12	Essex	ILFORD, Hippodrome	*The Wow-Wows*
September 12	London	SHOREDITCH, Olympia	*The Wow-Wows*
September 12	London	TOTTENHAM, Palace	*Jimmy the Fearless*
September 22	Hampshire	SOUTHAMPTON	Karno Company sails for America.

Stan Jefferson appeared at all the venues listed in dark print.

o-o-0-o-o

FRED KARNO COMPANY
SS Cairnrona - 20th September 1910
Back L-R: Albert Austin, Fred Palmer, Bert Williams, George Seaman, Frank Melroyd
Stan Jefferson, Fred Westcott, Charlie Chaplin, Arthur Dandoe
Muriel Palmer, Mike Asher, Amy Minister, Capt. C.J. Slooke

MAP of STATES in NORTH AMERICA, and Border States of CANADA

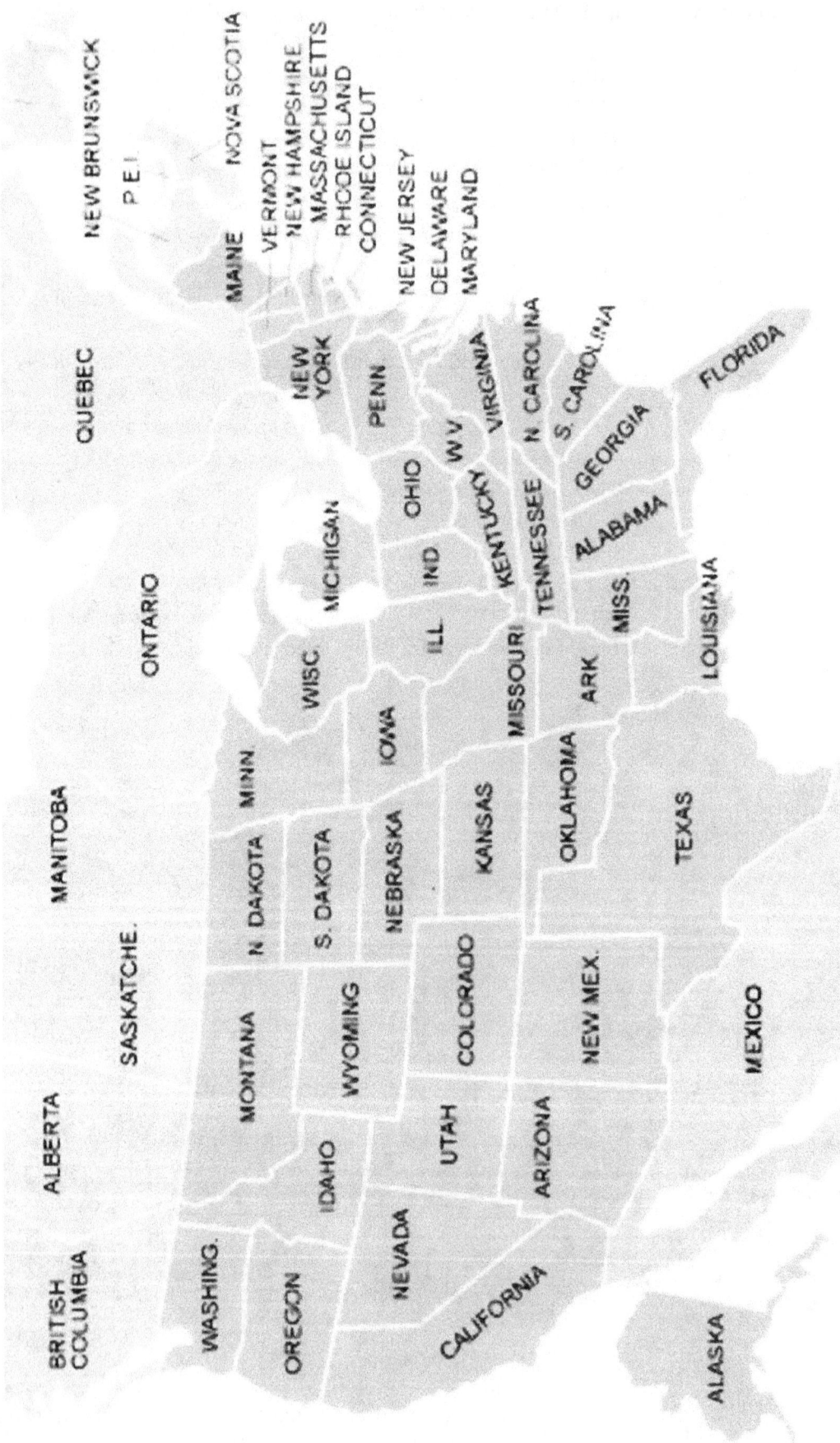

Stan Jefferson — Date-Sheets

FRED KARNO COMPANY
The American Tours 1910-1911

KEY: For the American tours, "*Mumming Birds*" was re-named: "*A Night in an English Music Hall*," but was often billed as: "*A Night in a London Music Hall*." In these listings, the abbreviated name "*Music Hall*" is used. Likewise, "*A Night in a London Club*," and similar derivatives, is abbreviated to "*London Club*."

1910 (continued)

Date	State/Province	Venue	Show	
Sep 26-Oct 02		Trans-Atlantic crossing on the *Cairnona*—SOUTHAMPTON to QUEBEC		
Oct 03	New York	NEW YORK CITY, Colonial	*The Wow-Wows*	
Oct 10	New York	NEW YORK CITY, Alhambra	*The Wow-Wows*	
Oct 17	New York	BROOKLYN, Orpheum	*The Wow-Wows*	
Oct 24	New York	BRONX, Bronx	*The Wow-Wows*	
Oct 31	New York	BROOKLYN, Greenpoint		
Nov 07	Massachusetts	FALL RIVER, Savoy	*Music Hall*	
Nov 14	New York	NEW YORK CITY, National		
Nov 21	Pennsylvania	PHILADELPHIA, Nixon	*Music Hall*	
Nov 28	New York	NY CITY, American Music Hall	*Music Hall*	
Dec 05	New York	NY CITY, American Music Hall	*The Wow-Wows*	
Dec 12	New York	NY CITY, American Music Hall	*London Club*	
Dec 19	New York	NY CITY, American Music Hall	*A Night in the Slums*	
Dec 26	New York	NY CITY, American Music Hall	*Harlequinade in Black & White*	
Dec 26	New York	NY CITY, American Music Hall	*Music Hall*	

Nixon-Nirdlinger Circuit

1911

Date	State	Venue	Show	
Jan 02	New York	NEW YORK CITY, Plaza	*The Wow-Wows* plus *A Harlequinade in Black & White*	
Jan 09	Pennsylvania	PHILADELPHIA, Nixon	*London Club*	
Jan 12	Pennsylvania	PHILADELPHIA, Academy	*London Club*	[1 night]
Jan 16	Pennsylvania	PHILADELPHIA, Park	*Music Hall*	
Jan 23	Pennsylvania	PHILADELPHIA, Nixon	*The Wow-Wows*	

Sullivan-Considine Circuit — East-West, California

Date	State/Province	Venue	Show	
Jan 30	Illinois	CHICAGO, American Music Hall	*London Club*	
Feb 06	Illinois	CHICAGO, American Music Hall	*The Wow-Wows*	
Feb 13	Illinois	CHICAGO, American Music Hall	*Music Hall*	
Feb 20		no trace	[possibly: Cleveland – Ohio, St. Louis – Missouri; or Detroit – Michigan]	
Feb 26-Mar 03	Ohio	CINCINNATI, Empress	*Music Hall*	
Mar 04	Illinois	CHICAGO, Empress	*Music Hall*	
Mar 12	Wisconsin	MILWAUKEE, Empress	*Music Hall*	
Mar 20	Minnesota	MINNEAPOLIS, Unique	*Music Hall*	
Mar 26-Apr 02	Minnesota	DULUTH, Empress	*Music Hall*	
Apr 03-08	Manitoba	WINNIPEG, Empress	*Music Hall*	
Apr 10-14		no trace	[possibly: Billings – Montana, or Miles City, or both]	
Apr 15-21	Montana	BUTTE, Majestic	*Music Hall*	
Apr 23-29	Washington	SPOKANE, Washington	*Music Hall*	
May 01	Washington	SEATTLE, Majestic	*Music Hall*	
May 08-13	British Columbia	VANCOUVER, Orpheum	*Music Hall*	
May 15	Washington	TACOMA, Majestic	*Music Hall*	
May 22	Oregon	PORTLAND, Grand	*Music Hall*	
May 29		no trace		
Jun 04	California	SAN FRANCISCO, Empress	*Music Hall*	
Jun 11-17	California	SACRAMENTO, Grand	*Music Hall*	[16th – Stan's 21st Birthday]
Jun 18-24	California	OAKLAND, Bell	*Music Hall*	
Jun 26	California	LOS ANGELES, Empress	*Music Hall*	
Jul 05-11	California	SAN DIEGO, Empress	*Music Hall*	
[Jul 10-13	`	no trace	[probably timeout between turnaround]	
Jul 15	Colorado	DENVER, Empress	*Music Hall*	
Jul 22-28	Colorado	COLORADO SPRINGS, Majestic	*Music Hall*	

Jul 29	Missouri	KANSAS CITY, Empress	*Music Hall*	

August 4, 1911 – Sullivan-Considine tour ENDS HERE. Jefferson and Dandoe leave.

[Aug 07   timeout, between turnaround]

Commencing August 14, 1911 the Karno Company (minus Jefferson and Dandoe) stay on in America to do a second tour on the Sullivan-Considine circuit – playing *A Night in a London Club*.

o-o-0-o-o

The WAX-WORKS
Chas. Baldwin's Company of 30

1911 (continued)

[August 14 (circa)   Stan Jefferson and Arthur Dando arrive back in England.]

September 4	LIVERPOOL	LIVERPOOL, Pavilion
September 11	MANCHESTER	HULME, Hippodrome
September 18	LANCASHIRE	ASHTON, Empire Hippodrome
September 25	MANCHESTER	QUEEN'S PARK, Hippodrome
October 02		vacant
October 09	YORKSHIRE	KEIGHLEY, Hippodrome

The run of *The Waxworks* ends here — October 14, 1911

-----0-----

The BARTO BROS – Stan Jefferson and Arthur Dandoe
"The Rum 'Uns From Rome"

1911

October 16-December 25	no trace

1912

January 01-29	no trace	
[February 05	[8 KOMIKS in 'MIXTURES'	where, when??]
[February 12	DENMARK HILL, 25 Allendale Road	Stan is living here]
February 19-May 20	no trace	

-----0-----

The 8 KOMIKS and The 4 BARTOS
"Het Dolle Hotel" ("The Crazy/Mad Hotel")

1912

May 25	HOLLAND	ROTTERDAM, Circus Variété	(Saturday and Sunday, and maybe Monday)
[June 01	HOLLAND	ROTTERDAM, Circus Variété	(Sat-Sun-Monday – CANCELLED)]
June 03			
June 10			
June 17			
June 25	BELGIUM	LIEGE, Palace	(may be 1 night only)
July 01 (circa)	BELGIUM	BRUSSELS	7 Jackley Wonders

-----0-----

"BEN-MY CHREE"

July 08	London	SHAFTESBURY AVENUE, Prince's	[not known when SJ starts]
July 15	London	SHAFTESBURY AVENUE, Prince's	
July 22	London	SHAFTESBURY AVENUE, Prince's	
July 29	London	SHAFTESBURY AVENUE, Prince's	
August 05	London	SHAFTESBURY AVENUE, Prince's	
August 12	London	SHAFTESBURY AVENUE, Prince's	
August 19	London	SHAFTESBURY AVENUE, Prince's	
August 26	London	SHAFTESBURY AVENUE, Prince's	
September 02	London	SHAFTESBURY AVENUE, Prince's	[not known when SJ leaves]

-----0-----

The BARTO BROS – Stan Jefferson and Ted Leo
"The Rum 'Uns From Rome"

1912

August 12			[not known when SJ starts]
August 19			
August 26			
September 02			
September 09	WALES	ABERTILLERY, Metropole	
September 16			
September 23			
September 28	London	LAMBETH, Royal Victoria Palace	[date may vary]

-----0-----

October 02	Southampton	Stan Jefferson sails for America on the *Oceanic*

o-o-0-o-o

FRED KARNO COMPANY
The American Tours 1912 – 1914

1912 (continued)

Oct 02	England	SOUTHAMPTON		*Oceanic* leaves Southampton
Oct 09	New York	NEW YORK CITY		*Oceanic* arrives at New York
Oct 10-13	New York	NEW YORK CITY		[rehearsals]
Oct 14-19	Massachusetts	FALL RIVER, Empress		[debut]

Sullivan-Considine Tour starts here.

Oct 20	Ohio	CINCINNATI, Empress	*The Wow-Wows*	
Oct 28	Illinois	CHICAGO, Empress	*The Wow-Wows*	
Nov 03	Wisconsin	MILWAUKEE, Empress	*The Wow-Wows*	
Nov 10-16	Minnesota	MINNEAPOLIS, Unique	*The Wow-Wows*	
Nov 17	Minnesota	ST. PAUL, Empress	*The Wow-Wows*	
Nov 25	Manitoba	WINNIPEG, Empress	*The Wow-Wows*	
Dec 02-03		no trace		[possibly Miles City – Montana]
Dec 04-05	Montana	BILLINGS, Babcock	*The Wow-Wows*	
Dec 07-13	Montana	BUTTE, Empress	*The Wow-Wows*	
Dec 15	Washington	SPOKANE, Empress	*The Wow Wows*	
Dec 23-28	Washington	SEATTLE, Empress	*The Wow-Wows*	
Dec 30-Jan 04	British Columbia	VANCOUVER, Orpheum	*The Wow-Wows*	

1913

Jan 06-11	Washington	TACOMA, Empress	*The Wow-Wows*	
Jan 13-19	Oregon	PORTLAND, Empress	*The Wow-Wows*	
Jan 20	California	OAKLAND, Empress		[unconfirmed]
Jan 26-Feb 01	California	SAN FRANCISCO, Empress	*The Wow-Wows*	
Feb 02-08	California	SACRAMENTO, Empress	*The Wow-Wows*	
Feb 10-15	California	LOS ANGELES, Empress	*The Wow-Wows*	
Feb 17-22	California	SAN DIEGO, Empress	*The Wow-Wows*	
Feb 23-25		no trace		
Feb 26-Mar 04	Utah	SALT LAKE CITY, Empress	*The Wow-Wows*	
Mar 05-09		time out		
Mar 10	Colorado	DENVER, Empress	*The Wow-Wows*	
Mar 17-18	Colorado	PUEBLO, Empress	*The Wow-Wows*	
Mar 19-21	Colorado	COLORADO SPRINGS, Empress	*The Wow-Wows*	
Mar 23-29	Missouri	KANSAS CITY, Empress	*The Wow-Wows*	

Sullivan-Considine Circuit ends here.

Mar 31	Pennsylvania	PHILADELPHIA	[week out]

Nixon-Nirdlinger Circuit starts here

1913 (continued)

Date	State	Venue	Show	Notes
Apr 07	Pennsylvania	PHILADELPHIA, People's		
Apr 14	Pennsylvania	PHILADELPHIA, People's		
Apr 21	Pennsylvania	PHILADELPHIA, Nixon	*Music Hall*	
Apr 28	Pennsylvania	PHILADELPHIA, Nixon	*London Club*	
May 05-10	Pennsylvania	PHILADELPHIA, Nixon	*The Wow-Wows*	
May 12	Pennsylvania	PHILADELPHIA, People's		
May 19	Pennsylvania	PHILADELPHIA, Metropolitan	*Music Hall*, and *London Club*	
May 26	Maryland	BALTIMORE, Victoria	*Music Hall*	
Jun 02	Maryland	BALTIMORE, Victoria	*London Club*	
Jun 09	Dist' of Columbia	WASHINGTON DC, Cosmos	*Music Hall*	
Jun 16-21	Dist' of Columbia	WASHINGTON DC, Cosmos	*London Club*	

Nixon-Nirdlinger Circuit ends here

| Jun 23 | | timeout | | |

Sullivan-Considine Tour starts here.

Date	State	Venue	Show	Notes
Jun 29	Michigan	DETROIT, Broadway		[unconfirmed]
Jul 06	Illinois	CHICAGO, Empress	*London Club*	
Jul 14		no trace		[possibly: Wisconsin, MILWAUKEE]
Jul 20	Minnesota	MINNEAPOLIS, Unique		[Stan's studio portraits]
Jul 27-Aug 02	Minnesota	ST. PAUL, Empress	*London Club*	
Aug 04-09	Manitoba	WINNIPEG, Empress	*London Club*	
Aug 11-13	Montana	MILES CITY, Liberty	*London Club*	
Aug 14-15	Montana	BILLINGS, Babcock	*London Club*	
Aug 16-22	Montana	BUTTE, Empress	*London Club*	
Aug 24-30	Washington	SPOKANE, Orpheum	*London Club*	
Sep 01	Washington	SEATTLE, Empress	*London Club*	
Sep 08	British Columbia	VANCOUVER, Orpheum	*London Club*	
Sep 15-20	Washington	TACOMA, Empress	*London Club*	
Sep 22-27	Oregon	PORTLAND, Empress	*London Club*	
Sep 28-Oct 04		no trace		[possibly: California, OAKLAND]
Oct 05-11	California	SAN FRANCISCO, Empress	*London Club*	
Oct 12	California	SACRAMENTO, Empress	*London Club*	
Oct 20-25	California	LOS ANGELES, Empress	*London Club*	
Oct 26	California	SAN DIEGO, Empress	*London Club*	
Nov 02-04		no trace		[Sun-Tue]
Nov 05-11	Utah	SALT LAKE CITY, Empress	*London Club*	[Wed-Tue]
Nov 12-15		no trace		
Nov 16-22	Colorado	DENVER, Empress	*London Club*	
Nov 23-29	Missouri	KANSAS CITY, Empress	*London Club*	

CHAPLIN leaves here, to go to Keystone.

Sullivan-Considine Tour ends here.

Date	State	Venue	Show	Notes
Dec 01			}	
Dec 08			}	[company laid off]
Dec 15			}	
[Dec 19		*SS Lusitania*		Dan Raynor arrives at New York.]
Dec 22	Pennsylvania	PHILADELPHIA, Grand	*Music Hall*	[Dan Raynor debut]
Dec 29	Pennsylvania	PHILADELPHIA, Colonial	*Music Hall*	week 1 of 2

1914

Date	State	Venue	Show	Notes
Jan 05	Pennsylvania	PHILADELPHIA, Colonial	*London Club*	week 2 of 2
Jan 12-17	Pennsylvania	PHILADELPHIA, Keystone		
Jan 19-24	Pennsylvania	PHILADELPHIA, Broadway		
Jan 26-31	Pennsylvania	PHILADELPHIA, Alleghenny		
Feb 02-07	Pennsylvania	PHILADELPHIA, Nixon		
Feb 09	New York	NEW YORK, Hammerstein's	*Music Hall*	
Feb 16		no trace		

Stan Jefferson — Date-Sheets

Feb 23	New Jersey	TRENTON,		[unconfirmed]
Mar 02	Massachusetts	BOSTON, Keith's	*Music Hall*	
Mar 09-14	Quebec (Canada)	MONTREAL, Orpheum	*Music Hall*	
Mar 16		no trace		
Mar 23	New York	Mount VERNON	*Music Hall*	[unconfirmed]
Mar 30		no trace		
Apr 06	Ohio	CANTON, Lyceum	*Music Hall*	
Apr 13		no trace		
Apr 20	New York	NEW YORK, American Roof	*Music Hall*	
Apr 27		no trace		
May 04-09	New York	BUFFALO, Shea's	*Music Hall*	[date may vary]
May 04	Ontario (Canada)	TORONTO, Shea's Hippodrome		[CHECK – CLASH]
		The Karno Company officially disbands here.		
May 14, 1914		Karno Company sail for England, aboard the *Adriatic*.		

THE THREE (ENGLISH) COMIQUES

aka: 'Hurley, Stan, and Wren' also 'Jefferson, Hurley, and Wren'
[Comprising: Stan Jefferson – Edgar Hurley – Ethel Hurley]
In the sketch: "*The Nutty Burglars*" aka: "*The Burglars*" aka: "*The Would-be Burglars*" and: "*Breaking-In*"

May 09		Stan Jefferson's last appearance with the Karno Company		
May 11	Illinois	CHICAGO		[unconfirmed]
[May 14 (Thu)			Karno Company sail for England on the *Adriatic*.]	
May 18-20		no trace		
May 21-23	Manitoba	WINNIPEG, Columbia		Three English Comiques
May 25	Manitoba	BRANDON, Sherman		Three English Comiques
Jun 01				
Jun 08				
Jun 15-20	Missouri	KANSAS CITY, Hippodrome	*Breaking In*	Stan Jefferson and Company
Jun 22				
Jun 29				
Jul 1914				
Jul 02-05	South Dakota	SIOUX FALLS, Majestic		Stan Jefferson and Company
Jul 06				
Jul 13				
Jul 19-22	Iowa	DES MOINES, Empress	*The Nutty Burglars*	Three English Comiques
Jul 23				
Jul 27				
Aug 03				
Aug 10				
Aug 17				
Aug 24	Missouri	ST. LOUIS, Hippodrome	*The Burglars*	Jefferson Hurley Wren
Aug 31				
Sep 07				
Sep 14				
Sep 21				
Sep 28				
Oct 05				
Oct 12				
Oct 19				
Oct 26				
Nov 02	Michigan	DETROIT, Palace		Three English Comiques
Nov 09				
Nov 16				
Nov 23				
Nov 30				
Dec 07				
Dec 14				
Dec 21				

1914 (continued)

Dec 30	Pennsylvania	PHILADELPHIA, Cross Keys	Keystone Comedy Four	[not confirmed as Stan]
[unknown	Ohio	CLEVELAND		meet Kalma]
[unknown	Pennsylvania	PITTSBURG		get Bostock's telegram]
[unknown	New York	DAVENPORT, Sherman Theatre		possibility]
[unknown	Saskatchewan	SASSKATOON, Sherman Theatre		possibility]

-----0------

THE KEYSTONE TRIO
aka: 'Hurley, Stan, and Wren' also 'Jefferson, Hurley, Wren' and 'Stanley, Hurley and Wren'
[Comprising: Stan Jefferson – Edgar Hurley – Ethel Wren (Hurley)]
In the Sketch: *"The Nutty Burglars"*

1915

[unknown	New York	NEW YORK CITY, Plaza 59th St & Madison Ave]	Keystone Trio]
[unknown	Connecticut	STAMFORD	Keystone Trio]
[unknown	ONTARIO	St. THOMAS	Keystone Trio]
Jan 04		no trace	
Jan 11		no trace	
Jan 18		no trace	
Jan 25-27	New Jersey	JERSEY CITY, B.F. Keith's	[debut]
Jan 28	New York	HARLEM, Opera House	
Jan 31	New York	NEW YORK CITY, Columbia	
Feb 01-03	New Jersey	NEW BRUNSWICK, Opera House	
Feb 04-06	New Jersey	BAYONNE, Opera House	
Feb 07	Ohio	YOUNGSTOWN,	[date check]
Feb 11-13	Ohio	AKRON, Colonial	
Feb 15-17	Pennsylvania	JOHNSTOWN	
Feb 18-20	Pennsylvania	ALTOONA, Orpheum	
Feb 22-24	Pennsylvania	ALLENTOWN, Orpheum	
Feb 25-27	Ohio	EAST LIVERPOOL, American	[date check]
Mar 01-03	New Jersey	JERSEY CITY, Hudson	
Mar 04-06	Pennsylvania	PITTSBURG, [Kenyon Street]	[date and theatre not found]
Mar 08-10	Pennsylvania	WILKES-BARRE, Poli's	
Mar 11-13	Pennsylvania	WILLIAMSPORT, Family	
Mar 15-17	Connecticut	BRIDGEPORT, Plaza	[*Crown Studios* photo]
Mar 18-20	Connecticut	NEW HAVEN, Bijou	
Mar 22-24	Connecticut	WATERBURY, Poli's	
Mar 25-27	Massachusetts	SPRINGFIELD, Poli's	
Mar 29-31	New York	NEW YORK CITY, 125th Street	
Apr 01-03	New York	NEW YORK CITY, Mount Vernon	
Apr 05-07	New York	AUBURN, Jefferson	Stanley, Hurley and Wren
Apr 08-10	New York	ITHICA, Star	
Apr 12-13	New York	TROY, Proctor's New	
Apr 15-17	New York	ALBANY, Proctor's Grand	confirmed [see May 27-29]
Apr 19-21	New York	NEW YORK CITY, 5th. Avenue City	["Hurley died a death."]
Apr 22-24	New York	SYRACUSE	[see May 17-23]
Apr 26-28	New York	SCHENECTADY, Proctor's	
Apr 29-May 01	New Jersey	ELIZABETH, Proctor's	
May 03-05	New Jersey	PLAINFIELD, Proctor's	
May 06-08	Massachusetts	PITTSFIELD, Union Square	
May 10-12	New York	NEW YORK CITY, 58th Street	
May 13-15	New York	NEW YORK CITY, 23rd Street	
May 17-23	New York	SYRACUSE, Temple	
May 24-26	New York	SCHENECTADY, Proctor's	
May 27-29	New York	ALBANY, Proctor's	[see Apr 15-17]
May 31-Jun 02	New York	RICHMOND, Lyric	
Jun 03-05	Virginia	NORFOLK, Academy of Music	
Jun 07-09	Virginia	ROANOKE, Roanoke Theatre	

Stan Jefferson — Date-Sheets

1915 (continued)

Jun 14-19	Georgia	ATLANTA, Forsyth
Jun 21-23	New Jersey	NEWARK, Proctor's

-----0-----

Stan Laurel leaves The Keystone Trio around this date, and goes on to form 'The Stan Jefferson Trio.'

Meanwhile, Edgar Hurley fulfils all 'The Keystone Trio' dates, taking over Stan's role as the Chaplin figure, and recruiting former Karno Company comedian Ted Banks to fill his former role.

-----0-----

STAN JEFFERSON TRIO — Universal Trio/Four — Hayden Sisters
"The Crazy Cracksman"
[Stan Jefferson – Baldwin Cooke – Alice Hamilton]

Date	State	Venue	Act	Notes
Jun 28				
Jul 05				
Jul 12				
Jul 19				
Jul 26				
Aug 02				
Aug 09				
Aug 16				
Aug 23				
Aug 30				
[Aug 30-Sep 01	New Jersey	JERSEY CITY, Keith's	Hayden Sisters]	
Sep 06				
Sep 13				
[Sep 16-17	Connecticut	NORWICH, Davis	*Nutty Burglars*	NEW Keystone Trio]
Sep 20-21	New York	NEW BRUNSWICK, Opera House	*The Would-be Burglars*	Stan Jefferson Co. (1st sighting)
[Sep 22	New York	SYRACUSE, Temple	Hayden Sisters]	
Sep 22-25				
Sep 27-29	New York	TROY, Proctor's New	*Crazy Cracksman*	Stan Jefferson Trio
[Sep 28	New York	CORTLAND, Temple	Hayden Sisters]	
[Sep 30-Oct 02	New York	TROY, Proctor's New	Hayden Sisters]	
Sep 30				
Oct 04-06	New York	ALBANY, Proctor's Grand	*Crazy Cracksman*	Stan Jefferson Co.
Oct 07				
Oct 11	New York	NEW YORK CITY, 125th Street		Stan Jefferson Trio
[Oct 14-16	New Jersey	BRIDGEWATER, Proctor's New	Hayden Sisters]	[Thu-Sat]
Oct 21				
Oct 28	New York	BROOKLYN, Keeney's		Universal Trio
Nov 01				
Nov 08				
Nov 11-13				
Nov 15				
Nov 18				
Nov 22-24	New Jersey			
Nov 25-27	New Jersey	TRENTON, State Street		Universal Four
Nov 30 (Tue)	Michigan	ESCABANA, St. Anne's Minstrel Show		Universal Trio
Dec 05				
Dec 13				
Dec 20				
[Dec 20-21	New York	GLOVERSVILLE, Family	Hayden Sisters & Ward]	
[Dec 22-23	New York	ROME, Family	Hayden Sisters & Ward]	
[Dec 27-29	Vermont	BURLINGTON, Strong	Hayden Sisters & Ward]	
Dec 30				
[Dec 31-Jan 01	New York	GLENS FALLS, Empire	Hayden Sisters & Ward]	

1916

Jan 03				
[Jan 10	New York	FLATBUSH, Olympic		Hayden Sisters & Ward]
Jan 10				
Jan 14	New York	ROME, Family		Universal Trio
Jan 17				
Jan 24				
Jan 31-Feb 02				
Feb 03-05	New York	YONKERS, Orpheum	*Crazy Cracksman*	Stan Jefferson Co.
				[Bessie Delberg, Barry Preston as 'Percy']
Feb 07				
Feb 07				
Feb 21				
[Feb 25	New York	MALONE, Grand	Crackles, Cooke, & Hamilton	Universal Trio]
[Feb 28-29	Vermont	BURLINGTON, Strong		Universal Trio]
[Mar 02-04	Ohio	TOLEDO, Palace		Universal Four]
[Mar 05		COLUMBIA, Bell		Universal Trio]
[Mar 06	Michigan	DETROIT, Columbia		Universal Trio]
[Mar 13	New York	BUFFALO, Olympic		Universal Trio]
Mar 16-18	Indiana	MUNCIE, Star		Stan Jefferson Trio
Mar 20-25	Pennsylvania	PITTSBURGH, Harris	*Crazy Cracksman*	Stan Jefferson Trio
Mar 27-29	Kentucky	LEXINGTON, Ada Meade	*Crazy Cracksman*	Stan Jefferson Trio
				[last known appearance of the SJT]
Apr 03-05		no trace		
[Apr 06-08	Pennsylvania	UNIONTOWN, Dixie	*Crazy Cracksman*	Universal Trio]
				[Crackles, Cooke, & Hamilton]
Apr 06-08				

o-o-0-o-o

MARTINI & MAXIMILLIAN
[Bob Martini and Stan Jefferson]

Mar 30-Apr 01	West Virginia	RICHMOND, Lyric	[Stan *could* have started here.]
Apr 03	Pennsylvania	UNIONTOWN, Dixie	
Apr 10			
Apr 17	Georgia	ATLANTA, Forsyth	[most probable debut for Stan]
Apr 24			
Apr 27-May 01	New York	BROOKLYN, Prospect	
May 01-03			
May 04-06	New York	YONKERS, Orpheum	
May 08			
May 15-17			
May 18-20	New Jersey	TRENTON, Taylor's Opera House	
May 22	New Jersey	JERSEY CITY, Keith's	
May 29	Pennsylvania	PITTSBURGH, Harris	
Jun 05	Pennsylvania	PITTSBURGH, Sheridan	
Jun 12-14	New York	BROOKLYN, Prospect	[Confirmed re-booking (see April 27)]
Jun 15-17			
Jun 19			
Jun 26	New York	NEW YORK CITY, Greely Square	
Jul 03-05	New York	BINGHAMTON, Stone	[Mon-Wed]
Jul 06-08	New York	ELMIRA, Majestic	[Thu-Sat]
Jul 10-15	New York	BUFFALO, Shea's }	[CLASH. When is this show?]
Jul 10-15	New York	LOCKPORT, Shea's }	
Jul 17-18	New York	GLOVERSVILLE, Family	
Jul 20	New York	SARATOGA SPRINGS, Broadway	
Jul 24			
Jul 31			
Aug 07			
Aug 14			

1916 (continued)

Date	State/Country	Venue	Act	Notes
Aug 21				
Aug 28				
Sep 04-06				
Sep 07-09	CANADA	OTTAWA, Dominion		
Sep 11-16	CANADA	HAMILTON, Temple		
Sep 18				
Sep 25				
Oct 02-04				
Oct 09				
Oct 16	Indiana	KOKOMO, Sipe's		
Oct 22	Wisconsin	RACINE, Orpheum		
Oct 23	Minnesota	MINNEAPOLIS, Palace		
Oct 23				
Oct 30-Nov 01	North Dakota	GRAND FORKS, Grand		
Nov 03	Dakota	BISMARK, Auditorium		
Nov 06				
Nov 12-14	Montana	BUTTE, Empress		
Nov 15				
Nov 20				
Nov 27	Washington	TACOMA, Regent		
Dec 04-06	Washington	SEATTLE, Palace Hippodrome		
Dec 07-09	Oregon	PORTLAND, Hippodrome		
Dec 10	Oregon	SALEM, Bligh		former Hippodrome [Sun only]
Dec 11				
Dec 14-16	California	SACRAMENTO, Empress		
[Dec 18	California	SAN FRANCISCO, Empress		[so when did Stan leave Martini?]
Dec 18	Michigan	DETROIT	Stan & Mae Laurel	[unconfirmed]

-----o-----

STAN & MAE LAUREL
"Raffles the Dentist"

Date	State	Venue	Act	Notes
Dec 24-25	Michigan	JACKSON, Temple	Stan & Mae Laurel	
[Dec 25	California	SAN JOSE, José	Martini & Maximillian]	

1917

Date	State	Venue	Act	Notes
Jan 01	Illinois	CHICAGO, Rialto??	Stan & Mae Laurel	[unconfirmed]
[Jan 03	California	LOS ANGELES, Hippodrome	Martini and Maximillian]	
[Jan 08	California	SAN DIEGO, Spreckels	Martini and Maximillian]	
[Jan 14-20	Texas	EL PASO, Crawford	Martini and Maximillian]	
[Jan 22-24	Kansas	TOPEKA, Auditorium	Martini and Maximillian]	
[Jan 25	Missouri	SPRINGFIELD, Electric	Martini and Maximillian]	
[Jan 29-31	Nebraska	LINCOLN, Lyric	Martini and Maximillian]	
[Feb 01-03	Nebraska	OMAHA, Empress	Martini and Maximillian]	
Feb 05				
[Feb 08-10	South Dakota	SIOUX FALLS, Orpheum	Martini and Maximillian]	[Thu-Sat]
Feb 12	Illinois	CHICAGO, Academy	Stan & Mae Laurel	[possible debut]
[Feb 12	Minnesota	ROCHESTER, Metro	"New" Martini and Maximillian]	
[Feb 23-25	Minnesota	DULUTH, Grand	"New" Martini and Maximillian	
Feb 22	Montana	GREAT FALLS, Palace	Stan & Mae Laurel	[Thu only]
Feb 25-27	Montana	ANACONDA, Empress	Stan & Mae Laurel	
Feb 28				
Mar 05				
Mar 11				
Mar 15-17	Washington	TACOMA, Regent	Stan & Mae Laurel	
Mar 18-21	Washington	SEATTLE, Palace Hippodrome		
Mar 22-24	Oregon	PORTLAND, Hippodrome		
Mar 25	Oregon	SALEM, Bligh		[Sun only]
Mar 26-28		??, Majestic		

1917 (continued)

Mar 29-31	California	SACRAMENTO, Empress		
Apr 02				
Apr 04-07	California	OAKLAND, Hippodrome		
Apr 08-14	California	SAN FRANCISCO, Casino		[Sun-Sat]
Apr 16				
Apr 21-22	Nevada	RENO, T&H Hippodrome		[Sat-Sun]
Apr 23-26	California	SAN FRANCISCO, ??		[CHECK]
Apr 27-28	California	BAKERSFIELD, Hippodrome		
Apr 30				
May 03-06	California	SAN DIEGO, Spreckels Hippodrome		
May 07-13	California	LOS ANGELES, Hippodrome		
May 14				
May 21				
May 28				
Jun 04				
Jun 11				
Jun 18-24				
[Late Jun	California	LOS ANGELES	*Nuts in May*	filming]
[Early Jul	California	LOS ANGELES	*Nuts in May*	filming]
Jul 09				
Jul 16				
Jul 23				
Jul 30				
Aug 06				
Aug 13				
Aug 20				
Aug 27				
Sep 03				
Sep 12				

[Sometime between August 6th and September 12th the film *Nuts in May* was previewed at the Hippodrome, Los Angeles — with Carl Laemmle and Charles Chaplin in attendance.]

Sep 17-23				
[late Sep	California	LOS ANGELES	*Phoney Photos*	filming for L-KO
[early Oct	California	LOS ANGELES	*Phoney Photos*	]
Oct 04-06				
Oct 08	California	LOS ANGELES		
[Oct 15	California	LOS ANGELES	*Hickory Hiram*	filming for Nestor]
Oct 15-20				
[Oct 22			*Whose Zoo?*	L-KO]
[Oct 29-Nov 01			*It's Great to Be Crazy*	Nestor]
Nov 05				
Nov 12				
Nov 19				
Nov 26				
Dec 03				
Dec 10				
Dec 17				
Dec 24				
Dec 31				

1918

Jan 07				
Jan 14				
[Jan 18	Oklahoma	TULSA, Broadway		Hurley & Wren]
Jan 21				
Jan 28				

STAN & MAE LAUREL
"Raffles the Dentist"

1918 (continued)

Date	State	Venue		
Feb 04-09	New Mexico	DEMING, Cody		
Feb 10-15	Texas	EL PASO, Texas Grand		
Feb 16				
Feb 18	Iowa	DES MOINES, Empress		
Feb 24-26	Montana	BUTTE, Empress (Bluebird)		[Anaconda??]
Feb 27				
Mar 04				
Mar 11-13				
Mar 14-16	Washington	SEATTLE, Palace Hippodrome		
Mar 17	Oregon	PORTLAND, Hippodrome		
Mar 24-30	California	SAN FRANCISCO, Hippodrome		[Sun-Sat]
Mar 31-Apr 02	California	SAN FRANCISCO, Wigwam		[Sun-Tue]
Apr 03-05				
Apr 07-13	California	SAN JOSE, José		[Sun-Sat]
Apr 14-16	Nevada	RENO, Majestic		[Sun-Tue]
Apr 22				
Apr 29				
May 01-02	California	BAKERSFIELD, Hippodrome		
May 03-04				
May 05-11	California	LOS ANGELES, Hippodrome		[Sun-Sat]
May 13	California	SAN DIEGO, Spreckels Hippodrome		
May 20-25	California	SANTA BARBABA, Portalo		
[May 26	California	LOS ANGELES, Main Street	test film	Rolin Studios]
May 27	California			
Jun 03	California			

STAN LAUREL
JUST ARRIVED
Starring in Rolin-Pathe Comedies
Address: 406 Streeet, Los Angeles

Date	State	Venue	Title	Studio
[Jun 11-15	California	LOS ANGELES	*Do You Love Your Wife*	Rolin]
[Jun 18-22	California	LOS ANGELES	*Just Rambling Along*	Rolin]
[Jun 24-29	California	LOS ANGELES	*Hoot Mon!*	Rolin]
[Jul 01-05	California	LOS ANGELES	*No Place Like Jail*	Rolin]
[Jul 06-11	California	LOS ANGELES	*Hustling For Health*	Rolin]
[Jul 12-13				retakes]
[late Jul	California	LOS ANGELES	*Huns and Hyphens*	Vitagraph/Semon]
[Jul 29 Jul	California			
[early Aug	California	LOS ANGELES	*Bears and Badmen*	Vitagraph/Semon]
[Aug 12	California			
[mid Aug	California	LOS ANGELES	*Frauds and Frenzies*	Vitagraph/Semon]
Aug 26				
Sep 02				
Sep 09				
Sep 16				
Sep 23		All the *California* film studios are closed down, owing to the flu epidemic.		
Sep 29	Missouri	KANSAS CITY, Globe	*Raffles, the Dentist*	Stan & Mae Laurel
Oct 04-05	Kansas	ATCHISON, Crystal	*Raffles, the Dentist*	Stan & Mae Laurel
Oct 06	Kansas	ATCHISON, Orpheum	*Raffles, the Dentist*	Stan & Mae Laurel
Oct 07-09	Kansas	TOPEKA, Novelty	*Raffles, the Dentist*	Stan & Mae Laurel
Oct 10-12	Kansas	WITCHITA, Princess	*Raffles, the Dentist*	Stan & Mae Laurel
Oct 14				
Oct 21				
Oct 28				
Nov 04		Studios and theatres re-open after the flu epidemic.		

STAN & MAE LAUREL
No Mother to Guide Her

1918 (continued)

Date	State	Venue	Notes
Nov 04-06	Illinois	CHICAGO, Kedzie	*No Mother to Guide Her* [debut]
Nov 07			
Nov 11			
Nov 14-16	Illinois	SPRINGFIELD, Majestic	
Nov 17-20	Indianapolis	FORT WAYNE, Palace	[Sun-Wed]
Nov 21	Michigan	BATTLE CREEK, Bijou	
Nov 24-27	Michigan	JACKSON, Orpheum	[Sun-Wed]
Nov 28-30	Michigan	LANSING, Bijou	[Thu-Sat]
Dec 01-02	Michigan	FLINT, Palace	[dates may vary]
Dec 03-04	Michigan		
Dec 05-07	Michigan	SAGINAW, Strand	
Dec 08-11	Michigan	BAY CITY, Bijou	
Dec 12-14	Michigan	SAGINAW	[see 5-7 Dec]
Dec 15-18	Michigan	MUSKEGON, Regent	[Sun-Wed]
Dec 19-21	Indiana	SOUTH BEND, Orpheum	
Dec 23	Nebraska	LINCOLN, Orpheum	[advert says 'Opens 25th']
Dec 24-25	Wisconsin	MADISON, Orpheum	[Stan & Mae missed first night, Monday]
Dec 26-28	Illinois	ROCKFORD, Palace	
Dec 30-Jan 01	Illinois	CHICAGO, Wilson	

1919

Date	State	Venue	Notes
Jan 02-04	Missouri	ST. LOUIS, Park	[CHECK]
Jan 06-08	Illinois	E. ST. LOUIS, Erber's	[CHECK]
Jan 09-10	Illinois	ALTON, Hippodrome	
Jan 13	Illinois		
Jan 16-18	Illinois	CHAMPAIGN, Orpheum	
Jan 19-22	Illinois	DECATUR, Empress	[Sun-Wed]
Jan 23	Illinois	PEORIA, Orpheum	
Jan 27-29	Indiana	EVANSVILLE, New Grand	
Jan 30-Feb 01	Indiana	TERRE HAUTE, Hippodrome	
Feb 03	Illinois	ST. LOUIS, Grand	
Feb 10			
Feb 17	Illinois	CHICAGO, Lincoln	
Feb 20-22	Illinois	MOLINE, Palace	[Rock Island]
Feb 23-26	Illinois	DES MOINES, Empress	[Sun-Wed]
Feb 27-Mar 01	Iowa	CEDAR RAPIDS, Majestic	
Mar 02-05	Iowa	DUBUQUE, Majestic	[Sun-Wed]
Mar 06	Iowa	DAVENPORT, Columbia	
Mar 09	Iowa	WATERLOO, Majestic	[Sunday only]
Mar 10-12	Nebraska	LINCOLN, Liberty	
Mar 13-15	Iowa	DAVENPORT, Columbia	[CHECK]
Mar 17-19	Iowa	SIOUX CITY, Orpheum	[CHECK]
Mar 20-22	Nebraska	OMAHA, Empress	
Mar 24			
Mar 31	Minnesota	ST. PAUL, New Palace	[CHECK]
Apr 03-05	Minnesota	MINNEAPOLIS, New Palace	[*Sussman* shoot]
Apr 06-08	Minnesota	DULUTH, New Grand	[Sun-Tue]
Apr 09-11	Wisconsin	SUPERIOR, New Palace	
Apr 14	Minnesota	MINNEAPOLIS, Palace	
Apr 17-19	Wisconsin	GREEN BAY, Orpheum	
Apr 21	Illinois	CHICAGO, Hippodrome	
Apr 28-30	Illinois	CHICAGO, American Academy	[Stan & Mae walk out]
May 01-03	Illinois	CHICAGO, Empress	
May 05-07	Indiana	KOKOMO, Snipe	
May 08-11	Indiana	LAFAYETTE, Family	
May 12-14			

Stan Jefferson — Date-Sheets

1919 (continued)

May 15-17	Indiana	LOGANSPORT, Colonial	
May 19-21	Missouri	ST. LOUIS, Rialto	
May 22-24	Missouri	ST. LOUIS, Skydome	
May 26-28			
May 29-31			
Jun 02	Michigan	OWOSSO, Strand	[CHECK]
Jun 09-11	ONTARIO	LONDON, Grand Opera House	Canada
Jun 12-14	ONTARIO	BRANTFORD, Brant	Canada
Jun 16-18	ONTARIO	PETERBOROUGH, Grand Opera House	Canada
Jun 19	ONTARIO		Canada
Jun 23	ONTARIO	KINGSTON, Grand Opera House	Canada
Jun 30	ONTARIO	TORONTO, Younge	Canada
Jul 07			
Jul 14			
Jul 21	Illinois	CHICAGO, Rialto	
Jul 26-27	Indiana	HAMMOND, Orpheum	
Jul 28			

PANTAGES

Aug 03	Minnesota	MINNEAPOLIS, Pantages	[Sunday start]
Aug 08-10	Manitoba	WINNIPEG, Pantages	Canada
Aug 18-20	Saskatchewan	REGINA, Pantages	Canada
Aug 21-23	Saskatchewan	SASKATOON, Pantages	Canada
Aug 25	Alberta	EDMONTON, Pantages	Canada
Sep 01-06	Alberta	CALGARY, Pantages	Canada
Sep 09-10	Montana	GREAT FALLS, Grand	
Sep 11-12	Montana	HELENA, Marlowe	
Sep 13-16	Montana	ANACONDA, Pantages	[unconfirmed]
Sep 17-18	Montana	BUTTE, Broadway	[unconfirmed]
Sep 19-20	Montana	MISSOULA, Pantages	[unconfirmed]
Sep 22-27	Washington	SPOKANE, Pantages	
Sep 29-Oct 04	Washington	SEATTLE, Pantages	
Oct 06-11	British Columbia	VANCOUVER, Pantages	Canada
Oct 13	British Columbia	VICTORIA, Pantages	Canada
Oct 20-25	Washington	TACOMA, Pantages	
Oct 27-Nov 01	Oregon	PORTLAND, Pantages	
Nov 03			
Nov 07-08	California	SAN JOSE, Victory	
Nov 09-15	California	SAN FRANCISCO, Pantages	[Sun-Sat]
Nov 17-22	California	OAKLAND, Pantages	
Nov 23-29	California	LOS ANGELES, Pantages	[Sun-Sat]
Dec 01	California	SAN DIEGO, Savoy	
Dec 08	California	LONG BEACH, Pantages	
Dec 15			
Dec 17-23	Utah	SALT LAKE CITY, Pantages	
Dec 24			
Dec 25-27	Utah	OGDEN, Pantages	[Mae is ill.]
Dec 29-Jan 03	Colorado	DENVER, Empress	

1920

Jan 05-06	Colorado	COLORADO SPRINGS, Burns	
Jan 07			
Jan 13-15	Oklahoma	MUSKOGEE, Broadway	
Jan 16-17	Texas	WACO, Orpheum	
Jan 19-24	Texas	SAN ANTONIO, Royal	
Jan 26-31	Texas	WITCHITA FALLS, Wichita	
Feb 02-07	Texas	DALLAS, Jefferson	
Feb 09			
Feb 16			

1920 (continued)
Feb 19   Michigan   DETROIT, Majestic
Feb 23-25

LOEW'S CIRCUIT starts here

Feb 26-28   New York   BROOKLYN, Fulton
Mar 01-03   New York   NEW YORK CITY, National   }
Mar 03   New York   KYRA, Century Roof   }   [cancelled through illness]
Mar 04-06   New York   NEW YORK CITY, Delancey St.   }
Mar 08-14   Washington DC   WASHINGTON, Cosmos
Mar 15-20   Ohio   AKRON, Colonial
Mar 22
Mar 25-26   ONTARIO   LONDON, Loew's
Mar 28-Apr 03   New York   ROCHESTER, Fays
Apr 05-10   ONTARIO   TORONTO, Loew's
Apr 12-17   ONTARIO   HAMILTON, Loew's
Apr 19-21   New York   NEW YORK CITY, American Roof
Apr 22-24   New York   NEW YORK CITY, Boulevard
Apr 26-28   New York   NEW YORK CITY, National   [rescheduled from March 1]
Apr 29-May 01   New York   NEW YORK, Lincoln Square
May 03-05   New York   NEW YORK CITY, DeKalb
May 06-09
May 10   New York   BROOKLYN, Metropolitan
May 13-15   New York   NEW YORK CITY, Delancey St.   [rescheduled from March 4]
May 17-19   Massachusetts   BOSTON, Loew's Orpheum
May 20-22   Massachusetts   FALL RIVER, Empire
May 24
May 27-29   Massachusetts   SPRINGFIELD, Broadway
May 31-Jun 02
Jun 03-05   New York   NEW YORK, Greeley Square   }
Jun 07-09   New York   NEW YORK, Victoria   }   [dates may vary]
Jun 10-12   New York   NEW YORK, Lincoln Square   }
Jun 14-16   Pennsylvania   PHILADELPHIA, Nixon
Jun 21
Jun 28
Jul 05
Jul 12
[Jul 17   New York   NEW YORK CITY, Times Square   Teddy Jefferson arrives]
Jul 19
Jul 26   New York   NEW YORK CITY, Orpheum

LOEW'S CIRCUIT ends here — July 31, 1920
-----0-----

Aug 02   }
Aug 09   }   no bookings found
Aug 16   }
Aug 23   }

POLI'S PROCTOR'S starts here

Aug 30   Connecticut   HARTFORD, Palace (Poli's)   }   [may be 23-28 CHECK]
Aug 30-Sep 01   Massachusetts   SPRINGFIELD, Palace (Poli's)   }   [CLASH]
Sep 02-04   Connecticut   BRIDGEPORT, Poli's
Sep 06   Pennsylvania   WILKES-BARRE, Poli's
Sep 9-11   Pennsylvania   SCRANTON, Poli's
Sep 13   New York   BROOKLYN, Chester   [CHECK date]
Sep 20   Pennsylvania   CHESTER, Edgemont
Sep 27-Oct 02   Pennsylvania   PHILADELPHIA, Keystone
Oct 04
Oct 11
Oct 14-16   New York   SYRACUSE, Temple

1920 (continued)

Oct 18-20	New York	SCHENECTADY, Proctor's
Oct 21-23	New York	TROY, Proctor's
Oct 25		
Oct 28-30	New York	POUGHKEEPSIE, Collingwood
Nov 01		
Nov 08-10	New York	ALBANY
Nov 11-13	New York	BINGHAMTON
Nov 15	}	
Nov 22	}	
Nov 29	}	
Dec 06	}	NO THEATRE BOOKINGS TRACED
Dec 13	}	
Dec 20	}	
Dec 27	}	

PANTAGES – ORPHEUM Circuit
"No Mother to Guide Her"

1921

[Jan 03	Oregon	PORTLAND, Pantages	Rubini	Stan and Mae NOT billed]
Jan 10				
[Jan 15-21	California	BERKELEY, Pantages	Rubini	Stan and Mae NOT billed]
Jan 24				
[Jan 31	California	LOS ANGELES	*The Lucky Dog*	filming]
[Feb 07	California	LOS ANGELES	*The Lucky Dog*	filming]
Feb 10-13	California	SAN DIEGO, Hippodrome	*No Mother to Guide Her*	Stan & Mae Laurel
Feb 14				
Feb 17-18	California	RIVERSIDE, Loring		
Feb 19-20	California	SAN BERNADINO, Opera House		
Feb 21				
Feb 25-26	California	BAKERSFIELD, Hippodrome		
Feb 28				
Mar 03-05	California	RIVERSIDE, Orpheum		
Mar 07				
Mar 10	California	SAN FRANCISCO		
Mar 14				
Mar 21				
Mar 28				
Apr 04				
Apr 06-12	Utah	SALT LAKE CITY, Pantages		
Apr 14-16	Utah	OGDEN, Pantages		
Apr 18-23	Colorado	DENVER, Empress		
Apr 25-26	Colorado	COLORADO SPRINGS, Burns		
Apr 27				
May 02	Oklahoma	MUSKOGEE, Broadway		[1 night]
May 04-07	Texas	WACO, Hippodrome		
May 08-14	Texas	SAN ANTONIO, Grand		
May 16				
May 22-28	Texas	DALLAS, Hippodrome		
May 30				
Jun 06		Pantages		
Jun 13				
Jun 20	Illinois	CHICAGO, Chateau		[CHECK]
Jun 21	Illinois	CHICAGO, Hippodrome		[CHECK]
Jun 27-29	Illinois	DETROIT, Regent		
Jun 30	Ohio	CLEVELAND, Miles		[CHECK]
04 Jul				
Jul 11				
Jul 18-23	Manitoba	WINNIPEG, Pantages		

1921 (continued)

Jul 25	Alberta	EDMONTON, Pantages	
Jul 26-27	Montana	GREAT FALLS, Grand	
Jul 28-29	Montana	HELENA, Marlowe	
Aug 01-05			
Aug 06-09	Montana	ANACONDA, Pantages	
Aug 10	Montana	BUTTE, Pantages	
Aug 11	Montana	MISSOULA, Pantages	
Aug 15-20	Washington	SEATTLE, Pantages	
Aug 22	Washington	SPOKANE	[CLASH – when is this?]
Aug 22-28	British Columbia	VANCOUVER, Pantages	
Aug 29	Washington	TACOMA, Pantages	
Sep 05-10	Oregon	PORTLAND, Pantages	
Sep 12			
Sep 16-17	California	SAN JOSE, Victory	
Sep 18-24	California	SAN FRANCISCO, Pantages	
Sep 25	California	OAKLAND, Pantages	
Oct 03	California	LOS ANGELES, Pantages	

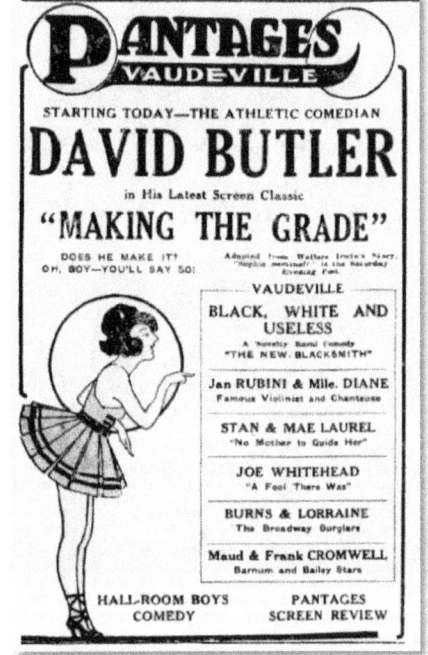 

Hey you, lady! What's the idea of pointing
out Jan Rubini on the bill?
Don't you know who this book is about?

That's better.
Thank you, Diane, for directing
readers to the best act on the bill.

Oct 10-16	California	CORONADO, Savoy	[SAN DIEGO, Pantages ??]
Oct 17	California	LONG BEACH, Hoyt	
Oct 24	Utah	SALT LAKE, Pantages	
Oct 31	Utah	OGDEN, Pantages	
Nov 07	Colorado	DENVER, Empress	
Nov 11	California	PETALUMA, Hill Opera House	[CHECK. Is this October??]
Nov 14			
Nov 21	Missouri	KANSAS CITY, Pantages	
Nov 28	Missouri	ST. LOUIS, Pantages	
Dec 05	Tennessee	MEMPHIS, Pantages	
Dec 12			
Dec 19			
Dec 26			

No further dates found for Laurel – on stage.

LAUREL & HARDY – The British Tours
Part 1 – Screen to Stage [1926 to 1951]

Second Edition – Extensively revised, reformatted and expanded

The story starts where our comedy heros meet up at the Hal Roach Studios, and become an inseparable partnership. We then fast forward to the promotional tour of major cities in England and Scotland, which they undertook in the summer of 1932.

Fast forward again to their 1947 British stage tour, for which readers are given a full account of every theatre engagement and every act they worked with; their travel arrangements; the hotels they stayed in; the people they met; previously undocumented public appearances. and descriptions of the crowds of thousands who mobbed them and left them reeling from the onslaught.

Second Edition. 210 pages. Lavishly illustrated — Softback — A4 [297mm x 210mm]
(ISBN 978-0-9521308-8-8) — Available via lulu.com

-----0-----

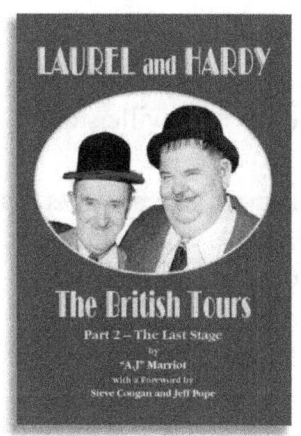

LAUREL & HARDY – The British Tours
Part 2 – 'The Last Stage.' [The 1952 and 1953-4 Tours]

Second Edition – Extensively revised, reformatted and expanded

This engaging book is the story of the love which the British and Irish retained for these two comedy legends after the USA had turned its back on them, and how they adapted from film- to stage-work, and survived through the changing *modes* of comedy, and the changing *moods* of theatre audiences. Readers are given a full account of the theatres they played, the acts they worked with, their travel arrangements; the hotels at which they stayed; the people they met; and their many public appearances – all complemented by scores of rare photographs from these tours.

Second Edition. 208 pages. Lavishly illustrated — Softback — A4 [297mm x 210mm]
(ISBN 978-0-9521308-8-8) — Available via lulu.com

-----0-----

LAUREL and HARDY – The European Tours

"The European Tours" details not only the 1947-48 stage tours Laurel and Hardy played around Denmark, Sweden, France, and Belgium, but the year the two Hollywood comedians spent in France, during the making of their 1950-51 film *Atoll K*. Included in this is a promotional visit to Italy; plus details of two earlier visits to France — one by Laurel in 1927, and one by both comedians in 1932.

Readers will get to see the real men behind the screen characters of "Stan and Ollie" — how they coped with being mobbed everywhere they went; the exhaustion of a life of touring; and how they both worked on through serious illness to complete their last film.

From it all, Stan Laurel and Oliver Hardy emerge as lovable, but vulnerable, men – and readers will experience their every emotion throughout these previously undocumented tours.

Second Print. 128 pages – 200 illustrations. Softback – A4 [297mm x 210mm]
(ISBN 978-0-9521308-4-0) — Available via lulu.com

LAUREL and HARDY – The U.S. Tours

Second Edition – Extensively revised, reformatted. and expanded

After the two comedians meet at the Hal Roach Studios, the story takes an unexpected route. Instead of following them through the making of their films, we are led into a parallel world of public appearances, show business events, theatre tours, wartime fund raising tours, and troop shows. Revealed for the first time ever are details of three major U.S. city-to-city stage tours; numerous trips from the West to the East coast; three junkets to Mexico; and even a tour of Caribbean islands. On their travels, Laurel and Hardy meet a whole constellation of Hollywood stars; befriend a future President; and are invited to the White House. Stan and Babe emerge as warm and lovable, but vulnerable, men – and the reader will experience their every highlight and emotion throughout their long partnership.

Second Edition. 334 pages. Lavishly illustrated. Softback – A4 [297mm x 210mm]

(ISBN 978-0-9521308-6-4) — Available via lulu.com

-----0-----

CHAPLIN – Stage by Stage

Contains every known stage appearance Chaplin made in the UK and, for the first time ever, the ones he made in Vaudeville, touring America with the Fred Karno Company of Comedians.

Along the way, many myths and mistakes from other works on Chaplin will be corrected, and many lies and legends exposed. But, in destroying the negative, a positive picture is built up of the very medium which created the man and the screen character "Chaplin."

Includes extracts from the scripts of the plays and sketches in which Chaplin appeared, complemented by reviews and plot descriptions, all of which help to complete the picture of the influences which affected Chaplin's later film work. Read and be Amazed!

[Although it is a companion to "LAUREL – Stage by Stage" it contains far more text relating to Chaplin, plus numerous different and previously unpublished photos of him.]

Chaplin Stage by Stage *provides a unique and indispensable record of Chaplin's career on the British stage and music hall and in American vaudeville in the formative fifteen years before he entered films. Marriot's phenomenal research gives us an exhaustive chronicle of Charlie's stage appearances – in addition to those of his father and his brother Sydney.* — [DAVID ROBINSON – Chaplin biographer.]

258 pages – 130 illustrations. Paperback – A4 [297mm x 210mm]

Second print (ISBN 978-1-78972-556-8) — Available via lulu.com

-----0-----

The many celebrities who have bought previous books written by "A.J" Marriot range from among Britain's best-loved British comedians; TV, film, and stage actors; and rock and pop stars, to some of Hollywood's most famous film directors and actors. Have you bought your copies yet?

A sincere "Thank You" to those who have.

"A.J" Marriot

For information on the First Editions, and how to purchase, go to the author's website:

www.laurelandhardybooks.com

OR e-mail: ajmarriot@aol.com for any enquiries.

o-o-0-o-o

www.ingramcontent.com/pod-product-compliance
Lightning Source LLC
Chambersburg PA
CBHW082005220426
43669CB00016B/2723